W9-ADV-300

AMERICA THROUGH
THE LOOKING GLASS

a historical reader in
popular culture
volume I

Edited by
DAVID BURNER
State University of New York at Stony Brook

ROBERT D. MARCUS
State University of New York at Stony Brook

JORJ TILSON

Prentice-Hall, Inc., Englewood Cliffs, New Jersey

Library of Congress Cataloging in Publication Data

BURNER, DAVID comp.
  America through the looking glass.

  1. United States—Popular culture—History—Sources.
I. Marcus, Robert D. joint comp.
II. Tilson, Jorj, joint comp. III. Title.
E169.1.B939   917.3'03   73-21852
ISBN 0-13-023911-9 (v. 1)

© 1974 by Prentice-Hall, Inc., Englewood Cliffs, New Jersey.

PRINTED IN THE UNITED STATES OF AMERICA

10 9 8 7 6 5 4 3 2 1

Cover *Illustration:* Mirror, c. 1865. Cast-iron frame, American flag, and monument
with eagle. Two female figures once painted red, white, and blue. Two weeping
willows and trophy of laurel, shield, ramrod, and arrow.—From *Index of American Design*

PRENTICE-HALL INTERNATIONAL, INC., LONDON
PRENTICE-HALL OF AUSTRALIA, PTY. LTD., SYDNEY
PRENTICE-HALL OF CANADA, LTD., TORONTO
PRENTICE-HALL OF INDIA PRIVATE LIMITED, NEW DELHI
PRENTICE-HALL OF JAPAN, INC., TOKYO

N 1 0 6

to
Arthur Marcus
the memory of Arthur Burner (1925–1973)
Robert Burner
Tim Tilson
brothers and friends

N 1 0 6

to
Arthur Marcus
the memory of Arthur Burner (1925–1973)
Robert Burner
Tim Tilson
brothers and friends

contents

RELIGION 176

EDUCATION 190

LIFE IN AMERICA 215

MANNERS 241

ENTERTAINMENT 251

AMERICA THROUGH
THE LOOKING GLASS

introduction

American popular culture is the mirror of American life; it is, in fact, the way most people see themselves. Like other mirrors, this one can give a true picture, a distorted one, or even a grotesque image. But we examine this reflection of American life, because it gives the only view that would be fully recognizable to the common men and women of the nation's past whose experience constitutes our history.

Culture is, quite simply, the subjective resources that members of a group possess: the body of beliefs, practices, rituals, goals, patterns of behavior that people have available to cope with life. It is the "inside" of which society or social structure is the "outside." No analysis of the activities of a people would be complete without examining both the objective structure of society—the institutions and actual relationships among people—and the culture, the way experience is subjectively organized.

In American history the backbone of every textbook is its account of the nation's institutions. Students come away with a shadowy vision of the people of the past "responding" to the frontier, to industrialism, to the rise of a welfare state, and to the country's role in world politics.

The past becomes what happened to people, not what people did or who they were. An introduction to their culture, to their sense of the world, to their amusements, customs, and passions is an obvious first step toward righting this balance.

The study of popular culture is a relatively recent intellectual discipline that has only begun to affect historical studies. It grew up since the 1930s, principally as a branch of literary criticism. Some custodians of high culture, convinced that they could no longer simply avoid the subject, embraced the distinction between serious and popular culture —in short to prevent the infection from spreading. Others applied the canons of serious criticism to popular culture to discover that popular entertainers like Charlie Chaplin were in fact artists or that tragedy, a traditional theme of high culture, could be found in popular media. Still, so long as esthetic standards dominated inquiry, the second-class character of popular culture could only be confirmed. And the emphasis on contemporary materials left historians with little of value to use when they sought to describe popular culture in the past.

The historical study of ideas often reinforced the tendency to ignore or isolate popular culture. Much intellectual history studied culture in the old nineteenth-century sense—the best that has been thought and felt. This, however, does little toward recapturing the way most people in the past encountered the world. The theory of virtual representation—that the elites of society can speak for the lowly—has long since vanished from political thought and ought to quit the cultural scene as well. The culture of the great and powerful is not the culture of the masses. Even the greatest works of art—Dante's poetry or Shakespeare's plays—do not speak for an age; they speak for less than that—a class or a group or a tendency, and they speak for more, transcending their age and touching the concerns of humanity in some way general and timeless. As humanists, we study them without worrying about what they tell us of the past. As historians, we study them as we would any other cultural artifact, for what they say about the man or woman who created them and the audience they reached. They provide a valuable entrée to one part of the past, not some royal road to broad insight.

Another discipline that has restricted inquiry into popular culture is the study of folklore. Like the literary critic, the folklorist saw popular culture as an alien force, undermining folk expression. He defined folklore as culture passed directly by word of mouth without the intermediaries of print or electronic media. Only such culture could be genuinely of the people. Popular culture using folk themes became known as "fakelore"—a pejorative term if there ever was one. Popular culture, then, became whatever was neither high culture nor folk culture, something both inferior and inauthentic; and most scholars gave it a rather wide berth. Only in the last few years have folklorists realized the artificial limits of their definition, recognizing that much vital folk culture moves in and out of print and electronic media without ceasing to be authentically of the common imagination.

Most of these problems of definition disappear when one focuses on historical rather than esthetic questions. Viewed historically, popular culture means any form of expression or custom that achieves popularity among a large group of people. It can include the high culture created by a single self-conscious artist (e.g., Shakespeare, whose plays were a staple of touring companies a century ago) and the folk artifacts that enter media such as print or phonograph records. Once into the consciousness of a substantial group both become indistinguishable parts of the community's cultural endowment. Transformed into popular culture, they function no differently from the products composed commercially for popular audiences.

In short, popular culture and all culture is a process, not a specific kind of product. Students of high culture call this process "tradition"; folklorists speak of "the folk process." Both mean something living and evolving out of the imaginations of specific groups of people. Still, popular culture, because of its low academic pedigree and its concentration on the present, achieved a far more limiting definition than is implied in the image of a free-flowing process. Most people, their gazes narrowed to the electronic media, the professional entertainer, and the mass-produced popular book, magazine, or comic, envision popular culture as a consumer item created by professionals for a passive audience.

This static definition does not at all conform to most historical experience and even eliminates a good deal of contemporary culture from consideration. Much popular culture was created wholly or in part by the people who enjoyed it. Transmission by the folk process meant a continuous modification of what was inherited. Even the transmission of commercially produced popular entertainment was once a more active process. Sheet music, for example, was printed for playing on the piano and singing at home. Similarly, in transmitting the culture of home economics, the cooking, and housekeeping, and childrearing books, and even the sex manuals that dot the American past and clot the American present assume a more active role on the part of the ultimate consumer than, say, the motion picture. Rituals such as quilting bees, barn raisings,

Fourth of July fireworks, cookouts, coffee klatches, garage sales, dormitory bull sessions, bar hopping, and neighborhood cancer fund drives reflect as much popular culture as listening to *Amos 'n' Andy* or watching *All in the Family*. The whole world of how-to-do-it books is a continuing index to the popular mind. Popular culture, then, is not simply mankind as a vast audience: it is whatever provides materials for people to use in their daily lives—to use to give meaning to their experience.

Popular culture so defined encompasses the whole cycle of human life from midwifery and childrearing practices through marriage rituals and success images to the art of tombstone inscriptions. Most beliefs about hygiene and health come through the conduit of popular culture augmented by, perhaps, less science than we like to think. Humor becomes a part of the culture as do religious practices and beliefs. Instruction comes in schoolbooks, etiquette manuals (extremely influential in the nineteenth century), and how-to-do-it books of every description (perhaps even more prevalent a hundred years ago than now). Even political life once had much the form of popular entertainment and then as now helped to mold people's perception of the world. Domestic architecture and fashions in clothing fixed some of the most basic parts of people's imaginations, teaching particular standards of beauty, of order, of seemliness. A wide range of materials addressed to both children and adults affected the meanings people found in work, the views they took of the environment, their visions of people they had never seen, or their stereotypes of people they encountered daily.

This broad and indefinite expanse of the American mind is the subject of the book before you. Its organization reflects no limiting theoretical definition of popular culture. Some of the selections—e.g., the various songs—appear for their obvious popularity. Other selections—occasionally rather obscure ones—represent customs and attitudes that had wide currency. The diary—written in French—of a budding scientist, Lester Frank Ward, was not a best seller: we include it because it recounts the feelings of a mid-nineteenth century young man in love. Some other items report on widespread practices: Mrs. Trollope would be highly insulted to find her writings included in a book on popular culture, but her rather clinical description of a revival is an invaluable portrait of Americans expressing themselves.

Historians have recently become aware of the degree to which they have concentrated on elites and neglected the "underside" of American history. This book aims at moving yet another step: to examine the "inside" of American history, of the way Americans experienced their world. Such an emphasis has the advantage of exposing many of the most interesting and readable documents that a culture produces as well as introducing new nonwritten sources, such as the everyday objects—toys, decorations, gadgets—displays in the illustrations taken from the Index of American Design. Since motion pictures, an important part of popular culture, can be readily available for classroom use in a way that radio or video tapes cannot, we have included an illustrated guide to movies and information on how to locate them. The authors have always found their students enthusiastic about having motion pictures as part of a course; the major problem in using films is relating them to other sources of information and preventing movies from dominating all discussion. Tying such media to other forms of popular culture and organizing them in a way that will supplement American history textbooks hopefully will help solve that problem and integrate popular culture sources into the broader consideration of the American past.

part 1 the colonial era: 1607-1800

English colonists accumulated about 150 years of experience in the New World before they came to be identifiably "American." In their earlier years, the scattered settlements hugging the coastline kept closer ties with the mother country than with the other colonies struggling to survive. Mail between colonies even travelled by way of Great Britain until well into the eighteenth century; settlers from different sections might seem wholly alien as the rude North Carolinians appeared to William Byrd of Virginia. With good reason, colonials took pride in being Englishmen despite their transplantation to new shores.

Gradually, however, settlers learned to recognize their neighbors who faced similar problems and developed comparable institutions. A set of sectional cultures began its slow evolution, and eventually people recognized distinctions between the civilizations of New England, the Middle States, and the South. New England's flavor derived in part from its harsh climate, rugged coast, and rocky soil, but even more from the common Puritan background of its leaders and most of its population—men and women who had labored to purify the Church of England and to live according to the strict laws of the Bible. The Middle States showed a polyglot mixture with a substantial sprinkling of non-English immigrants, a diversified economy, and several growing cities. In the course of the seventeenth century the South became a staple-producing area in which involuntary black slave labor cultivated large tobacco plantations. The differences among the three sections became increasingly apparent early in the eighteenth century. New England's regional culture based on Puritanism had taken form long before; the South assumed its clear coloration once the plantation system triumphed late in the seventeenth century; the Middle States remained too variegated to achieve as sharp an image, with mostly Dutch in New York, Quakers in Pennsylvania, Swedes along the Delaware, and Scotch-Irish on the Frontier. Yet in some ways the Middle States' melting pot produced the most American section of all: subsequent generations have viewed its representative man, Benjamin Franklin, as the archetypical American.

In the twentieth century the New England Puritans have had a bad press. We tend to see them at their gloomiest: grim-visaged, dark-garmented prudes minding other people's business. Certainly the popularity of a poem like Michael Wigglesworth's "The Day of Doom," the Puritan treatment of Quakers, and Samuel Sewall's lugubrious ruminations in the family mausoleum offer evidence for the sad sack view of Puritanism. But much else lightened New England life: joyous Psalm singing, bundling, student insurrections, even the deep current of macabre humor in wills and epitaphs. Divorce was rare in New England, and the proportion of bad marriages probably no more or less than in the present, so these parting shots at the end of life could sometimes constitute getting in the last word on half a century or more of bickering.

In the South, the plantation shaped the aspirations of almost the entire white population. Hospitality, grandeur, political power and elevated notions of rights made up a good part of the style. The Virginia aristocrat was supposed to be adventurous and martial, showing equal aplomb in dealing with Indians, rabble, or Frenchmen. Hospitality on the plantation ascended to grand peaks on election days when the gentry treated their supporters to huge quantities of food and alcohol. The ideal of the English country gentlemen defending King, land, and country somehow took root amid slaves and the rude farmers of the New World.

The middle colonies had a wider cast of characters from which to evolve popular stereotypes and fashions. Urban gentleman enjoyed as many frills as the Southern gentry, but once on the road he might have to sleep among a crowd of drunks and rowdies. The Indian frontier posed a real threat and tales of Indian wars and captivities entertained and warned men raising their tankards in the taverns. The foibles of Dutchmen and Scots and Germans proved a source of many an anecdote. Newspapers and almanacs amused and instructed, bringing news from outside the communities, offering bits of folk wisdom, and teaching new ways of viewing the world. The achievements of Benjamin Franklin—establishing a mail system, publishing a widely read almanac, experimenting as a scientist, creating libraries, learned societies, and other amenities for his city—aptly symbolized the cultural activities that gradually pulled people together into a new culture of their own—an American culture.

The Revolutionary War culminated a vast and unplanned cultural movement. People from all sections glimpsed the outlines of a common heritage tying them more closely to their fellow colonials than to the people of the mother country. Newspapers during the half century before the revolution, for example, increasingly referred to *American* rather than imperial questions with each passing year. The revolution itself was another giant step toward the creation of this national culture. The history of modern nationalism begins with the emotions flowing out of the war experience. Events leading up to and taking place in the war—mobs, captivities, battles—became the stuff of popular legend, the themes of melodrama, and the subject of songs for the next century. A colonial people found its myths, and heroes, and identities in rebellion. This process, begun in America, would spread during the next two centuries to every part of the world that Europe had touched.

The *Bay Psalm Book* (1640), while it suffers by comparison to the roughly contemporary King James version of the Bible, is noteworthy as the first book printed in English America. Its publication in Cambridge, Massachusetts, came as no accident, for the exceptionally literate Puritans had a great zeal for education. They founded such institutions as Harvard University and the Boston Latin School as early as the settlement's first decade. More important still, their poetry and prose worked its way into the churches and even the households of ordinary folk. The Bay Psalms in particular affected the lives and faith of most of the colonists. Its Preface defends the singing of psalms—"If any be afflicted, let him pray, and if any be merry let him sing psalmes"—and then apologizes (below) in typical Puritan fashion for the work's supposed literary shortcomings. But its alleged weakness—what is called the "plain style"—could sometimes be a towering strength. (Selections from *The Whole Booke of Psalmes Faithfully Translated into English Metre,* Cambridge, 1640.)

THE BAY PSALM BOOK

If therefore the verses are not alwayes so smooth and elegant as some may desire or expect; let them consider that Gods Altar needs not our pollishings: Ex. 20. for wee have respected rather a plaine translation, then to smooth our verses with the sweetnes of any paraphrase, and soe have attended Conscience rather then Elegance, fidelity rather then poetry, in translating the hebrew words into english language, and Davids poetry into english meetre; that so wee may sing in Sion the Lords songs of prayse according to his owne will; untill hee take us from hence, and wipe away all our teares, & bid us enter into our masters ioye to sing eternall Halleluiahs.

The 23rd Psalm

23 A Psalme of David.
The Lord to mee a shepheard is,
want therefore shall not I.
2   Hee in the folds of tender-grasse,

doth cause mee downe to lie:
To waters calme me gently leads
3   Restore my soule doth hee:
he doth in paths of righteousness:
for his names sake leade mee.
4   Yea though in valley of deaths shade
I walk, none ill I'le feare:
because thou art with mee, thy rod,
and staffe my comfort are.
5   For mee a table thou hast spread,
in presence of my foes:
thou dost annoynt my head with oyle,
my cup it over-flowes.
6   Goodnes & mercy surely shall
all my dayes follow mee:
and in the Lords house I shall dwell
so long as dayes shall bee.

A PSALM IN TIME SAVES WISHART

The covenanters in the time of the civil wars [1642–66] were passionately addicted to psalm singing. When the great Montrose was taken prisoner, his chaplin, Wishart, the elegant historian of his exploits, shared the same fate, and was condemned to the same punishment with his patron. Being desired on the scaffold to name the psalm he wished to be sung, previous to his execution, he pitched upon the 119th, consisting of twenty-four parts. He made a good choice; for before two-thirds of the psalm was sung, a pardon arrived. Any other psalm would, in all probability, have hanged him.—From *New England Farmer* (Boston), Nov. 11, 1825.

Because the Puritans and Pilgrims considered themselves a chosen people, they had special need to understand everything that took place in their society to see if it accorded with their ideals. As a result, William Bradford, sometimes governor of the Plymouth Colony, wrote some excellent social history to explain the various outbreaks of "wickedness" in his colony. (Selection from William Bradford, *Of Plymouth Plantations*, 1856.)

OF PLYMOUTH PLANTATIONS

1642 [Wickedness Breaks Forth]

Marvelous it may be to see and consider how some kind of wickedness did grow and break forth here, in a land where the same was so much witnessed against and so narrowly looked unto, and severely punished when it was known, as in no place more, or so much, that I have known or heard of; insomuch that they have been somewhat censured even by moderate and good men for their severity in punishments. And yet all this could not suppress the breaking out of sundry notorious sins (as this year, besides other, gives us too many sad precedents and instances), especially drunkenness and uncleanness. Not only incontinency between persons unmarried, for which many both men and women have been punished sharply enough, but some married persons also. But that which is worse, even sodomy and buggery (things fearful to name) have broke forth in this land oftener than once.

I say it may justly be marveled at and cause us to fear and tremble at the consideration of our corrupt natures, which are so hardly, subdued and mortified; nay, cannot by any other means but the powerful work and grace of God's Spirit. But (besides this) one reason may be that the Devil may carry a greater spite against the churches of Christ and the gospel here, by how much the more they endeavour to preserve holiness and purity amongst them and strictly punisheth the contrary when it ariseth either in church or commonwealth; that he might cast a blemish and stain upon them in the eyes of [the] world, who use to be rash in judgment. I would rather think thus, than that Satan hath more power in these heathen lands, as some have thought, than in more Christian nations, especially over God's servants in them.

2. Another reason may be, that it may be in this case as it is with waters when their streams are stopped or dammed up. When they get passage they flew with more violence and make more noise and disturbance than when they are suffered to run quietly in their own channels; so wickedness being here more stopped by strict laws, and the same more nearly looked unto so as it cannot run in a common road of liberty as it would and is inclined, it searches everywhere and at last breaks out where it gets vent.

3. A third reason may be, here (as I am verily persuaded) is not more evils in this kind, nor nothing near so many by proportion as in other places; but they are here more discovered and seen and made public by due search, inquisition and due punishment; for the churches look narrowly to their members, and the magistrates over all, more strictly than in other places. Besides, here the people are but few in

comparison of other places which are full and populous and lie hid, as it were, in a wood or thicket and many horrible evils by that means are never seen nor known; whereas here they are, as is were, brought into the light and set in the plain field, or rather on a hill, made conspicuous to the view of all.

But to proceed. There came a letter from the Governor in the Bay to them here, touching matters of the forementioned nature which, because it may be useful, I shall here relate it and the passages thereabout.

> Sir: Having an opportunity to signify the desires of our General Court in two things of special importance, I willingly take this occasion to impart them to you, that you may impart them to the rest of your magistrates and also to your Elders for counsel, and give us your advice in them. The first is concerning heinous offenses in point of uncleanness; the particular cases with the circumstances and the questions thereupon, you have here enclosed.

> The second thing is concerning the Islanders at Aquidneck. That seeing the chiefest of them are gone from us in offenses either to churches or commonwealth or both, others are dependents on them, and the best sort are such as close with them in all their rejections of us. Neither is it only in faction that they are divided from us, but in very deed they rend themselves from all the true churches of Christ.

[A Horrible Case of Bestiality]

And after the time of the writing of these things befell a very sad accident of the like foul nature in this government, this very year, which I shall now relate. There was a youth whose name was Thomas Granger. He was servant to an honest man of Duxbury, being about 16 or 17 years of age. (His father and mother lived at the same time at Scituate.) He was this year detected of buggery, and indicted for the same, with a mare, a cow, two goats, five sheep, two calves and a turkey. Horrible it is to mention, but the truth of the history requires it. He was first discovered by one that accidentally saw his lewd practice towards the mare. (I forbear particulars.) Being upon it examined and committed, in the end he not only confessed the fact with that beast at that time, but sundry times before and at several times with all the rest of the forenamed in his indictment. And this his free confession was not only in private to the magistrates (though at first he strived to deny it) but to sundry, both ministers and others; and afterwards, upon his indictment, to the whole Court and jury; and confirmed it at the execution. And whereas some of the sheep could not so well be known by his description of them, others with them were brought before him and he declared which were they and which were not. And accordingly he was cast by the jury and condemned, and after executed about the 8th of September, 1642. A very sad spectacle it was. For first the mare and then the cow and the rest of the lesser cattle were killed before his face, according to the law, Leviticus xx.15; and then he himself was executed. The cattle were all cast into a great and large pit that was digged of purpose for them, and no use made of any part of them.

Upon the examination of this person and also of a former that had made some sodomitical attempts upon another, it being demanded of them how they came first to the knowledge and practice of such wickedness, the one confessed he had long used it in old England; and this youth last spoken of said he was taught it by another that had heard of such things from some in England when he was there, and they kept cattle together. By which it appears how one wicked person may infect many, and what care all ought to have what servants they bring into their families.

But it may be demanded how came it to pass that so many wicked persons and profane people should so quickly come over into this land and mix themselves amongst them? Seeing it was religious men that began the work and they came for religion's sake? I confess this may be marveled at, at least in time to come, when the reasons thereof should not be known; and the more because here was so many hardships and wants met withal. I shall therefore endeavour to give some answer hereunto.

1. And first, according to that in the gospel, it is ever to be remembered that where the Lord begins to sow good seed, there the envious man will endeavour to sow tares.

2. Men being to come over into a wilderness, in which much labour and service was to be done about building and planting, etc., such as wanted help in that respect, when they could not have such as they would, were glad to take such as they could; and so, many untoward servants, sundry of them proved, that were thus brought over, both men and womenkind who, when their times were expired, became families of themselves, which gave increase hereunto.

3. Another and a main reason hereof was that men, finding so many godly disposed persons willing to come into these parts, some began to make a trade of it, to transport passengers and their goods, and hired ships for that end. And then, to make up their freight and advance their profit, cared not who the persons were, so they had money to pay them. And by this means the country became pestered with many unworthy persons who, being come over, crept into one place or other.

4. Again, the Lord's blessing usually following His people as well in outward as spiritual things (though afflictions be mixed withal) do make many to adhere to the People of God, as many followed Christ

for the loaves' sake (John vi.26) and a "mixed multitude" came into the wilderness with the People of God out of Egypt of old (Exodus xii.38). So also there were sent by their friends, some under hope that they would be made better; others that they might be eased of such burthens, and they kept from shame at home, that would necessarily follow their dissolute courses. And thus, by one means or other, in 20 years' time it is a question whether the greater part be not grown the worser?

Not the best, but certainly the most popular Puritan poet in his day, Michael Wigglesworth literally scared the hell out of young and old Puritans in Massachusetts Bay. (Selection from Michael Wigglesworth, *The Day of Doom*, stanzas 1-34, 201-205, 1701.)

THE DAY OF DOOM

1

Still was the night, Serene and Bright,
  when all Men sleeping lay;
Calm was the season, and carnal reason
  thought so 'twould last for ay.
Soul, take thine ease, let sorrow cease,
  much good thou hast in store:
This was their Song, their Cups among,
  the Evening before.

2

Wallowing in all kind of sin,
  vile wretches lay secure:
The best of men had scarcely then
  their Lamps kept in good ure.
Virgins unwise, who through disguise
  amongst the best were number'd,
Had clos'd their eyes; yea, and the wise
  through sloth and frailty slumber'd.

3

Like as of old, when Men grow bold
  Gods' threatnings to contemn,
Who stopt their Ear, and would not hear,
  when Mercy warned them:
But took their course, without remorse,
  till God began to powre
Destruction the World upon
  in a tempestuous showre.

4

They put away the evil day,
  And drown'd their care and fears,
Till drown'd were they, and swept away
  by vengeance unawares:
So at the last, whilst Men sleep fast
  in their security,
Surpriz'd they are in such a snare
  as cometh suddenly.

5

For at midnight brake forth a Light,
  which turn'd the night to day,
And speedily an hideous cry
  did all the world dismay.
Sinners awake, their hearts do ake,
  trembling their loynes surprizeth;
Amaz'd with fear, by what they hear,
each one of them ariseth.

6

They rush from Beds with giddy heads,
  and to their windows run,
Viewing this light, which shines more bright
  then doth the Noon-day Sun.

Straightway appears (they see't with tears)
    the Son of God most dread;
Who with his Train comes on amain
    To Judge both Quick and Dead.

7

Before his face the Heav'ns gave place,
    and Skies are rent asunder,
With mighty voice, and hideous noise,
    more. terrible than Thunder.
His brightness damps heav'ns glorious lamps
    and makes then hide their heads,
As if afraid and quite dismay'd,
    they quit their wonted steads.

8

Ye sons of men that durst contemn
    the Threatnings of Gods Word,
How cheer you now? your hearts, I trow,
    are thrill'd as with a sword.
Now Atheist blind, whose brutish mind
    a God could never see,
Dost thou perceive, dost now believe,
    that Christ thy Judge shall be?

9

Stout Courages, (whose hardiness
    could Death and Hell out-face)
Are you as bold now you behold
    your Judge draw near apace?
They cry, no, no: Alas! and wo!
    our Courage all is gone:
Our hardiness (fool hardiness)
    hath us undone, undone.

10

No heart so bold, but now grows cold
  and almost dead with fear:
No eye so dry, but now can cry,
  and pour out many a tear.
Earths Potentates and pow'rful States,
  Captains and Men of Might
Are quite abasht, their courage dasht
  at this most dreadful sight. . . .

14

The Judge draws nigh, exalted high
  upon a lofty Throne,
Amidst the throngs of Angels strong,
  lo, Israel's Holy One!
The excellence of whose presence
  and awful Majesty,
Amazeth Nature, and every Creature,
  doth more than terrify.

15

The Mountains smoak, the Hills are shook,
  the Earth is rent and torn,
As if she should be clean dissolv'd,
  or from the Center born.
The Sea doth roar, forsakes the shore,
  and shrinks away for fear;
The wild Beasts flee into the Sea,
  so soon as he draws near.

16

Whose Glory bright, whose wondrous might,
  whose Power Imperial,
So far surpass whatever was
  in Realms Terrestrial;

That tongues of men (nor Angels pen)
    cannot the same express,
And therefore I must pass it by,
    lest speaking should transgress.

17

Before his Throne a Trump is blown,
    Proclaiming th' Day of Doom:
Forthwith he cries, *Ye Dead arise,*
    and unto Judgment come.
No sooner said, but 'tis obey'd;
    Sepulchers open'd are:
Dead Bodies all rise at his call,
    and's mighty power declare.

18

Both Sea and Land, at his Command,
    their Dead at once surrender:
The Fire and Air constrained are
    also their dead to tender
The mighty word of this great Lord
    links Body and Soul together
Both of the Just, and the unjust,
    to part no more for ever.

27

At Christ's left hand the Goats do stand,
    all whining hypocrites,
Who for self-ends did seem Christ's friends,
    but foster'd guileful sprites;
Who Sheep resembled, but they dissembled
    (their hearts were not sincere);
Who once did throng Christ's Lambs among,
    but now must not come near.

28

Apostates and Run-awayes,
   such as have Christ forsaken,
Of whom the Devil, with seven more evil,
   hath fresh possession taken:
Sinners in grain, reserv'd to pain
   and torments most severe:
Because 'gainst light they sinn'd with spight,
   are also placed there.

29

There also stand a num'rous band,
   that no Profession made
Of Godliness, nor to redress
   their wayes at all essay'd:
Who better knew, but (sinful Crew)
   Gospel and Law despised;
Who all Christ's knocks withstood like blocks
   and would not be advised.

30

Moreover, there with them appear
   a number, numberless
Of great and small, vile wretches all,
   that did Gods Law transgress:
Idolaters, false worshippers,
   Prophaners of Gods Name,
Who not at all thereon did call,
   or took in vain the same.

31

Blasphemers lewd, and Swearers shrewd,
   Scoffers at Purity,
That hated God, contemn'd his Rod,
   and lov'd Security;

Sabbath-polluters, Saints persecuters,
   Presumptuous men and Proud,
Who never lov'd those that reprov'd;
   all stand amongst this Crowd.

32

Adulterers and Whoremongers
   were there, with all unchast:
There Covetous, and Ravenous,
   that Riches got too fast:
Who us'd vile ways themselves to raise
   t'Estates and worldly wealth,
Oppression by, or Knavery,
   by force, or fraud, or stealth.

33

Moreover, there together were
   Children flagitious,
And Parents who did them undo
   by Nurture vicious,
False-witness-bearers, and self-forswearers,
   Murd'rers, and Men of blood,
Witches, Inchanters, and Ale-house-haunters,
   beyond account there stood.

34

Their place there find all Heathen blind,
   that Natures light abused,
Although they had no tydings glad,
   of Gospel-grace refused.
There stands all Nations and Generations
   of *Adam's* Progeny,
Whom Christ redeem'd not, who Christ esteem'd not,
   through Infidelity. . . .

201

Ye sinful wights, and cursed sprights,
  that work Iniquity,
Depart together from me for ever
  to endless Misery;
Your portion take in yonder Lake,
  where Fire and Brimstone flameth:
Suffer the smart, which your desert
  as it's due wages claimeth.

202

Oh piercing words more sharp than swords!
  what, to depart from *Thee,*
Whose face before for evermore
  the best of Pleasures be!
What? to depart (unto our smart)
  from thee *Eternally:*
To be for aye banish'd away,
  with *Devils* company!

203

What? to be sent to *Punishment,*
  and flames of *Burning Fire,*
To be surrounded, and eke confounded
  with Gods *Revengful ire.*
What? to abide, not for a tide
  these Torments, but for *Ever:*
To be released, or to be eased,
  not after years, but *Never.*

204

Oh, *fearful Doom!* now there's no room
  for hope or help at all:

Sentence is past which aye shall last,
  Christ will not it recall.
There might you hear them rent and tear
  the Air with their out-cries:
The hideous noise of their sad voice
  ascendeth to the Skies.

205

Their wring their hands, their caitiff-hands
  and gnash their teeth for terrour;
They cry, they roar for anguish sore,
  and gnaw their tongues for horrour.
But get away without delay,
  Christ pitties not your cry:
Depart to Hell, there may you yell,
  and roar Eternally.

College students have long complained about the quality of food in university
dining rooms. If this very first American instance of an incipient food riot is
typical, they have had good reason for their complaint. Mistress Eaton, the cook,
was wife of Harvard's first headmaster, Nathaniel Eaton. Both lost their jobs
when students protested the severe discipline that Mr. Eaton dispensed and the
atrocious food that his wife served. (Selection from William Bentinck-Smith, ed.,
The Harvard Book: Selections from Three Centuries, 1935.)

AN EARLY HARVARD RIOT (1639)

For their breakfast, that it was not so well ordered, the flour not
so fine as it might, nor so well boiled or stirred, at all times that it was
so, it was my sin of neglect, and want of that care that ought to have
been in one that the Lord had intrusted with such a work. Concerning
their beef, that was allowed them, as they affirm, which, I confess, had
been my duty to have seen they should have had it, and continued to
have had it, because it was my husband's command; but truly I must
confess, to my shame, I cannot remember that ever they had it, nor that

ever it was taken from them. And that they had not so good or so much provision in my husband's absence as presence, I conceive it was, because he would call sometimes for butter or cheese, when I conceived there was no need of it; yet, forasmuch as the scholars did otherways apprehend, I desire to see the evil that was in the carriage of that as well as in the other, and to take shame to myself for it. And that they sent down for more, when they had not enough, and the maid should answer, if they had not, they should not, I must confess, that I have denied them cheese, when they sent for it, and it have been in the house; for which I shall humbly beg pardon of them, and own the shame, and confess my sin. And for such provoking words, which my servants have given, I cannot own them, but am sorry any such should be given in my house. And for bad fish, that they had it brought to table, I am sorry there was that cause of offence given them. I acknowledge my sin in it. And for their mackerel, brought to them with their guts in them, and goat's dung in their hasty pudding, it's utterly unknown to me; but I am much ashamed it should be in the family, and not prevented by myself or servants, and I humbly acknowledge my negligence in it. And that they made their beds at any time, were my straits never so great, I am sorry they were ever put to it. For the Moor his lying in Sam. Hough's sheet and pillow-bier, it hath a truth in it: he did so one time, and it gave Sam. Hough just cause of offence; and that it was not prevented by my care and watchfulness, I desire [to] take the shame and sorrow for it. And that they eat the Moor's crusts, and the swine and they had share and share alike, and the Moor to have beer, and they denied it, and if they had not enough, for my maid to answer, they should not, I am an utter stranger to these things, and know not the least footsteps for them so to charge me; and if my servants were guilty of such miscarriages, had the boarders complained of it unto myself, I should have thought it my sin, if I had not sharply reproved my servants, and endeavored reform. And for bread made of heated, sour meal, although I know of but once that it was so, since I kept house, yet John Wilson affirms it was twice; and I am truly sorry, that any of it was spent amongst them. For beer and bread, that it was denied them by me betwixt meals, truly I do not remember, that ever I did deny it unto them; and John Wilson will affirm, that, generally, the bread and beer was free for the boarders to go unto. And that money was demanded of them for washing the linen, it's true it was propounded to them, but never imposed upon them. And for their pudding being given the last day of the week without butter or suet, and that I said, it was miln of Manchester in Old England, it's true that I did say so, and am sorry, they had any cause of offence given them by having it so. And for their wanting beer, betwixt brewings, a week or half a week together, I am sorry that it was so at any time, and should tremble to have it so, were it in my hands to do again.

Hair, oddly enough, is a perennial social problem. (Selection from Hutchinson Papers, I, 151–152, Massachusetts State Archives, Boston.)

A MANIFESTO AGAINST LONG HAIR

Forasmuch as the wearing of long hair, after the manner of ruffians and barbarous Indians, has begun to invade New England, contrary to the rule of God's word, which says it is a shame for a man to wear long hair (I Cor. xi. 14), as also the commendable custom generally of all the godly of our nation, until within this few years.

We the magistrates who have subscribed this paper (for the showing of our innocence in this behalf) do declare and manifest our dislike and detestation against the wearing of such long hair, as against a thing uncivil and unmanly, whereby men do deform themselves and offend sober and modest men, and do corrupt good manners. We do thereby earnestly entreat all the elders of this jurisdiction (as they often shall see cause) to manifest their zeal against it in their public administration, and to take care that the members of their respective churches be not defiled therewith; that so, such as shall prove obstinate and will not reform themselves, may have God and man to witness against them. The third month, 10th day, 1649.

Jo. Endicott, Governor,   William Hibbins,
Tho. Dudley, Dep. Gov.,   Thomas Flint,
Rich. Bellingham,   Robert Bridges,
Richard Saltonstall,   Simon Bradstreet
Increase Nowell,

Bundling was an eminently sensible custom for people living in cold climates with little indoor space to allow any privacy for courting. Prudent mothers tied their daughter's pantaloon legs before they abandoned them to the protection of the bundling board placed in the bed between the young woman and her beau. The seventeenth and eighteenth century did not look with any great opprobrium on "six-month babies," some of whom must have come from bundling. (Selections from Henry Stiles, *Bundling*, 1869.)

POEM ON BUNDLING

Whether they must be hugg'd or kiss'd when sitting by the fire
Or whether they in bed may lay, which doth the Lord require?
In Genesis no knowledge is of this thing to be got,
Whether young men did bundle then, or whether they did not.
The sacred book says wives they took, it don't say how they
    courted.
Whether that they in bed did lay, or by the fire sported.
But some do hold in times of old, that those about to wed,
Spent not the night, nor yet the light by fire, or in the bed.
They only meant to say they sent a man to choose a bride,
Isaac did so, but let me know of anyone beside.
Man don't pretend to trust a friend to choose him sheep and cows,
Much less a wife which all his life he doth expect to house. . . .

Young miss, if this your habit be, I'll teach you now yourself to see:
You plead you're honest, modest too, but such a plea will never do;
For how can modesty consist, with shameful practice such as this?
I'll give your answer to the life: You don't undress, like man and
    wife.
That is your plea, I'll freely own, but who's your bondsman when
    alone,
That further rules you will not break, and marriage liberties
    partake?
But you will say that I'm unfair, that some who bundle take
    more care,
For some we may in truth suppose, bundle in bed with all their
    clothes.
But bundler's clothes are no defense, unruly horses push the fence.

Cate, Nance and Sue proved just and true,
    Tho' bundling did practise;
But Ruth beguil'd and proved with child,
    Who bundling did dispise.

Whores will be whores, and on the floor
    Where many has been laid,
To set and smoke and ashes poke,
    Wont keep awake a maid.

Bastards are not at all times got
    In feather beds we know;
The strumpet's oath convinces both
    Oft times it is not so.

One whorish dame, I fear to name
    Lest I should give offence,
But in this town she was took down
    Not more than eight months sence.

She was the first, that on snow crust,
    I ever knew to gender
I'll hint no more about this whore
    For fear I should offend her.

'Twas on the snow when Sol was low,
    And was in Capricorn,
A child was got, and it will not
    Be long ere it is born.

Now unto those that do oppose
    The bundling traid, I say
Perhaps there's more got on the floor,
    Than any other way.

The Puritans have a reputation for being prudes, but in reality they were only fussbudgets. They were not against sex and not against people enjoying themselves. But they did believe in an Old Testament morality—rules by which everything had to be done—and therefore they fussed endlessly about what was and what was not allowable. (Selection from Increase Mather, *An Arrow*, 1684.)

PURITAN RULES

An Arrow Against Profane and Promiscuous Dancing

Concerning the Controversy about *Dancing*, the Question is not, whether all *Dancing* be in it self sinful. It is granted, that *Pyrrhical* or *Polemical Saltation:* i.e. when men vault in their Armour, to shew their strength and activity, may be of use. Nor is the question, whether a sober and grave *Dancing* of Men with Men, or of Women with Women, be not allowable; we make no doubt of that, where it may be done without offence, in due season, and with moderation. The Prince of Philosophers has observed truly, that *Dancing* or *Leaping*, is a natural expression of joy: So that there is no more Sin in it, than in laughter, or any outward expression of inward Rejoicing.

But our question is concerning *Gynecandrical Dancing*, or that which is commonly called *Mixt* or *Promiscuous Dancing, viz.* of Men and Women (be they elder or younger persons) together: Now this we affirm to be utterly unlawful, and that it cannot be tollerated in such a place as *New England*, without great Sin. And that it may appear, that we are not transported by Affection without Judgment, let the following Arguments be weighed in the Ballance of the Sanctuary.

Arg. 1. *That which the Scripture condemns is sinful.* None but Atheists will deny this *Proposition:* But the Scripture condemns *Promiscuous Dancing.* This *Assumption* is proved, 1. *From the Seventh Commandment.* It is an Eternal Truth to be observed in expounding the Commandments, that whenever any sin is forbidden, not only the highest acts of that sin, but all degrees thereof, and all occasions leading thereto are prohibited. Now we cannot find one Orthodox and Judicious Divine, that writeth on the Commandments, but mentions *Promiscuous Dancing*, as a breach of the seventh Commandment, as being an occasion, and an incentive to that which is evil in the sight of God. Yea, this is so manifest as that the *Assembly* in the *larger Cathechism,* do expresly take notice of *Dancings*, as a violation of the Commandments. It is sad, that when in times of Reformation, Children have been taught in their C[a]techism, that such *Dancing* is against the Commandment of God, that now in *New-England* they should practically be learned the contrary. The unchast Touches and Gesticulations used by *Dancers*, have a palpable tendency to that which is evil. Whereas some object, that they are not sensible of any ill motions occasioned in them, by being Spectators or Actors in such *Saltations;* we are not bound to believe all which some pretend concerning their own Mortification. . . .

Now they that frequent Promiscuous Dancings, or that send their Children thereunto, walk disorderly, and contrary to the Apostles Doctrine. It has been proved that such a practice is a *Scandalous Immorality,* and therefore to be removed out of Churches by Discipline, which is the Broom of Christ, whereby he keeps his Churches clean. . . .

And shall Churches in *N[ew] E[ngland]* who have had a Name to be stricter and purer than other Churches, suffer such a scandalous evil amongst them? if all that are under Discipline be made sensible of this matter, we shall not be much or long infested with a *Choreutical Dæmon.* . . .

The Catechism which Wicked men teach their Children is to Dance and to Sing. Not that Dancing, or Musick, or Singing are in themselves sinful: but if the Dancing Master be wicked they are commonly abused to lasciviousness, and that makes them to become abominable. But will you that are Professors of Religion have your Children to be thus taught? the Lord expects that you should give the Children who are Baptized into his Name another kind of Education, that you should bring them up in the nurture and admonition of the Lord: And do you not hear the Lord Expostulating the case with you, and saying, you have taken my Children, the Children that were given unto me; the Children that were solemnly engaged to renounce the Pomps of Satan; but is this a light matter that you have taken these my Children, and initiated them in the Pomps and Vanities of the Wicked one, contrary to your Covenant? What will you say in the day of the Lords pleading with you? we have that charity for you as to believe that you have erred through Ignorance, and not wickedly: and we have therefore accounted it our Duty to inform you in the Truth. If you resolve not on Reformation, you will be left inexcusable. However it shall be, we have now given our Testimony and delivered our own souls. *Consider what we say, and the Lord give you understanding in all things.*

In later times the Massachusetts Bay colony became famous for its lack of tolerance. Religious freedom—if it meant anything then—meant the freedom to practice one's own religion, not freedom for anyone to practice his. Most seventeenth-century sects were intolerant, but the Puritan mistreatment of the Quakers near the end of the century is a classic part of the popular image of the grim-visaged Puritan. (Selection from Joseph Beese, *A Collection of the Sufferings of the People Called Quakers*, 1753.)

PERSECUTION OF QUAKERS

During the continuance under so rigorous a persecution here in England, the popular prejudice against them spread itself also into foreign countries, especially the English Plantations in America, where falsehood and calumny had anticipated their arrival, and prepossessed the minds of those in Authority against them: hence it came to pass that in New-England a set of fiery zealots, who, through impatience under sufferings from the Bishops in Old-England, had fled from thence, being invested with power, and placed at the helm of government, exceeded all others in their cruelty towards this people, the barbarity of whose reception soon after their first arrival there, is well described in a summary account thereof drawn up by some of the sufferers, and presented to King Charles the Second after his Restoration, by Edward Burrough, being as follows, viz.

"A DECLARATION OF SOME PART OF THE SUFFERINGS OF THE PEOPLE OF GOD IN SCORN CALLED QUAKERS, FROM THE PROFESSORS IN NEW-ENGLAND, ONLY FOR THE EXERCISE OF THEIR CONSCIENCES TO THE LORD, AND OBEYING AND CONFESSING TO THE TRUTH, AS IN HIS LIGHT HE HAD DISCOVERED IT TO THEM.

"1. Two honest and innocent women stripped stark naked, and searched after such an inhuman manner, as modesty will not permit particularly to mention.

"2. Twelve strangers in that country, but free-born of this nation, received twenty-three whippings, the most of them being with a whip of three cords with knots at the ends, and laid on with as much strength as could be by the arm of their executioner, the stripes amounting to three hundred and seventy.

"3. Eighteen inhabitants of the country, being free-born English, received twenty-three whippings, the stripes amounting to two hundred and fifty. . . .

"5. Two beaten with pitched ropes, the blows amounting to an hundred and thirty-nine, by which one of them brought near unto death, much of his body being beaten like unto a jelly, and one of their doctors, a member of their church, who saw him, said, *it would be a miracle if ever he recovered, he expecting the flesh should rot off the bones,* who afterwards was banished upon pain of death. There are many witnesses of this there. . . .

"10. One laid neck and heels in irons for sixteen hours.

"11. One very deeply burnt in the right hand with the letter H after he had been whipt with above thirty stripes.

"12. One chained to a log of wood the most part of twenty days, in an open prison, in the winter-time. . . .

"14. Three had their right ears cut by the hangman in the prison, the door being barred, and not a Friend suffered to be present while it was doing, though some much desired. . . .

"18. Also three of the servants of the lord they put to death, all of them for obedience to the truth, in the testimony of it, against the WICKED RULERS and LAWS at Boston. . . .

"These things, O King! from time to time have we patiently suffered, and not for the transgression of any just or righteous law, either pertaining to the worship of God, or the civil government of England, but simply and barely for our consciences to God. . . .

"And this, O King! we are assured of, that in time to come it will not repent thee, if by a close rebuke thou stoppest the BLOODY PROCEEDINGS of these BLOODY PERSECUTORS, for in so doing thou wilt engage the heart of many honest people unto thee both there and here, and for such works of mercy the blessing is obtained; and shewing it is the way to prosper; we are witnesses of these things, who

"Besides many long imprisonments, and many cruel whippings, had our ears cut,

JOHN ROUSE   JOHN COPELAND."

Often diaries are the best way to view day-to-day life in the past. As is usually the case, the people who keep diaries are hardly common folk, but part of the elites of society. This was the case with Samuel Sewall, one of the officials responsible for the Salem witchcraft trials. His account of the omnipresence of death in an era before modern medicine gives his diary a universal quality. (Selection from Samuel Sewall, *Diary*, 1692-1695.)

DIARY OF SAMUEL SEWALL

April 11 [1692]

Went to Salem, where in the meeting-house, the persons accused of witchcraft were examined. Was a very great assembly. 'Twas awful to see how the afflicted persons [hysterical young girls who alleged they had been bewitched] were agitated.

August 19

[In the margin appear the words, "Doleful Witchcraft!"]
This day George Burroughs, John Willard, John Procter, Martha Carrier and George Jacobs were executed at Salem, a very great number of spectators being present. Mr. Cotton Mather was there, Mr. Sims, Hale, Noyes, Cheever and others. All of them [the accused] said they were innocent, Carrier and all. Mr. Mather says they all died by a righteous sentence. Mr. Burroughs, by his speech, prayer, protestation of innocence, did much move unthinking persons, which occasions their speaking hardly concerning his being executed.

September 19

About noon, at Salem, Giles Cory was pressed to death for standing mute [refusing to plead to an indictment on the charge of witchcraft].

Much pains was used with him two days, one after another, by the court and Captain Gardner of Nantucket who had been of his acquaintance, but all in vain.

September 21

A petition is sent to town in behalf of Dorcas Hoar, who now confesses. Accordingly an order is sent to the sheriff to forbear her execution, notwithstanding her being in the warrant to die tomorrow. This is the first condemned person who has confessed.

November 22

I prayed that God would pardon all my sinful wanderings and direct me for the future; that God would bless the Assembly in their debates, and that he would assist our judges and save New England as to enemies and witchcrafts and vindicate the late judges.

December 22

Betty being sick, lies abed and sweats.

December 23

She takes a vomit and brings up two worms, one about six inches and the other above eight inches long; a third about eleven inches in length.

March 9 [1693]

Joseph puts his grandmother and mother in great fear by swallowing a bullet which for a while stuck in his throat. He had quite got it down before I knew what the matter was. When I come home my wife shows me the bullet Joseph swallowed, which he voided in the orchard. The Lord help us to praise him for his distinguished favor.

August 7

About 4 in the morning I go for the midwife. About 4 P.M. my wife is brought to bed of a daughter. Thanks be to God.

September 9

I return from Point Judith, having been gone from home ever since the 28 of August. At my return find Jane [his new daughter] not well.

September 12

Call Mr. Willard [Rev. Samuel, of Old South Church, Boston] to pray with little Jane. Went to Roxbury lecture. Mr. Hobart came home with me, who also prayed with Jane. Both excellently. By Dr. Oakes's advice I gave her a little manna. The good Lord prepare her and us for the issue and help us to choose the things that please him. Nurse Judd watches.

September 13

Between 12 and 1 at night following that day, Jane expires in neighbor Smith's lap, Nurse Hill and I being by.

November 21 [1694]

My wife is brought to bed of a daughter between 9 and 10 of the clock in the morn.

November 12

I set Betty to read Ezekiel 37, and she weeps so that she can hardly read. I talk with her and she tells me of the various temptations she had; as that she was a reprobate, loved not God's people as she should.

December 12

A very great show of snow in on the ground. I go in the morn to Mr. Willard to entreat him choose his own time to come and pray with little Sarah. He comes a little before night and prays very fully and well. Mr. Mather, the president, had prayed with her in the time of the court's sitting.

December 22

Being catechising day, I give Mr. Willard a note to pray for my daughter publicly, which he did. This day I remove poor little Sarah into my bedchamber, where about break of day December 23 she gives up the ghost in Nurse Cowell's arms. Born November 21, 1694.

Neither I nor my wife were by, nurse not expecting so sudden a change, and having promised to call us. I thought of Christ's words, "Could you not watch with me one hour!" and would fain have sat up with her, but fear of my wife's illness, who is very valetudinarious, made me to lodge with her in the new hall, where she was called by Jane's cry, to take notice of my dead daughter.

Nurse did long and pathetically ask our pardon that she had not called us, and said she was surprised.

Thus this very fine day is rendered foul to us by reason of the general sorrow and tears in the family.

Master Cheever was here the evening before. I desired him to pray for my daughter. The chapter read in course was Deuteronomy 22, which made me sadly reflect that I had not been so thoroughly tender of my daughter, nor so effectually careful of her defense and preservation, as I should have been. The good Lord pity and pardon and help for the future as to those God has still left me.

December 24

Sam recites to me in Latin, Matthew 12 from the 6th to the end of the 12th verse. The 7th verse did awfully bring to mind the Salem tragedy. ["If ye had known what this meaneth, I will have mercy and not sacrifice, ye would not have condemned the guiltless."]

March 18 [1695]

Last night I dreamed that all my children were dead except Sarah [the infant daughter] which did distress me sorely with reflections on my omission of duty towards them, as well as breaking oft the hopes I had of them. The Lord help me thankfully and fruitfully to enjoy them and let that be a means to awaken me.

April 29

The morning is very warm and sunshiny. In the afternoon there is thunder and lightning, and about 2 p.m. a very extraordinary storm of hail, so that the ground was made white with it, as with blossoms when fallen. 'Twas as big as pistol and musket bullets. It broke of the glass of the new house about 480 quarrels [squares] of the front.

Mr. Cotton Mather dined with us and was with me in the new kitchen when this was. He had just been mentioning that more ministers' houses than others proportionably had been smitten with lightning, inquiring what the meaning of God should be in it.

Many hailstones broke through the glass and flew to the middle of the room or farther. People afterward gazed upon the house to see its ruins.

I got Mr. Mather to pray with us after this awful providence. He told God he had broken the brittle part of our house and prayed that we might be ready for the time when our clay tabernacles should be broken.

'Twas a sorrowful thing to me to see the house so far undone again before 'twas finished.

June 21

About one at night, Jane comes up with an unusual gate and gives us an account of mother's illness, not being able to speak a considerable time.

I went to Captain Davis' and fetched some treacle water and syrup of saffron. Dame Ellis made a cake of herbs to strengthen mother's stomach. In the morn Roger Judd is sent to Cambridge for Dr. Oliver, mother choosing to speak with him and no other. When he comes he advises to a plaster for the stomach, which is applied, and a potion made of bezar [a concretion from the alimentary tract of an animal, thought to be an antidote for poisoning] to be taken in syrup of saffron and treacle water, of which she took once or twice.

About 8 or 9 I called Mr. Willard at her desire, who prays with her. Finding the room free once, and observing her very great weakness, I took the opportunity to thank her for all her labors of love to me and mine and asked her pardon for our undutifulness. She, after a while, said, God pity 'em; which was the last prayer I heard her make. A little before sunset she expired.

July 26

Poor little Mary falls down into the cellar of Matthias Smith's house and cuts her head against the stones, making a large orifice of more than two inches long. 'Twas about six past meridian. The Lord sanctify me to this bloody accident.

August 8

About 9 P.M. little Sarah has a convulsion fit. I and Mr. Torrey were sent for to see it. It lasted not long. When all quiet, Mr. Torrey went to prayer. A little after lecture Sarah has another sore fit. My wife and I take her to bed with us.

August 9

About six in the morn Sarah has another sore fit in her mother arms presently after she was brought down.

August 13

We have a fast kept in our new chamber. Mr. Willard begins with prayer and preaches from II Chron. 34:27. Mr. Allen prays. P.M., Mr. Bayley begins with prayer, preaches from Luke 1:50 and then concludes with prayer. Sung the 27 Psalm 7-10. I set the tune and burst so into tears that I could scarce continue singing.

From this attack Sarah recovers.

Baptisms, wills, and epitaphs are a prime source for reconstructing life in the past, but few are as interestingly written as these are. New England particularly excelled in giving those who died an interesting sendoff.

BAPTISMS, WILLS, AND EPITAPHS

"O, Ye of Little Faith . . ."

During this unnatural ceremony [a baptism by immersion in freezing weather], I was no less entertained with the remarks of the spectators. On[e] of them observed that, severe as the discipline was, they seldom took cold, or suffered subsequently bodily pains; adding, that their enthusiasm was so great, and their minds were wrought up to such a degree of religious phrenzy, that no room was left for reflection, or sense of danger. Another related a story of a public baptism of this nature in Connecticut, which was attended with a fatal circumstance. "It was about the same time of year," continued the narrator, (for the severer the weather the greater their faith) "when I was present at one of these *duckings*, (as he termed it.) It was performed in a small but rapid river, then covered with ice, except a place cut for the purpose. The minister, with his followers, advanced to the proper distance into the water: after the usual introductory prayer, being in the act of immersing the first, he accidentally lost his hold of the unfortunate person, who was in an instant carried down the stream, still running under the ice, and irrecoverably lost. The good man finding his subject gone, with a happy serenity of mind exclaimed, "The Lord hath given, the Lord hath taken away, blessed be the name of the Lord:—come another of you, my children." The remainder, astonished and confounded, lost their faith, and fled. (From Charles William Janson, *The Stranger in America,* London, 1807.

The Estate of True Love

Cambridge, Decemb. 1731.

Some time since died here Mr. *Matth. A———y,* in a very advanc'd Age, he had for a great Number of Years served the College here, in Quality of Bed maker and Sweeper, Having left no Child, his Wife inherits his whole Estate which he bequeathed to her by his last Will and Testament as follows,

1.
To my dear Wife,
My Joy of Life,
I freely now do give her
My whole Estate,
With all my Plate
Being just about to leave her.

2.
A Tub of Soap,
A long Cart Rope,
A Frying Pan & Kettle,
An Ashes Pail, A threshing Flail,
An iron Wedge & Beetle.

3.
Two painted Chairs,
Nine Warden Pairs,
A large old dripping Platter,
The Bed of Hay
On which I lay,
An old Sauce Pan for Butter.

4.
A little Mugg,
A Two Quart Jugg,
A Bottle full of Brandy,
A Looking Glass
To see your Face
You'll find it very handy.

5.
A Musket true
As ever flew,

A pound of Shot and Wallett
A leather Sash
My Calabash
My Powder Horn & Bullet.

6.
An old Sword Blade,
A Garden Spade
A Ho, a Rake, a Ladder,
A wooden Cann,
A Close Stool Pan,
A Clyster Pipe and Bladder.

7.
A greazy Hat,
My old Ram Cat,
A yard & half of Linnen,
A Pot of Greaze,
A woollen Fleece,
In order for your spinning.

8.
A small Tooth Comb,
An ashen Broom,
A Candlestick & Hatchet,
A Coverlid
Strip'd down with Red.
A Bagg of Rags to patch it.

9.
A ragged Mat,
A Tub of Fat,
A Book put out by *Bunnian,*
Another Book
By *Robin Rook,*
A Skain or two of Spunyarn.

10.
An old black Muff,
Some Garden Stuff,
A Quantity of Burrage,
Some Devil's Weed
And Burdock Seed
To season well your Porridge.

11.
A Chafing Dish
With one Salt Fish,
If I am not mistaken,
A leg of Pork,
A broken Fork
And half a Flitch of Bacon.

12.
A spinning Wheel,
One Peck of Meal,
A Knife without a handle,
A rusty lamp,
Two Quarts of Samp,
And half a Tallow Candle.

13.
My Pouch and Pipes,
Two Oxen Tripes,
An oaken Dish well carved,
My little Dog,
And spotted Hog,
With two young Pigs just starv'd.

14.
This is my Store
I have no more,
I heartily do give it,
My Years are spun
My Days are done,
And so I think to leave it.

(*The* [Boston] *Weekly Rehearsal*, January 3, 1732.)

Grass, smoke, a flower, a vapor, a shade, a span,
Serve to illustrate the frail life of man;
And they, who longest live, survive to see
The certainty of death, of life the vanity. . . .

Under the sod and under the trees
Here lies the body of Solomon Pease

The Pease are not here there's only the pod
The Pease shelled out and went to God.

Our father lies beneath the sod,
His spirit's gone unto his God;
We never more shall hear his tread,
Nor see the wen upon his head. . . .

Beneath this little mound of clay
    Lies Captain Ephraim Daniels,
Who chose the dangerous month of May
    To change his winter flannels. . . .

Here lies the body of Saphronia Proctor,
    Who had a cold, but wouldn't doctor.
She couldn't stay, she had to go,
    Praise God from whom all blessings flow. . . .

Shed not for her the bitter tear,
    Nor give the heart to vain regret;
Tis but the casket that lies here:
    The gem that filled it sparkles yet. . . .

To all my friends I bid adieu,
    A more sudden death you never knew.
As I was leading the old mare to drink.
    She kicked and killed me quicker'n a wink. . . .

Molly, tho' pleasant in her day,
Was sudd'nly seized and sent away.
How soon she's ripe, how soon she's rotten,
Laid in the grave and soon forgott'n. . . .

Here lies the best of slaves,
    Now turning into dust.
Caesar, the Ethiopian, craves
    A place among the just.

His faithful soul is fled
    To realms of heavenly light;
And by the blood that Jesus shed,
    Is changed from black to white. . . .

I was drowned, alas! in the deep, deep seases.
The blessed Lord does as he pleases.
But my Kittery friends did soon appear,
And laid my body right down here.

To death he fell a helpless prey,
On April V and Twentieth Day,
In Seventeen Hundred Seventy-Seven
Quitting this world, we hope, for heaven.

Behold the amazing alteration,
Effected by inoculation;
The means empowered his life to save,
Hurried him headlong to the grave.

(From New England graveyards.)

A Family Affair

I
Ye Witty Mortals! as you're passing by,
    Remark, that near this Monument doth lie,
        Center'd in Dust,
    Two Husbands, Two Wives,
    Two Sisters, Two Brothers;
    Two Fathers, a Son
    Two Daughters, Two Mothers;
A Grandfather, Grandmother, and a Grand-daughter,
An Uncle, an Aunt, and their Niece follow'd after.
    This Catalogue of Persons, mention'd here,
    Was only Five, and all from incest clear.

(From *Maryland Gazette* (Annapolis), Aug. 16, 1749.)

the south

John Smith, a founder of the Virginia colony, was one of its most effective administrators. His accounts of the Virginia adventure and of his relations with the local Indian chief Powhatan may well suffer from his habit of exaggeration. But the tale of his encounter with the Indian princess Pocahontas, however near or far from the truth, became one of the first enduring popular romantic legends of the English experience in the New World. (Selections from John Smith, *A True Relation*, 1608, and *The Generall Historie of Virginia*, 1624.)

ON VIRGINIA

[1607]

. . . The first land we made, we fell with Cape Henry, the very mouth of the Bay of Chesapeake, which at that present we little expected, having by a cruel storm been put to the northward. Anchoring in this bay, twenty or thirty went ashore with the Captain, and in coming aboard they were assaulted with certain Indians which charged them within pistolshot, in which conflict Captain Archer and Mathew Morton were shot. Whereupon Captain Newport, seconding them, made a shot at them which the Indians little respected, but having spent their arrows retired without harm. And in that place was the box opened wherein the Council for Virginia was nominated. And arriving at the place where we are now seated, the Council was sworn and the president elected . . . where was made choice for our situation a very fit place for the erecting of a great city. All our provision was brought ashore, and with as much speed as might be we went about our fortification. . . .

Captain Newport, having set things in order, set sail for England the 22d of June, leaving provision for thirteen or fourteen weeks. The day before the ship's departure, the king of Pamaunkee sent the Indian that had met us before, in our discovery, to assure us of peace. Our fort being then palisaded round, and all our men in good health and comfort, albeit that through some discontented humors it did not so long continue. God (being angry with us) plagued us with such famine and sickness that the living were scarce able to bury the dead—our want of sufficient and good victuals, with continual watching, four or five each night at three bulwarks, being the chief cause. Only of sturgeon had we great store, whereon our men would so greedily surfeit as it cost many lives. . . . Shortly after it pleased God, in our extremity, to move the Indians to bring us corn, ere it was half ripe, to refresh us when we rather expected they would destroy us. About the 10th of September there were about forty-six of our men dead. . . .

Our provisions being now within twenty days spent, the Indians brought us great store both of corn and bread ready-made, and also there came such abundance of fowls into the rivers as greatly refreshed our weak estates, whereupon many of our weak men were presently able to go abroad. As yet we had no houses to cover us, our tents were rotten, and our cabins worse than nought. Our best commodity was iron, which we made into little chisels. The president and Captain Martin's sickness constrained me to be cape merchant, and yet to spare no pains in making houses for the company, who, notwithstanding our misery, little ceased their malice, grudging and muttering.

As at this time most of our chiefest men were either sick or discontented, the rest being in such despair as they would rather starve and rot with idleness than be persuaded to do anything for their own relief without constraint, our victuals being now within eighteen days spent, and the Indian trade decreasing, I was sent to the mouth of the river, to Kegquouhtan and Indian town, to trade for corn and try the river for fish; but our fishing we could not effect by reason of the stormy weather. With fish, oysters, bread, and deer they kindly traded with me and my men. . . .

And now [1608], the winter approaching, the rivers became so covered with swans, geese, ducks, and cranes, that we daily feasted with good bread, Virginia peas, pumpkins, and putchamins, fish, fowl, and divers sorts of wild beasts as fat as we could eat them: so that none of our tuftaffety humorists desired to go for England.

But our comedies never endured long without a tragedy; some idle exceptions being muttered against Captain Smith for not discovering the head of Chickahamania River, and taxed by the Council to be too slow in so worthy an attempt. The next voyage he proceeded so far that with much labor by cutting of trees asunder he made his passage; but when his barge could pass no farther, he left her in a broad bay out of danger of shot, commanding none should go ashore till his return: himself with two English and two savages went up higher in a canoe; but he was not long absent but his men went ashore, whose want of government gave both occasion and opportunity to the savages to surprise one George Cassen, whom they slew, and much failed not to have cut off the boat and all the rest.

Smith, little dreaming of that accident, being got to the marshes at the river's head, twenty miles in the desert, had his two men slain, as is supposed, sleeping by the canoe, whilst himself by fowling sought them victual: finding he was beset with 200 savages, two of them he slew, still defending himself with the aid of a savage his guide, whom he bound to his arm with his garters, and used him as a buckler, yet he was shot in his thigh a little, and had many arrows that stuck in his clothes; but no great hurt, till at last they took him prisoner. When this news came to Jamestown, much was their sorrow for his loss, few expecting what ensued.

Six or seven weeks those barbarians kept him prisoner, many strange triumphs and conjurations they made of him, yet he so demeaned himself amongst them, as he not only diverted them from surprising the fort but procured his own liberty, and got himself and his company such estimation amongst them that those savages admired him more than their own Quiyouckosucks.

The manner how they used and delivered him is as follows. . . .

He demanding for their captain, they showed him Opechankanough, king of Pamaunkee, to whom he gave a round ivory double compass dial. Much they marveled at the playing of the fly and needle, which they could see so plainly and yet not touch it because of the glass that covered them. But when he demonstrated by that globe-like jewel the roundness of the earth and skies, the sphere of the sun, moon, and stars, and how the sun did chase the night round about the world continually; the greatness of the land and sea, the diversity of nations, variety of complexions, and how we were to them antipodes, and many other such like matters, they all stood as amazed with admiration. Notwithstanding, within an hour after they tied him to a tree, and as many as could stand about him prepared to shoot him: but the king holding up the compass in his hand, they all laid down their bows and arrows, and in a triumphant manner led him to Orapaks, where he was after their manner kindly feasted, and well used.

At last they brought him to Werowocomoco, where was Powhatan, their emperor. Here more than two hundred of those grim courtiers stood wondering at him, as he had been a monster; till Powhatan and his train had put themselves in their greatest braveries. Before a fire upon a seat like a bedstead, he sat covered with a great robe, made of raccoon skins, and all the tails hanging by. On either hand did sit a young wench of sixteen or eighteen years, and along on each side the house, two rows of men, and behind them as many women, with all their heads and shoulders painted red, many of their heads bedecked with the white down of birds, but every one with something, and a great chain of white beads about their necks. At his entrance before the king, all the people gave a great shout. The queen of Appamatuck was appointed to bring him water to wash his hands, and another brought him a bunch of feathers, instead of a towel to dry them. Having feasted him after their best barbarous manner they could, a long consultation was held, but the conclusion was, two great stones were brought before Powhatan: then as many as could laid hands on him, dragged him to them, and thereon laid his head, and being ready with their clubs to beat out his brains, Pocahontas, the king's dearest daughter, when no entreaty could prevail, got his head in her arms, and laid her own upon his to save his from death: whereat the emperor was contented he should live to make him hatchets, and her bells, beads, and copper; for they thought him as well of all occupations as themselves. For the king himself will make his own robes, shoes, bows, arrows, pots; plant, hunt, or do anything so well as the rest.

Two days after, Powhatan having disguised himself in the most fearfulest manner he could, caused Captain Smith to be brought forth to a great house in the woods, and there upon a mat by the fire to be left alone. Not long after, from behind a mat that divided the house was made the most dolefulest noise he ever heard; then Powhatan, more like a devil than a man, with some two hundred more as black as himself, came unto him and told him now they were friends, and presently he should go to Jamestown, to send him two great guns, and a grindstone, for which he would give him the county of Capahowosick, and for ever esteem him as his son Nantaquoud.

William Byrd, II, of the Virginia Byrds was an amateur naturalist as well as the owner of a plantation and man of affairs. He also wrote a number of diaries and travel accounts which offer one of the better pictures of eighteenth-century life. While running a boundary line between Virginia and North Carolina in 1746, he received a rather jaundiced impression of the denizens of Virginia's neighboring state. (Excerpts from William Byrd, *Histories of the Dividing Line*, 1728-29.)

WILLIAM BYRD, THE DIVIDING LINE

12. Complaint was made to Me this Morning, that the Men belonging to the Periauga, had stole our People's Meat while they Slept. This provoked me to treat them a la Dragon, that is to swear at them furiously; & by the good Grace of my Oaths, I might have past for an Officer in his Majesty's Guards. I was the more out of Humour, because

it disappointed us in our early March, it being a standing Order to boil
the Pot over Night, that we might not be hinder'd in the Morning. This
Accident, & Necessity of drying our Bed-Cloaths kept us from decamp-
ing til near 12 a Clock. By this delay the Surveyors found time to plot
off their Work, and to observe the Course of the River. Then they past
it over against Northern's Creek, the Mouth of which was very near our
Line. But the Commissioners made the best of their way to the Bridge,
and going ashoar walkt to Mr Ballance's Plantation. I retir'd early to our
Camp at some distance from the House, while my Collegues tarry'd
within Doors, & refresh't themselves with a Cheerful Bowl. In the Gaiety
of their Hearts, they invited a Tallow-faced Wench that had sprain'd
her Wrist to drink with them, and when they had rais'd her in good
Humour, they examined all her hidden Charms, and play'd a great many
gay Pranks. While Firebrand who had the most Curiosity, was ranging
over her sweet Person, he pick't off several Scabs as big as Nipples, the
Consequence of eating too much Pork. The poor Damsel was disabled
from making any resistance by the Lameness of her Hand; all she cou'd
do, was, to sit stil, & make the Fashionable Exclamation of the Country,
Flesh a live & tear it, & by what I can understand she never spake so
properly in her Life. . . .

16. The Line was this day carry'd one Mile and half and 16 Poles.
The Soil continued soft and Miry, but fuller of Trees, especially White
cedars. Many of these too were thrown down and piled in Heaps, high
enough for a good Muscovite Fortification. The worst of it was, the Poor
Fellows began now to be troubled with Fluxes, occasion'd by bad Water
and moist Lodgings: but chewing of Rhubarb kept that Malady within
Bounds.

In the mean time the Commissioners decampt early in the Morning,
and made a March of 25 Miles, as far as Mr. Andrew Mead's, who lives
upon Nansimand River. They were no sooner got under the Shelter of
that Hospitable Roof, but it began to rain hard, and continued so to do
great part of the Night. This gave them much Pain for their Friends in
the Dismal, whose sufferings spoilt their Taste for the good Chear, where-
with they were entertain'd themselves.

However, late that Evening, these poor Men had the Fortune to
come upon another Terra-firma, which was the Luckyer for them, because the Lower ground, by the rain that fell, was made a fitter Lodging
for Tadpoles than men.

In our Journey we remarkt that the North Side of this great Swamp
lies higher than either the East on the West, nor were the approaches to
it so full of Sunken Grounds. We passt by no less than two Quaker
Meeting Houses, one of which had an Awkward Ornament on the West

End of it, that seem'd to Ape a Steeple. I must own I expected no such Piece of Foppery from a Sect of so much outside Simplicity.

That persuasion prevails much in the lower end of Nansimond county, for want of Ministers to Pilot the People a decenter way to Heaven.

The ill Reputation of Tobacco planted in those lower Parishes makes the Clergy unwilling to accept of them, unless it be such whose abilities are mean as their Pay. Thus, whether the Churches be quite void or but indifferently filled, the Quakers will have an Opportunity of gaining Proselytes. Tis a wonder no Popish Missionaries are sent from Maryland to labour in this Neglected Vineyard, who we know have Zeal enough to traverse Sea and Land on the Meritorious Errand of making converts.

Nor is it less Strange that some Wolf in Sheep's cloathing arrives not from New England to lead astray a Flock that has no shepherd. People uninstructed in any Religion are ready to embrace the first that offers. Tis natural for helpless man to adore his Maker in Some Form or other, and were there any exception to this Rule, I should expect it to be among the Hottentots of the Cape of Good Hope and of North Carolina.

There fell a great deal of Rain in the Night, accompany'd with a Strong Wind. The fellow-feeling we had for the poor Dismalites, on Account of this unkind. Weather, render'd the Down we laid upon uneasy. We fancy'd them half-drown'd in their Wet Lodging, with the Trees blowing down about their Ears. These Were the Gloomy Images our Fears Suggested; tho' twas so much uneasiness clear again. They happen'd to come of much better, by being luckily encampt on the dry piece of Ground afore-mention'd.

17. They were, however, forct to keep the Sabbath in Spite of their Teeth, contrary to the Dispensation our good Chaplain had given them. Indeed, their Short allowance of Provision would have justify'd their making the best of their way, without Distinction of days. Twas certainly a Work both of Necessity and Self-preservation, to save themselves from Starving. Nevertheless, the hard Rain had made everything so thoroughly wet, that it was quite impossible to do any Business. They therefore made a vertue of what they could not help, and contentedly rested in their dry situation.

Since the Surveyors had enter'd the Dismal they had laid Eyes on no living Creature: neither Bird nor Beast, Insect nor Reptile came in View. Doubtless, the Eternal Shade that broods over this mighty Bog, and hinders the sun-beams from blessing the Ground, makes it an uncomfortable Habitation for any thing that has life. Not so much as a Zealand Frog cou'd endure so Aguish a Situation.

It had one Beauty, however, that delighted the Eye, tho' at the Expense of all the other Senses: the Moisture of the Soil preserves a continual Verdure, and makes every Plant an Evergreen, but at the same time the foul Damps ascend without ceasing, corrupt the Air, and render it unfit for Respiration. Not even a Turkey-Buzzard will venture to fly over it, no more than the Italian Vultures will over the filthy Lake Avernus, or the Birds in the Holy-Land over the Salt Sea, where Sodom and Gomorrah formerly stood.

In these sad Circumstances, the Kindest thing we cou'd do for our Suffering Friends was to give them a place in the Litany. Our Chaplain, for his Part, did his Office, and rubb'd us up with a Seasonable Sermon. This was quite a new thing to our Brethren of North Carolina, who live in a climate where no clergyman can Breathe, any more than Spiders in Ireland.

For want of men in Holy Orders, both the Members of the Council and Justices of the Peace are empower'd by the Laws of that Country to marry all those who will not take One another's Word; but for the ceremony of Christening their children, they trust that to chance. If a Parson come in their way, they will crave a Cast of his office, as they call it, else they are content their Offspring should remain as Arrant Pagans as themselves. They account it among their greatest advantages that they are not Priest-ridden, not remembering that the Clergy is rarely guilty of Bestriding such as have the misfortune to be poor.

One thing may be said for the Inhabitants of that Province, that they are not troubled with any Religious Fumes, and have the least Superstition of any People living. They do not know Sunday from any other day, any more than Robinson Crusoe did, which would give them a great Advantage were they given to be industrious. But they keep so many Sabbaths every week, that their disregard of the Seventh Day has no manner of cruelty in it, either to Servants or Cattle.

It was with some difficulty we cou'd make our People quit the good chear they met with at this House, so it was late before we took our Departure; but to make us amends, our Landlord was so good as to conduct us Ten Miles on our Way, as far as the Cypress Swamp, which drains itself into the Dismal. Eight Miles beyond that we forded the Waters of Coropeak, which tend the same way as do many others on that side. In Six Miles more we reacht the Plantation of Mr. Thomas Spight, a Grandee of N Carolina. We found the good Man upon his Crutches, being crippled with the Gout in both his Knees. Here we flatter'd ourselves we should by this time meet with good Tydings of the

Surveyors, but had reckon'd, alas! without our Host: on the Contrary, we were told the Dismal was at least Thirty Miles wide at that Place. However, as nobody could say this on his own Knowledge, we Order'd Guns to be fired and a Drum to be beaten, but receiv'd no Answer, unless it was from that prating Nymph Echo, who, like a loquacious Wife, will always have the last Word, and Sometimes return three for one.

18. It was indeed no Wonder our Signal was not heard at that time, by the People in the Dismal, because, in Truth they had not then penetrated one Third of their way. They had that Morning fallen to work with great Vigour; and, finding the Ground better than Ordinary, drove on the Line 2 Miles and 38 poles. This was reckon'd an Herculean day's Work, and yet they would not have Stopp'd there, had not an impenetrable cedar Thicket chekt their Industry. Our Landlord had seated Himself on the Borders of this Dismal, for the Advantage of the Green Food His Cattle find there all Winter, and for the Rooting that Supports His Hogs. This, I own, is some convenience to his Purse, for which his whole Family pay dear in their Persons, for they are devoured by musketas all the Summer, and have Agues every Spring and Fall, which Corrupt all the Juices of their Bodies, give them a cadaverous complexion, and besides a lazy, creeping Habit, which they never get rid of.

19. We Ordered Several Men to Patrole on the Edge of the Dismal, both towards the North and towards the South, and to fire Guns at proper Distances. This they perform'd very punctually, but cou'd hear nothing in return, nor gain any Sort of Intelligence. In the mean time whole Flocks of Women and Children flew hither to Stare at us, with as much curiosity as if we had Landed from Bantam or Morocco.

Some Borderers, too, had a great Mind to know where the Line wou'd come out, being for the most part Apprehensive lest their Lands Should be taken into Virginia. In that case they must have submitted to some Sort of Order and Government; whereas, in N Carolina, every One does what seems best in his own Eyes. There were some good Women that brought their children to be Baptiz'd, but brought no Capons along with them to make the solemnity cheerful. In the mean time it was Strange that none came to be marry'd in such a Multitude, if it had only been for the Novelty of having their Hands Joyn'd by one in Holy Orders. Yet so it was, that tho' our chaplain Christen'd above an Hundred, he did not marry so much as one Couple dureing the whole Expedition. But marriage is reckon'd a Lay contract in Carolina, I said before, and a Country Justice can tie the fatal Knot there, as fast as an Arch-Bishop. . . .

25. The air was chill'd this Morning with a Smart North-west Wind, which favour'd the Dismalites in their Dirty March. They return'd by the Path they had made in coming out, and with great Industry arriv'd in the Evening at the Spot where the Line had been discontinued.

After so long and laborious a Journey, they were glad to repose themselves on their couches of Cypress-bark, where their sleep was as sweet as it wou'd have been on a Bed of Finland Down.

In the mean time, we who stay'd behind had nothing to do, but to make the best observations we cou'd upon that Part of the Country. The Soil of our Landlord's Plantation, tho' none of the best, seem'd more fertile than any thereabouts, where the Ground is near as Sandy as the Desarts of Affrica, and consequently barren. The Road leading from thence to Edenton, being in distance about 27 Miles, lies upon a Ridge call'd Sandy-Ridge, which is so wretchedly Poor that it will not bring Potatoes.

The Pines in this Part of the country are of a different Species from those that grow in Virginia: their bearded Leaves are much longer and their Cones much larger. Each Cell contains a Seed of the Size and Figure of a black-ey'd Pea, which, Shedding in November, is very good Mast for Hogs, and fattens them in a Short time.

The Smallest of these Pines are full of Cones, which are 8 or 9 Inches long, and each affords commonly 60 or 70 Seeds. This Kind of Mast has the Advantage of all other, by being more constant, and less liable to be nippt by the Frost, or Eaten by the Caterpillars. The Trees also abound more with Turpentine, and consequently yield more Tarr, than either the Yellow or the White Pine; And for the same reason make more durable timber for building. The Inhabitants hereabouts pick up Knots of Lightwood in Abundance, which they burn into tar, and then carry it to Norfolk or Nansimond for a Market. The Tar made in this method is the less Valuable, because it is said to burn the Cordage, tho' it is full as good for all other uses, as that made in Sweden and Muscovy.

Surely there is no place in the World where the Inhabitants live with less Labour than in N Carolina. It approaches nearer to the Description of Lubberland than any other, by the great felicity of the Climate, the easiness of raising Provisions, and the Slothfulness of the People.

Indian Corn is of so great increase, that a little Pains will Subsist a very large Family with Bread, and then they made have meat without any pains at all, by the Help of the Low Grounds, and the great Variety of Mast that grows on the High-land. The Men, for their Parts, just like the Indians, impose all the Work upon the poor Women. They make their Wives rise out of their Beds early in the Morning, at the same time that they lye and Snore, till the Sun has run one third of his course, and disperst all the unwholesome Damps. Then, after Stretching and Yawning for half an Hour, they light their Pipes, and, under the Protection of a cloud of Smoak, venture out into the open Air; tho', if it happens to be never so little cold, they quickly return Shivering into the Chimney corner. When the weather is mild, they stand leaning with both their arms upon the corn-field fence, and gravely consider whether they had best go and take a Small Heat at the Hough: but generally find reasons to put it off till another time.

Thus they loiter away their Lives, like Solomon's Sluggard, with their Arms across, and at the Winding up of the Year Scarcely have Bread to Eat.

To speak the Truth, tis a thorough Aversion to Labor that makes People file off to N Carolina, where Plenty and a Warm Sun confirm them in their Disposition to Laziness for their whole Lives.

This play, written by Robert Munford, a Virginia politician active from the 1750s through the Revolution, was never produced and has little enough literary merit. Yet scholars agree that it is the best portrait of mid-eigheenth-century political life that we have. Politics was a splendid game until it turned into a serious business in the 1770s. (From Robert Munford, "The Candidates," *William and Mary Quarterly*, 5 (1948), 229-45; 252-57.)

"THE CANDIDATES"

Act I. Scene I

Mr. Wou'dbe's house.
Enter Wou'dbe with a newspaper in his hand.

WOU'DBE.   I am very sorry our good old governor Botetourt has left us. He well deserved our friendship, when alive, and that we should for years to come, with gratitude, remember his mild and affable deportment. Well, our little world will soon be up, and very busy towards our next election. Must I again be subject to the humours of a fickle croud? Must I again resign my reason, and be nought but what each voter pleases? Must I cajole, fawn, and wheedle, for a place that brings so little profit?

Enter Ralpho (his Servant).

RALPHO.   Sir John Toddy is below, and if your honour is at leisure, would beg to speak to you.

WOU'DBE. My compliments to Sir John, and tell him, I shall be glad of his company. So—Sir John, some time ago, heard me say I was willing to resign my seat in the house to an abler person, and he comes modestly to accept of it.

Enter Sir John Toddy (a Candidate for Office).

SIR JOHN. Mr. Wou'dbe, your most obedient servant, sir; I am proud to find you well. I hope you are in good health, sir?

WOU'DBE. Very well, I am obliged to you, Sir John. Why, Sir John, you surely are practising the grimace and compliments you intend to make use of among the freeholders in the next election, and have introduced yourself to me with the self-same common-place expressions that we candidates adopt when we intend to wheedle a fellow out of his vote—I hope you have no scheme upon me, Sir John?

SIR JOHN. No, sir, upon my honour, sir, it was punctually to know how your lady and family did, sir, 'pon honour, sir, it was.

WOU'DBE. You had better be more sparing of your honour at present, Sir John; for, if you are a candidate, whenever you make promises to the people that you can't comply with, you must say upon honour, otherwise they won't believe you.

SIR JOHN. Upon honour, sir, I have no thought to set up for a candidate, unless you say the word.

WOU'DBE. Such condescension from you, Sir John, I have no reason to expect: you have my hearty consent to do as you please, and if the people choose you their Representative, I must accept of you as a colleague.

SIR JOHN. As a colleague, Mr. Wou'dbe! I was thinking you did not intend to stand a poll, and my business, sir, was to get the favour of you to speak a good word for me among the people.

WOU'DBE. I hope you have no occasion for a trumpeter, Sir John? If you have, I'll speak a good word to you, and advise you to decline.

SIR JOHN. Why, Mr. Wou'dbe, after you declin'd, I thought I was the next *fittenest* man in the country, and Mr. Wou'dbe, if you would be ungenerous, tho' you are a laughing man, you would tell me so.

WOU'DBE. It would be ungenerous indeed, Sir John, to tell you what the people could never be induced to believe. But I'll be ingenuous to tell you, Sir John, if you expect any assistance from me, you'll be disappointed, for I can't think you the *fittenest* man I know.

SIR JOHN. Pray, sir, who do you know besides? Perhaps I may be thought as fit as your honour. But, sir, if you are for that, the hardest fend off: damn me, if I care a farthing for you; and so, your servant sir.

Exit Sir John.

WOU'DBE. So, I have got the old knight, and his friend Guzzle, I suppose, against me, by speaking so freely; but their interest, I believe, has not weight enough among the people, for me to lose any thing, by making them my enemies. Indeed, the being intimate with such a fool as Sir John, might tend more to my discredit with them, for the people of Virginia have too much sense not to perceive how weak the head must be that is always filled with liquor. Ralpho!—

Enter Ralpho.

RALPHO.   Sir, what does your honour desire?

WOU'DBE.   I'm going into my library, and if any gentleman calls, you may introduce him to me there.

RALPHO.   Yes, sir. But, master, as election-times are coming, I wish you would remember a poor servant, a little.

WOU'DBE.   What do you want?

RALPHO.   Why, the last suit of clothes your honour gave me is quite worn out. Look here, (*shewing his elbows*) the insigns, (as I have heard your honour say, in one of your fine speeches) the insigns of faithful service. Now, methinks, as they that set up for burgesses, cut a dash, and have rare sport, why might not their servants have a little decreation?

WOU'DBE.   I understand you, Ralpho, you wish to amuse yourself, and make a figure among the girls this Election, and since such a desire is natural to the young, and innocent if not carried to excess, I am willing to satisfy you; you may therefore, have the suit I pulled off yesterday, and accept this present as an evidence that I am pleased with your diligence and fidelity, and am ever ready to reward it.

Exit Wou'dbe.

RALPHO.   God bless your honour! what a good master! who would not do every thing to give such a one pleasure? But, e'gad, it's time to think of my new clothes: I'll go and try them on. Gadso! this figure of mine is not reconsiderable in its delurements, and when I'm dressed out like a gentleman, the girls, I'm a thinking, will find desistible.

Exit.

Scene II

A porch of a tavern: a Court-house on one side, and an high road behind.

Captain Paunch, Ned, and several freeholders discovered.

NED.   Well, gentlemen, I suppose we are all going to the barbecue together.

CAPT. PAUNCH.   Indeed, sir, I can assure you, I have no such intention.

NED.   Not go to your friend Wou'dbe's treat! He's such a pretty fellow, and you like him so well, I wonder you won't go to drink his liquor.

CAPT. P. Aye, aye, very strange: but your friends Strutabout and Smallhopes, I like so little as never to take a glass from them, because I shall never pay the price which is always expected for it, by voting against my conscience: I therefore don't go, to avoid being asked for what I won't give.

NED. A very distress motive, truly, but for the matter of that, you've not so much to boast of your friend Wou'dbe, if what I have been told of him is true; for I have heard say, he and the fine beast of a gentleman, Sir John Toddy, have joined interess. Mr. Wou'dbe, I was creditly 'formed, was known for to say, he wouldn't serve for a burgess, unless Sir John was elected with him.

1ST FREEHOLDER. What's that you say, neighbor? has Mr. Wou'dbe and Sir John joined interest?

NED. Yes, they have; and ant there a clever fellow for ye? a rare burgess you will have, when a fellow gets in, who will go drunk, and be a sleeping in the house! I wish people wouldn't pretend for to hold up their heads so high, who have such friends and associates. There's poor Mr. Smallhopes, who isn't as much attended to, is a very proper gentleman, and is no drunkard, and has no drunken companions.

1ST FREEHOLDER. I don't believe it. Mr. Wou'dbe's a cleverer man than that, and people ought to be ashamed to vent such slanders.

2D FREEHOLDER. So I say: and as we are of one mind, let's go strait, and let Mr. Wou'dbe know it.

Exeunt two Freeholders.

3D FREEHOLDER. If Mr. Wou'dbe did say it, I won't vote for him, that's sartain.

4TH FREEHOLDER. Are you sure of it, neighbour?

(To Ned.)

NED. Yes, I am sure of it: d'ye think I'd speak such a thing without having good authority?

4TH FREEHOLDER. I'm sorry for't; come neighbour, *(to the 3d Free-holder)* this is the worst news that I've heard for a long time.

Exeunt 3rd & 4th Freeholder.

5TH FREEHOLDER. I'm glad to hear it. Sir John Toddy is a clever openhearted gentleman as I ever knew, one that wont turn his back upon a poor man, but will take a chearful cup with one as well as another, and it does honour to Mr. Wou'dbe to prefer such a one, to any of your whifflers who han't the heart to be generous, and yet despise poor folks. Huzza! for Mr. Wou'dbe and for Sir John Toddy.

6TH FREEHOLDER. I think so too, neighbour. Mr. Wou'dbe, I always thought, was a man of sense, and had larning, as they call it, but he did not love diversion enough, I like him the better for't. Huzza for Mr. Wou'dbe and Sir John Toddy.

BOTH.   Huzza for Mr. Wou'dbe and Sir John Toddy. Wou'dbe and Toddy, for ever, boys!

Exeunt.

Scene III

Wou'dbe's house.
Enter Wou'dbe, looking at a letter.

WOU'DBE.   This note gives me information, that the people are much displeased with me for declaring in favour of Sir John Toddy. Who could propagate this report, I know not, but was not this abroad, something else would be reported, as prejudicial to my interest; I must take an opportunity of justifying myself in public.

Enter Ralpho.

RALPHO.   Mr. Strutabout waits upon your honour.

WOU'DBE.   Desire him to walk in.

Enter Mr. Strutabout (another Candidate).

STRUTABOUT.   Mr. Wou'dbe, your servant. Considering the business now in hand I think you confine yourself too much at home. There are several little reports circulating to your disadvantage, and as a friend, I would advice you to shew yourself to the people, and endeavour to confute them.

WOU'DBE.   I believe, sir, I am indebted to my brother candidates, for most of the reports that are propagated to my disadvantage, but I hope, Mr. Strutabout is a man of too much honour, to say anything in my absence, that he cannot make appear.

STRUTABOUT.   That you may depend on, sir. But there are some who are so intent upon taking your place, that they will stick at nothing to obtain their ends.

WOU'DBE.   Are you in the secret, sir?

STRUTABOUT.   So far, sir, that I have had overtures from Mr. Small-hopes and his friends, to join my interest with their's, against you. This, I rejected with disdain, being conscious that you were the properest person to serve the county; but when Smallhopes told me, he intended to prejudice your interest by scatering a few stories among the people to your disadvantage, it raised my blood to such a pitch, that had he not promised me to be silent, I believe I should have chastised him for you myself.

WOU'DBE.   If, sir, you were so far my friend, I am obliged to you:

though whatever report he is the author of, will, I am certain, gain little credit with the people.

STRUTABOUT. I believe so; and therefore, if you are willing, we'll join our interests together, and soon convince the fellow, that by attacking you he has injured himself.

WOU'DBE. So far from joining with you, or any body else, or endeavouring to procure a vote for you, I am determined never to ask a vote for myself, or receive one that is unduly obtained.

Enter Ralpho.

RAL. Master, rare news, here's our neighbour Guzzle, as drunk as ever Chief Justice Cornelius was upon the bench.

WOU'DBE. That's no news, Ralpho: but do you call it rare news, that a creature in the shape of man; and endued with the faculties of reason, should so far debase the workmanship of heaven, by making his carcase a receptacle for such pollution?

RALPHO. Master, you are hard upon neighbour Guzzle: our Justices gets drunk and why not poor Guzzle? But sir, he wants to see you.

WOU'DBE. Tell him to come in. (*exit Ralpho*). All must be made welcome now.

Re-enter Ralpho and Guzzle, with an empty bottle.

GUZZLE. Ha! Mr. Wou'dbe, how is it?

WOU'DBE. I'm something more in my senses than you, John, tho' not so sensible as you would have me, I suppose.

GUZZLE. If I can make you sensible how much I want my bottle filled, and how much I shall love the contents, it's all the senses I desire you to have.

RALPHO. If I may be allowed to speak, neighbour Guzzle, you are wrong; his honour sits up for a burgess, and should have five senses at least.

GUZZLE. Five senses! how, what five?

RALPHO. Why, neighbour, you know, eating, drinking, and sleeping are three; t'other two are best known to myself.

WOU'DBE. I'm sorry Mr. Guzzle, you are so ignorant of the necessary qualifications of a member of the house of burgesses.

GUZZLE. Why, you old dog, I knew before Ralpho told me. To convince you, eating, drinking, and sleeping, are three; fighting and lying are t'others.

WOU'DBE. Why fighting and lying?

GUZZLE. Why, because you are not fit for a burgess, unless you'll fight; suppose a man that values himself upon boxing, should stand in the lobby, ready cock'd and prim'd, and knock you down, and bung up both your eyes for a fortnight, you'd be ashamed to shew your face in the house, and be living at our expence all the time.

Wou'dbe. Why lying?

Guzzle. Because, when you have been at Williamsburg, for six or seven weeks, under pretence of serving your county, and come back, says I to you, what news? none at all, says you; what have you been about? says I,—says you—and so out must tell some damned lie, sooner than say you have been doing nothing.

Wou'dbe. No, Guzzle, I'll make it a point of duty to dispatch the business, and my study to promote the good of my county.

Guzzle. Yes, damn it, you all promise mighty fair, but the devil a bit do you perform; there's Strutabout, now, he'll promise to move mountains. He'll make the rivers navigable, and bring the tide over the tops of the hills, for a vote.

Strutabout. You may depend, Mr. Guzzle, I'll perform whatever I promise.

Guzzle. I don't believe it, damn me if I like you.
Looking angry.

Wou'dbe. Don't be angry, John, let our actions hereafter be the test of our inclinations to serve you.
Exit Strutabout.

Guzzle. Agreed, Mr. Wou'dbe, but that fellow that slunk off just now, I've no opinion of.

Wou'dbe. (*Looking about*) what, is Mr. Strutabout gone? why, surely, Guzzle, you did not put him to flight?

Guzzle. I suppose I did, but no matter, (*holding up his bottle, and looking at it,*) my bottle never was so long a filling in this house, before; surely, there's a leak in the bottom, (*looks at it again*).

Wou'dbe. What have you got in your bottle, John, a lizard?

Guzzle. Yes, a very uncommon one, and I want a little rum put to it, to preserve it.

Wou'dbe. Hav'n't you one in your belly, John?

Guzzle. A dozen, I believe, by their twisting, when I mentioned the rum.

Wou'dbe. Would you have rum to preserve them, too?

Guzzle. Yes, yes, Mr. Wou'dbe, by all means; but, why so much talk about it, if you intend to do it, do it at once, man, for I am in a damnable hurry.

Wou'dbe. Do what? Who are to be burgesses, John?

Guzzle. Who are to be what? (*looking angry*).

Wou'dbe. Burgesses, who are you for?

Guzzle. For the first man that fills my bottle: so Mr. Wou'dbe, your servant.
Exit Guzzle.

Wou'dbe. Ralpho, go after him, and fill his bottle.

Ralpho. Master, we ought to be careful of the rum, else 'twill not hold out, (*aside*) it's always a feast or a famine with us; master has just got a little Jamaica for his own use, and now he must spill it, and spare it till there's not a drop left.

Exit.

Wou'dbe. (*pulling out his watch.*) 'Tis now the time a friend of mine has appointed for me to meet the freeholders at a barbecue; well, I find, in order to secure a seat in our august senate, 'tis necessary a man should either be a slave or a fool; a slave to the people, for the privilege of serving them, and a fool himself, for thus begging a troublesome and expensive employment.

> To sigh, while toddy-toping sots rejoice,
> To see you paying for their empty voice,
> From morn to night your humble head decline,
> To gain an honour that is justly thine,
> Intreat a fool, who's your's at this day's treat,
> And next another's, if another's meat,
> Is all the bliss a candidate acquires,
> In all his wishes, or his vain desires.

Exit.

End of the First Act.

The South is always mysterious to outsiders. Philip Fithian, a tutor on the giant Carter estate of 330,000 acres, worked hard at understanding his hosts. (From Philip Fithian, *Journal*, 1773.)

PHILIP FITHIAN, *Journal*

Monday 13 [December 1773]

The people are extremly hospitable, and very polite, both of which are most certainly universal Characteristics of the Gentlemen in Virginia —some swear bitterly, but the practice seems to be generally disapproved —I have heard that this Country is notorious for Gaming; however this be, I have not seen a Pack of Cards, nor a Die, since I left home, nor gaming nor Betting of any kind except at the Richmond Race. Almost every Gentleman of Condition keeps a Chariot and Four; many drive with six Horses.

Saturday 18

When the candles were lighted we all repaired, for the last minute, into the dancing Room; first each couple danced a Minuet; then all joined as before in the country Dances, these continued till half after Seven when we played *Button,* to get Pauns for Redemption; here I could join with them, and indeed it was carried on with sprightliness, and Decency; in the course of redeeming my Pauns, I had several Kisses of the Ladies!— Early in the Evening came colonel Philip Lee, in a traveling Chariot from Williamsburg—Half after eight we were rung into Supper; The room looked luminous and splendid; four very large candles burning on the table where we supp'd, three others in different parts of the Room; a gay, sociable Assembly, & four well instructed waiters!

Thursday 23

This Evening, after I had dismiss'd the Children, & was sitting in the School-Room cracking Nuts, none present but Mr. Carter's Clerk, a civil, inoffensive, agreeable young Man, who acts both in the character of a Clerk and Steward, when the Woman who makes my Bed asked me for the key of my Room, and on seeing the young Man, sitting with me, she told him that her Mistress had this afternoon given orders that their [the slaves'] Allowance of Meat should be given out to them to-morrow.

She left us; I then asked the young man what their allowance is? He told me that excepting some favourites about the table, their weekly allowance is a peck of Corn, & a pound of Meat a Head! And Mr. Carter is allow'd by all, & from what I have already seen of others, I make no Doubt at all but he is, by far the most humane to his Slaves of any in these parts! Good God! are these Christians?

When I am on the Subject, I will relate further, what I heard Mr. George Lees Overseer, one Morgan, say the other day that he himself had often done to Negroes, and found it useful; He said that whipping of any kind does them no good, for they will laugh at your greatest Severity; But he told us he had invented two things, and by several experiments had proved their success.

For Sulleness, Obstinacy, or Idleness, says he, take a Negro, strip him, tie him fast to a post; take then a sharp Curry-Comb, & curry him severely til he is well scrap'd; & call a Boy with some dry Hay, and make the Boy rub him down for several Minutes, then salt him, & unlose him. He will attend to his Business (said the inhuman Infidel) afterwards!

But savage Cruelty does not exceed His next diabolical Invention— To get a Secret from a Negro, says he, take the following Method—Lay upon your Floor a large thick plank, having a peg about eighteen Inches long, of hard wood, & very Sharp, on the upper end, fixed fast in the plank—then strip the Negro, tie the Cord to a staple in the Ceiling, so that his foot may just rest on the sharpened Peg, then turn him briskly around, and you would laugh (said our informer) at the Dexterity of the Negro, while he was releiving his Feet on the sharpen'd Peg!

The way of the artist is hard. (From *Maryland Gazette* (Annapolis), Sept. 8, 15, 22, 1774, *Middletown, Del.*)

THE ARTIST IN AMERICA

Annapolis, September 6, 1774

If a certain E. V. does not immediately pay for his family picture, his name shall be published at full length in the next paper.

CHARLES PEALE

Annapolis, September 13, 1774

Mr. Elie Vallette, pay me for painting your family picture.

CHARLES PEALE

Mr. Elie Vallette, pay me for painting your family picture.

CHARLES PEALE

Mr. Charles Wilson Peale, alias Charles Peale—yes, you shall be paid; but not before you have learned to be less insolent.

ELIE VALLETTE

The diary of William Winstan Fontaine, a mid-nineteenth-century Virginian, contains this secondhand account of a firsthand observation of Patrick Henry's famous remark in the Virginia House of Burgesses in 1775—one of the enduring events celebrated in story and song. (From William Winstan Fontaine, *Diary*, 1859.)

LIBERTY OR DEATH

Saturday, February 19, 1859, Williamsburg

I met an old friend of my father, Mr. Hugh Blair Grigsby, the Historian of the Virginia Convention of 1776. He introduced me to Ex-President John Tyler, as the great-grandson of Patrick Henry. Mr. Tyler asked me if I was the son of Colonel Wm. Spotswood Fontaine, of King William; and on my saying yes, he invited me to call at his room, as he wished to tell me something about Colonel Henry, which, perhaps, I had never heard. I accompanied Mr. Tyler to the house where he was staying.

On reaching his room, he said that his father had given him the following account of Colonel Henry's address delivered in March, 1775, in which he said: "Give me libery, or give me death."

There were, said Mr. Tyler, many in the Convention who opposed the resolution of Mr. Henry to organize the militia and put the colony into a posture of defense; these gentlemen by some were unjustly called submissionists.

Mr. Henry was holding a paper-cutter in his right hand; and when he came to that part of his speech in which he said, "I know not what course others may take," he cast a glance at these gentlemen, and bending his head forward, and with stooping shoulders, and with submissive expression of countenance, he crossed his wrists, as if to be bound; then suddenly straightening up, a bold, resolute purpose of soul flashed over his countenance and then, struggling as if trying to burst his bonds, his voice swelled out in boldest, vibrant tone; "Give me liberty!" Then wrenching his hands apart, and raising aloft his hand with the clenched paper-cutter, he exclaimed: "Or give me death!" And aimed at his breast, as with a dagger, and dropped to his seat.

The effect, continued Mr. Tyler, was electrical. There was more in the tones and the action than in the words. The house was still as death. The members felt as if they had witnessed a real tragedy of the noblest days of the Roman Republic.

Then the members started from their seats. "The cry 'to arms' seemed to quiver on every lip and gleam in every eye."

the middle states

Not until the nineteenth century did a writer of the first order recapture something of the Dutch "Knickerbockers" of seventeenth-century New Amsterdam.
Employing a kindly humor and pardonable exaggeration, Washington Irving
draws here a portrait of the honest simplicity of New York's first inhabitants.
(From Washington Irving, A History of New York—By Diedrich Knickerbocker,
1809.)

WOUTER VAN TWILLER AND HIS FINE LADY

In this dulcet period of my history, when the beauteous island of
Manna-hata presented a scene, the very counterpart of those glowing
pictures drawn of the golden reign of Saturn, there was, as I have before
observed, a happy ignorance, an honest simplicity prevalent among its
inhabitants, which, were I even able to depict, would be but little understood by the degenerate age for which I am doomed to write. Even the
female sex, those arch innovators upon the tranquillity, the honesty, and
gray-beard customs of society, seemed for a while to conduct themselves with incredible sobriety and comeliness.

Their hair, untortured by the abominations of art, was scrupulously
pomatumed back from their foreheads with a candle, and covered with
a little cap of quilted calico, which fitted exactly to their heads. Their
petticoats of linsey-woolsey were striped with a variety of gorgeous dyes
—though I must confess these gallant garments were rather short, scarce
reaching below the knee; but then they made up in the number, which
generally equalled that of the gentleman's small clothes; and what is
still more praiseworthy, they were all of their own manufacture—of
which circumstances, as may well be supposed, they were not a little vain.

These were the honest days in which every woman staid at home,
read the Bible, and wore pockets—ay, and that too of a goodly size,
fashioned with patchwork into many curious devices, and ostentatiously
worn on the outside. These, in fact, were convenient receptacles, where
all good housewives carefully stored away such things as they wished
to have at hand; by which means they often came to be incredibly
crammed—and I remember there was a story current when I was a boy
that the Lady of Wouter Van Twiller once had occasion to empty her
right pocket in search of a wooden ladle, when the contents filled a

couple of corn baskets, and the utensil was discovered lying among some rubbish in one corner—but we must not give too much faith to all these stories; the anecdotes of those remote periods being very subject to exaggeration.

Besides these notable pockets, they likewise wore scissors and pincushions suspended from their girdles by red ribands, or among the more opulent and showy classes, by brass, and even silver chains—indubitable tokens of thrifty housewives and industrious spinsters. I cannot say much in vindication of the shortness of the petticoats; it doubtless was introduced for the purpose of giving the stockings a chance to be seen, which were generally of blue worsted with magnificent red clocks —or perhaps to display a well-turned ankle, and a neat, though serviceable foot, set off by a high-heeled leathern shoe, with a large and splendid silver buckle. Thus we find that the gentle sex in all ages have shown the same disposition to infringe a little upon the laws of decorum, in order to betray a lurking beauty, or gratify an innocent love of finery.

From the sketch here given, it will be seen that our good grandmothers differed considerably in their ideas of a fine figure from their scantily dressed descendants of the present day. A fine lady, in those times, waddled under more clothes, even on a fair summer's day, than would have clad the whole bevy of a modern ball-room. Nor were they the less admired by the gentlemen in consequence thereof. On the contrary, the greatness of a lover's passion seemed to increase in proportion to the magnitude of its object—and a voluminous damsel arrayed in a dozen of petticoats, was declared by a Low Dutch sonneteer of the province to be radiant as a sunflower, and luxuriant as a full-blown cabbage. Certain it is, that in those days the heart of a lover could not contain more than one lady at a time; whereas the heart of a modern gallant has often room enough to accommodate half a dozen. The reason of which I conclude to be, that either the hearts of the gentlemen have grown larger, or the persons of the ladies smaller—this, however, is a question for physiologists to determine.

But there was a secret charm in these petticoats, which, no doubt, entered into the consideration of the prudent gallants. The wardrobe of a lady was in those days her only fortune; and she who had a good stock of petticoats and stockings, was as absolutely an heiress as is a Kamschatka damsel with a store of bearskins, or a Lapland belle with a plenty of reindeer. The ladies, therefore, were very anxious to display these powerful attractions to the greatest advantage; and the best rooms in the house, instead of being adorned with caricatures of dame Nature, in water colors and needle work, were always hung round with abundance of homespun garments, the manufacture and the property of the females—a piece of laudable ostentation that still prevails among the heiresses of our Dutch villages.

The gentlemen, in fact, who figured in the circles of the gay world in these ancient times, corresponded, in most particulars, with the beauteous damsels whose smiles they were ambitious to deserve. True it is, their merits would make but a very inconsiderable impression upon the heart of a modern fair; they neither drove their curricles, nor sported their tandems, for as yet those gaudy vehicles were not even dreamt of—neither did they distinguish themselves by their brilliancy at the table, and their consequent recontres with watchmen, for our forefathers were of too pacific a disposition to need those guardians of the night, every soul throughout the town being sound asleep before nine o'clock. Neither did they establish their claims to gentility at the expense of their tailors—for as yet those offenders against the pockets of society, and the tranquillity of all aspiring young gentlemen, were unknown in New Amsterdam; every good housewife made the clothes of her husband and family, and even the goede vrouw of Van Twiller himself thought it no disparagement to cut out her husband's linsey-woolsey galligaskins.

Not but what there were some two or three youngsters who manifested the first dawning of what is called fire and spirit; who held all labor in contempt; skulled about docks and market-places; loitered in the sunshine, squandered what little money they could procure at hustle-cap and chuck-farthing; swore, boxed, fought cocks, and raced their neighbor's horses—in short, who promised to be the wonder, the talk, and abomination of the town, had not their stylish career been unfortunately cut short by an affair of honor with a whipping-post.

Far other, however, was the truly fashionable gentleman of those days—his dress, which served for both morning and evening, street and drawing-room, was a linsey-woolsey coat, made, perhaps, by the fair hands of the mistress of his affections, and gallantly bedecked with abundance of large brass buttons—half a score of breeches heightened the proportions of his figure—his shoes were decorated by enormous copper buckles—a low-crowned broad-rimmed hat overshadowed his burly visage, and his hair dangled down his back in a prodigious queue of eelskin.

Thus equipped, he would manfully sally forth with pipe in mouth to besiege some fair damsel's obdurate heart—not such a pipe, good reader, as that which Acis did sweetly tune in praise of his Galatea, but one of true Delft manufacture, and furnished with a charge of fragrant tobacco. With this would he resolutely set himself down before the fortress, and rarely failed, in the process of time, to smoke the fair enemy into a surrender, upon honorable terms.

Such was the happy reign of Wouter Van Twiller, celebrated in many a long forgotten song as the real golden age, the rest being nothing but counterfeit copper-washed coin. In that delightful period, a sweet and holy calm reigned over the whole province. The burgomaster smoked his pipe in peace—the substantial solace of his domestic cares, after her daily toils were done, sat soberly at the door, with her arms crossed over her apron of snowy white, without being insulted with ribald street walkers or vagabond boys—those unlucky urchins who do so infest our streets, displaying, under the roses of youth, the thorns and briers of iniquity. Then it was that the lover with ten breeches, and the damsel with petticoats of half a score, indulged in all the innocent endearments of virtuous love without fear and without reproach; for what had that virtue to fear, which was defended by a shield of good linsey-woolseys, equal at least to the seven bull hides of the invincible Ajax?

Ah blissful, and never to be forgotten age! when every thing was better than it has ever been since, or ever will be again—when Buttermilk Channel was quite dry at low water—when the shad in the Hudson were all salmon, and when the moon shone with a pure and resplendent whiteness, instead of that melancholy yellow light which is the consequence of her sickening at the abominations she every night witnesses in this degenerate city!

Happy would it have been for New Amsterdam could it always have existed in this state of blissful ignorance and lowly simplicty, but alas! the days of childhood are too sweet to last! Cities, like men, grow out of them in time, and are doomed alike to grow into the bustle, the cares, and miseries of the world. Let no man congratulate himself, when he beholds the child of his bosom or the city of his birth increasing in magnitude and importance—let the history of his own life teach him the dangers of the one, and this excellent little history of Mannahata convince him of the calamities of the other.

Benjamin Franklin's *Poor Richard's Almanac,* which he published annually from 1732 to 1757, was one of the early journalistic successes of American history and among the most important expositions of a value system that has come to be identified more closely with American culture than any other. Franklin's collection of proverbs expressed the practical, time-is-money spirit of American capitalism with a thoroughness that has left all subsequent boosters as small footnotes to his central text. (From *Poor Richard's Almanac,* 1757.)

THE WAY TO WEALTH

Courteous Reader:

I have heard that nothing gives an author so great pleasure as to find his works respectfully quoted by other learned authors. This pleasure I have seldom enjoyed, for though I have been, if I may say it without vanity, an eminent author of *Almanacks* annually now a full quarter of a century, my brother authors in the same way, for what reason I know not, have ever been very sparing in their applauses, and no other author has taken the least notice of me, so that, did not my writings produce me some solid *pudding*, the great deficiency of *praise* would have quite discouraged me.

I concluded at length that the people were the best judges of my merit, for they buy my works; and, besides, in my rambles where I am not personally known, I have frequently heard one or other of my adages repeated, with, "as *Poor Richard* says," at the end of it; this gave me some satisfaction, as it showed not only that my instructions were regarded, but discovered likewise some respect for my authority; and I own that to encourage the practice of remembering and repeating those wise sentences I have sometimes *quoted myself* with great gravity.

Judge, then, how much I must have been gratified by an incident I am going to relate to you. I stopped my horse lately where a great number of people were collected at a vendue of merchant goods. The hour of sale not being come, they were conversing on the badness of the times and one of the company called to a plain clean old man with white locks, "Pray, father Abraham, what think you of the times? Won't these heavy taxes quite ruin the country? How shall we be ever able to pay them? What would you advise us to?" Father Abraham stood up and replied, "If you'd have my advice, I'll give it you in short, for 'A word to the wise is enough,' and 'Many words won't fill a bushel,' as *Poor Richard* says." They joined in desiring him to speak his mind, and gathering round him, he proceeded as follows:

"Friends," says he, "and neighbors, the taxes are indeed very heavy, and if those laid on by the government were the only ones we had to pay, we might more easily discharge them; but we have many others, and much more grievous to some of us. We are taxed twice as much by our *idleness*, three times as much by our *pride,* and four times as much by our *folly;* and from these taxes the commissioners cannot ease or deliver us by allowing an abatement. However let us hearken to good advice, and something may be done for us; 'God helps them that help themselves,' as *Poor Richard* says, in his *Almanack* of 1733.

"It would be thought a hard government that should tax its people one-tenth part of their *time*, to be employed in its service. But *idleness* taxes many of us much more, if we reckon all that is spent in absolute *sloth*, or doing of nothing, with that which is spent in idle employments or amusements that amount to nothing. Sloth, by bringing on diseases, absolutely shortens life. 'Sloth, like rust, consumes faster than labor wears; while the used key is always bright,' as *Poor Richard* says. 'But dost thou love life, then do not squander time, for that's the stuff life is made of,' as *Poor Richard* says. How much more than is necessary do we spend in sleep, forgetting that 'The sleeping fox catches no poultry,' and that 'There will be sleeping enough in the grave,' as *Poor Richard* says.

" 'If time be of all things the most precious, wasting time must be,' as *Poor Richard* says, 'the greatest prodigality'; since, as he elsewhere tells us, 'Lost time is never found again; and what we call time enough, always proves little enough.' Let us then up and be doing, and doing to the purpose; so by diligence shall we do more with less perplexity. 'Sloth makes all things difficult, but industry all easy,' as *Poor Richard* says; and 'He that riseth late must trot all day, and shall scarce overtake his business at night'; while 'Laziness travels so slowly that poverty soon overtakes him,' as we read in *Poor Richard*, who adds, 'Drive thy business, let not that drive thee'; and 'Early to bed and early to rise makes a man healthy, wealthy, and wise.'

"So what signifies *wishing* and *hoping* for better times. We may make these times better if we bestir ourselves. 'Industry need not wish,' as *Poor Richard* says, 'and he that lives upon hope will die fasting. There are no gains without pains; then help hands, for I have no lands,' or if I have, they are smartly taxed. And, as *Poor Richard* likewise observes, 'He that hath a trade hath an estate; and he that hath a calling hath an office of profit and honor'; but then the *trade* must be worked at, and the *calling* well followed, or neither the *estate* nor the *office* will enable us to pay our taxes. If we are industrious, we shall never starve; for, as *Poor Richard* says, 'At the workingman's house hunger looks in, but dares not enter.' Nor will the bailiff or the constable enter, for 'Industry pays debts, while despair increaseth them,' says *Poor Richard*. What though you have found no treasure, nor has any rich relation left you a legacy, 'Diligence is the mother of good luck,' as *Poor Richard* says, 'and God gives all things to industry. Then plough deep, while sluggards sleep, and you shall have corn to sell and to keep,' says *Poor Dick*. Work while it is called today, for you know not how much you may be hindered tomorrow, which makes *Poor Richard* say, 'One today is worth two tomorrows,' and further, 'Have you somewhat to do tomorrow, do it today.' If you were a servant, would you not be ashamed that a good master should catch you idle? Are you then your own master, 'be ashamed to catch yourself idle,' as *Poor Dick* says. When there is so much to be done for yourself, your family, your country, and your gracious king, be up by peep of day; 'Let not the sun look down and say, inglorious here he lies.' Handle your tools without mittens; remember that 'The cat in gloves catches no mice,' as *Poor Richard* says. 'Tis true there is much to be done, and perhaps you are weakhanded, but stick to it steadily; and you will see great effects, for 'Constant dropping wears away stones,' and by 'diligence and patience the mouse ate in two the cable'; and 'Little strokes fell great oaks,' as *Poor Richard* says in his *Almanack,* the year I cannot just now remember.

"Methinks I hear some of you say, 'Must a man afford himself no leisure? I will tell thee, my friend, what *Poor Richard* says: 'Employ thy time well, if thou meanest to gain leisure; and, since thou art not sure of a minute, throw not away an hour.' Leisure is time for doing something useful; this leisure the diligent man will obtain, but the lazy man never; so that, as *Poor Richard* says, 'A life of leisure and a life of laziness are two things.' Do you imagine that sloth will afford you more comfort than labor? No, for as *Poor Richard* says, 'Trouble springs from idleness, and grievous toil from needless ease. Many without labor would live by their wits only, but they break for want of stock.' Whereas industry gives comfort and plenty and respect: 'Fly pleasures, and they'll follow you. The diligent spinner has a large shift; and now I have a sheep and a cow, everybody bids me good morrow'; all which is well said by *Poor Richard.*

"But with our industry, we must likewise be *steady, settled,* and *careful,* and oversee our own affairs 'with our own eyes,' and not trust too much to others; for, as *Poor Richard* says,

> I never saw an oft-removed tree,
> Nor yet an oft-removed family,
> That throve so well as those that settled be.

and again, 'Three removes is as bad as a fire'; and again, 'Keep thy shop, and thy shop will keep thee'; and again, 'If you would have your business done, go; if not, send.' And again,

> He that by the plough would thrive,
> Himself must either hold or drive.

And again, 'The eye of a master will do more work than both his hands'; and again, 'Want of care does us more damage than want of knowledge'; and again, 'Not to oversee workmen, is to leave them your purse open.' Trusting too much to others' care is the ruin of many; for, as the *Al-*

manack says, 'In the affairs of this world, men are saved, not by faith, but by the want of it'; but a man's own care is profitable; for, says *Poor Dick*, 'Learning is to the studious,' and 'riches to the careful,' as well as 'power to the bold,' and 'Heaven to the virtuous.' And further, 'If you would have a faithful servant and one that you like, serve yourself.' And again, he advises to circumspection and care, even in the smallest matters, because sometimes 'A little neglect may breed great mischief'; adding, 'for want of a nail the shoe was lost; for want of a shoe the horse was lost; and for want of a horse the rider was lost, being overtaken and slain by the enemy; all for want of care about a horseshoe nail.'

"So much for industry, my friends, and attention to one's own business; but to these we must add *frugality*, if we would make our *industry* more certainly successful. A man may, if he knows not how to save as he gets, 'keep his nose all his life to the grindstone,' and die not worth a 'groat' at last. 'A fat kitchen makes a lean will,' as *Poor Richard* says; and

> Many estates are spent in the getting,
> Since women for tea forsook spinning and knitting,
> And men for punch forsook hewing and splitting.

'If you would be wealthy,' says he in another *Almanack*, 'think of saving as well as of getting: The Indies have not made Spain rich, because her outgoes are greater than her incomes.'

"Away then with your expensive follies, and you will not then have so much cause to complain of hard times, heavy taxes, and chargeable families; for, as *Poor Dick* says,

> Women and wine, game and deceit,
> Make the wealth small and the wants great.

And further, 'What maintains one vice would bring up two children.' You may think, perhaps, that a *little* tea or a *little* punch now and then, diet a *little* more costly, clothes a *little* finer, and a *little* entertainment now and then, can be no *great* matter; but remember what *Poor Richard* says, 'Many a little makes a mickle'; and further, 'Beware of little expenses; a small leak will sink a great ship'; and again, 'Who dainties love shall beggars prove'; and moreover, 'Fools make feasts, and wise men eat them.'

"Here you are all got together at this vendue of *fineries* and *knick-knacks*. You call them *goods*; but if you do not take care, they will prove *evils* to some of you. You expect they will be sold *cheap*, and perhaps they may for less than they cost; but if you have no occasion for them, they must be *dear* to you. Remember what *Poor Richard* says; 'Buy what thou hast no need of, and ere long thou shalt sell thy necessaries.' And again, 'At a great pennyworth pause a while'; he means that perhaps the cheapness is *apparent* only, and not *real;* or the bargain, by straitening thee in thy business, may do thee more harm than good. For in another place he says, 'Many have been ruined by buying good pennyworths.' Again, *Poor Richard* says, 'tis 'foolish to lay out money in a purchase of repentance'; and yet this folly is practiced every day at vendues, for want of minding the *Almanack.* 'Wise men,' as *Poor Dick* says, 'learn by others' harms, fools scarcely by their own; but *felix quem faciunt aliena pericula cautum.*' Many a one, for the sake of finery on the back, have gone with a hungry belly, and half-starved their families. 'Silks and satins, scarlet and velvets,' as *Poor Richard* says, 'put out the kitchen fire.'

"These are not the *necessaries* of life; they can scarcely be called the *conveniences;* and yet only because they look pretty, how many *want* to *have* them! The *artificial* wants of mankind thus become more numerous than the *natural;* and, as *Poor Dick* says, "for one poor person, there are a hundred indigent.' By these and other extravagances the genteel are reduced to poverty, and forced to borrow of those whom they formerly despised, but who through industry and frugality have maintained their standing; in which case it appears plainly that 'A ploughman on his legs is higher than a gentleman on his knees,' as *Poor Richard* says. Perhaps they have had a small estate left them, which they knew not the getting of; they think, ' 'Tis day, and will never be night'; that a little to be spent out of *so much* is not worth minding; 'A child and a fool,' as *Poor Richard* says, 'imagine twenty shillings and twenty years can never be spent' but, 'Always taking out of the meal-tub, and never putting in, soon comes to the bottom'; as *Poor Dick* says, 'When the well's dry, they know the worth of water.' But this they might have known before if they had taken his advice: 'If you would know the value of money, go and try to borrow some; for he that goes aborrowing goes asorrowing'; and indeed so does he that lends to such people, when he goes *to get it in again. Poor Dick* further advises, and says,

> Fond pride of dress is sure a very curse;
> E'er fancy you consult, consult your purse.

And again, 'Pride is as loud a beggar as want, and a great deal more saucy.' When you have bought one fine thing, you must buy ten more, that your appearance may be all of a piece; but *Poor Dick* says, ' 'Tis easier to suppress the first desire than to satisfy all that follow it.' And 'tis as truly folly for the poor to ape the rich, as for the frog to swell in order to equal the ox.

Great estates may venture more,
But little boats should keep near shore.

At the mention of lynching, we think of the South. At the mention of courts putting people to death on the testimony of unstable witnesses, we think of the Salem witchcraft madness. Yet New York City was the site of one of the most terrible episodes of bigotry and hysteria in all American history. The punishments meted out to those accused of conspiring to burn down New York in 1741 —hanging, burning at the stake, leaving bodies in chains on the gallows to rot —were far more terrible than anything done at Salem in 1692. One cannot help but wonder how well-known this incident would be had its victims not been black. (From Joel Tyler Headley, *The Great Riots of New York, 1712 to 1873*, 1873.)

THE GREAT ANTI-BLACK RIOT OF 1741

Probably no event of comparatively modern times—certainly none in our history—has occurred so extraordinary in some it its phases, as the negro riot of 1741.

The population numbered only about ten thousand, one-fifth of which was negroes, who were slaves. Their education being wholly neglected, they were ignorant and debased, and addicted to almost every vice. They were, besides, restive under their bondage and the severe punishments often inflicted on them, which caused their masters a great deal of anxiety. Not isolated as an inland plantation, but packed in a narrow space, they had easy communication with each other, and worse than all, with the reckless and depraved crews of the vessels that came into port. It is true, the most stringent measures were adopted to prevent them from assembling together; yet, in spite of every precaution, there would now and then come to light some plan or project that would fill the whites with alarm. They felt half the time as though walking on the crust of a volcano, and hence were in a state of mind to exaggerate every danger, and give credit to every sinister rumor.

The experience of the past, as well as the present state of feeling among the slaves, justified this anxiety and dread; for only thirty years before occurred just such an outbreak as they now feared. On the 7th of April, in 1712, between one and two o'clock in the morning, the house of Peter Van Tilburgh was set on fire by negroes, which was evidently meant as a signal for a general revolt.

The cry of fire roused the neighboring inhabitants, and they rushed out through the unpaved muddy streets, toward the blazing building. As they approached it, they saw, to their amazement, in the red light of the flames, a band of negroes standing in front, armed with guns and long knives. Before the whites could hardly comprehend what the strange apparition meant, the negroes fired, and then rushed on them with knives, killing several on the spot. The rest, leaving the building to the mercy of the flames, ran to the fort on the Battery, and roused the Governor. Springing from his bed, he rushed out and ordered a cannon to be fired from the ramparts to alarm the town. As the heavy report boomed over the bay and shook the buildings of the town, the inhabitants leaped from their beds, and looking out of the windows, saw the sky lurid with flames. Their dread and uncertainty were increased, when they heard the heavy splash of soldiers through the mud, and the next moment saw their bayonets gleam out of the gloom, as they hurried forward towards the fire. In the meantime, other negroes had rushed to the spot, so that soon there were assembled, in proportion to the white population, what in the present population of the city would be fully 10,000 negroes.

The rioters stood firm till they saw the bayonets flashing in the fire-light, and then, giving one volley, fled into the darkness northward, towards what is now Wall Street. The scattered inhabitants they met, who, roused by the cannon, were hastening to the fire, they attacked with their knives, killing and wounding several. The soldiers, firing at random into the darkness, followed after them, accompanied by a crowd of people. The negroes made for the woods and swamps near where the Park now stands, and disappearing in the heavy shadows of the forest, were lost to view. Knowing it would be vain to follow them into the thickets, the soldiers and inhabitants surrounded them and kept watch till morning. Many, of course, got off and buried themselves in the deeper, more extensive woods near Canal Street, but many others were taken prisoners. Some, finding themselves closely pressed and all avenues of escape cut off, deliberately shot themselves, preferring such a death to the one they knew awaited them. How many were killed and captured during the morning, the historian does not tell us. We can only infer that the number must have been great, from the statement he incidentally makes, that "during the day *nineteen more were* taken, tried, and executed—some that turned State's evidence were transported." "Eight or ten whites had been murdered," and many more wounded.

It was a terrible event, and remembered by the present inhabitants with horror and dismay. To the little handful occupying the point of the island, it was a tragedy as great as a riot in New York to-day would be, in which was a loss of 5,000 or more on each side.

Many middle-aged men, in 1741, were young men at that time, and remembered the fearful excitement that prevailed, and it was a common topic of conversation.

The state of things, therefore, which we have described, was natural. This was rendered worse by the arrival, in the winter of 1741, of a Spanish vessel, which had been captured as a prize, the crew of which was composed in part of negroes, who were sold at auction as slaves. These became very intractable, and in spite of the floggings they received, uttered threats that they knew would reach their masters' ears. Still, no evidence of any general plot against the inhabitants was suspected, and things were moving on in their usual way, when, on the 18th of March, a wild and blustering day, the Governor's house in the fort was discovered to be on fire. Fanned by a fierce south-east wind, the flames spread to the King's chapel, the secretary's house, barracks, and stables; and in spite of all efforts to save them, were totally consumed. The origin of the fire was supposed to be accidental, but a few days after, Captain Warren's house, near the fort, was found to be on fire. Two or three days later, the storehouse of Mr. Van Zandt was discovered on fire. Still, no general suspicions were aroused. Three more days passed, when a cow-stall was reported on fire, and a few hours later, the house of Mr. Thompson; the fire in the latter case originating in the room where a negro slave slept. The very next day, live coals were discovered under the stable of John Murray, on Broadway. This, evidently, was no accident, but the result of design, and the people began to be alarmed. The day following, the house of a sergeant near the fort was seen to be on fire, and soon after, flames arose from the roof of a dwelling near the Fly Market. The rumor now spread like wildfire through the town that it was the work of incendiaries. It seems to us a small foundation to base such a belief on, but it must be remembered that the public mind was in a state to believe almost anything.

The alarm was increased by the statement of Mrs. Earle, who said that on Sunday, as she was looking out of her window, she saw three negroes swaggering up Broadway, engaged in earnest conversation. Suddenly she heard one of them exclaim, "Fire! fire! Scorch! scorch; a little d—n by and by!" and then throwing up his hands, laughed heartily. Coupled with the numerous fires that had occurred, and the rumors afloat, it at once excited her suspicions that this conversation had something to do with a plot to burn the city. She therefore immediately reported it to an alderman, and he, next day, to the justices.

Although the number of buildings thus mysteriously set on fire was, in reality, small, yet it was as great in proportion to the town then, as three hundred would be in New York to-day. Less than that number, we imagine, would create a panic in the city, especially if the public mind was in a feverish state, as, for instance, during the recent civil war.

Some thought the Spanish negroes had set the buildings on fire from revenge, especially as those of the Government were the first to suffer. Others declared that it was a plot of the entire negro population to burn down the city. This belief was strengthened by the fact that, in one of the last fires, a slave of one of the most prominent citizens was seen to leap from the window, and make off over garden fences. A shout was immediately raised by the spectators, and a pursuit commenced. The terrified fugitive made desperate efforts to escape, but being overtaken, he was seized, and, pale as death, lifted on men's shoulders and carried to jail.

Added to all this, men now remembered it lacked but a few days of being the anniversary of the bloody riot of thirty years ago. They began to watch and question the negroes, and one of the Spanish sailors, on being interrogated, gave such unsatisfactory, suspicious answers, that the whole crew were arrested, and thrown into prison. But that same afternoon, while the magistrates, whom the alarming state of things had called together, were in consultation about it, the cry of "Fire!" again startled the entire community. The ringing of the alarm-bell had now become almost as terrifying as the sound of the last trumpet, and the panic became general. The first step was to ascertain if there were any strangers in town who might be concealed enemies, and a thorough search was made—the militia being ordered out, and sentries posted at the ends of all the streets, with orders to stop all persons carrying bags and bundles. This was done on the 13th of April. None being found, the conclusion became inevitable that some dark, mysterious plot lay at the bottom of it all, and the inhabitants thought the city was doomed, like Sodom. First, the more timorous packed up their valuable articles and fled into the country, up toward Canal Street. This increased the panic, which swelled until almost the entire population were seen hurrying through the streets, fleeing for their lives. The announcement of an approaching army would not have created a greater stampede. Every cart and vehicle that could be found was engaged at any price, into which whole families were piled, and hurried away to the farms beyond Chambers Street, in the neighborhood of Canal Street. It was a strange spectacle, and the farmers could hardly believe their senses, at his sudden inundation into their quiet houses of the people of the city. The town authorities were also swept away in the general excitement, and negroes of all ages and sexes were arrested by the wholesale, and hurried to prison. The Supreme Court was to sit in the latter part of April, and the interval of a few days was spent in efforts to get at the guilty parties. But nothing definite could be ascertained, as the conspirators, whoever they were, kept their own secret. At length, despairing of getting at the truth in any other way, the authorities offered a reward of a hundred pounds, and a full pardon to any one who would turn State's evidence, and reveal the names of the ringleaders. This was pretty sure to bring out the facts, if there were any to disclose, and almost equally sure to obtain a fabricated story, if there was nothing to tell. A poor, ignorant slave, shaking with terror in his cell, would hardly be proof against such an inducement as a free pardon, and to him or her an almost fabulous sum of money, if he had anything to reveal, while the temptation to invent a tale that would secure both liberty and money was equally strong.

On the 21st of April the court met, Judges Philips and Horsmander presiding. A jury was impanelled, but although there was no lack of prisoners, there was almost a total want of evidence sufficient to put a single man on trial. The reward offered had not borne its legitimate fruits, and no one offered to make any revelations.

Among the first brought up for examination was Mary Burton, a colored servant girl, belonging to John Hughson, the keeper of a low, dirty negro tavern over on the west side of the city, near the Hudson River. This was a place of rendezvous for the worst negroes of the town; and from some hints that Mary had dropped, it was suspected it had been the head-quarters of the conspirators. But when brought before the Grand Jury, she refused to be sworn. They entreated her to take the oath and tell the whole truth, but she only shook her head. They then threatened her, but with no better success; they promised she should be protected from danger and shielded from persecution, but she still maintained an obstinate silence. They then showed her the reward, and attempted to bribe her with the wealth in store for her, but she almost spat on it in her scorn. This poor negro slave showed an independence and stubbornness in the presence of the jury that astonished them. Finding all their efforts vain, they ordered her to be sent to jail. This terrified her, and she consented to be sworn. But after taking the oath, she refused to say anything about the fire. A theft had been traced to Hughson, and she told all she knew about that, but about the fires would neither deny nor affirm anything. They then appealed to her conscience; painted before her the terrors of the final judgment, and the torments of hell, till at last she broke down, and proposed to make a clean breast of it. She commenced by saying that Hughson had threatened to take her life if she told, and then again hesitated. But at length, by persistent efforts, the following facts were wrenched from her by piecemeal. She said that three negroes—giving their names—had been in the habit of meeting at the tavern, and talking about burning of the fort and city and murdering the people, and that Hughson and his wife had promised to help them; after which Hughson was to be governor and Cuff Phillipse king. That the first part of the story was true, there is little doubt. How much, with the imagination and love of the marvellous peculiar to her race, she added to it, it is not easy to say. She said, moreover, that but one white person beside her master and mistress was in the conspiracy, and that was an Irish girl known as Peggy, "the Newfoundland Beauty." She had several *aliases*, and was an abandoned character, being a prostitute to the negroes, and at this time kept as a mistress by a bold, desperate negro named Cæsar. This revelation of Mary's fell on the Grand Jury like a bombshell. The long-sought secret they now felt was out. They immediately informed the magistrates. Of course the greatest excitement followed. Peggy was next examined, but she denied Mary Burton's story *in toto*—swore that she knew nothing of any conspiracy or of the burning of the stores; that if she should accuse any one it would be a lie, and blacken her own soul.

It is rather a severe reflection on the courts of justice of that period, or we might rather say, perhaps, a striking illustration of the madness that had seized on all, that although the law strictly forbade any slave to testify in a court of justice against a white person, yet this girl Mary Burton was not only allowed to appear as evidence against Peggy, but her oath was permitted to outweigh hers, and cause her to be sentenced to death. The latter, though an abandoned, desperate character, was seized with terror at the near approach of death, and begged to be allowed another examination, which was granted, and she professed to make a full confession. It is a little singular that while she corroborated Mary Burton's statement as to the existence of a conspiracy, she located the seat of it not in Hughson's tavern, but in a miserable shanty near the Battery, kept by John Romme, who, she said, had promised to carry them all to a new country, and give them their liberty, if they would murder the whites and bring him the plunder. Like Mary Burton's confession, if truthful at all, it evidently had a large mixture of falsehood in it.

On Saturday, May 9th, Peggy was again brought in, and underwent a searching examination. Some of her statements seemed improbable, and they therefore tested them in every possible way. It lasted for several hours, and resulted in a long *detailed* confession, in which she asserted, among other things, that it was the same plot that failed in 1712, when the negroes designed to kill all the whites, in fact, exterminate them from the island. She implicated a great many negroes in the conspiracy; and every one that she accused, as they were brought before her, she identified as being present at the meetings of the conspirators in Romme's house. The court seemed anxious to avoid any collusion between the prisoners, and therefore kept them apart, so that each story should rest on its own basis. By this course they thought they would be able to distinguish what was true and what was false.

Either from conscious guilt, or from having got some inkling of the charge to be brought against him, Romme fled before he could be arrested. His wife, however, and the negroes whose names Peggy gave, were sent to jail.

On the 11th of May, or twenty days after the court convened, the executions commenced. On this day, Cæsar and Prince, two of the three negroes Mary Burton testified against, were hung, though not for the conspiracy, but for theft. They were abandoned men, and died recklessly. Peggy and Hughson and his wife were next condemned. The former, finding that her confession did not, as had been promised, secure her pardon, retracted all she had said, and exculpated entirely the parties whose arrest she had caused.

An atmosphere of gloom now rested over the city; every face showed signs of dread. In this state of feeling the Lieutenant-governor issued a proclamation, appointing a day of fasting and humiliation, not only in view of this calamity, but on account also of the want and loss caused by the past severe winter, and the declaration of war by England against Spain. When the day arrived, every shop was closed and business of all kinds suspended, and the silence and repose of the Sabbath rested on the entire community. Without regard to sect, all repaired to the places of worship, where the services were performed amid the deepest solemnity.

The day of execution appointed for Hughson, his wife, and Peggy was a solemn one, and almost the entire population turned out to witness it. The former had declared that some extraordinary appearance would take place at his execution, and every one gazed on him as he passed in a cart from the prison to the gallows. He was a tall, powerful man, being six feet high. He stood erect in the cart all the way, his piercing eye fixed steadily on the distance, and his right hand raised high as his fetters would permit, and beckoning as though he saw help coming from afar. His face was usually pale and colorless, but to-day it was noticed that two bright red spots burned on either cheek, which added to the mystery with which the superstitious spectators invested him. When the sad procession arrived at the place of execution, the prisoners were helped to the ground, and stood exposed to the gaze of the crowd. Hughson was firm and self-possessed; but Peggy, pale, and weeping, and terrorrstruck, begging for life; while the wife, with the rope round her neck, leaned against a tree, silent and composed, but colorless as marble. One after another they were launched into eternity, and the crowd, solemn and thoughtful, turned their steps homeward.

Hughson was hung in chains; and in a few days a negro was placed beside him, and here they swung, "blind and blackening," in the April air, in full view of the tranquil bay, a ghastly spectacle to the fishermen as they plied their vocation near by. For three weeks they dangled here in sunshine and storm, a terror to the passers-by. At length a rumor passed through the town that Hughson had turned into a negro, and the negro into a white man. This was a new mystery, and day after day crowds would come and gaze on the strange transformation, some thinking it supernatural, and others trying to give an explanation. Hughson had threatened to take poison, and it was thought by many that he had, and it was the effect of this that had wrought the change in his appearance. For ten days the Battery was thronged with spectators, gazing on these bloated, decomposing bodies, many in their superstitious fears expecting some new transformation. Under the increasing heat of the sun, they soon began to drip, till at last the body of Hughson burst asunder, filling the air with such an intolerable stench that the fishermen shunned the locality.

As simple hanging was soon thought not sufficient punishment, and they were left to swing, and slowly rot in chains, so this last was at length thought to be too lenient, and the convicts were condemned to be burned at the stake. Two negroes, named Quack and Cuffee, were the first doomed to this horrible death. The announcement of this sentence created the greatest excitement. It was a new thing to the colonists, this mode of torture being appropriated by the savages for prisoners taken in war. Curious crowds gathered to see the stake erected, or stare at the loads of wood as they passed along the street, and were unloaded at its base. It was a strange spectacle to behold—the workmen carefully pilling up the fagots under the spring sun; the spectators looking on, some horrified, and others fierce as savages; and over all the blue sky bending, while the gentle wind stole up from the bay and whispered in the tree-tops overhead. On the day of execution an immense crowd assembled. The two negroes were brought forward, pale and terrified, and bound to the stake. As the men approached with the fire to kindle the pile, they shrieked out in terror, confessed the conspiracy, and promised, if released, to tell all about it. They were at once taken down. This was the signal for an outbreak, and shouts of "burn 'em, burn 'em" burst from the multitude. Mr. Moore then asked the sheriff to delay execution till he could see the Governor and get a reprieve. He hurried off, and soon returned with a conditional one. But, as he met the sheriff on the common, the latter told him that it would be impossible to take the criminals through the crowd without a strong guard, and before that could arrive, they would be murdered by the exasperated populace. They were then tied up again, and the torch applied. The flames arose around the unhappy victims. The curling smoke soon hid their dusky forms from view, while their shrieks and cries for mercy grew fainter and fainter, as the fierce fire shrivelled up their forms, till at last nothing but the crackling of the flames was heard, and the shouting, savage crowd grew still. As the fire subsided, the two wretched creatures, crisped to a cinder, remained to tell, for the hundredth time, to what barbarous deeds terror and passion may lead men.

Some of the negroes went laughing to the place of execution, indulging in all sorts of buffoonery to the last, and mocking the crowd which surrounded them.

All protested their innocence to the last, and if they had confessed previously, retracted before death their statements and accusations. But this contradiction of themselves, to-morrow denying what to-day they had solemnly sworn on the Bible to be true, instead of causing the authorities to hesitate, and consider how much terror and the hope of pardon had to do with it, convinced them still more of the strength and dangerous nature of the conspiracy, and they went to work with a determination and recklessness which made that summer the bloodiest and most terrific in the annals of New York. No lawyer was found bold enough to step forward and defend these poor wretches, but all volunteered their services to aid the Government in bringing them to punishment. The weeks now, as they rolled on, were freighted with terror and death, and stamped with scenes that made the blood run cold. This little town on the southern part of Manhattan Island was wholly given to panic, and a nameless dread of some mysterious, awful fate, extended even to the scattered farm-houses near Canal Street. Between this and the last of August, a hundred and fifty-four negroes, exclusive of whites, were thrown into prison, till every cell was crowded and packed to suffocation with them. For three months, sentence of condemnation was on an average of one a day. The last execution was that of a Catholic priest, or rather a schoolmaster of the city, who was charged with being one. Mary Burton, after an interval of three months, pretended to remember that he was present with the other conspirators she had first named as being in Hughson's tavern.

His trial was long, and apparently without excitement. He conducted his own case with great ability, and brought many witnesses to prove his good character and orderly conduct; but he, of course, could not disprove the assertion of Mary, that she had some time or other seen him with the conspirators at Hughson's tavern—for the latter, with his wife and Peggy, and the negroes she had before named, had all been executed. Mary Burton alone was left, and her evidence being credited, no amount of testimony could avail him.

Although the proceedings were all dignified and solemn, as became an English court, yet the course the trial took showed how utterly unbalanced and one-sided it had become. To add weight to Mary's evidence, many witnesses were examined to prove that Ury, though a schoolmaster, had performed the duties of a Catholic priest, as though this were an important point to establish. The attorney-general, in opening the case, drew a horrible picture of former persecutions by the Papists, and their cruelties to the Protestants, until it was apparent that all that the jury needed to indorse a verdict of guilty was evidence that he was a Catholic priest. Still it would be unfair to attribute this feeling wholly to religious intolerance or the spirit of persecution. England was at this time at war with Spain, and a report was circulated that the Spanish priests in Florida had formed a conspiracy to murder the English colonists. A letter from Ogilthorpe, in Georgia, confirmed this. Ury, who was an educated Englishman, but had led an adventurous life in different countries, could not disprove this, and he was convicted and sentenced to be hung. He met his fate with great composure and dignity, asserting his innocence to the last. He made the eighteenth victim hung, while thirteen had been burned at the stake, and seventy-one transported to various countries.

At the average rate of two every week, one hanged and one burned alive, they were hurried into eternity amid prayers, and imprecations, and shrieks of agony. The hauling of wood to the stake, and the preparation of the gallows, kept the inhabitants in a state bordering on insanity. Business was suspended, and every face wore a terrified look. The voice of pity as well as justice was hushed, and one desire, that of swift vengeance, filled every heart. Had the press of to-day, with its system of interviewing, and minuteness of detail and description, existed then, there would have been handed down to us a chapter in human history that could be paralleled only in the dark ages.

A swift massacre, a terrible slaughter, comes and goes like an earthquake or a tornado, and stuns rather than debases; but this long, steady succession of horrible executions and frightful scenes changed the very nature of the inhabitants, and they became a prey to a spirit demoniacal rather than human. The prayers and tears of those led forth to the stake, their heart-rending cries as they were bound to it, and their shrieks of agony that were wafted out over the still waters of the bay, fell on hard and pitiless hearts. The ashes of the wood that consumed one victim would hardly grow cold before a new fire was kindled upon them, and the charred and blackened posts stood month after month, hideous monuments of what man may become when judgment and reason are surrendered to fear and passion. The spectacle was made still more revolting by the gallows standing near the stake, on which many were hung in chains, and their bodies left to swing, blacken, and rot in the summer air, a ghastly, horrible sight.

Where this madness, that had swept away court, bar, and people together, would have ended, it is impossible to say, had not a new terror seized the inhabitants. Mary Burton, on whose accusation the first victims had been arrested and executed, finding herself a heroine, sought new fields in which to win notoriety. She ceased to implicate the blacks, and turned her attention to the whites, and twenty-four were arrested and thrown into prison. Elated with her success, she began to ascend in the social scale, and criminated some persons of the highest social standing in the city, whose characters were above suspicion. This was turning the tables on them in a manner the upper class did not expect, and they began to reflect what the end might be. The testimony that was sufficient to condemn the slaves was equally conclusive against them. The stake and the gallows which the court had erected for the black man, it could not pull down because a white gentleman stood under their shadow.

Robespierre and his friends cut off the upper-crust of society without hesitation or remorse; but unfortunately the crust next below this became in turn the upper-crust, which also had to be removed, until at last they themselves were reached, when they paused. They had advanced up to their necks in the bloody tide of revolution, and finding that to proceed farther would take them overhead, they attempted to wade back to shore. So here, so long as the accusations were confined to the lowest class, it was all well enough, but when *they* were being reached, it was high time to stop. The proceedings were summarily brought to a close, further examinations were deemed unnecessary, and confessions became flat and unprofitable; and this strange episode in American history ended.

That there had been cause for alarm, there can be no doubt. That threats should be uttered by the slaves, is natural; for this would be in keeping with their whole history in this country. Nor is it at all improbable that a consiparcy was formed; for this, too, would only be in harmony with the conduct of slaves from time immemorial. The utter folly and hopelessness of such a one as the blacks testified to, has been urged against its existence altogether. If the argument is good for anything, it proves that the conspiracy thirty years before never existed, and that the Southampton massacre was a delusion, and John Brown never hatched his utterly insane conspiracy in Harper's Ferry. There have been a good many servile insurrections plotted in this country, not one of which was a whit more sensible or easier of execution than this, which was said to look to the complete overthrow of the little city. That the fires which first started the panic were the work of negro incendiaries, there is but little doubt; but how far they were a part of a wide-laid plan, it is impossible to determine.

Unquestionably, success at the outset would have made the movement general, so that nothing but military force could have arrested it.

There is one thing, however, about which there is no doubt—that a panic seized the people and the courts, and made them as unreliable as in the days of the Salem witchcraft. But these striking exhibitions of the weakness of human nature under certain circumstances have been witnessed since the world was made, and probably will continue to the end of time, or until the race enters on a new phase of existence. Panics, even among the most veteran soldiers, sometimes occur, and hence we cannot wonder they take place amid a mixed population. Popular excitements are never characterized by reason and common-sense, and never will be. In this case, there was more reason for a panic than at first sight seems to be.

In the first place, the proportion of slaves to the whites was large. In the second place, they were a turbulent set, and had shown such a dangerous spirit, that the authorities became afraid to let them assemble together in meetings. This restriction they felt sorely, and it made them more restive. All were aware of this hostile state of feeling, and were constantly anticipating some outbreak or act of violence. Besides, it was but a few years since the thing they now feared did actually take place. And then, too, the point first aimed at was significant, and showed a boldness founded on conscious strength. Right inside the fort itself, and to the Governor's house, the torch was applied. It certainly looked ominous. Besides, the very wholesale manner in which the authorities thought it best to go to work increased the panic. In a very short time over a hundred persons were thrown into prison. The same proportion to the population to-day would be over ten thousand. Such a wholesale arrest would, of itself, throw New York into the wildest excitement, and conjure up all sorts of horrible shapes. Add to this, an average of two hundred burned at the stake, and two hundred hung every week, or more than fifty a day, and nearly three times that number sentenced to transportation, and one can faintly imagine what a frightful state of things would exist in the city. The very atmosphere grew stifling from the smoke of burning men and women, while the gallows groaned under its weight of humanity. Had this been the wild work of a mob it would have been terrible enough, but when it was the result of a deliberate judicial tribunal, which was supposed to do nothing except on the most conclusive evidence, the sense of danger was increased tenfold. The conclusion was inevitable, that the conspiracy embraced every black man in the city, and was thoroughly organized. In short, the whole place was, beyond doubt, resting over a concealed volcano, and the instinct of self-preservation demanded the most summary work. Let the inhabitants of any city become thoroughly possessed of such an idea, and they will act with no more prudence or reason than the people of New York at that time did. An undoubted belief in such a state of things will confuse the perceptions and unbalance the judgment of a community anywhere and everywhere on the globe.

Still, consistent as it is with human history, one can hardly believe it possible, as he stands in New York to-day, that men have there been burned at the stake under the sanction of English law, or left to swing and rot in the winds of heaven, by order of the Supreme Court of the city.

"Captured by Indians!" Few things struck such a mixture of terror and adventure into white American hearts. Mrs. Jemison contemplates below the many possible outcomes of being captured—she fell among the Iroquois in 1755—and realizes one of the more surprising ones. These narratives were a popular literary form during the whole period in which Indians constituted a danger. (From James E. Seaver, *A Narrative of the Life of Mrs. Mary Jemison*, 1824.)

CAPTURED BY INDIANS

The night was spent in gloomy forebodings. What the result of our captivity would be, it was out of our power to determine or even imagine.—At times we could almost realize the approach of our masters to butcher and scalp us;—again we could nearly see the pile of wood kindled on which we were to be roasted; and then we would imagine ourselves at liberty; alone and defenceless in the forest, surrounded by wild beasts that were ready to devour us. The anxiety of our minds drove sleep from our eyelids; and it was with a dreadful hope and painful impatience that we waited for the morning to determine our fate.

The morning at length arrived, and our masters came early and let us out of the house, and gave the young man and boy to the French, who immediately took them away. Their fate I never learned; as I have not seen nor heard of them since.

I was now left alone in the fort, deprived of my former companions, and of everything that was near or dear to me but life. But it was not long before I was in some measure relieved by the appearance of two pleasant looking squaws of the Seneca tribe, who came and examined me attentively for a short time, and then went out. After a few minutes absence they returned with my former masters, who gave me to them to dispose of as they pleased.

The Indians by whom I was taken were a party of Shawanees, if I remember right, that lived, when at home, a long distance down the Ohio.

My former Indian masters, and the two squaws, were soon ready to leave the fort, and accordingly embarked; the Indians in a large canoe, and the two squaws and myself in a small one, and went down the Ohio.

When we set off, an Indian in the forward canoe took the scalps of my former friends, strung them on a pole that he placed upon his shoulder, and in that manner carried them, standing in the stern of the canoe, directly before us as we sailed down the river, to the town where the two squaws resided.

On our way we passed a Shawanee town, where I saw a number of heads, arms, legs, and other fragments of the bodies of some white people who had just been burnt. The parts that remained were hanging on a pole which was supported at each end by a crotch stuck in the ground, and were roasted or burnt black as a coal. The fire was yet burning; and the whole appearance afforded a spectacle so shocking, that, even to this day, my blood almost curdles in my veins when I think of them!

At night we arrived at a small Seneca Indian town, at the mouth of a small river, that was called by the Indians, in the Seneca language, She-nan-jee, where the two Squaws to whom I belonged resided. There we landed, and the Indians went on; which was the last I ever saw of them.

Having made fast to the shore, the Squaws left me in the canoe while they went to their wigwam or house in the town, and returned with a suit of Indian clothing, all new, and very clean and nice. My clothes, though whole and good when I was taken, were now torn in pieces, so that I was almost naked. They first undressed me and threw my rags into the river; then washed me clean and dressed me in the new suit they had just brought, in complete Indian style; and then led me home and seated me in the center of their wigwam.

I had been in that situation but a few minutes, before all the Squaws in the town came in to see me. I was soon surrounded by them, and they immediately set up a most dismal howling, crying bitterly, and wringing their hands in all the agonies of grief for a deceased relative.

Their tears flowed freely, and they exhibited all the signs of real mourning. At the commencement of this scene, one of their number began, in a voice somewhat between speaking and singing, to recite some words to the following purport, and continued the recitation till the ceremony was ended; the company at the same time varying the appearance of their countenances, gestures and tone of voice, so as to correspond with the sentiments expressed by their leader:

"Oh our brother! Alas! He is dead—he has gone; he will never return! Friendless he died on the field of the slain, where his bones are yet lying unburied! Oh, who will not mourn his sad fate? No tears dropped around him; oh, no! No tears of his sisters were there! He fell in his prime, when his arm was most needed to keep us from danger! Alas! he has gone! and left us in sorrow, his loss to bewail: Oh where is his spirit? His spirit went naked, and hungry it wanders, and thirsty and wounded it groans to return! Oh helpless and wretched, our brother has gone! No blanket nor food to nourish and warm him; nor candles to light him, nor weapons of war:—Oh, none of those comforts had he! But well we remember his deeds!—The deer he could take on the chase! The panther shrunk back at the sight of his strength! His enemies fell at his feet! He was brave and courageous in war! As the fawn he was harmless; his friendship was ardent: his temper was gentle: his pity was great! Oh! our friend our companion is dead! Our brother, our brother, alas! he is gone! But why do we grieve for his loss? In the strength of a warrior, undaunted he left us, to fight by the side of the Chiefs! His war-whoop was shrill! His rifle well aimed laid his enemies low: his tomahawk drank of their blood: and his knife flayed their scalps while yet covered with gore! And why do we mourn? Though he fell on the field of the slain, with glory he fell, and his spirit went up to the land of his fathers in war! Then why do we mourn? With transports of joy they received him, and fed him, and clothed him, and welcomed him there! Oh friends, he is happy; then dry up your tears! His spirit has seen our distress, and sent us a helper who with pleasure we greet. Dickewamis has come: then let us receive her with joy! She is handsome and pleasant! Oh! she is our sister, and gladly we welcome her here. In the place of our brother she stands in our tribe.; With care we will guard her from trouble; and may she be happy till her spirit shall leave us."

In the course of that ceremony, from mourning they became serene —joy sparkled in their countenances, and they seemed to rejoice over me as over a long lost child. I was made welcome amongst them as a sister to the two Squaws before mentioned, and was called Dickewamis; which being interpreted, signifies a pretty girl, a handsome girl, or a pleasant, good thing. That is the name by which I have ever since been called by the Indians.

I afterwards learned that the ceremony I at that time passed through, was that of adoption. The two squaws had lost a brother in Washington's war, sometime in the year before, and in consequence of his death went up to Fort Pitt, on the day on which I arrived there, in order to receive a prisoner or an enemy's scalp, to supply their loss.

It is a custom of the Indians, when one of their number is slain or taken prisoner in battle, to give to the nearest relative to the dead or absent, a prisoner, if they have chanced to take one, and if not, to give him the scalp of an enemy. On the return of the Indians from conquest, which is always announced by peculiar shoutings, demonstrations of joy, and the exhibition of some trophy of victory, the mourners come forward and make their claims. If they receive a prisoner, it is at their option either to satiate their vengeance by taking his life in the most cruel manner they can conceive of; or, to receive and adopt him into the family, in the place of him whom they have lost. All the prisoners that are taken in battle and carried to the encampment or town by the Indians, are given to the bereaved families, till their number is made good. And unless the mourners have but just received the news of their bereavement, and are under the operation of a paroxysm of grief, anger and revenge; or, unless the prisoner is very old, sickly, or homely, they generally save him, and treat him kindly. But if their mental wound is fresh, their loss so great that they deem it irreparable, or if their prisoner or prisoners do not meet their approbation, no torture, let it be ever so cruel, seems sufficient to make them satisfaction. It is family, and not national, sacrifices amongst the Indians, that has given them an indelible stamp as barbarians, and identified their character with the idea which is generally formed of unfeeling ferocity, and the most abandoned cruelty.

It was my happy lot to be accepted for adoption; and at the time of the ceremony I was received by the two squaws, to supply the place of their brother in the family; and I was ever considered and treated by them as a real sister, the same as though I had been born of their mother.

During my adoption, I sat motionless, nearly terrified to death at the appearance and actions of the company, expecting every moment to feel their vengeance, and suffer death on the spot. I was, however, happily disappointed, when at the close of the ceremony the company retired, and my sisters went about employing every means for my consolation and comfort.

Being now settled and provided with a home, I was employed in nursing the children, and doing light work about the house. Occasionally I was sent out with the Indian hunters, when they went but a short distance, to help them carry their game. My situation was easy; I had no particular hardships to endure. But still, the recollection of my parents, my brothers and sisters, my home, and my own captivity, destroyed my happiness, and made me constantly solitary, lonesome and gloomy.

My sisters would not allow me to speak English in their hearing; but remembering the charge that my dear mother gave me at the time I left her, whenever I chanced to be alone I made a business of repeating my prayer, catechism, or something I had learned in order that I might not forget my own language. By practising in that way I retained it till I came to Genesee flats, where I soon became acquainted with English people with whom I have been almost daily in the habit of conversing.

My sisters were diligent in teaching me their language; and to their great satisfaction I soon learned so that I could understand it readily, and speak it fluently. I was very fortunate in falling into their hands; for they were kind good natured women; peaceable and mild in their dispositions; temperate and decent in their habits, and very tender and gentle towards me. I have great reason to respect them, though they have been dead a great number of years.

The town where they lived was pleasantly situated on the Ohio, at the mouth of the Shenanjee: the land produced good corn; the woods furnished a plenty of game, and the waters abounded with fish. Another river emptied itself into the Ohio, directly opposite the mouth of the Shenanjee. We spent the summer at that place, where we planted, hoed, and harvested a large crop of corn, of an excellent quality.

About the time of corn harvest, Fort Pitt was taken from the French by the English.

The corn being harvested, the Indians took it on horses and in canoes, and proceeded down the Ohio, occasionally stopping to hunt a few days, till we arrived at the mouth of Sciota river; where they established their winter quarters, and continued hunting till the ensuing spring, in the adjacent wilderness. While at that place I went with the other children to assist the hunters to bring in their game. The forests on the Sciota were well stocked with elk, deer, and other large animals; and the marshes contained large numbers of beaver, muskrat, &c. which made excellent hunting for the Indians; who depended, for their meat, upon their success in taking elk and deer; and for ammunition and clothing, upon the beaver, muskrat, and other furs that they could take in addition to their peltry.

The season for hunting being passed, we all returned in the spring to the mouth of the river Shenanjee, to the houses and fields we had left in the fall before. There we again planted our corn, squashes, and beans, on the fields that we occupied the preceding summer.

About planting time, our Indians all went up to Fort Pitt, to make peace with the British, and took me with them. We landed on the opposite side of the river from the fort, and encamped for the night. Early the next morning the Indians took me over to the fort to see the white people that were there. It was then that my heart bounded to be liberated from the Indians and to be restored to my friends and my country. The white people were surprized to see me with the Indians, enduring the hardships of a savage life, at so early an age, and with so delicate a constitution as I appeared to possess. They asked me my name; where and when I was taken—and appeared very much interested on my behalf. They were continuing their inquiries, when my sisters became alarmed, believing that I should be taken from them, hurried me into their canoe and recrossed the river—took their bread out of the fire and fled with me, without stopping, till they arrived at the river Shenanjee. So great was their fear of losing me, or of my being given up in the treaty, that they never once stopped rowing till they got home.

Shortly after we left the shore opposite the fort, as I was informed by one of my Indian brothers, the white people came over to take me back; but after considerable inquiry, and having made diligent search to find where I was hid, they returned with heavy hearts. Although I had then been with the Indians something over a year, and had become considerably habituated to their mode of living, and attached to my sisters, the sight of white people who could speak English inspired me with an unspeakable anxiety to go home with them, and share in the blessings of civilization. My sudden departure and escape from them, seemed like a second captivity, and for a long time I brooded the thoughts of my miserable situation with almost as much sorrow and dejection as I had done those of my first sufferings. Time, the destroyer of every affection, wore away my unpleasant feelings, and I became as contented as before.

We tended our cornfields through the summer; and after we had harvested the crop, we again went down the river to the hunting ground on the Sciota, where we spent the winter, as we had done the winter before.

Early in the spring we sailed up the Ohio river, to a place that the Indians called Wiishto, where one river emptied into the Ohio on one side, and another on the other. At that place the Indians built a town, and we planted corn.

We lived three summers at Wiishto, and spent each winter on the Sciota.

The first summer of our living at Wiishto, a party of Delaware Indians came up the river, took up their residence, and lived in common with us. They brought five white prisoners with them, who by their conversation, made my situation much more agreeable, as they could all speak English. I have forgotten the names of all of them except one, which was Priscilla Ramsay. She was a very handsome, good natured girl, and was married soon after she came to Wiishto to Capt. Little Billy's uncle, who went with her on a visit to her friends in the states. Having tarried with them as long as she wished to, she returned with her husband to Can-a-ah-tua, where he died. She, after his death, married a white man by the name of Nettles, and now lives with him (if she is living) on Grand River, Upper Canada.

Not long after the Delawares came to live with us, at Wiishto, my sisters told me that I must go and live with one of them, whose name was She-nin-jee. Not daring to cross them, or disobey their commands, with a great degree of reluctance I went; and Sheninjee and I were married according to Indian custom.

Sheninjee was a noble man; large in stature; elegant in his appearance; generous in his conduct; courageous in war; a friend to peace, and a great lover of justice. He supported a degree of dignity far above his rank, and merited and received the confidence and friendship of all the tribes with whom he was acquainted. Yet, Sheninjee was an Indian. The idea of spending my days with him, at first seemed perfectly irreconcilable to my feelings: but his good nature, generosity, tenderness, and friendship towards me, soon gained my affection; and, strange as it may seem, I loved him!—To me he was ever kind in sickness, and always treated me with gentleness; in fact, he was an agreeable husband, and a comfortable companion. We lived happily together till the time of our final separation, which happened two or three years after our marriage, as I shall presently relate.

In the second summer of my living at Wiishto, I had a child at the time that the kernels of corn first appeared on the cob. When I was taken sick, Sheninjee was absent, and I was sent to a small shed, on the bank of the river, which was made of boughs, where I was obliged to stay till my husband returned. My two sisters, who were my only companions, attended me, and on the second day of my confinement my child was born; but it lived only two days. It was a girl: and notwithstanding the shortness of the time that I possessed it, it was a great grief to me to lose it.

After the birth of my child, I was very sick, but was not allowed to go into the house for two weeks; when, to my great joy, Sheninjee returned, and I was taken in and as comfortably provided for as our situation would admit of. My disease continued to increase for a number of days; and I became so far reduced that my recovery was despaired of by my friends, and I concluded that my troubles would soon be finished. At length, however, my complaint took a favorable turn, and by the time that the corn was ripe I was able to get about. I continued to gain my health, and in the fall was able to go to our winter quarters, on the Sciota, with the Indians.

From that time, nothing remarkable occurred to me till the fourth winter of my captivity, when I had a son born, while I was at Sciota.

Before the days of the camera, travellers had to keep journals to remember where they had been and what they had seen. Alexander Hamilton, a colonial traveller, observed his fellow countrymen and found them heavily under the influence of alcohol most of the time. Until the temperance crusades of the nineteenth century, Americans were among the most formidable drinkers in the world. (From Alexander Hamilton, *Diary*, 1744.)

ALEXANDER HAMILTON, *Diary*

Thursday, May 31 [1744]

I put up att one Tradaway's about 10 miles from Joppa [Maryland].

Just as I dismounted att Tradaway's, I found a drunken club dismissing. Most of them had got upon their horses and were seated in an oblique situation, deviating much from a perpendicular to the horizontal plane, a posture quite necessary for keeping the center of gravity within its proper base for the support of the superstructure; hence we deduct the true physicall reason why our heads overloaded with liquor become too ponderous for our heels.

Their discourse was as oblique as their position; the only thing intelligible in it was oaths and God dammes; the rest was an inarticulate sound like Rabelais' frozen words a thawing, interlaced with hickupings and belchings. I was uneasy till they were gone, and my landlord, seeing me stare, made that trite apology—that indeed he did not care to have such disorderly fellows come about his house; he was always noted far and near for keeping a quiet house and entertaining only gentlemen or such like, but these were country people, his neighbours, and it was not prudent to dissoblige them upon slight occasions. "Alas, sir!" added he, "we that entertain travelers must strive to oblige every body, for it is our dayly bread."

While he spoke thus, our bacchanalians, finding no more rum in play, rid off helter skelter as if the devil had possessed them, every man sitting his horse in a see-saw manner like a bunch of rags tyed upon the saddle.

I found nothing particular or worth notice in my landlord's character or conversation, only as to his bodily make. He was a fat pursy man and had large bubbies like a woman.

I supped upon fry'd chickens and bacon, and after supper the conversation turned upon politicks, news, and the dreaded French war. This learned company consisted of the landlord, his overseer and miller, and another greasy-thumbed fellow who, as I understood, professed physick and particularly surgery. In the drawing of teeth, he practiced upon the housemaid, a dirty piece of lumber, who made such screaming and squalling as made me imagine there was murder going forwards in the house. However, the artist got the tooth out att last with a great clumsy pair of black-smith's forceps; and indeed it seemed to require such an instrument, for when he showed it to us, it resembled a horse-nail more than a tooth.

After having had my fill of this elegant company, I went to bed att 10 o'clock.

Tuesday, June 5 [Wilmington]

After dinner we fell upon politicks, and the expected French war naturally came in, whence arose a learned dispute which was about settling the meaning of the two words, declaration and proclamation.

Mr. Smith asserted that a proclamation of war was an impropper phraze, and that it ought to be a declaration of war, and on the other hand a proclamation of peace.

Mr. Morison affirmed with a bloody oath that there might be such a thing as a proclamation of a declaration and swore heartily that he knew it to be true both by experience and hearsay. They grew very loud upon it as they put about the bowl, and I retired into a corner of the room to laugh a little, handkerchief fashion, pretending to be busied in blowing my nose; so I slurd a laugh with nose blowing as people sometimes do a fart with coughing.

Saturday, June 9th [Philadelphia]

At six in the evening I went to my lodging, and looking out att the window, having been led there by a noise in the street, I was entertained by a boxing match between a master and his servant. The master was an unwieldy, pott-gutted fellow, the servant muscular, rawbon'd, and tall; therefor tho he was his servant in station of life, yet he would have been his master in single combat had not the bystanders assisted the master and holp him up as often as the fellow threw him down. The servant, by his dialect, was a Scotsman; the names he gave his master were no better than little bastard, and shitten elf, terms ill apply'd to such a pursy load of flesh.

Friday, June 15 [New York]

After supper they set in for drinking, to which I was averse and therefor sat upon nettles. They filled up bumpers att each round, but I would drink only three which were to the King, Governour Clinton, and Governour Bladen, which last was my own.

Two or three toapers in the company seemed to be of opinion that a man could not have a more sociable quality or enduement than to be able to pour down seas of liquor and remain unconquered while others sunk under the table. I heard this philosophical maxim but silently dissented to it.

I left the company att 10 att night pritty well flushed with my three bumpers and, ruminating on my folly, went to my lodging att Mrs. Hogg's in Broadstreet.

Sunday, June 17th [The Battery, New York]

Mr. Jefferys told me that to walk out after dusk upon this platform was a good way for a stranger to fit himself with a courtezan, for that place was the generall rendezvous of the fair sex of that profession after sun set. He told me there was a good choice of pritty lasses among them, both Dutch and English. However, I was not so abandoned as to go among them but went and supped with the Club att Todd's.

It appeared that our landlord was drunk, both by his words and actions. When we called for one thing he hastily pulled the bell rope, and when the servants came up, Todd had by that time forgot what was called for.

Then he gave us a discourse upon law and gospell and swore by God that he would prove that law was founded upon gospell and gospell upon law, and that reason was depending upon both and therefor to be a good lawer it was substituted to be a good gospeller. We asked him what such a wicked dog as he had to do with gospell. He swore by God that he had a soul to be saved as well as the King, and he would neither be hang'd nor damn'd for all the Kings in Christendome.

We could not get rid of him till we put him in a passion by affirming he had no soul and offering to lay him a dozen of wine that he could not prove he had one. Att which, after some taggs of incoherent argument, he departed the room in wrath, calling us heathens and infidels. I went home att 12 o'clock.

Friday, July 6

I dined at Todd's, where there was a mixed company. After dinner they went to the old trade of bumpering.

In this company there was one of these despicable fellows whom we may call court spies, a man, as I understand, pretty intimate with Governour Clinton who might perhaps share some favour for his dexterity in intelligence. This fellow I found made it his business to foist himself into all mixed companies to hear what was said and to inquire into the business and character of strangers.

After dinner I happened to be in a room near the porch fronting the street, and overheard this worthy intelligencer a-pumping of Todd, the landlord. Todd informed him who I was, upon his asking the question. "You mean the pockfretten man," said he, "with the dark-coloured silk coat. One Hamilton from Maryland. They say he is a doctor, and traveling for his health."

Just as the inquisitor was desiring Todd to speak lower (he was not deaf) I bolted out upon them and put an end to the inquiry, and the inquisitor went about his business.

At five I went to the coffeehouse, and there meeting with Mr. Dupeyster, he carried me to the tavern, where in a large room were convened a certain club of merry fellows.

But the most remarkable person in the whole company was one Wendall, a young gentleman from Boston. He entertained us mightily by playing on the violin the quickest tunes upon the highest keys, which he accompanied with his voice, so as even to drown the violin, with such nice shakings and gracings that I thought his voice outdid the instrument.

I sat for some time immovable with surprise. The like I never heard, and the thing seemed to me next a miracle. The extent of his voice is impossible to describe or even to imagine unless by hearing him.

The whole company were amazed that any person but a woman or eunuch could have such a pipe, and began to question his virility; but he swore if the company pleased he would show a couple of as good witnesses as any man might wear.

Sunday, July 8th

I spent the morning att home and att one o'clock went to dine with Mr. Bayard. Among some other gentlemen there was my old friend Dr. McGraa who to day seemed to have more talk and ostentation than usuall, but he did not shine quite bright till he had drunk half a dozen glasses of wine after dinner. He spoke now in a very arbitrary tone as if his opinion was to pass for an ipse dixit.

He and I unhappily engaged in a dispute which I was sorry for, it being dissonant to good manners before company, and what none but rank pedants will be guilty of. We were obliged to use hard physicall terms, very discordant and disagreeable to ears not accustomed to them. I wanted much to drop it, but he keept teizing of me.

The subject of this dispute, effect which the moon has upon all fluids, as well as the ocean, in a proportionable ratio by the law of gravitation or her attractive power, and even upon the fluids in the vessels of animals.

The thing that introduced this was an action of McGraa's which exceded every thing I had seen for nastiness, impudence, and rusticity. He told us he was troubled with the open piles and with that, from his breeches, pulled out a linnen handkercheff all stained with blood and showed it to the company just after we had eat dinner.

After my astonishment att this piece of clownish impudence was over, I asked him if that evacuation att any particular times was greater or less such as the full or change of the moon in the same manner as the catamene in women. I intended only to play upon him. He answered with a sneer that he did not believe the moon had anything to do with us or our distempers and said that such notions were only superstitious nonsense, wondering how I could give credit to any such stuff.

There was another doctor at dinner with us who went away before this dispute began. His name was Ascough. When he came first he told Mr. Bayard he would dine with him provided he had no green pease for dinner. Mr. Bayard told him there were some, but that they should not come to table, upon which, with some entreaty, the doctor sat down and eat pritty heartily of bacon, chickens, and veal, but just as he had begun upon his veal, the stupid wench, forgetting her orders to the contrary, produced the pease, att which the doctor began to stare and change colour in such a manner that I thought he would have been convulsed, but he started up and ran out of doors so fast that we could never throw salt on his tail.

Mr. Bayard was so angry that he had almost oversett the table, but we had a good dish of pease by the bargain which otherwise we should not have tasted. This was the oddest antipathy ever I was witness to.

Monday, July 9th

The people of New York att the first appearance of a stranger are seemingly civil and courteous but this civility and complaisance soon relaxes if he be not either highly recommended or a good toaper. To drink stoutly with the Hungarian Club, who are all bumper men, is the readiest way for a stranger to recommend himself, and a sett among them are very fond of making a stranger drunk. To talk bawdy and to have a knack att punning passes among some there for good sterling wit. Govr. Clinton himself is a jolly toaper and gives good example and, for that one quality, is esteemed among these dons.

The *Almanac,* full of wit, wisdom, snappy sayings, and guesses about the weather was particularly popular in the eighteenth and nineteenth centuries. Like Franklin's *Poor Richard's Almanac,* most took a highly moral tone. (Selection, An American Tavern in 1776, *Houghton's Almanac,* 1810.)

A DESCRIPTION OF A TAVERN

A Tavern is a little *Sodom,* where as many vices are practised as ever were known in the great one. Thither Libertines repair to drink away their brains, and piss away their estates; *Alderman* to talk treason, and bewail the loss of trade; *Saints* to elevate the spirit, hatch calumnies, coin false news, and reproach the Church; *Gamesters* to shake their elbows, and pick the pockets of such cullies who have no more wit than to play with them; *Rakes* with their *Whores,* that by the help of wine they may be more impudent and more wicked, and do those things in their cups, that would be a scandal to sobriety; *Lovers* with their *Mistresses,* in hopes to wash away that modesty with the soothing juice, which had been a hindrance to their happiness, so that they may fall to without grace, and give a pleasing earnest to each other of their future affections. Thither *Sober Knaves* walk with *Drunken Fools,* to make cunning bargains, and overreach them in their dealings, where cloaking their mental reservations with a grave countenance, they will tell more lies about a hogshead of tobacco, than *Tavernier* in his travels does about Mount *Etna.* Thither *Young Quality* retire to spend their tradesmen's money, and to delight themselves with the impudence of lewd harlots, free from the reflections or remarks of their own servants, whilst their Ladies at home are doing themselves justice after the like manner, and perhaps, for want of better opportunity, are glad to break a commandment with their own footmen. Thither *Bullies* coach it to kick drawers, and invent new oaths and curses, and in feasting, rattling and blustering, to lavish away that scandalous income called a petticoat-pension, though doomed the next day to a three-penny ordinary. Thither run *Sots* purely to be drunk, that they may either wash away the reflections of their own past follies, or forget the treachery of their friends, the falsehood of their wives, the disobedience of their children, the roguery of their lawyers, the bitchery of their paramours, or the ingratitude of the world, that they may drown the remembrance of past evils in the enjoyment of the present.

the revolution

Almost every army goes to battle singing something. Among the most popular of the Revolutionary War were this air, by Nathaniel Niles, and the eternal "Yankee Doodle." (From National Magazine, *Heart Songs*, 1909.)

The Sword of Bunker Hill

1 He lay upon his dying bed;
His eye was growing dim,
When with a feeble voice he call'd
His weeping son to him:
"Weep not, my boy!" the vet'ran said,
"I bow to Heav'n's high will,—
But quickly from yon antlers bring
The Sword of Bunker Hill;
But quickly from yon antlers bring
The Sword of Bunker Hill."

2 The sword was bro't, the soldier's eye
Lit with a sudden flame;
And as he grasp'd the ancient blade,
He murmured Warren's name:
Then said, "My boy, I leave you gold,—
But what is richer still,
I leave you, mark me, mark me now—
The Sword of Bunker Hill;
I leave you, mark me, mark me now—
The Sword of Bunker Hill.

3 " 'Twas on that dread, immortal day,
I dared the Briton's band,
A captain raised this blade on me—
I tore it from his hand;
And while the glorious battle raged,
It lightened freedom's will—
For boy, the God of freedom blessed

The Sword of Bunker Hill;
For, boy the God of freedom blessed
The Sword of Bunker Hill.

4 "Oh, keep the sword!"—his accents broke—
A smile—and he was dead!
His wrinkled hand still grasped the blade
Upon that dying bed.
The son remains; the sword remains—
Its glory growing still—
And twenty millions bless the sire,
And Sword of Bunker Hill;
And twenty millions bless the sire,
And Sword of Bunker Hill.

Yankee Doodle

1 Fath'r and I went down to camp
Along with Captain Goodwin,
And there we saw the men and boys,
As thick as hasty pudding.

Chorus

Yankee doodle keep it up,
Yankee doodle dandy,
Mind the music and the step,
And with the girls be handy.

2 And there was Captain Washington
Upon a slapping stallion,
A giving orders to his men,
I guess there was a million.

3 And then the feathers on his hat,
They look'd so tarnal finey,
I wanted peskily to get,
To give to my Jemima.

4 And there they had as wamping gun,
As big as a log of maple,
On a deuced little cart,—
A load for father's cattle.

5 And ev'ry time they fired it off
It took a horn of power;

It made a noise like father's gun,
Only a nation louder.

6   I went as near to it myself,
As Jacob's underpinin',
And father went as near again,—
I tho't the deuce was in him.

7   It scared me so, I ran the streets,
Nor stopped, as I remember,
Till I got home, and safely locked
In granny's little chamber.

8   And there I see a little keg,
Its heads were made of leather,
They knocked upon't with little sticks,
To call the folks together.

9   And there they'd fife away like fun,
And play on corn-stalk fiddles,
And some had ribbons red as blood,
All bound around their middles.

10   The troopers too, would gallop up,
And fire in our faces;
It scared me almost half to death
To see them run such races.

11   Uncle Sam came there to change
Some pancakes and some onions,
For 'lasses cakes to carry home
To give his wife and young ones.

12   But I can't tell you half I see,
They kept up such a smother;
So I took my hat off, made a bow,
And scampered home to mother.

Hail! Columbia

1   Hail! Columbia, happy land!
Hail! ye heroes, heav'n-born band,
Who fought and bled in freedom's cause,
Who fought and bled in freedom's cause,
And when the storm of war was gone,
Enjoyed the peace your valor won;
Let Independence be your boast,
Ever mindful what it cost,

Ever grateful for the prize,
Let its altar reach the skies.

Chorus
Firm, united, let us be,
Rallying round our liberty,
As a band of brothers joined,
Peace and safety we shall find.

2 Immortal patriots, rise once more!
Defend your rights, defend your shore;
Let no rude foe, with impious hand,
Let no rude foe, with impious hand
Invade the shrine where sacred lies,
Of toil and blood, the well-earned prize;
While off'ring peace, sincere and just,
In heav'n we place a manly trust,
That truth and justice may prevail,
And ev'ry scheme of bondage fail!

3 Sound, sound the trump of fame!
Let Washington's great name
Ring through the world with loud applause!
Ring through the world with loud applause!
Let ev'ry clime, to freedom dear,
Listen with a joyful ear;
With equal skill, with steady pow'r,
He governs in the fearful hour
Of horrid war, or guides with ease,
The happier time of honest peace.

4 Behold the chief who now commands,
Once more to serve his country stands,
The rock on which the storm will beat!
The rock on which the storm will beat!
But armed in virtue, firm and true,
His hopes are fixed on Heav'n and you;
When hope was sinking in dismay,
When gloom obscured Columbia's day,
His steady mind, from changes free,
Resolved on death or Liberty.

Bunker Hill, or The American Hero, 1775

Why should vain mortals tremble at the sight of
Death and destruction in the field of battle,

Where blood and carnage clothe the ground in crimson,
   Sounding with death-groans?

Death will invade us by the means appointed
And we must all bow to the King of Terrors;
Nor am I anxious, if I am preparéd,
   What shape he comes in.

Infinite goodness teaches us submission;
Bids us be quiet under all His dealings:
Never repining, but forever praising
   God our Creator.

Well may we praise Him, all His ways are perfect;
Though a resplendence infinitely glowing
Dazzles in glory on the sight of mortals,
   Struck blind by lustre!

Good is Jehovah in bestowing sunshine,
Nor less His goodness in the storm and thunder:
Mercies and judgments both proceed from kindness—
   Infinite kindness.

O then exult that God forever reigneth.
Clouds, which around Him hinder our perception,
Bind us the stronger to exalt His name, and
   Shout louder praises!

Then to the wisdom of my Lord and Master
I will commit all that I have or wish for:
Sweetly as babes sleep will I give my life up
   When called to yield it.

Now, Mars, I dare thee, clad in smoky pillars,
Bursting from bomb-shells, roaring from the cannon,
Rattling in grape shot, like a storm of hailstones,
   Torturing Aether!

Up the black heavens, let the spreading flames rise,
Breaking like Aetna through the smoky columns,
Low'ring like Egypt o'er the falling city,
   Wantonly burnt down.

While all their hearts quick palpitate for havock,
Let slip your blood hounds, named the British lyons:
Dauntless as Death stares; nimble as the whirlwind;
   Dreadful as demons!

Let Oceans waft on all your floating castles,
Fraught with destruction, horrible to nature:
Then, with your sails filled by a storm of vengeance,
    Bear down to battle!

From the dire caverns made by ghostly miners,
Let the explosion, dreadful as vulcanoes,
Heave the broad town, with all its wealth and people,
    Quick to destruction!

Still shall the banner of the King of Heaven
Never advance where I'm afraid to follow:
While that precedes me with an open bosom,
    War, I defy thee.

Fame and dear freedom lure me on to battle,
While a fell despot, grimmer than a death's-head,
Stings me with serpents, fiercer than Medusa's,
    To the encounter.

Life, for my country and the cause of freedom,
Is shut a trifle for a worm to part with;—
And if preservéd in so great a contest,
    Life is redoubled.

(From Stedman and Hutchinson, *Library of American Literature*, III, 263-264.)

Tories and English troops sang too, mostly drinking songs. Few had the fervor of the patriot music. No question here that the side with the best songs won. (Selections from Dolph, *Sound Off*; Moore, ed., *Songs and Ballads*, pp. 196-99 and p. 253.)

1. How Happy the Soldier

How happy the soldier who lives on his pay
And spends half a crown out of six-pence a day;
Yet fears neither justices, warrants, nor bums,
But pays all his debts with the roll of his drums.
With row de dow, row de dow, row de dow, dow;
And he pays all his debts with the roll of his drums.

He cares not a marnedy how the world goes;
His King finds his quarters, and money, and clothes;
He laughs at all sorrow whenever it comes,
And rattles away with the roll of his drums,
With row de dow, row de dow, row de dow, dow;
And he pays all his debts with the roll of his drums.

The drum is his glory, his joy and delight,
It leads him to pleasure as well as to fight;
No girl, when she hears it, tho' ever so glum,
But packs up her tatters and follows the drum.
With row de dow, row de dow, row de dow, dow;
And he pays all his debts with the roll of his drums.

2. The Rebels, 1778

Ye brave, honest subjects, who dare to be loyal
And have stood the brunt of every trial
        Of hunting-shirts and rifle-guns:
Come listen awhile, and I'll sing you a song;
I'll show you those Yankees are all in the wrong,
Who, with blustering look and most awkward gait,
'Gainst their lawful sovereign dare for to prate,
        With their hunting-shirts and rifle-guns.
The arch-rebels, barefooted tatterdemalions,
In baseness exceed all other rebellions,
        With their hunting-shirts and rifle-guns.
To rend the empire, the most infamous lies
Their mock-patriot Congress do always devise;
Independence, like the first of rebels, they claim,
But their plots will be damned in the annals of fame,
        With their hunting-shirts and rifle-guns.
Forgetting the mercies of Great Britain's king,
Who saved their forefathers' necks from the string;
        With their hunting-shirts and rifle-guns.
They renounce allegiance and take up their arms,
Assemble together like hornets in swarms.
So dirty their backs and so wretched their show
That carrion-crow follows wherever they go,
        With their hunting-shirts and rifle-guns.

With loud peals of laughter, your sides, sirs, would crack
To see General Convict and Colonel Shoe-black,
        With their hunting-shirts and rifle-guns.

See cobblers and quacks, rebel priests and the like,
Pettifoggers and barbers, with sword and with pike,
All strutting, the standard of Satan beside,
And honest names using, their black deeds to hide.
    With their hunting-shirts and rifle-guns.

This perjured banditti now ruin this land,
And o'er its poor people claim lawless command,
    With their hunting-shirts and rifle-guns.
Their pasteboard dollars prove a common curse;
They don't chink like silver and gold in our purse.
With nothing their leaders have paid their debts off;
Their honor's dishonor, and justice they scoff,
    With their hunting-shirts and rifle-guns.

For one lawful ruler, many tyrants we've got,
Who force young and old to their wars, to be shot,
    With their hunting-shirts and rifle-guns.
Our good king, God speed him! never uséd men so;
We then could speak, act, and like freemen could go;
But committees enslave us, Liberty's gone,
Our trade and church murdered, our country's undone,
    By hunting-shirts and rifle-guns.

Come take up your glasses, each true loyal heart,
And may every rebel meet his due desert,
    With his hunting-shirt and rifle-gun.
May Congress, Conventions, those damn'd inquisitions,
Be fed with hot sulphur, from Lucifer's kitchens,
May commerce and peace again be restored,
And Americans own their true sovereign lord!
    Then oblivion to shirts and rifle-guns.
        God save the King!

3. A Convivial Song, 1779

"A song written by a refugee on reading the King's Speech, and sung at the Refugee Club in the City of New York."

Here's a bumper, brave boys, to the health of our king,
Long may he live, and long may we sing
In praise of a monarch who boldly defends
The laws of the realm and the cause of his friends.
    CHORUS

Then cheer up, my lads, we have nothing to fear
    While we remain steady
    And always keep ready
To add to the trophies of this happy year.

The Congress did boast of their mighty ally,
But George doth both France and the Congress defy,
And when Britons unite, there's no force can withstand
Their fleets and their armies, by sea and on land.
    CHORUS

Thus supported, our cause we will ever maintain,
And all treaties with rebels will ever disdain;
Till, reduced by our arms, they are forced to confess
While ruled by Great Britain they ne'er knew distress.
    CHORUS

Then let us, my boys, Britain's right e'er defend.
Who regards not her rights, we esteem not our friend;
Then, brave boys, we both France and the Congress defy,
And we'll fight for Great Britain and George till we die.
    CHORUS

Songs honoring George Washington began to be sung at the very beginning of the Revolutionary War and continued to echo for at least the next century. (Selections from F. Hopkinson, *Miscellaneous Essays*, III, 176; *Columbia Magazine*, August 1789.)

WASHINGTONIANA

A. The Toast, Francis Hopkinson

'Tis Washington's health—fill a bumper around,
For he is our glory and pride;
Our arms shall in battle with conquest be crowned,
Whilst virtue and he's on our side.

'Tis Washington's health—and cannons should roar,
And trumpets the truth should proclaim;
There cannot be found, search the world all o'er,
His equal in virtue and fame.

'Tis Washington's health—our hero to bless,
May Heav'n look graciously down!
Oh! long may he live our hearts to possess,
And freedom still call him her own.

B. A New Song (Tune: "The British Grenadiers")

Vain Britons, boast no longer with proud indignity
By land your conquering legions, your matchless strength at sea!
Since we your braver sons, incensed, our swords have girded on,
Huzza, huzza, huzza, huzza, for War and Washington!

Urged on by North and Vengeance, these valiant champions came,
And bellowing "Tea and Treason!" and George was all on flame!
As sacrilegious as it seems, we Rebels still live on
And laugh at all your empty puffs, and so does Washington!

Still deaf to mild intreaties, still blind to England's good,
You have for thirty pieces betrayed your country's blood;
Like Aesop's greedy cur, you'll gain a shadow for your bone,
Yet find us fearful shades indeed, inspired by Washington.

Mysterious! unexampled! incomprehensible!
The blundering schemes of Britain, their folly, pride and zeal!
Like lions how ye growl and threat! mere asses have ye shown,
And ye shall share an ass's fate and drudge for Washington!

Your dark, unfathomed councils our weakest heads defeat,
Our children rout your armies, our boats destroy your fleet!
And to compleat the dire disgrace, cooped up within a town,
You live the scorn of all our host, the slaves of Washington!

Great Heaven! is this the nation whose thundering arms were
    hurled
Thro' Europe, Afric, India? Whose Navy ruled the world?
The lustre of your former deeds—whole ages of renown—
Lost in a moment—or transferred to us and Washington!

Yet think not thirst of glory unsheaths our vengeful swords
To rend your bands asunder and cast away your cords.
'Tis Heaven-born Freedom fires us all and strengthens each brave
    son,
From him who humbly guides the plough to god-like Washington!

For this, O could our wishes your ancient rage inspire,
Your armies should be doubled in numbers, force and fire!

Then might the glorious conflict prove which best deserved the
boon—
America or Albion—a George or Washington!

Fired with the great idea our fathers' shades would rise!
To view the stern contention, the gods desert their skies,
And Wolfe, mid hosts of heroes, superior, bending down,
Cry out with eager transport, "Well done, brave Washington!"

Should George, too choice of Britons, to foreign realms apply
And madly arm half Europe, yet still we would defy
Turk, Russian, Jew and Infidel, or all those powers in one,
While Hancock crowns our Senate—our camp great Washington.

Tho' warlike weapons failed us, disdaining slavish fears,
To swords we'd beat our plough-shares, our pruning hooks to spears,
And rush all desperate on our foe, nor breathe, till battle won;
Then shout and shout, "America and conquering Washington!"

Proud France should view with terror, and haughty Spain should
fear,
While every warlike nation would court alliance here—
And George, his minions trmebling round, dismounted from his
Throne,
Pay homage to America and glorious Washington!

"The People out of doors" was a major political instrument in the eighteenth
century, if one which was brandished only in time of crisis. Rioting and disturbance was the main form of politics for the urban poor and—obviously—an
important means of self-expression.

THE PEOPLE OUT OF DOORS: THE MOB AT WORK

"The Tories! The Tories Will Yet Be the Ruin of You!"

Appeal to the Inhabitants of Philadelphia, 1779.

Rouse, America! Your danger is great—great from a quarter where
you least expect it. The Tories, the Tories will yet be the ruin of you!
'Tis high time they were separated from among you. They are now busy
engaged in undermining your liberties. They have a thousand ways of

doing it, and they make use of them all. Who were the occasion of this war? The Tories. Who persuaded the tyrant of Britain to prosecute it in a manner before unknown to civilized nations, and shocking even to barbarians? The Tories! Who prevailed on the savages of the wilderness to join the standard of the enemy? The Tories! . . . Who advised and who assisted in burning your towns, ravaging your country and violating the chastity of your women? The Tories! Who are the occasion that thousands of you now mourn the loss of your dearest connections? The Tories. Who have always counteracted the endeavors of Congress to secure the liberties of this country? The Tories! . . . Who take the oaths of allegiance to the States one day and break them the next? The Tories! Who prevent your battalions from being filled? The Tories! Who dissuade from entering the army? The Tories! Who persuade those who have enlisted to desert? The Tories! Who harbor those who do desert? The Tories!

In short, who wish to see us conquered, to see us slaves, to see us hewers of wood and drawers of water? The Tories! (From Moore, *Diary of the American Revolution*, II, 166.

"The Unhappy Wretch Still Cried: 'Curse All Traitors!' "

Ann Hulton to Mrs. Lightbody

Boston, January 31, 1774

. . . But the most shocking cruelty was exercised a few nights ago, upon a poor old man, a tidesman, one Malcolm. He is reckoned creasy, a quarrel was picked with him, he was afterward taken and tarred and feathered. Theres no law that knows a punishment for the greatest crimes beyond what this is of cruel torture. And this instance exceeds any other before it. He was stript stark naked, one of the severest cold nights this winter, his body covered all over with tar, then with feathers, his arm dislocated in tearing off his cloaths. He was dragged in a cart with thousands attending, some beating him with clubs and knocking him out of the cart, then in again. They gave him several severe whippings, at different parts of the town. This spectacle of horror and sportive cruelty was exhibited for about five hours.

The unhappy wretch they say behaved with the greatest intrepidity and fortitude all the while. Before he was taken, [he] defended himself a long time against numbers, and afterwards when under torture they demanded of him to curse his masters, the King, Governor, etc., which they could not make him do, but he still cried, "Curse all traitors!" They brought him to the gallows and put a rope about his neck, saying they would hang him. He said he wished they would, but that they could not, for God was above the Devil. The doctors say that it is impossible this poor creature can live. They say his flesh comes off his back in stakes.

It is the second time he has been tarred and feathered and this is looked upon more to intimidate the judges and others than a spite to the unhappy victim tho' they owe him a grudge for some things particularly. He was with Govr. Tryon in the battle with the Regulators and the Governor has declared that he was of great servise to him in that affair, by his undaunted spirit encountering the greatest dangers.

Govr. Tryon had sent him a gift of ten guineas just before this inhuman treatment. He has a wife and family and an aged father and mother who, they say, saw the spectacle which no indifferent person can mention without horror.

These few instances amongst many serve to shew the abject state of government and the licentiousness and barbarism of the times. There's no majestrate that dare or will act to suppress the outrages. No person is secure. There are many objects pointed at, at this time, and when once marked out for vengeance, their ruin is certain.

The judges have only a weeks time allowed them to consider whether they will take the salaries from the Crown or no. Govr. Hutchinson is going to England as soon as the season will permit.

We are under no apprehension at present on our own account but we can't look upon our safety secure for long. (From Hulton, *Letters of a Loyalist Lady*, pp. 70-72.)

"The New Fashion Dress of Tar and Feathers"

Joseph Spencer to Governor Trumbull.

East Haddam, [Connecticut], September 14, 1774

Honoured Sir: Doctor Beebe, who will deliver this, will wait on your Honour in hopes of the favour of your Honour's advice with respect to an unhappy affair that concerns himself. The zeal of people here, in general, runs very high for what is called Liberty; and there being a few amongst us that don't agree with the rest, who are called Tories, many people here have thought proper to visit the Tories and demand some satisfaction with relation to their principles and practices; and they have accordingly visited several in this society, and I think they have, except Doctor Beebe, given them satisfaction. They have, a large number of them, visited the Doctor this week, and he refused to say any thing that gave satisfaction, and the people have been so rough with him as to give him the new fashion dress of tar and feathers; and he thinks himself extremely abused, and has been desirous that I would grant surety of the peace against a few of them, but I declined; he seems to think he is obliged, in duty, to prosecute some of them; but, however, has finally applied to your Honour for advice as to the necessity or expediency of his prosecuting in this case.

I hope also, myself, to have your Honour's advice as to my duty with respect to signing a precept for the Doctor in this case. I believe if one should be granted, it will not be executed to any advantage without force from abroad to govern our people; for although these rough measures lately taken place with us are contrary to my mind, yet I am not able to prevent it at present.

I am, honoured sir, your Honour's most obedient and humble servant,

JOSEPH SPENCER

(From FORCE, *American Archives*, 4th Series, I, 787.)

The Mobs Cry: "Down with the Church, the Rags of Popery!"

The Reverend Samuel Peters to the Reverend Doctor Achmuty of New York.

Boston, October 1, 1774

Reverend Sir: The riots and mobs that have attended me and my house, set on by the Governour of Connecticut, have compelled me to take up my abode here; and the clergy of Connecticut must fall a sacrifice, with the several churches, very soon to the rage of the puritan nobility, if the old serpent, that dragon, is not bound. Yesterday I waited on his Excellency, the Admiral, etc., Doctor Canner, Mr. Troutbeck, Doctor Byles, etc. I am soon to sail for England; I shall stand in great need of your letters, and the letters of the clergy of New-York; direct to Mr. Rice Williams, woollen draper, in London, where I shall put up. Judge Achmuty, etc., etc., will do all things reasonable for the neighbouring charter; necessity calls for such friendship, as the head is sick and the heart faint, and spiritual iniquity rides in high places with halberts, pistols and swords. See the Proclamation I send you by my nephew, and their pious Sabbath day, the 4th of last month, when the preachers and magistrates left the pulpits, etc., for the gun and drum, and set off for Boston, cursing the King and Lord North, General Gage, the Bishops and their cursed Curates, and the Church of England. And for my telling the church people not to take up arms, etc., it being high treason, etc., the Sons of Liberty have almost killed one of my church, tarred and feathered two, abused others; and on the sixth day destroyed my windows, and rent my clothes, even my gown, etc., crying out, "Down with the church, the rags of Popery," etc. Their rebellion is obvious; treason is common; and robbery is their daily diversion; the Lord deliver us from anarchy! The bounds of New-York may directly extend to Connecticut River, Boston meet them, and New-Hampshire take the Province of Maine, and Rhode Island be swallowed up as Dathan. Pray lose no time, nor fear worse times than attend,

Reverend sir, your very humble servant,

SAMUEL PETERS

(From FORCE, American Archives, 4th Series, I, 716.)

"A Poor Man Was Tarred and Feathered Ten Times"

Lord William Campbell to Lord Dartmouth.

Charlestown [S. C.], August 19, 1775

. . . This is a very disagreeable subject for me to dwell on, but my duty requires I should represent the true state of this Province, and of my unfortunate vicinage of N. Carolina, and Georgia, which is equally neglected, equally abandoned. Your Lordship will, I am sure, excuse my warmth when I acquaint that yesterday under colour of law they hanged and burned an unfortunate wretch, a free Negro of considerable property, one of the most valuable and useful men in his way in the Province, on suspicion of instigating an insurrection, for which I am convinced there was not the least ground.

I could not save him, my Lord! the very reflection harrows my soul! I have only the comfort to think I left no means untried to preserve him.

They have now dipt their hands in blood. God Almighty knows where it will end, but I am determined to remain till the last extremity in hope to promote the King's service, tho my familys being here adds not a little to my distress.

Another act of barbarity, tho happily of not so tragical a nature, was committed a few days ago on a poor man, the gunner of Fort Johnson, who for expressing his loyalty was tarred and feathered 10 or 12 times, in different parts of the town, and otherwise treated with great cruelty, stopping him at the doors of those Crown officers who were most obnoxious; and the mob so grossly insulted Mr. Milligan, in particular, who is surgeon to the forts and garrisons in this Province, that he was under a necessity of taking refuge on board the King's ship till the packet boat sails. (From GR. BRIT. HIST. MSS. COMM., *Dartmouth Papers*, II, 354.)

Tar and Feathers Make Thomas Randolph Repent

From the records of the Committee of Safety.

New York, December 28, 1775

The 6th of December, at Quibbletown, Middlesex County, Piscataway Township, New-Jersey, Thomas Randolph, cooper, who had publickly proved himself an enemy to his country, by reviling and using his utmost endeavours to oppose the proceedings of the Continental and Provincial Conventions and Committees, in defence of their rights and liberties; and he, being judged a person of not consequence enough for a severer punishment, was ordered to be stripped naked, well coated with tar and feathers, and carried in a wagon publickly round the town; which punishment was accordingly inflicted. And as he soon became duly sensible of his offense, for which he earnestly begged pardon, and promised to atone, as far as he was able, by a contrary behaviour for the future, he was released, and suffered to return to his house in less than half an hour. The whole was conducted with that regularity and decorum that ought to be observed in all publick punishments. (From FORCE, *American Archives*, 4th Series, IV, 203.)

Ethan Allen, the Vermont patriot, was also author of the most popular captivity narrative to come out of the Revolutionary War. Like all such examples of the genre, this one has much about ill treatment by captors and courageous deportment by captives. (From *The Narrative of Ethan Allen*, 1779.)

PRISONER OF WAR

I next invite the reader to a retrospect sight and consideration of the doleful scene of inhumanity exercised by Gen. Sir Wm. Howe, and the army under his command, towards the prisoners taken on Long Island, on the 27th day of August, 1776, sundry of whom were in an inhuman and barbarous manner, murdered after they had surrendered their arms, particularly a Gen. Odel, (or Woodhul) of the militia, who was hacked to pieces with cutlasses (when alive) by the light horsemen, and a Captain Fellows, of the Continental army, who was thrust through with a bayonet, of which wound he died instantly.

Sundry others were hanged up by the neck till they were dead, 5 on the limb of a white oak tree, and without any reason assigned, (except that they were fighting in defence of the only blessing worth preserving), and indeed those who had the misfortune to fall into their hands at fort Washington, in the month of November following, met with but very little better usage, except that they were reserved from immediate death to famish and die with hunger, in fine the word rebel applied to any vanquished persons, without regard to rank, who were in the continental service, on the 27th of August aforesaid, was thought (by the enemy) sufficient to sanctify whatever cruelties they were pleased to inflict death itself not excepted: but to pass over particulars which would swell my narrative far beyond my design.

The private soldiers who were brought to New York, were crowded into churches, and environed with slavish Hessian guards, a people of a strange language, who were sent to America for no other design but cruelty and desolation; and at others, by merciless Britons, whose mode of communicating ideas being intelligible in this country, served only to tantalize and insult the helpless and perishing; but above all the hellish delight and triumph of the tories over them, as they were dying by hundreds: This was too much for me to bear as a spectator; for I saw the tories exulting over the dead bodies of their murdered countrymen. I have gone into the churches, and seen sundry of the prisoners in the agonies of death, in consequence of very hunger, and others speechless and near death, biting pieces of chips; others pleading for God's sake, for something to eat, and at the same time shivering with the cold. Hollow groans saluted my ears, and despair seemed to be imprinted on every of their countenances. The filth of these churches (in consequence of the fluxes) was almost beyond description. The floors were covered with excrements, I have carefully sought to direct my steps so as to avoid it, but could not. They would beg for God's sake for one copper, or morsel of bread. I have seen in one of these churches seven dead at the same time, lying among the excrements of their bodies.

It was a common practice with the enemy, to convey the dead from these filthy places, in carts, to be slightly buried, and I have seen whole gangs of tories making derision, and exulting over the dead, saying there goes another load of damned rebels. I have observed the British soldiers to be full of their blackguard jokes, and vaunting on those occasions, but they appeared to me less malignant than tories.

The provision dealt out to the prisoners was by no means sufficient for the support of life: it was deficient in quantity, and much more so in quality. The prisoners often presented me with a sample of their bread, which I certify was damaged to that degree, that it was loathsome and unfit to be eaten, and I am bold to aver it, (as my opinion) that it had been condemned, and was of the very worst sort. I have seen and been fed upon damaged bread, (in the course of my captivity) and observed the quality of such bread as has been condemned by the enemy, among which was very little so effectually spoiled as what was dealt out to these prisoners. Their allowance of meat (as they told me) was quite trifling, and of the basest sort, I never saw any of it, but was informed (bad as it was) it was swallowed almost as quick as they got hold of it. I saw some of them sucking bones after they were speechless; others who could yet speak, and had the use of their reason, urged me in the strongest and most pathetic manner, to use my interest in their behalf, for you plainly see (say they) that we are devoted to death and destruction; and after I had examined more particularly into their truly deplorable condition, and had become more fully apprized of the essential facts, I was persuaded that it was a premeditated and systematical plan of the British council, to destroy the youths of our land, with a view thereby to deter the country, and make it submit to their despotism; but that I could not do them any material service, and that by any public attempt for that purpose I might endanger myself by frequenting places the most nauseous and contagious that could be conceived of. I refrained going into the churches, but frequently conversed with such of the prisoners as were admitted to come out into the yard, and found that the systematical usage still continued. The guard would often drive me away with their fixed bayonets. A Hessian (one day) followed me five or six rods, but by making use of my legs, got rid of the lubber. Sometimes I could obtain a little conversation, notwithstanding their severities.

I was in one of the church yards, and it was rumoured among those in the church, and sundry of the prisoners came with their usual complaints to me, and among the rest a large boned tall young man, (as he told me from Pennsylvania) who was reduced to a mere skeleton; said he was glad to see me before he died, which he had expected to have done last night, but was a little revived; he furthermore informed me, that he and his brother had been urged to enlist in the British service, but had both resolved to die first; that his brother had died last night, in consequence of that resolution, and that he expected shortly to follow him; but I made the other prisoners stand a little off, and told him, with a low voice, to list; he then asked, whether it was right in the sight of God? I assured him that it was, and that duty to himself obliged him to deceive the British by enlisting, and deserting the first opportunity: upon which he answered with transport, that he would list. I charged him not to mention my name as his adviser, least it should get air, and I should be closely confined, in consequence of it. The integrity of these suffering prisoners is hardly credible. Many hundreds, I am confident, submitted to death, rather than enlist in the

British service, which (I am informed) they most generally were pressed to do. I was astonished at the resolution of the two brothers particularly; it seems that they could not be stimulated to such exertions of heroism from ambition, as they were but obscure soldiers; strong indeed must the internal principle of virtue be, which supported them to brave death, and one of them went through the operation, as did many hundred others. I readily grant, that instances of public virtue are no excitement to the sordid and vicious, nor on the other hand, with all the barbarity of Britain and Heshland awaken them to a sense of their duty to the public; but these things will have their proper effect on the generous and brave . . . The officers on parole were most of them zealous, if possible, to afford the miserable soldiery relief, and often consulted, with one another on the subject, but to no effect, being destitute of the means of subsistence, which they needed; nor could the officers project any measure, which they thought would alter their fate, or so much as be a means of getting them out of those filthy places to the privilege of fresh air. Some projected that all the officers should go in procession to Gen. Howe, and plead the cause of the perishing soldiers; but this proposal was negatived for the following reasons, viz. because that general Howe must needs be well acquainted and have a thorough knowledge of the state and condition of the prisoners in every of their wretched apartments, and that much more particular and exact than any officer on parole could be supposed to have, as the general had a return of the circumstances of the prisoners, by his own officers every morning, of the number which were alive, as also the number which died every 24 hours, and consequently the bill of mortality, as collected from the daily returns, lay before him with all the material situations and circumstances of the prisoners; and provided the officers should go in procession to gen. Howe, according to the projection, it would give him the greatest affront, and that he would either retort upon them; that it was no part of their parole to instruct him in his conduct to prisoners; that they were mutinying against his authority, and by affronting him, had forfeited their parole: or that more probably, instead of saying one word to them, would order them all into as wretched a confinement as the soldiers whom they sought to relieve; for at that time, the British, from the general to the private centinel, were in full confidence, nor did they so much as hesitate but that they should conquer the country. Thus the consultation of the officers was confounded and broken to pieces, in consequence of the dread, which at that time lay on their minds, of offending gen. Howe; for they conceived so murderous a tyrant would not be too good to destroy even the officers, on the least pretence of an affront, as they were equally in his power with the soldiers; and as gen. Howe perfectly understood the condition of the private soldiers, it was argued that it was exactly such as he and his council had devised, and as he meant to destroy them it would be to no purpose for them to try to dissuade him from it, as they were helpless and liable to the same fate, on giving the least affront; indeed anxious apprehensions disturbed them in their then circumstances.

Mean time mortality raged to such an intolerable degree among the prisoners, that the very school boys in the streets knew the mental design of it in some measure, at least they knew that they were starved to death. Some poor women contributed to their necessity, till their children were almost starved, and all persons of common understanding knew that they were devoted to the cruelest and worst of deaths. It was also proposed by some to make a written representation of the condition of the soldiery, and the officers to sign it, and that it should be couched in such terms, as though they were apprehensive that the General was imposed upon by his officers, in their daily returns to him of the state and condition of the prisoners, and that therefore the officers moved with compassion, were constrained to communicate to him the facts relative to them, nothing doubting but that they would meet with a speedy redress; but this proposal was most generally negatived also, and for much the same reason offered in the other case, for it was conjectured that General Howe's indignation would be moved against such officers as should attempt to whip him over his officers backs, that he would discern that himself was really struck at, and not the officers, who made the daily returns, and therefore self preservation deterred the officers from either petitioning or remonstrating to General Howe, either verbally or in writing, as also the consideration that no valuable purpose to the distressed would be obtained.

I made several rough drafts on the subject, one of which I exhibited to Cols. Magaw, Miles and Atlee, and they said that they would consider the matter, soon after I called on them, and some of the gentlemen informed me, that they had wrote to the Gen. on the subject, and I concluded that the gentlemen thought it best that they should write without me, as there was such spirited aversion subsisting between the British and me.

A tradition, as constant as it is probably unreliable, asserts that this marvellously fitting ditty was sung when Cornwallis surrendered at Yorktown. (From *Gentleman's Magazine*, XXXVI, 140-41.)

THE WORLD TURNED UPSIDE DOWN

Goody Bull and her daughter together fell out.
Both squabbled, and wrangled, and made a damned rout,
But the cause of the quarrel remains to be told.
Then lend both your ears, and a tale I'll unfold.

The old lady, it seems, took a freak in her head
That her daughter, grown woman, might earn her our bread:
Self-applauding her scheme, she was ready to dance;
But we're often too sanguine in what we advance.

For mark the event: thus by fortune we're crossed,
Nor should people reckon without their good host;
The daughter was sulky, and wouldn't come to,
And pray, what in this case could the old woman do?

In vain did the matron hold forth in the cause
That the young one was able; her duty, the laws;
Ingratitude vile, disobedience far worse;
But she might e'en as well sung psalms to a horse.

Young, forward and sullen, and vain of her beauty,
She tartly replied that she knew well her duty,
That other folks' children were kept by their friends,
And that some folks loved people but for their own ends.

"Zounds, neighbor!" quoth Pitt, "what the devil's the matter?
A man cannot rest in his house for your clatter."
"Alas!" cries the daughter, "here's dainty fine work.
The old woman grown harder than a Jew or than Turk."

"She be damned," says the farmer, and to her he goes,
First roars in her ears, then tweaks her old nose.
"Hallo, Goody, what ails you? Wake! woman, I say;
I am come to make peace in this desperate fray.

"Adzooks, ope thine eyes, what a pother is here!
You've no right to compel her, you have not, I swear;
Be ruled by your friends, kneel down and ask pardon,
You'd be sorry, I'm sure, should she walk Covent Garden."

"Alas!" cries the old woman, "and must I comply?
But I'd rather submit than the huzzy should die."
"Pooh, prithee be quiet, be friends and agree,
You must surely be right, *if you're guided, by me.*"

Unwillingly awkward, the mother knelt down,
While the absolute farmer went on with a frown,
"Come, kiss the poor child, there come, kiss and be friends!
There, kiss your poor daughter, and make her amends."

"No thanks to you, Mother," the daughter replied;
"But thanks to my friend here, I've humbled your pride."

TRIVIA

Next to Godliness

"June 30, 1771: . . . went this afternoon into the Bath, I found the shock much greater than I expected. . . .

July 1, 1799; Nancy came here this evening. she and self went into the Shower bath. I bore it better than I expected, not having been wett all over at once, for 28 years past." (From *Journal of Elizabeth Drinker of Philadelphia,* 1771–99.)

Certain Contrarieties and Decisions

I: JUST PUBLISHED
And for sale at this office, price 25 cents per pack,
    A neat edition of the much admired
    Courting, or Conversation Cards.
Each pack contains 60 cards, 30 questions in black,
    and 30 answers in red, and are so constructed
    as to cause each answer to suit any question,
    if played indiscriminately.

From billiards, cards and dice, much mischief springs,
These cards have neither *aces, treys,* nor *kings,*
Nor *knave,* nor *queen,* nor *diamond, club* or *spade,*
For LOVE'S pure purpose they are wholly made:
Of gaming cards they don't possess one part,
Save that at times they tend to win the *heart.*
LOVE'S language soft, and all its sweet contents,
With these you buy for *five and twenty cents.*

Two thousand packs of these cards have actually met
with a rapid sale in Baltimore.
Also may be had
A few elegant copies of Burkitt on the New Testament,
Neatly bound and lettered, price 8 dollars each copy.

(*The Maryland Gazette,* July 11, 1799.)

II

Whereas Mary the Wife of Richard Leadame, hath misused her
said Husband, and doth run him into debt unnecessarily; this is to warn
all Persons against trusting her on his Account, for he will not pay any
Debts she shall contract after the Date hereof.

RICHARD LEADAME.
Phila. Dec. 14, 1742.
(*Pennsylvania Gazette,* Dec. 14, 1742.)

Friend *Benjamin Franklin,*

I desire thee to stop the Advertisement in thy last Week's Paper,
concerning my Wife; and Print to the Contrary, that my Friends may
give her Credit on my Account as usual. I acknowledge I had no Reason
to do what I have done: For what I did was entirely thro' others Per-
swasion, and my own Passion.

RICHARD LEADAME.
Dec. 21, 1742.
Pennsylvania Gazette, Dec. 21, 1742.

Friend *Franklin,*

I have again Necessity for troubling thy News-Paper, about *Mary*
my Wife: It was Force that made me comply with publishing the last
Advertisement in thy Paper. Pray insert in thy Paper now, that she
abuses me her Husband so much that I cannot live with her: And I
forwarn all Persons from Trusting her on my Account, after the Date
hereof.

RICHARD LEADAME.
March 15, 1743.
(*Pennsylvania Gazette,* March 17, 1743.)

III

The following very curious advertisement is copied from the
Bahama Gazette, of June the 30th.

Whereas the subscriber, through a pernicious habit of drinking for many years, has greatly hurt himself in purse and person, and rendered himself odious to all his acquaintance; finding there is no possibility of breaking off from the said practice, but through impossibility to find the liquor, he therefore earnestly begs and prays, that in future no person will sell him either for money or on trust, any sort of spiritous liquors, as he will not in future pay it, but will prosecute any one for action of damage against the temporal and external interest of the public's humble, serious, sober servant.

JAMES CHALMERS
WILLIAM ANDREW, Witness to my signing.
Nassau, June 21, 1795.
(*Litchfield Monitor*, Dec. 23, 1795.)

How to Die

I: BEAUTIFULLY

Died in the flower of her age, Miss Mary Harrison, daughter of the late Mr. Thomas Harrison, of Wheldon Bridge House.—If boundless benevolence be the basis of beatitude, and harmless humility the harbinger of a hallowed heart, these christian concomitants composed her characteristic, and conciliated the esteem of her contemporary acquaintances, who mean to model their manners by the mould of their meritorious monitor.

(*Newcastle Journal*, July 12, 1788, quoted in *State Gazette of North Carolina* (Edenton), III, No. 155, Dec. 25, 1788.)

II: WITH UNSPEAKABLE SATISFACTION

A new tontine—not for the benefit of survivorship—has just started up in Birmingham (England). It may be called a Dead Club, or Funeral Association, where every member, from the small deposit of a single penny per week, will have *the unspeakable satisfaction* of being decently put under the sod. The Secretary of this social set is said to be an Apothecary and the two Stewards, an undertaker and a Sexton!

(*Norristown Gazette*, Apr. 4, 1800.)

III: PLASTERED

John Tatson, an Indian native of Lyme, being found dead on a winter's morning, not far from a tavern, where he had been drinking freely of spiritous liquors the evening before, the Indians immediately assembled a jury of their own tribe, who, after examining the corpse of the defunct, unanimously agreed, that "the said Tatson's death was occasioned by the freezing of the large quantity of water in his body that had been mixed with the rum he drank."

> (Claypoole's *American Daily Advertiser* (Philadelphia, Pa.), No. 5873, Feb. 1, 1798.)

A Receipt for A Long Life

I: *Drink this*

"Doctor Eales Pouder agst ye Stone—1702

"Take anniseeds, Sweet fennel Seeds, dill Seed, [illeg.] Tops, ye Root of white Saxifrage, ye husk rub off, of each an ounce, beat them fine, & sift them thro a Tiffany Seive, mix them together, then add crabs Eyes, ye Seeds of wild Briar heps & Jaw bone of a Pike, of each in fine Pouder as much as wil Lye upon ye Point of a knife at twice, mix this with ye Rest, take ye quantity of a Drahm of this Pouder ye day before ye new moon, & ye day after & So at ye full in white wine, or ale."

> (Livingston-Redmond MSS., Franklin D. Roosevelt Library, Hyde Park.)

II: *Whiff this*

"Hannah Chapman makes and sells a Smell in Mixture, that will cure the itch or any other breaking out, by the smell of it. Enquire for me at the Sign of the Staves at the head of Seven Star Lane."

> (*Boston Evening-Post,* March 21, 1748.)

III: *View this*

"A famous *Bolognian* Physician in Publish'd Bills profess'd a Sovereign *Antidote* against an horrible *Distemper* which Men bring upon themselves by their *Uncleanness*. But when Multitudes flock'd unto him for his *Antidote*, he only gave 'em the Picture of a *Gallant* with his Nose eaten off. He bid 'em, that when they were going to debauch themselves, they would look upon that Picture; and if that would not preserve 'em, nothing would."

> (Cotton Mather, *Magnalia Christi Americana,* Book VI, p. 34.)

IV: *And get a good doctor*

To Phelim Donance, Whitesmith, Boston
"Egg-Harbour, mouth of the Delaware, May 12, 1789.
    My Dear Friend,
    You will, no doubt, be greatly astonished at receiving a letter from one whom you so lately saw, in all appearance, numbered with the dead, with all the ignominy of a public and shameful execution. But though strange as it may appear, it is no less strange than true, that, blessed be God for his infinite goodness, I am now among the living to praise him. It was my fervent desire that you should have been made acquainted with the steps which were taken to recover me to life immediately after my being hanged. But the doctor who managed the affair would not admit of more than five persons in the secret, as he feared a discovery, and said a crowd around me would be fatal, and prevent the air getting into my lungs, and O'Donnell and Tector had been told of it before I saw you; and they, with the doctor, his young man, and person he brought with him, made the five. I therefore take this early opportunity to let you know of my being alive, and in health, blessed be God! as I hope these lines will find you: as also the circumstances which attend my execution and recovery to life; as also my present frame of mind and resolution, through the grace of God, to sin no more, but endeavour after new obedience.
    You remember that you among other friends had great hopes of my being pardoned, on account of my youth; but when their Honors sat, I soon found I must be made an example of, as they were determined never to pardon highway-men. I then began to prepare for death, but must needs say, though I had many affecting conferrences with the reverend parsons who visited me in gaol, I never, even after my condemnation, realized that I was suddenly to die in so awful a manner, until a gentleman, who I afterwards found was a doctor, came and talked privately with the late unhappy sufferer, and my fellow convict. Archibald Taylor, who, when the gentleman was gone, came to me with money in his hand, and so smiling a countenance, that I thought he had received it in charity. But he soon undeceived me, telling me with an air of gaiety, that it was the price of his body; and then added a shocking speech, which I sincerely hope is blotted out of the book of God's remembrance against his poor soul.
    This was the first time since my condemnation that I thought what it was to die. The shock was terrible, and Taylor increased it saying that the doctor had desired him to bargain with me for my body also. The thoughts of my bones not being permitted to remain in the grave in peace, and my body, which my poor mother had so often caressed and

dandled on her knee, and which had been so pampered by my friends in my better days, being slashed and mangled by the doctors, was too much for me. I had been deaf to the pious exhortations of the priests; but now my conscience was awakened, and hell seemed indeed to yawn for me.

What a night of horror was the next night!

—When the doctor came in the morning to bargain for my body, I was in a cold sweat; my knees smote together, and my tongue seemed to cleave to the roof of my mouth. He perceived the agony of my soul and asked me some questions of the state of my mind. I found utterance, and poured out my heart to him. He seemed affected with my distress, especially as my conduct was so different from that of A. Taylor's; and after pausing he left me without mentioning the sale of my body, and he would call again the next day. He came and asked me privately whether I had two or three friends I could depend upon to assist in any thing for my benefit. He communicated his design of attempting to recover me to life if my body could be carried immediately after I was cut down, to some convenient place, out of the reach of the people; assuring me by all that was sacred, that if he failed in his attempt, he would give my body a christian burial. I closed with it, without hesitating. . . .

Soon after they left us, the doctor's young man came (under pretence of a message from Mrs. Ranger, who had shown me much kindness in gaol the Lord reward her for it) to renew the Doctor's directions how to conduct my body so as not to suffer the least shock: He left me the following paper.

'Thursday morning, May 8th, 1789.

'TAYLOR, every thing depends on your presence of mind. Remember that the Human Machine may be put in tune again, if you preserve the spinal muscle from injury, and do not dislocate the Vertebrae of the neck: As the Colli Spinalis is deduced from the transverse processes of the Vertebrae of the throat, and is latterly inserted into the Vertebrae of the neck, its connection with the whole human frame is material; so that you must endeavour to work the knot behind your neck, and press your throat upon the halter, which will prevent the neck's breaking, and likewise the compressions of the Jugular, and preserve the circulations in some degree. *Keep up your Spirits.*'

My hopes were now raised, and my former terror did not return upon me; which I doubt not was observed by the Reverend Parson who attended me, by the officers of justice, and the multitude, who doubtless compared my behaviour with that of my fellow-sufferer. It is true, when

I mounted the stage, I dreaded the pain of hanging as I should any other bodily pain equally severe; but the far greatest distress of meeting an offended, inexorable Judge, and being consigned to endless misery, was done away: For the nearer the time of execution approached, the more my reliance on the Doctor increased. . . .

But to return to my particular feelings—I preserved my presence of mind, and when the halter was fastened, remembered the Doctor's directions, and while the prayer was making I kept gently turning my head so as to bring the knot on the back of my neck, nearly, as O'Donnell afterwards informed, and as you and others observed. When the trap fell I had all my senses about me; and though I have no remembrance of hearing any sounds among the people, yet I believe I did not lose my senses until some minutes after. My first feelings after the shock of falling, was a violent strangling and oppression for want of breath: this soon gave way to a pain in my eyes, which seemed to be burned by two balls of fire which appeared before them, which seemed to dart on and off like lightning; settling ever and anon upon my shoulders as if they weighed ten hundred tons, and after one terrible flash, in which the two balls seemed to join in one, I sunk away without pain, like one falling to sleep.

What followed after I was turned off you know, as I was informed you kindly assisted my other friends in taking the body down as soon as you were permitted, and conveying it across the salt works to the small boat: I was from thence carried on board the two mast boat, to the Doctor, to all appearance dead: for O'Donnell, who was directed by the Doctor to cut and loosen my clothes, and rub me, throwing water on me, could perceive no life in me, but told the Doctor it was too late. But the Doctor was not discouraged; and in one and twenty-two minutes after I was brought on board the boat, making two hours and forty-three minutes after I was turned off, he perceived sign of life in me, by a small motion and warmth in my bosom: In twenty minutes after, I gave a violent deep groan. Here description fails! I cannot describe the intolerable agony of that moment. Ten thousand stranglings are trifling to it! The first confused thoughts I had, were, that it was the moment of my desolation; for I had no knowledge of my removal from the gallows, but was quite insensible from the time I first lost myself, to that in which I recovered—except some faint glimmerings of a scene, which, faint and confused as they were, I shall never forget, but which I feel impressed upon my heart I ought to communicate *to no man living.* I was soon after this violent anguish, made sensible where I was; the Doctor's stuff, and sight of my friends, restored me in a great measure to my senses. The Doctor would not allow me to talk much; but feeling fatigued he permitted me to lie down, having two persons by me to rub me with a brush while I slept. When I awoke it was dark. I felt somewhat light-headed and confused, from the dreadful scene I had passed through. All hands were now called, and a solemn oath was taken by all present, not to tell any thing which had happened until they should know that I was safe out of the country; and then not to discover the Doctor, his friend, or apprentice. I was then put on shore, and went from thence on board the vessel which brought me here. . . .

So I remain your assured friend,
until death shall indeed come,
JOSEPH TAYLOR."
(*Pennsylvania Packet,* Jannary 11, 1790.)

index of american design

The Index of American Design, now housed in the National Gallery of Art in Washington, D.C., was one of the most ambitious cultural projects of the Works Projects Administration (WPA) of the New Deal.

This collection of 20,000 plates, each an original rendering of an object by an accomplished artist, is the best single guide to what one scholar has called the "vernacular tradition" in American art. It represents a sampling of popular artistic expression—in handicrafts, commercial design, and simple ingenuity from the beginning of American history until about the 1890s. The *Index of American Design Manual* (1938), instructing artists on how to prepare their plates, explains the purposes of the project:

> The aim of the Index is to compile material for a nation-wide pictorial survey of design in the American decorative, useful and folk arts from their inception to about 1890.
>
> It seeks especially:—
>
> 1. To record material of historical significance which has not heretofore been studied and which, for one reason or another, stands in danger of being lost.
>
> 2. To gather a body of traditional material which may form the basis of an organic development of American design.
>
> 3. To make usable source records of this material accessible to artists, designers, manufacturers, museums, libraries, and art schools.
>
> 4. To give employment to painters, graphic artists, photographers and commercial artists who might not otherwise find employment.

The Index was by every standard an enormous success. Critics acclaimed the quality of the artwork and the selection of objects. The availability of this material encouraged—just as its sponsor had hoped—a revival of interest in American designs. It was a remarkable example of successful cultural nationalism and remains a splendid resource valuable both for historical and design purposes. One longs only for an updating of the Index and for the opportunity to present some of these plates in full color, since the black and white reproductions below do only partial justice to the many cultural excellences of the objects.

Material from the Index is readily available to teachers. Erwin O.

Christensen, *The Index of American Design* (Macmillan Co. for the National Gallery of Art, 1950) contains excellent color illustrations and an illuminating text. Clarence P. Hornung, *Treasury of American Design* (Harry N. Abrams, New York, n.d., L.C. #76–142742) is a recently published, large two-volume work, splendidly illustrated with many hundreds of plates from the Index. Finally, and most extraordinary to relate, the Extension Service of the National Gallery of Art has twenty-three different slide sets plus lecture notes for the use of teachers, which can be loaned without charge. For information write to Extension Service, National Gallery of Art, Washington, D.C. 20565.

Numerals, wrought iron; made by original Dutch settlers for the Old Tile House, New Castle, Delaware, 1687.

Dress, imported brocaded silk,
made in Boston about 1770.

Clog, ash sole, leather toe and heel piece; eighteenth century.

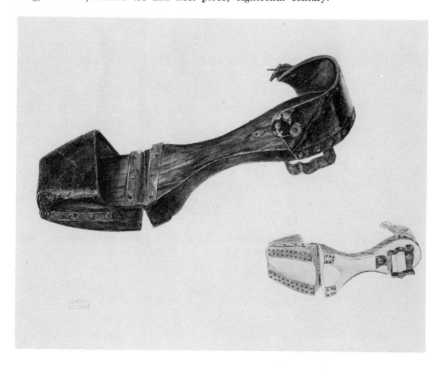

"Mercury," carved and gilded wood, 3½ feet high; attributed to Simeon Skillin; second half of eighteenth century.

Lantern of pierced tin called a "Paul Revere"; probably made in New England; eighteenth to nineteenth century.

Windsor chair, reputed to be the sort used by Thomas Jefferson while he wrote the Declaration of Independence; probably made in New England; mid-eighteenth century.

"Hessian Soldier" andiron, one of a pair; cast iron, painted; late eighteenth century.

Dowry chest, Pennsylvania German; inscribed with name of first owner, Jacob Rickert, dated 1782.

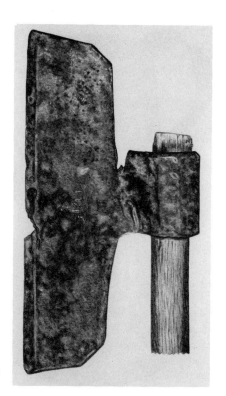

Broadax, wrought iron, oak handle, dated 1745.

Settler's wagon; length, over 14 feet; wagon bed, 10½ feet; wheel diameters, 42 inches and 33½ inches; about 1800.

Toleware coffee pot from Lebanon, Pennsylvania.

Birth and Baptismal Certificate, Fraktur writing, Pennsylvania German, dated 1808.

Tall clock, Shaker; made by Benjamin Youngs in Watervliet, New York in 1806.

Fire engine, hand pump, built by Patrick Lyon in 1806 for the Pennsylvania Fire Company No. 22, Philadelphia; side panels from the Weccaco Fire Company No. 19.

Whirligig, painted pine, Pennsylvania German; nineteenth century.

Chicken, reputedly carved by slave of Jean Laffite; first quarter of nineteenth century.

Figurehead, "The Quaker"; Boston, nineteenth century.

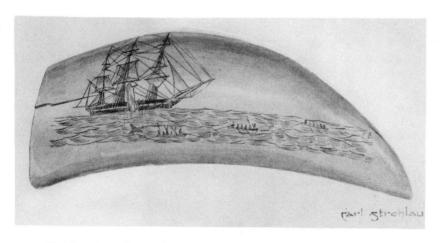

"Whaling Scene," scrimshaw engraving on whale tooth; New Bedford, Massachusetts, nineteenth century.

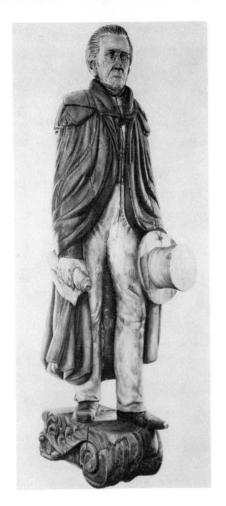

Figurehead, "Andrew Jackson"; carved in Boston Navy Yard about 1834.

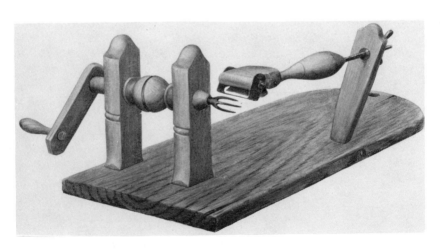

Apple corer, Delaware, nineteenth century.

Police rattle, oak, nineteenth century.

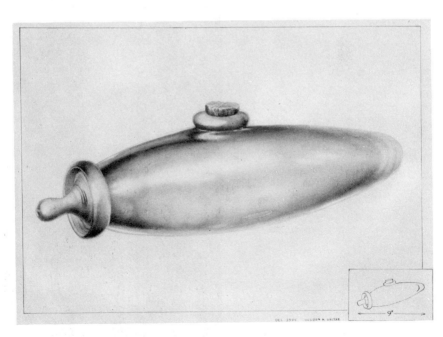

Nursing bottle, hand-blown; first half of nineteenth century.

Rag doll, Pennsylvania; made about 1830.

Calendar, painted wood; made by Shakers, Zoar, Ohio, 1836.

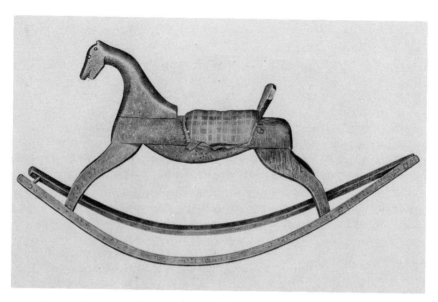

Rocking horse, wood, nineteenth century.

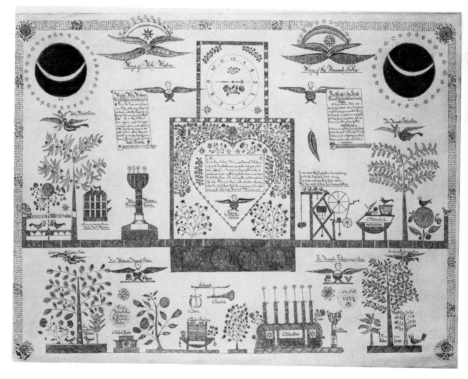

Religious picture, Ohio, 1847.

Dutch oven, cast iron; made in Ohio, mid-nineteenth century.

Basket, made in 1822 by Anna Mari Marta, San Buenaventura Mission, California.

Saint Acacius, *bulto*, painted wood; made in New Mexico, eighteenth century.

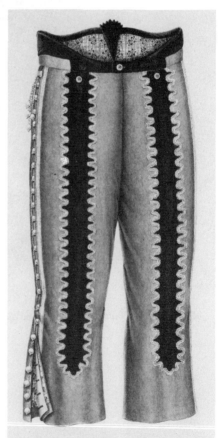

Caballero suit, owned by Don Antonio Franco de Coronel; southern California, mid-nineteenth century.

Spur with leather toe strap; made in southern California, nineteenth century.

Head, wood; made in California
about 1849; later a saloon ornament.

Cigar-store Indian, wood, carved and painted; nineteenth century.

Fire hat with portrait of Zachary Taylor; made about 1850–60.

Carrousel rooster, wood; made
in St. Johnsbury, Vermont, nineteenth century.

Roller skates; mid-nineteenth century.

Ice cream freezer, cedar with iron handle; Delaware, 1860.

Coverlet (detail); woven on jaquard loom by Harry Tyler, in Butterville, Jefferson County, New York in 1853.

Quilt, appliqué; made in Virginia in 1853.

Flatiron stand, cast iron; "W" advertises maker; nineteenth century.

"Lumberjacks Sawing a Log," woodcarving, 19 inches long; made in Eau Claire, Wisconsin, nineteenth century.

Black mammy doll; Wisconsin, nineteenth century.

"Simon Legree" marionette, carved and painted wood, fabric shirt and trousers; California, nineteenth century.

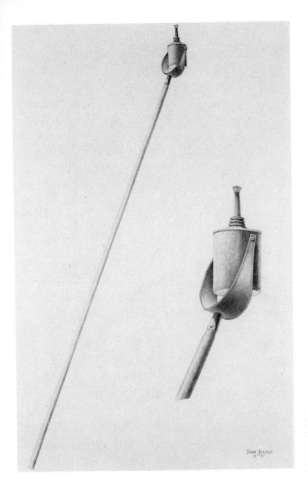

Election torch, tin, used oil or lard fuel; made in Nauvoo, Illinois; used in Lincoln's 1860 campaign for "Wide Awake" parades.

Civil War drum, Ninth Regiment, Vermont Volunteers, U. S. infantry, made about 1860.

Historical printed textile. Event handkerchief printed on silk. American flags, golden eagle, purple mourning stripes, portraits of Lincoln and his generals with views of New York, Philadelphia, Baltimore and New Orleans; nineteenth century.

Deer, hollow cast zinc, 3½ feet high; made by J. W. Fiske Ornamental Iron Works, New York City in 1870.

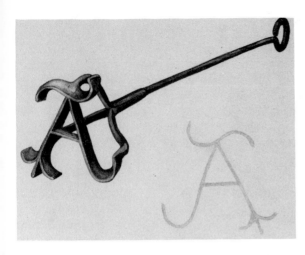

Branding iron, cast iron about 34 inches long; made in Arizona in 1891.

Mechanical toy bank, "Teddy and the Bear," cast iron; made in the Stevens Foundry, Cromwell, Connecticut about 1900.

part 2 evangelical america: 1800-1870

An evangel means literally a "good messenger" or a bearer of good news. Citizens of the young republic before the tragedy of sectional conflict viewed themselves as bearers of good news on every front. Religious revivals beginning in the West in 1797 and never wholly ceasing before the Civil War set an overtly evangelical tone for all of American culture. This new republic, facing its own problems, nevertheless possessed the energy and resources for major missionary efforts in taming the Western frontier, bringing religion to the freethinking cities, and spreading the word about evangelical Protestantism to "heathens" in Asia, Africa, and the islands of the Pacific.

Republicanism became another item of good news. Every foreign traveller heard about our institutions. Self-government, a nation without kings, the heroic and patriotic Washington: these were moral commodities ready for export. Americans took credit for the French Revolution (but not, of course, for its excesses) and for each subsequent revolution in Latin America and Europe. These official patrons of revolution actively sided with liberals and nationalists in 1830 and 1848 when Europe went to the barricades. Americans did not consider their patriotism a narrow chauvinism, but an example, a sermon, to the peoples of the world. As a result, they could be blithely unself-conscious in their assertions of American superiority.

The "rise of the common man" was another message spread by many (but by no means all) Americans. This democratization had many meanings: some members of older elites saw it as a dangerous tendency to level all of society; but the mass of people viewed it as an opportunity to rise. This "rising" did not mean simply becoming richer; it meant becoming better: more educated and ethical, more polished and graceful. The country's passion for books on manners began in this period as Americans avidly absorbed lessons in etiquette, in household management, in childrearing, and in improving their habits and institutions. Equality, especially in popular culture, threatened far less than conservatives feared.

"Reform," another popular subject, inspired great oratory, writing, and popular concern. Temperance became a prime enthusiasm and bit deeply into popular habits. In these years, Americans went from being one of the hardest drinking people in the world to a relatively temperate society in which, as foreign travellers often noticed, a young woman could travel about freely without fear of alcohol-soaked rowdies insulting or molesting her. But antislavery eventually achieved even greater importance in the North and West and more spectacular results. Fiery agitators like William Lloyd Garrison became household names; the underground railroad formed an enduring folk legend in many parts of the country, one which often exaggerated the role of the "trainmen" and "conductors" and underestimated what runaway slaves themselves did. Phrenology and communitarian experiments and reforms in land ownership, prisons, and education left profound traces not only on the country's institutions but also on its temperament.

Americans shouted their good news and whispered their bad. This mobile, striving world inevitably produced not only overt and physical discomfort like the factories and cities rising as smoky contradictions to the nation's romantic agrarian ideals, but also those more psychological: the emphasis on self-improvement betrayed people struggling with new forms of society and behavior, new lessons to learn and obsolete ones to forget. An etiquette instruction manual might relieve some anxiety about possible mistakes, but knowing what to do did not automatically enable one to do it on the spot. As a result, much popular culture revolved about problems of manners or turned sentimentally to those who did not have to worry about "rising." Minstrel shows, the most popular entertainment of the middle half of the century, presented black-faced actors (usually white men) clowning as they would not dare to do in their natural white skin. Dialect humor—old "Down East" Yankees or unassimilated Irish—provided the stage and literature with a staple for a century. The master showman, Phineas T. Barnum, sold the public amusement in the form of "education" in his American Museum. A middle-brow popular culture of romantic sentimentality moved Americans—mostly women—into realms of fantasy and pathos where the mundane crudities of life did not intrude.

This sentimentality reflected a yearning for the past. Modern Americans, raised with a nostalgia for the "good old days" of the nineteenth century, may be surprised that people then suffered the same longings for a simpler world. Recollections of rural neighborliness or of venturesome frontier days before the custodians of manners took control appealed to men and women rising from rural origins and making their way in the towns and cities. Stephen Collins Foster's longing for "The Old Folks at Home" moved millions who had no intention of ever returning.

A recognizable popular culture had emerged in the United States by the time of the Civil War. Rapidly spreading literacy and great improvements in transportation and communications had brought much folk culture into the medium of print; a vigorous political life had made oratory a great popular art; the war itself, an event touching every citizen, renewed the nationalist impulse of the revolution. Meanwhile, industrialism spread the technological base for a fully nationalized popular culture. More and more, Americans could vicariously experience events together and move together in their responses toward a common culture.

politics and nationality

Parson Weems, itinerant bookseller and book writer, gave a giant boost to the creation of legends that turned George Washington from an interesting human being to an insufferable moral ideal. Anyone can appreciate a boy who doesn't tell lies, but one who "can't" seems a bit much. (Selection from Mason L. Weems, *The Life of Washington*, 1800.)

LIFE OF WASHINGTON

Birth and Education

To this day numbers of good Christians can hardly find faith to believe that Washington was, bone fide, *"a Virginian! What! a buckskin!"* say they with a smile, *"George Washington a buckskin! pshaw! impossible! he was certainly an European: So great a man could never have been born in America."*

So great a man could never have been born in America! Why that's the very *prince of reasons* why he should have been born here! Nature, we know, is fond of *harmonies;* and *paria paribus*, that is, *great things to great*, is the rule she delights to work by. Where, for example, do we look for the *whale* "the biggest born of nature?" not, I trow, in a *mill-pond*, but in the main ocean; *"there go the great ships,"* and there are the spoutings of whales amidst their boiling foam.

By the same rule, where shall we look for Washington, the greatest among men, but in *America?* That greatest Continent, which, rising from beneath the frozen pole, stretches far and wide to the south, running almost *"whole the length of this vast terrene,"* and sustaining on her ample sides the roaring shock of half the watery globe. And equal to its size, is the furniture of this vast continent, where the Almighty has reared his cloud-capt mountains, and spread his sea-like lakes, and poured his mighty rivers, and hurled down his thundering cataracts in a style of the *sublime,* so far superior to any thing of the kind in the other continents, that we may fairly conclude that great men and great deeds are designed for America.

This seems to be the verdict of honest analogy; and accordingly we find America the honoured cradle of Washington, who was born on Pope's creek, in Westmoreland county, Virginia, the 22nd of February,

1732. His father, whose name was Augustin Washington, was also a Virginian, but his grandfather (John) was an Englishman, who came over and settled in Virginia in 1657.

His father fully persuaded that a marriage of virtuous love comes nearest to angelic life, early stepped up to the *altar* with glowing cheeks and joy sparkling eyes, while by his side, with soft warm hand, sweetly trembling in his, stood the angel form of the lovely Miss Dandridge.

After several years of great domestic happiness, Mr. Washington was separated by death, from this excellent woman, who left him and two children to lament her early fate.

Fully persuaded still, that *"it is not good for man to be alone,"* he renewed, for the second time, the chaste delights of matrimonial love. His consort was Miss Mary Ball, a young lady of fortune, and descended from one of the best families in Virginia.

. . . . By his first wife, Mr. Washington had two children, both sons —Lawrence and Augustin. By his second wife, he had five children, four sons and a daughter—George, Samuel, John, Charles, and Elizabeth. Those *over delicate* ones, who are ready to faint at thought of a second marriage, might do well to remember, that the greatest man that ever lived was the son of his second marriage! . . .

To assist his son to overcome that selfish spirit which too often leads children to fret and fight about trifles, was a notable care of Mr. Washington. For this purpose, of all the presents, such as cakes, fruit, &c. he received, he was always desired to give a liberal part to his play-mates. To enable him to do this with more alacrity, his father would remind him of the love which he would hereby gain, and the frequent presents which would in return be made *to him;* and also would tell of that great and good God, who delights above all things to see children love one another, and will assuredly reward them for acting so amiable a part. . . .

Never did the wise Ulysses take more pains with his beloved Telemachus, than did Mr. Washington with George, to inspire him with an *early love of truth.* "Truth, George," (said he) "is the loveliest quality of youth. I would ride fifty miles, my son, to see the little boy whose heart is so *honest,* and his lips so *pure,* that we may depend on every word he says. O how lovely does such a child appear in the eyes of every body! His parents doat on him; his relations glory in him; they are constantly praising him to their children, whom they beg to imitate him. They are often sending for him, to visit them; and receive him, when he comes, with as much joy as if he were a little angel, come to set pretty examples to their children.

"But, Oh! how different, George, is the case with the boy who is so given to lying, that nobody can believe a word he says! He is looked at with aversion wherever he goes, and parents dread to see him come among their children. Oh, George! my son! rather than see you come to this pass, dear as you are to my heart, gladly would I assist to nail you up in your little coffin, and follow you to your grave. Hard, indeed, would it be to me to give up my son, whose little feet are always so ready to run about with me, and whose fondly looking eyes and sweet prattle make so large a part of my happiness: but still I would give him up, rather than see him a common liar.

"Pa, (said George very seriously) do I ever tell lies?"

"No, George, I *thank God* you do not, my son; and I rejoice in the hope you never will. At least, you shall never, from me, have cause to be guilty of so shameful a thing. Many parents, indeed, even compel their children to this vile practice, by barbarously beating them for every little fault; hence, on the next offence, the little terrified creature slips out a *lie!* just to escape the rod. But as to yourself, George, you know I have *always* told you, and now tell you again, that, whenever by accident you do anything wrong, which must often be the case, as you are but a poor little boy yet, without *experience* or *knowledge*, never tell a falsehood to conceal it; but come *bravely* up, my son, like a *little man*, and tell me of it: and instead of beating you, George, I will but the more honour and love you for it, my dear."

This, you'll say, was sowing good seed!—Yes, it was: and the crop thank God, was, as I believe it ever will be, where a man acts the true parent, that is, the *Guardian Angel*, by his child.

The following anecdote is a *case in point*. It is too valuable to be lost, and too true to be doubted; for it was communicated to me by the same excellent lady to whom I am indebted for the last.

"When George," said she, "was about six years old, he was made the wealthy master of a *hatchet!* of which, like most little boys, he was immoderately fond, and was constantly going about chopping every thing that came in his way. One day, in the garden, where he often amused himself hacking his mother's pea-sticks, he unluckily tried the edge of his hatchet on the body of a beautiful young English cherry-tree, which he barked so terribly, that I don't believe the tree ever got the better of it. The next morning the old gentleman finding out what had befallen his tree, which, by the by, was a great favourite, came into the house, and with much warmth asked for the mischievous author, declaring at the same time, that he would not have taken five guineas for his tree. Nobody could tell him any thing about it. Presently George and his hatchet made their appearance. *George,* said his father, *do you know who killed that beautiful little cherry-tree yonder in the garden?* This was a *tough question;* and George staggered under it for a moment; but quickly recovered himself: and looking at his father, with the sweet face of youth brightened with the inexpressible charm of all-conquering truth, he bravely cried out, *"I can't tell a lie, Pa; you know I can't tell a lie. I did cut it with my hatchet."—Run to my arms, you dearest boy,* cried his father in transport, *run to my arms; glad am I, George, that you killed my tree; for you have paid me for it a thousand fold. Such an act of heroism in my son, is more worth than a thousand trees, though blossomed with silver, and their fruits of purest gold. . . .*

Many Americans look back with nostalgia on the uncomplicated and hearty nationalism of the nineteenth century. Beginning immediately with the Revolutionary War, Americans marched and sang and celebrated "The Glorious Fourth" with shameless enthusiasm. (From National Magazine, *Heart Songs,* 1909.)

PATRIOTIC SONGS AND SLOGANS

The Glorious Fourth

1 We'll march and shout hurrah!
  With flags and banners gay!
  For is it not the glorious Fourth
  We celebrate today?
  This day gave Freedom birth;
  Its fame now fills the earth.
  For this th'embatled heroes stood
  To serve their country's good.

2 Columbia's freemen brave
  Rejoice to do and dare!
  This day the winds exult to wave
  The stars and stripes in air!
  'Tis North and South no more;
  One Country we adore.
  No stars have from our banner fled,—
  What glorious light they shed!

3 Our land is broad and fair,
  Sweet freedom ev'rywhere.
  We welcome others to our shores,
  This home with us to share.

Though wealth in goods we own,
True freemen prize alone
The laws upheld by ev'ry one—
The peace our fathers won.

The Glorious Fourth!—real joy of independence and citizenship, mingled with an older, deferential social system in the early years of nationhood. This rollicking ballad catches the revelry of Independence Day celebrations and describes, incidentally, rural social relations. The poem is said to be "composed for the 4th of July, calculated for the meridian of some country towns in Massachusetts, and Rye, in New Hampshire." (From *Farmer's Museum*, Massachusetts, 1800.)

Squeak the Fife and Beat the Drum
"Squeak the fife and beat the drum,
Independence day is come!!
Let the roasting pig be bled,
Quick twist off the rooster's head,
Quickly rub the pewter platter,
Heap the nut cakes fried in butter,
Set the cups and beaker glass,
The pumpkin and the apple sauce.
Send the keg to shop for brandy;
Maple sugar we have handy.
Independent, staggering Dick,
A noggin mix of *swinging thick*;
Sal, put on your *russel skirt*,
Jotham, get your *boughten* shirt,
To-day we dance to tiddle-diddle—
Here comes Sambo with his fiddle;
Sambo, take a draw of whiskey,
And play up Yankee Doodle frisky—
Moll, come leave your witched tricks,
And let us have a reel of six—
Father and mother shall make two;
Sall, Moll, and I stand all a row,
Sambo, play and dance with polity;
This is the day of blest equality,—
Father and mother are but men,
And Sambo is a *citizen*.
Come, foot it, Sal; Moll, figure in,

And, mother, you dance up to him;
Now saw as fast as e'er you can do,
And, father, you cross over to Sambo.
—Thus we dance and thus we play,
On glorious Independence Day.
Rub more rosin on your bow,
And let us have another go—
Zounds! as sure as eggs and bacon,
Here's Ensign Sneak and uncle Deacon,
Aunt Thiah, and their Bet's behind her
On blundering mare, than beetle blinder—
And there's the Squire, too, with his lady—
Sal, hold the beast! I'll take the baby!
Moll, bring the Squire our great arm-chair,
Good folks, we're glad to see you here—
Jotham, get the great case bottle,
Your teeth can draw the corn-cob stopple—
Ensign, Deacon, never mind;
Squire, drink until you're blind."

"Uncle Sam" is one of the most constant symbols of American nationality. The following obituary in the Albany *Evening Journal* explains its origin. (From the Albany *Evening Journal*, August 1, 1854.)

The Real Uncle Sam

"UNCLE SAM"—The death of Samuel Wilson, an aged, worthy and formerly enterprising citizen of Troy, will remind those who were familiar with the incidents of the War of 1812, of the origin of the popular sobriquet for the "United States." Mr. Wilson was an extensive packer, had the contract for supplying the northern army with beef and pork. He was everywhere known and spoken of as "Uncle Sam," and the "U. S." branded on the heads of barrels for the army were at first taken to be the initials of "Uncle Sam" Wilson, but finally lost their local significance and became, throughout the army, the familiar term for "United States." . . .

The 1840 campaign brought all the folklore of mass politics to the fore. Whig singers celebrated the humble origins of their candidate. (Daniel Webster actually apologized for his failure to be born in a log cabin!) (Selection is a Whig campaign song, 1840.)

TIPPECANOE AND TYLER TOO

The Log Cabin and Hard Cider Candidate

Tune, "Auld Lang Syne'
Should good old cider be despised,
    And ne'er regarded more?
Should plain log cabins be despised,
    Our fathers built of yore?
For the true old style, my boys!
    For the true old style?
Let's take a mug of cider, now,
    For the true old style.

We've tried experiments enough
    Of fashions new and vain,
And now we long to settle down
    To good old times again.
For the good old ways, my boys!
    For the good old ways,
Let's take a mug of cider, now,
    For the good old ways.

We've tried your purse-proud lords, who love
    In palaces to shine;
But we'll have a plowman President
    Of the Cincinnatus line.
For old North Bend, my boys!
    For old North Bend,
We'll take a mug of cider, yet,
    For old North Bend.

We've tried the "greatest and the best,"
    And found him bad enough;
And he who "in the footsteps treads"
    Is yet more sorry stuff.
For the brave old Thames, my boys!
    For the brave old Thames,
We'll take a mug of cider, yet,
    For the brave old Thames.

Then give's a hand, my boys!
    And here's a hand for you,
And we'll quaff the good old cider yet
    For Old Tippecanoe.
For Old Tippecanoe, my boys!
    For Old Tippecanoe,
We'll take a mug of cider, yet,
    For Old Tippecanoe.

And surely you'll give your good vote,
    And surely I will, too;
And we'll clear the way to the White House, yet,
    For Old Tippecanoe.
For Tip-pe-canoe, my boys,
    For Tip-pe-canoe,
We'll take a mug of cider, yet,
    For Tippecanoe.

The merchandising of political candidates by hoopla and emotional appeals was first practiced early in the nineteenth century. The St. Louis *New Era* description of a rally for William Henry Harrison in 1840 is typical of the highly partisan nature of contemporary newspapers and fully conveys the fanfaronade of contrived political events. (Selection from A. B. Norton, ed., *The Election of 1840*, 1840.)

THE LOG CABIN CAMPAIGN

Rally for William Henry Harrison in St. Louis, Missouri,
as Reported by the St. Louis New Era

We cannot believe that any friend of Harrison could, in his most sanguine moments, have anticipated so glorious a day, such a turn-out of the people, as was witnessed on Tuesday last in this city. Everything was auspicious. The heavens, the air, the earth, all seemed to have combined to assist in doing honor to the services, the patriotism and the virtues of William Henry Harrison. Never have we seen so much enthusiasm, so much honest, impassioned and eloquent feeling displayed in the countenances and bursting from the lips of freemen. It was a day of jubilee. The people felt that the time had come when they could breathe freely—when they were about to cast from them the incubus of a polluted and abandoned party, and when they could look forward to better and happier days in store for them and for the country. The city itself bore, in some respects, the remarkable character of a Sabbath day. By the Whigs, and even among the Democrats, there was little work done. The doors of all places of business were closed, and nothing was thought of on this carnival day but joy and gratitude. We shall, ourselves, give such an account of the proceedings as our time and opportunities permitted us to gather, leaving it to the imagination to fill up the *tout ensemble* of the picture.

Preparations had been made for the reception and entertainment of the company, by the proper committees, at Mrs. Ashley's residence. The extensive park was so arranged as to accommodate the throng of persons who were expected. Seats were erected for the officers of the day, for the speakers and for the ladies. At the hour appointed by the marshal of the day, the people commenced to assemble at the court house, and several associations and crafts were formed in the procession as they advanced on the ground. While this was going on, the steamboats bringing delegations from St. Charles, Hannibal, Adams county, Ill., and Alton, arrived at the wharf, with banners unfurled to the breeze, and presenting a most cheering sight. The order of procession, so far as we have been able to obtain it, was as follows:

Music: Brass band.
1. Banner, borne by farmers from the northern part of St. Louis township. This banner represented the "Raising of the Siege of Fort Meigs" and bore as its motto, "It Has Pleased Providence, We Are Victorious." (Harrison's dispatch.)
2. Officers and members of the Tippecanoe club, preceded by the president, Col. John O'Fallon, with a splendid banner, representing a hemisphere surmounted by an American eagle, strangling with his beak a serpent, its folds grasped within its talons, and its head having the face of a fox in the throes of death. Above was a rainbow, emblematic of hope, in which was the name of the club. Below the hemisphere was the motto, "The Victor in '11, Will be the Victor in '40." On the reverse side, the letters "T.C." The members six abreast.
3. Log cabin committee, six abreast.
4. The president and vice-presidents of the day.
5. Soldiers who served under Harrison in the late war—in a car, adorned with banners on each side—one, a view of a steamboat named Tippecanoe, with a sign board, "For Washington City." On the other, a view of the cabin at North Bend, the farmer at his plow, with the inscription, "Harrison, the Old Soldier, Honest Man, and Pure Patriot."
6. Invited guests in carriages.
7. Citizens on foot, six abreast, bearing banners inscribed, "Harrison, the Friend of Pre-emption Rights," "One Term for the Presidency;"

"Harrison, the People's Candidate;" "Harrison, the People's Sober Second Thought;" "Harrison, He Never Lost a Battle;" "Harrison, the Protector of the Pioneers of the West;" "Harrison, Tyler and Reform;" "Harrison, the Poor Man's Friend;" "Harrison, the Friend of Equal Laws and Equal Rights."

8. Citizens on horseback, six abreast.
9. Delegation from Columbia Bottom.
10. Canoe, "North Bend."
11. Boys with banners, upon one of which was inscribed, "Our Country's Hope," and on another, "Just as the Twig is Bent, the Tree's Inclined."

   These boys belonged to the several schools of the city; were regularly marshaled, and presented, by the regularity of their conduct, a most interesting spectacle.

12. Laborers, with their horses and carts, shovels, picks, etc., with a banner bearing the inscription, "Harrison, the Poor Man's Friend—We Want Work."
13. A printing press on a platform with banners, and the pressman striking off Tippecanoe songs, and distributing them to the throng of people as they passed along, followed in order by the members of the craft.
14. Drays, with barrels of hard cider.
15. A log cabin mounted on wheels, and drawn by six beautiful horses, followed by the craft of carpenters in great numbers. Over the door of the cabin, the words, "The String of the Latch Never Pulled In."
16. The blacksmiths, with forge, bellows, etc., mounted on cars, the men at work. Banner, "We Strike for Our Country's Good."
17. The joiners and cabinet-makers; a miniature shop mounted on wheels; men at work; the craft following it.
18. A large canoe, drawn by six horses, and filled with men.
19. Two canoes, mounted, and filled with sailors.
20. Fort Meigs, in miniature, 40 by 15 feet, drawn by nine yoke of oxen. The interior filled with soldiers, in the usual dress of that day, hunting shirts, leggins, leather breeches, etc.; and one of the men a participant in the defense of Fort Meigs. At every bastion of the fort the muzzle of a piece of ordnance protruded itself, and from another point a piece of artillery was fired, at short intervals, during the day. The whole was most admirably got up, and reflects much credit upon the friends of "Old Tip," to be found at the "Floating Dock."
21. Delegation of brickmakers, with apparatus, clay, etc., and men at work.
22. Delegation of bricklayers, with a beautiful banner, representing a log cabin, brick house going up, etc., and followed by the craft, six abreast.

   Band of music.
23. Delegation from Carondelet.
24. Delegation from Belleville, Ill., with banners.
25. Delegation from Alton, with canoe, drawn by four horses, and banners representing the state of the country, the peculiar notions of the Loco Foco party about the reduction of the prices of labor to the

standard of the hard-money countries of Europe and Cuba; a sub-treasury box, with illustrations, etc. One of the banners bore the inscription, "Connecticut Election, 4,600 Majority; Rhode Island, 1,500 Majority;" and a cunning looking fellow, with his thumb on his nose, and twisting his fingers in regular Samuel Weller style, saying, "You Can't Come It, Matty." This delegation numbered about two hundred men.

26. Delegations from Hannibal and Pike counties with banners, etc.
27. Delegation from Rockport with a log cabin, canoe, banners, etc.
28. Delegation from St. Charles, with banners bearing the names of the twenty-six States, borne by as many individuals, and having with them a handsome canoe drawn by four horses.

Arrived at the southern extremity of the park, the procession halted and formed in open order, the rear passing to the front.

The people were then successively addressed by Mr. John Hogan, of Illinois.

Colonel John O'Fallon was then called for, and mounted on Fort Meigs, he thus addressed the people:

My Fellow Citizens:

I feel deeply sensible of the honor you confer upon me by calling me to address this vast concourse of intelligent freemen. My pursuits in life have led me into retirement; I am wholly unused to speaking in public.

Aware that my known acquaintance with the eventful scenes which we have this day assembled to commemorate, is the only reason for this call, I shall, consequently, in responding to it, state something of what I know in relation to them.

I had the honor of serving under General Harrison at the battle of Tippecanoe, during the siege of Fort Meigs, and at the battle of the Thames. I can say that, from the commencement to the termination of his military services in the last war, I was almost constantly by his side. I was familiar with his conduct as governor and superintendent of Indian affairs of the Territory of Indiana, and after the return of peace, as commissioner to treat with all the hostile Indians of the last war in the Northwest, for the establishment of a permanent reconciliation and peace. I saw also much of General Harrison whilst he was in the Congress of the United States.

Opportunities have thus been afforded me of knowing him in all the relations of life, as an officer and as a man, and of being enabled to form a pretty correct estimate of his military and civil services, as well as his qualifications and fitness for office. I know him to be open and brave in his disposition, of active and industrious habits, uncompromizing in his principles, above all guile and intrigue, and a pure, honest, noble-minded man, with a heart ever overflowing with warm and generous sympathies for his fellow-man. As a military man, his daring, chivalrous courage inspired his men with confidence and spread dismay and terror to his enemies. In all his plans he was successful. In all his engagements he was victorious. He has filled all the various civil and military offices committed to him by his country, with sound judgment and spotless fidelity. In every situation he was cautious and prudent, firm and energetic, and his decisions always judicious. His acquirements as a scholar are varied and extensive, his principles as a statesman sound, pure and republican.

If chosen President he will be the President of the people rather than of a party. The Government will then be administered for the general good and welfare.

His election will be the dawn of a new era! The reform of the abuses of a most corrupt, prolifigate and oppressive Government. Then will end the ten years' war upon the currency and institutions of the country. The hard-money cry and hard times will disappear together. Then will cease further attempts to increase the wages of the office-holders and reduce the wages of the people to the standard of European labor.

Then shall we see restored the general prosperity of the people, by giving them a sound local currency, mixed with a currency of a uniform value throughout the land. The revival of commerce, of trade, enterprise and general confidence. Then the return of happier, more peaceful and more prosperous days, when cheerfulness and plenty will, once more, smile around the poor man's table.

About the close of the meeting the following resolutions were adopted with three cheers:

Resolved, That the Whig young men of St. Louis county will respond to the call for a young men's convention at Rocheport on the 20th of June, and that the cause of old Tippecanoe shall not suffer because they are not on the ground.

Resolved, That five hundred of the real "log cabin and hard cider boys" of St. Louis county will stand at a corner of the Rocheport cabin on the 18th, and join in the convention of the 20th, when they hope to meet ten thousand of their brethren and join with them in doing honor to the farmer-statesmen of the West.

Resolved, That a committee of twenty be appointed to select the five hundred who shall go.

After the adoption of these resolutions, a song was sung, and the company dispersed.

The political role of saloons is older than the American republic. (Selection from Matthew P. Breen, *Thirty Years of New York Politics Up-to-Date,* New York, 1899, p. 112.)

THE POLITICAL SALOON

. . . It was part of the original charter of New York, according to oldtime records, that the officials of the city government should be paid from an excise tax. It can therefore be seen that, from the beginning, it was the policy of the city authorities to encourage, not to oppress, taverns and public houses. In New Amsterdam the taverns were under the special control and protection of the city government, which regulated all their details and protected their proprietors in all their rights. The law even regulated the precise amount of liquor which was given or could be demanded for a drink. Any man who "beat" the barkeeper, or did not pay his bill, was ostracized as well as punished. Originally, the New York taverns were, in fact, used as District Courts. The magistrates decided local disputes at the local taverns. And as the Court held its sessions and rendered its decisions at the taverns, so the fines imposed by the courts were often taken out in drinks. The Judges, witnesses, and all concerned, including the plaintiff and defendant, would order their drinks, and take them together, and then the party against whom decisions were rendered would pay for them—a pleasant way of paying a fine, especially for the landlord! When the Dutch surrendered New Amsterdam to the English, the courts became more dull and dignified. Regular halls of justice were established, and the tap-room ceased to be a court-room; nevertheless, under the English as under the Dutch, the New York tavern continued to be a political center, and it has so remained down to our own day.

These effusions of patriotism come from The Wide-Awake Gift: A Know-Nothing Token for 1855, edited by "One of 'Em." The anti-Catholic Know-nothing movement was at its peak in the early and mid-1850s when this ladies' gift book was published. Politics by that time could reach anywhere, even into the presents that young men were expected to offer their ladies. (Selections from The Wide-Awake Gift: A Know-Nothing Token for 1855.)

THE AMERICAN FLAG

When Freedom, from her mountain height,
    Unfurled her standard to the air,
She tore the azure robe of night,
    And set the stars of glory there.

She mingled with its gorgeous dyes,
The milky baldrick of the skies,
And striped its pure, celestial white,
With streakings of the morning light;
Then, from his mansion in the sun,
She called her eagle-bearer down,
And gave into his mighty hand
The symbol of her chosen land.

Majestic monarch of the cloud!
    Who rear'st aloft thy eagle form,
To hear the tempest trumping loud,
And see the lightning-lances driven,
    When strides the warrior of the storm,
And rolls the thunder-drum of heaven;
Child of the sun! to thee 'tis given
    To guard the banner of the free,
To hover in the sulphur smoke,
To ward away the battle-stroke,
And bid its blendings shine afar,
Like rainbows in the cloud of war,
    The harbinger of victory.

Flag of the brave! thy folds shall fly
The sign of hope and triumph high.
When speaks the signal-trumpet tone,
And the long line comes gleaming on,
Ere yet the life-blood, warm and wet,
Has dimmed the glistening bayonet,
Each soldier's eye shall brightly turn
To where thy meteor glories burn,
And as his springing steps advance,
Catch war and vengeance from the glance;
And when the cannon's mouthings loud,
Heave, in wild wreaths, the battle shroud,
And gory sabres rise and fall,
Like shoots of flame on midnight's pall,
There, shall thy victor glances glow,
And cowering foes shall sink below
Each gallant arm, that strikes beneath
That awful messenger of death.

Flag of the seas! on ocean's wave
Thy stars shall glitter o'er the brave.

When death, careering on the gale,
Sweeps darkly round the bellied sail,
And frighted waves rush wildly back,
Before the broadside's reeling rack.
The dying wanderer of the sea
Shall look at once to heaven and thee,
And smile, to see thy splendors fly
In triumph o'er his closing eye.

Flag of the free heart's only home!
    By angel hands to valor given,
Thy stars have lit the welkin dome,
    And all thy hues were born in heaven.
Forever float that standard sheet!
    Where breathes the foe but falls before us,
With freedom's soil beneath our feet,
    And Freedom's banner waving o'er us!

—J. R. Drake

AMERICA FOR AMERICANS

Well, why not? Is there another country under the sun, that does not belong to its own, native-born people? Is there another country where the alien by birth, and often by openly boasted sympathy, is permitted to fill the most responsible offices, and preside over the most sacred trusts of the land? Is there another country that would place its secret archives and its diplomacy with foreign states, in other than native hands—with tried and trusty native hearts to back them? Is there another country that would even permit the foreigner to become a citizen, shielded by its laws and its flag, on terms such as we exact, leaving the political franchise out of sight? More than all else, is there a country, other than ours, that would acknowledge as a citizen, a patriot, a republican, or a safe man, one who stood bound by a religious oath or obligation, in political conflict with, and which he deemed temporarily higher than, the Constitution and Civil Government of that country—to which he also professes to swear fealty?

America for the Americans, we say. And why not? Didn't they plant it, and battle for it through bloody revolution—and haven't they developed it, as only Americans could, into a nation of a century, and yet mightier than the oldest empire on earth? Why shouldn't they shape and rule the destinies of their own land—the land of their birth, their love, their altars, and their graves; the land red and rich with the blood and ashes, and hallowed by the memories of their fathers? Why not rule their own, particularly when the alien betrays the trust that should never have been given him, and the liberties of the land are thereby imperilled?

Lacks the American numbers, that he may not rule by the right of majority, to which is constitutionally given the political sovereignty of this land? Did he not, at the last numbering of the people, count seventeen and a half millions, native to the soil, against less than two and a half millions of actually foreign born, and those born of foreigners coming among us for the last three quarters of a century? Has he not tried the mixed rule, with a tolerance unexampled, until it has plagued him worse than the lice and locust plagued the Egyptian? Has he not shared the trust of office and council, until foreign-born pauperism, vice and crime, stain the whole land—until a sheltered alien fraction have become rampant in their ingratitude and insolence? Has he not suffered burdens of tax, and reproach, and shame, by his ill-bestowed division of political power?

America for the Americans! That is the watchword that should ring through the length and breath of the land, from the lips of the whole people. America for the Americans—to shape and to govern; to make great, and to keep great, strong and free, from home foes and foreign demagogues and hierarchs. In the hour of Revolutionary peril, Washington said, "Put none but Americans on guard to-night." At a later time, Jefferson wished "an ocean of fire rolled between the Old World and the New." To their children, the American people, the fathers and builders of the Republic, bequeathed it. "Eternal vigilance is the price of liberty!"—let the American be vigilant that the alien seize not his birthright.

America for the Americans! Shelter and welcome let them give to the emigrant and the exile, and make them citizens in so far as civil privileges are concerned. But let it be looked to that paupers and criminals are no longer shipped on us by foreign states. Let it be looked to that foreign nationalities in our midst are rooted out; that foreign regiments and battalions are disarmed; that the public laws and schools of the country are printed and taught in the language of the land; that no more charters for foreign titled or foreign charactered associations —benevolent, social or other—are granted by our Legislatures; that all National and State support given to Education, have not the shadow of sectarianism about it. There is work for Americans to do. They have slept on guard—if, indeed, they have been on guard—and the enemy have grown strong and riotous in their midst.

America for the Americans! We have had enough of "Young Irelands," "Young Germanys," and "Young Italys." We have had enough of insolent alien threat to suppress our "Puritan Sabbath," and amend our Constitution. We have been a patient camel, and borne foreign burden even to the back-breaking pound. But the time is come to right the wrong; the occasion is ripe for reform in whatever we have failed. The politico-religious foe is fully discovered—he must be squarely met, and put down. We want in this free land none of this political dictation. We want none of his religious mummeries—let him keep his "holy shirt of Treves," his "winking (pictorial) damsel of Rimini," his "toe-nails of the Apostle Peter," and his travail about the "Immaculacy of the Virgin Mary," in those lands that have been desolated with persecution, and repeopled with serfs and lazzaroni by the hierarchy to which he owes supreme religious and temporal obedience. Our feeling is earnest, not bitter. The matters of which we have written are great and grave ones, and we shall not be silent until we have aided in wholly securing *America for the Americans*—From *The New York Mirror.*

religion

Sabbath breaking could lead to murder, solitary vices, or even jaywalking in this antebellum tract. (From J. A. Ackley, *Pictorial Narratives*, n.d.)

WARNING TO SABBATH BREAKERS

As I was walking down ———— street, on my way to church, I saw a party of young people going on before me, whose volatile manners ill accorded with the sanctity of the day; and just as I was passing them I heard one say, "Indeed I think we shall do wrong—my conscience condemns me—I must return." "There can be no harm," replied another, "in taking an excursion on the water; especially as we have resolved to go to church in the evening." "I must return," rejoined a female voice, "my conscience condemns me. What will father say, if he hear of it?" By this time they had reached the river, and one of the party was busily engaged with a waterman, while the rest stood in close debate for the space of the five minutes, when they all moved forward towards the water.

I watched them going down the stairs, and thought I perceived an air of peculiar melancholy in the countenance of the female who had objected to the excursion, but whose firmness gave way to the ardor of importunity. Two of the gentlemen stepped into the boat, two more stood at the water's edge, and the females were handed in, one after another; but still I could perceive great reluctance on the part of the one who had previously objected; till, at length, being surrounded by all the gentlemen of the party, she yielded, and the boat was pushed off.

It was a fine morning, though rather cold; the tide was running in at its usual rate; many were gazing on them, like myself, when a naval officer, standing near to me, called to them and said, "A pleasant voyage to you." One of the gentlemen suddenly arose to return the compliment; but, from some cause which I could not perceive, he unfortunately fell into the water. This disaster threw the whole party into the utmost consternation; and each one, instead of retaining his seat, rushed to the side of the boat over which their companion had fallen, which upset it, and all were instantaneously plunged into the deep. The shriek which the multitude of spectators gave, when they beheld this calamity, exceeded any noise I had ever heard; several females fainted;

boats immediately put off; and in a few minutes I had the gratification of seeing the watermen rescuing one—and another—and another, from a premature grave. Having picked up all that they could find, the different boats rowed to shore, where some medical gentlemen were in waiting; but when the party met together, no language can describe the horror which was depicted on every countenance, when they found that two were still missing. "Where's my sister?" said the voice which had said, only a few minutes before, "There can be no harm in taking an excursion on the water; especially as we have resolved to go to church in the evening." "Where's my Charles?" said a female, who had appeared the most gay and sprightly when I first saw them.

At length, two boats, which had gone a considerable distance up the river, were seen returning; and, on being asked if they had picked up any, they replied, "Yes, two." This reply electrified the whole party; they embraced each other with the tenderest emotions; they wept for joy, and so did many others who stood around them. "Here's a gentleman," said the waterman, as he was coming up to the foot of the stairs, "but I believe he's dead." "Where's the lady?" said her brother, "is she safe?" "She is in the other boat, sir!" "Is she alive? Has she spoken?" "No sir, she has not spoken, I believe." "Is she dead? O tell me!" "I fear she is, sir."

The bodies were immediately removed from the boats to a house in the vicinity, and every effort was employed to restore animation; and some faint hopes were entertained by the medical gentlemen that they should succeed. In the space of little more than ten minutes they announced the joyful news that the gentleman began to breathe, but they made no allusion to the lady. Her brother sat motionless, absorbed in the deepest melancholy, till the actual decease of his sister was announced, when he started up, and became almost frantic with grief; and, though his companions tried to comfort him, yet he refused to hear the words of consolation. "O my sister! my sister! would to God I had died for thee!" They were all overwhelmed in trouble, and knew not what to do. "Who will bear the heavy tidings to our father?" said the brother, who paced backwards and forwards the room, like a maniac broke loose from the cell of misery—"O, who will bear the heavy tidings to our father?" He paused—a deathlike silence pervaded the whole apartment: he again burst forth, in the agonies of despair—"I forced her to go against the dictates of her conscience—I am her murderer—I ought to have perished, and not my sister. Who will bear the heavy tidings to our father?" "I will," said a gentleman who had been unremitting in his attention to the sufferers. "Do you know him, sir?" "Yes, I know him." "Oh, how can I ever appear in his presence? I enticed the best of children to an act of disobedience which has destroyed her!"

How the old man received the intelligence, or what moral effect resulted from the disaster, I never heard; but it may furnish me with a few reflections, which I wish to press upon the attention of my readers. As the Sabbath is instituted for the purpose of promoting your moral improvement and felicity, never devote its sacred hours to the recreations of pleasure. He who has commanded you to keep it holy, will not suffer you to profane it with impunity. He may not bring down upon you the awful expressions of his displeasure while you are in the act of setting at open defiance his authority; but there is a day approaching when you must stand before him. And can you anticipate the solemnities of that day, while going on in a course of sin, but with the most fearful apprehensions? You may, like many others, suppose that that day is very far off; but you may be undeceived by a sudden visitation of Providence, and in a moment be removed from amongst your gay companions to appear in his presence. If you should, with what terror-struck amazement will you look on the awful scene around you! with what agonizing despair will you listen to the final sentence—*Depart!*

Resist the *first* temptation to evil, or your ruin may be the inevitable consequence. "Indeed, I think we shall do wrong—my conscience condemns me—I must return," said the unfortunate female, when she got near the edge of the water; but, having yielded to the first temptation, she was induced to overcome all her scruples—and, within the space of half an hour from that time she entered the eternal world. Had she refused when her brother solicited her to leave her father's house, she had still lived to bless and comfort him in his old age; but, by complying, she lost her strength to withstand temptation—and then her life. What a warning!

And is this the only one which the history of crime has given us? Alas, no! Have not many, who have ended their days on the gallows, traced up their ruin to their profanation of the Sabbath? This is the day in which the foul spirits are abroad, enticing the young and the thoughtless to evil; and if you wish to avoid the misery and degradation in which others have been involved, devote its sacred hours to the purpose for which they were appointed. Attend some place of worship, where the pure evangelical truth of the Scriptures is preached with pathos and with power; and attend regularly. He who regularly attends a place of worship—who engages with reverence in its devotional exercises, and receives the truth which is preached, under a deep conviction of its excellence and importance, enjoys a high mental feast on the Sabbath, and becomes imperceptibly fortified to resist the fascinating seductions of the world; while he who spends the consecrated hours in the society of the impure, amidst scenes of gayety and dissipation, becomes an easy prey to the worst of temptations—often retires to rest reproaching himself for his folly and impiety; and is gradually led on, from one crime to another, till "iniquity proves his ruin."

By any European standard, American revivals and camp meetings were crude beyond belief. Mrs. Trollope, who did not like Americans very much and whom Americans did not like at all, thought she had found the key to understanding revivals in the lack of other society and amusement for women in America. (Selection from Frances Trollope, *Domestic Manners of the Americans*, 1832.)

A FRONTIER REVIVAL: A FOREIGNER'S VIEW

I never saw any people who appeared to live so much without amusement as the Cincinnatians. Billiards are forbidden by law, so are cards. To sell a pack of cards in Ohio subjects the seller to a penalty of fifty dollars. They have no public balls, excepting, I think, six, during the Christmas holidays. They have no concerts. They have no dinner parties.

They have a theatre, which is, in fact, the only public amusement of this triste little town; but they seem to care little about it, and either from economy or distaste, it is very poorly attended. Ladies are rarely seen there, and by far the larger proportion of females deem it an offence against religion to witness the representation of a play. It is in the churches and chapels of the town that the ladies are to be seen in full costume: and I am tempted to believe that a stranger from the continent of Europe would be inclined, on first reconnoitring the city, to suppose that the places of worship were the theatres and cafés of the place. No evening in the week but brings throngs of the young and beautiful to the chapels and meeting-houses, all dressed with care, and sometimes with great pretension; it is there that all display is made, and all fashionable distinction sought. The proportion of gentlemen attending these evening meetings is very small, but often, as might be expected, a sprinkling of smart young clerks makes this sedulous display of ribbons and ringlets intelligible and natural. Were it not for the churches, indeed, I think there might be a general bonfire of best bonnets, for I never could discover any other use for them.

The ladies are too actively employed in the interior of their houses to permit much parading in full dress for morning visits. There are no public gardens or lounging shops of fashionable resort, and were it not for public worship, and private tea-drinkings, all the ladies in Cincinnati would be in danger of becoming perfect recluses.

The influence which the ministers of all innumerable religious sects throughout America have on the females of their respective congregations, approaches very nearly to what we read of in Spain, or in other strictly Roman Catholic countries. There are many causes for this peculiar influence. Where equality of rank is affectedly acknowledged by the rich, and clamorously claimed by the poor, distinction and preeminence are allowed to the clergy only. This gives them high importance in the eyes of the ladies. I think, also, that it is from the clergy only that the women of America receive that sort of attention which is so dearly valued by every female heart throughout the world. With the priests of America the women hold that degree of influential importance which, in the countries of Europe, is allowed them throughout all orders and ranks of society, except, perhaps, the very lowest; and in return for this they seem to give their hearts and souls into their keeping. I never saw, or read of, any country where religion had so strong a hold upon the women, or a slighter hold upon the men.

I mean not to assert that I met with no men of sincerely religious feelings, or with no women of no religious feelings at all; but I feel perfectly secure of being correct as to the great majority in the statement I have made.

We had not been many months in Cincinnati when our curiosity was excited by hearing the "revival" talked of by every one we met throughout the town. "The revival will be very full," "We shall be constantly engaged during the revival," were the phrases we constantly heard repeated, and for a long time without in the least comprehending what was meant; but at length I learnt that the un-national church of America required to be roused, at regular intervals, to greater energy and exertion. At these seasons the most enthusiastic of the clergy travel the country, and enter the cities and towns by scores, or by hundreds, as the accommodation of the place may admit, and for a week or fortnight, or, if the population be large, for a month, they preach and pray all day, and often for a considerable portion of the night, in the various churches and chapels of the place. This is called a Revival.

I took considerable pains to obtain information on this subject; but in detailing what I learnt I fear that it is probable I shall be accused of exaggeration; all I can do is cautiously to avoid deserving it. The subject is highly interesting, and it would be a fault of no trifling nature to treat it with levity.

These itinerant clergymen are of all persuasions, I believe, except the Episcopalian, Catholic, Unitarian, and Quaker. I heard of Presbyterians of all varieties; of Baptists of I know not how many divisions; and

of Methodists of more denominations than I can remember; whose innumerable shades of varying belief it would require much time to explain
and more to comprehend. They enter all the cities, towns, and villages
of the Union in succession; I could not learn with sufficient certainty to
repeat, what the interval generally is between their visits. These Itinerants
are, for the most part, lodged in the houses of their respective followers,
and every evening that is not spent in the churches and meeting-houses,
is devoted to what would be called parties by others, but which they
designate as prayer-meetings. Here they eat, drink, pray, sing, hear confessions, and make converts. To these meetings I never got invited, and
therefore I have nothing but hearsay evidence to offer, but my information comes from an eye-witness, and one on whom I believe I may
depend. If one half of what I heard may be believed, these social prayer-
meetings are by no means the least curious, or the least important part
of the business.

It is impossible not to smile at the close resemblance to be traced
between the feelings of a first-rate Presbyterian or Methodist lady,
fortunate enough to have secured a favourite Itinerant for her meeting,
and those of a first-rate London Blue, equally blest in the presence of
a fashionable poet. There is a strong family likeness among us all the
world over.

The best rooms, the best dresses, the choicest refreshments sol-
emnise the meeting. While the party is assembling, the lode-star of the
hour is occupied in whispering conversations with the guests as they
arrive. They are called brothers and sisters, and the greetings are very
affectionate. When the room is full, the company, of whom a vast
majority are always women, are invited, entreated, and coaxed to confess
before their brothers and sisters, all their thoughts, faults, and follies.

These confessions are strange scenes; the more they confess, the
more invariably are they encouraged and caressed. When this is over,
they all kneel, and the Itinerant prays extempore. They then eat and
drink; and then they sing hymns, pray, exhort, sing, and pray again, till
the excitement reaches a very high pitch indeed. These scenes are going
on at some house or other every evening during the revival, nay, at many
at the same time, for the churches and meeting-houses cannot give occupation to half the Itinerants, though they are all open throughout the
day, and till a late hour in the night, and the officiating ministers succeed
each other in the occupation of them.

It was at the principal of the Presbyterian churches that I was
twice witness to scenes that made me shudder; in describing one, I
describe both, and every one; the same thing is constantly repeated.

It was in the middle of summer, but the service we were recommended to attend did not begin till it was dark. The church was well

lighted, and crowded almost to suffocation. On entering, we found three priests standing side by side, in a sort of tribune, placed where the altar usually is, handsomely fitted up with crimson curtains, and elevated about as high as our pulpits. We took our places in a pew close to the rail which surrounded it.

The priest who stood in the middle was praying; the prayer was extravagantly vehement, and offensively familiar in expression; when this ended, a hymn was sung, and then another priest took the centre place and preached. The sermon had considerable eloquence, but of a frightful kind. The preacher described, with ghastly minuteness, the last feeble fainting moments of human life, and then the gradual progress of decay after death, which he followed through every process up to the last loathsome stage of decomposition. Suddenly changing his tone, which had been that of sober accurate description, into the shrill voice of horror, he bent forward his head, as if to gaze on some object beneath the pulpit. And as Rebecca made known to Ivanhoe what she saw through the window, so the preacher made known to us what he saw in the pit that seemed to open before him. The device was certainly a happy one for giving effect to his description of hell. No image that fire, brimstone, molten lead, or red hot pincers could supply, with flesh, nerves, and sinews quivering under them, was omitted. The perspiration ran in streams from the face of the preacher; his eyes rolled, his lips were covered with foam, and every feature had the deep expression of horror it would have borne, had he, in truth, been gazing at the scene he described. The acting was excellent. At length he gave a languishing look to his supporters on each side, as if to express his feeble state, and then sat down, and wiped the drops of agony from his brow.

The other two priests arose, and began to sing a hymn. It was some seconds before the congregation could join as usual; every upturned face looked pale and horror-struck. When the singing ended, another took the centre place, and began in a sort of coaxing affectionate tone, to ask the congregation if what their dear brother had spoken had reached their hearts? Whether they would avoid the hell he had made them see? "Come, then!" he continued, stretching out his arms towards them; "come to us and tell us so, and we will make you see Jesus, the dear gentle Jesus, who shall save you from it. But you must come to him! You must not be ashamed to come to him! This night you shall tell him that you are not ashamed of him; we will make way for you; we will clear the bench for anxious sinners to sit upon. Come, then! come to the anxious bench, and we will show you Jesus! Come! Come! Come!"

Again a hymn was sung, and while it continued, one of the three was employed in clearing one or two long benches that went across the rail, sending the people back to the lower part of the church. The singing ceased, and again the people were invited, and exhorted not to be ashamed of Jesus, but to put themselves upon "the anxious benches," and lay their heads on his bosom. "Once more we will sing," he concluded, "that we may give you time." And again they sung a hymn.

And now in every part of the church a movement was perceptible, slight at first, but by degrees becoming more decided. Young girls arose, and sat down, and rose again; and then the pews opened, and several came tottering out, their hands clasped, their heads hanging on their bosoms, and every limb trembling, and still the hymn went on; but as the poor creatures approached the rail their sobs and groans became audible. They seated themselves on the "anxious benches"; the hymn ceased, and two of the three priests walked down from the tribune, and going, one to the right, and the other to the left, began whispering to the poor tremblers seated there. These whispers were inaudible to us, but the sobs and groans increased to a frightful excess. Young creatures, with features pale and distorted, fell on their knees on the pavement, and soon sunk forward on their faces; the most violent cries and shrieks followed, while from time to time a voice was heard in convulsive accents, exclaiming "O Lord!," "O Lord Jesus!," "Help me, Jesus!" and the like.

Meanwhile the two priests continued to walk among them; they repeatedly mounted on the benches, and trumpet-mouthed proclaimed to the whole congregation "the tidings of salvation," and then from every corner of the building arose in reply, short sharp cries of "Amen!," "Glory!," "Amen!," while the prostrate penitents continued to receive whispered comfortings, and from time to time a mystic caress. More than once I saw a young neck encircled by a reverend arm. Violent hysterics and convulsions seized many of them, and when the tumult was at the highest, the priest who remained above again gave out a hymn as if to drown it.

It was a frightful sight to behold innocent young creatures, in the gay morning of existence, thus seized upon, horror-struck, and rendered feeble and enervated for ever. One young girl, apparently not more than fourteen, was supported in the arms of another some years older; her face was pale as death; her eyes wide open, and perfectly devoid of meaning; her chin and bosom wet with slaver; she had every appearance of idiotism. I saw a priest approach her, he took her delicate hand. "Jesus is with her! Bless the Lord!" he said, and passed on.

Did the men of America value their women as men ought to value their wives and daughters, would such scenes be permitted among them?

It is hardly necessary to say, that all who obeyed the call to place themselves on the "anxious benches" were women, and by far the greater number, very young women. The congregation was, in general, extremely well-dressed, and the smartest and most fashionable ladies of the town were there; during the whole revival, the churches and meeting-houses were every day crowded with well-dressed people.

It is thus the ladies of Cincinnati amuse themselves: to attend the theatre is forbidden; to play cards is unlawful; but they work hard in their families, and must have some relaxation. For myself, I confess that I think the coarsest comedy every written would be a less detestable exhibition for the eyes of youth and innocence than such a scene.

Charles Grandison Finney transfixed a generation with his glowing eyes and soaring voice. He led the great revival that erupted in the 1820s and soon spilled over into a variety of reform causes, notably antislavery. Finney obviously believed in manmade revivals, not in waiting for them to descend from heaven when people were least prepared. Revivalism like Finney's became a recurrent part of American culture. (From Charles Grandison Finney, *Lectures on Revivals of Religion*, 1835.)

REMARKS ON REVIVALS

1. Revivals were formerly regarded as miracles. And it has been so by some even in our day. And others have ideas on the subject so loose and unsatisfactory, that if they would only *think*, they would see their absurdity. For a long time, it was supposed by the church, that a revival was a miracle, an interposition of Divine power which they had nothing to do with, and which they had no more agency in producing, than they had in producing thunder, or a storm of hail, or an earthquake. It is only within a few years that ministers generally have supposed revivals were to be *promoted*, by the use of means designed and adapted specially to that object. Even in New England, it has been supposed that revivals came just as showers do, sometimes in one town, and sometimes in another, and that ministers and churches could do nothing more to produce them, than they could to make showers of rain come on their own town, when they are falling on a neighboring town.

It used to be supposed that a revival would come about once in fifteen years, and all would be converted that God intended to save, and then they must wait until another crop came forward on the stage of life. Finally, the time got shortened down to five years, and they supposed there might be a revival about as often as that.

I have heard a fact in relation to one of these pastors, who supposed revivals might come about once in five years. There had been a revival in his congregation. The next year, there was a revival in a neighboring town, and he went there to preach, and staid several days, till he got his soul all engaged in the work. He returned home on Saturday, and went into his study to prepare for the Sabbath. And his soul was in an agony. He thought how many adult persons there were in his congregation at enmity with God—so many still unconverted—so so many persons *die* yearly—such a portion of them unconverted—if a revival does not come under five years, so many adult heads of families will be in hell. He put down his calculations on paper, and embodied them in his sermon for the next day, with his heart bleeding at the dreadful picture. As I understood it, he did not do this with any expectation of a revival, but he felt deeply, and poured out his heart to his people. And that sermon awakened *forty heads of families*, and a powerful revival followed; and so his theory about a revival once in five years was all exploded.

Thus God has overthrown, generally, the theory that revivals are miracles.

2. Mistaken notions concerning the sovereignty of God, have greatly hindered revivals.

Many people have supposed God's sovereignty to be something very different from what it is. They have supposed it to be such an arbitrary disposal of events, and particularly of the gift of his Spirit, as precluded a rational employment of means for promoting a revival of religion. But there is no evidence from the Bible, that God exercises any such sovereignty as that. There are no facts to prove it. But every thing goes to show, that God has connected means with the end through all the departments of his government—in nature and in grace. There is no *natural* event in which his own agency is not concerned. He has not built the creation like a vast machine, that will go on alone without his further care. He has not retired from the universe, to let it work for itself. This is mere atheism. He exercises a universal superintendence and control. And yet every event in nature has been brought about by means. He neither administers providence nor grace with that sort of sovereignty, that dispenses with the use of means. There is no more sovereignty in one than in the other.

And yet some people are terribly alarmed at all direct efforts to promote a revival, and they cry out, "You are trying to get up a revival in your own strength. Take care, you are interfering with the sovereignty of God. Better keep along in the usual course, and let God give a revival when he thinks it is best. God is a sovereign, and it is very wrong for you to attempt to get up a revival, just because *you think* a revival is needed." This is just such preaching as the devil wants. And men cannot do the devil's work more effectually, than by preaching up the sovereignty of God, as a reason why we should not put forth efforts to produce a revival.

3. You see the error of those who are beginning to think that religion can be better promoted in the world without revivals, and who are disposed to give up all efforts to produce religious excitements. Because there are evils arising in some instances out of great excitements on the subject of religion, they are of opinion that it is best to dispense with them altogether. This cannot, and must not be. True, there is danger of abuses. In cases of great *religious* as well as all other excitements, more or less incidental evils may be expected of course. But this is no reason why they should be given up. The best things are always liable to abuses. Great and manifold evils have originated in the providential and moral governments of God. But these *foreseen* perversions and evils were not considered a sufficient reason for giving them up. For the establishment of these governments was on the whole the best that could be done for the production of the greatest amount of happiness. So in revivals of religion, it is found by experience, that in the present state of the world, religion cannot be promoted to any considerable extent without them. The evils which are sometimes complained of, when they are real, are incidental, and of small importance when compared with the amount of good produced by revivals. The sentiment should not be admitted by the church for a moment, that revivals may be given up. It is fraught with all that is dangerous to the interests of Zion, is death to the cause of missions, and brings in its train the damnation of the world.

Finally—I have a proposal to make to you who are here present. I have not commenced this course of Lectures on Revivals to get up a curious theory of my own on the subject. I would not spend my time and strength merely to give you instructions, to gratify your curiosity, and furnish you something to talk about. I have no idea of preaching *about* revivals. It is not my design to preach so as to have you able to say at the close, "We *understand* all about revivals now," while you do *nothing*. But I wish to ask you a question. What do you hear lectures on revivals for? Do you mean that whenever you are convinced what your duty is in promoting a revival, you will go to work and practise it?

Will you follow the instructions I shall give you from the word of God, and put them in practice in your own hearts? Will you bring them to bear upon your families, your acquaintainces, neighbors, and through the city? Or will you spend the winter in learning *about* revivals, and do nothing *for* them? I want you, as fast as you learn any thing on the subject of revivals, to put it in practice, and go to work and see if you cannot promote a revival among sinners here. If you will not do this, I wish you to let me know at the beginning, so that I need not waste my strength. You ought to decide *now* whether you will do this or not. You know that we call sinners to decide on the spot whether *they* will obey the gospel. And we have no more authority to let you take time to deliberate whether *you* will obey God, than we have to let sinners do so. We call on you to unite now in a solemn pledge to God, that you will do your duty as fast as you learn what it is, and to pray that He will pour out his Spirit upon this church and upon all the city this winter.

Americans in the early republic did a great deal of worrying over "antidemocratic" secret societies. The Catholic Church, Mormonism, and Masonry all fell under their opprobrium. In the late 1820s, an antimasonry movement, originating in a mysterious abduction in upstate New York, produced near hysteria and generated an Anti-Masonic Party which, determined to avoid secrecy, held the first open presidential nominating convention in American history. Antimasonry thereby made a large contribution to the popularization of national politics as a kind of spectator sport. (Selection from *Light on Masonry*, 1829.)

THE MASONS

In justice to myself, I cannot present this work to the public, without a brief exhibition of the facts which have led to its publication.

Soon after I commenced the service of Christ, Free Masonry was commended to my attention as an institution from heaven; moral, benevolent, of great antiquity, the twin sister of Christianity, possessing the patronage of the wise, the great, and good, and highly important to the ministers of the Lord Jesus. Wishing to avail myself of every auxiliary in promoting the glory of God and the happiness of my fellow men, I readily received the three first degrees. My disappointment none can know but those who have, in similar circumstances, been led in the same path of folly and sin. I silently retired from the institution, and for three years was hardly known as a Mason. I was not, however, without my reflections on the subject. I considered what I had taken as frivolous and wicked; but was unwilling to believe that there existed no substantial good in the order; and this idea was strengthened from the fact that many of my friends of a higher grade in Masonry taught me, that what

I had received was not the "magnum bonum" of the institution, but that this was yet to be attained. Not being able to advocate its cause from the knowledge I had derived of its principles, and supposing that the obligations I had received were morally binding, I could not say "pro nor con" concerning it, without a violation of my conscience. With these views I embraced an offer to advance into the higher orders of mysticism, and reached forward to attain the desired end. In the reception of the Chaptoral degrees, my embarrassment increased. When I came to the oath of a Royal Arch Mason, which obligates to deliver a companion, "*right or wrong*," I made a full stop and objected to proceeding. I was then assured in the most positive terms, that all would in the end be explained to my full satisfaction. But no such explanation took place. Thought I—Is this free Masonry? Is this the ancient and honorable institution, patronized by thousands of the great and good? Upon my suggesting some queries to a Masonic friend, he gravely informed me, that the first seven degrees were founded on the Old Testament, and were but a shadow of good things to come; that if I wished to arrive at *perfection*, I must proceed to the sublime and ineffable degrees. These assurances, the awful oaths I had taken, with their penalties, and the vengeance of this most powerful institution, combined to deter me from renouncing it as evil. After much deliberation, hoping to find something in the higher orders to redeem the character of the institution in my estimation, I entered the lodge of Perfection and took the ineffable degrees.

About this time I learned that William Morgan was writing Masonry for publication. My informer was *then* a Baptist minister in high standing, and a Royal Arch Mason. He remarked that Morgan's writing Masonry was the greatest piece of depravity he ever knew; that some measures must be taken to stop it; that he would be one of a number to put him out of the way; that God looked upon the institution with so much complacency, he would never bring the perpetrators to light; that there had already been two meetings on the subject; and that he expected there would be another on that day; and finally attempted to justify his murder from Masonry and the word of God!

This conversation took place in Covington (where I then lived), five weeks before Morgan was murdered; and I should at this early period have informed him of his danger, had I not understood that he was on his guard and prepared for a defence.

The next week I left home for my health, and was absent some weeks. I returned on the 16th of September, and soon learned that Morgan was kidnapped and probably murdered! I conversed with the Masons on the subject, and they *justified both his abduction and murder!* I now read the first production of Elder Stearns on Masonry with peculiar interest. I also examined the Monitor and other Masonic writings, and reflected deeply on the nature and tendency of the institution. I compared the murder of Morgan and the conduct of the fraternity in relation to his abduction with the oaths and principles of the order, and became fully satisfied that to continue longer with the institution was not my duty. I expressed my opposition to its principles and the recent conduct of the fraternity in a free and open manner, which caused much excitement among the brotherhood. A meeting of the lodge in Covington was soon called, the object of which was to concert measures for an agreement among the fraternity, in what they should say in relation to their outrages, and to attend to members who were disaffected with their proceedings. I attended for the purpose of freeing my mind. When the lodge was duly opened and the subject introduced, I arose and in the most decisive manner disapproved the conduct of the fraternity, in their violation of civil and moral law. The meeting was long and *horribly* interesting! The true spirit of the institution was peculiarly manifest, especially towards me. For the introduction of Elder Stearns' book, and the honest expression of my sentiments, I was most shamefully abused. The murder of Morgan was justified, and every thing said that was calculated to harrow up the feelings of a patriot or Christian. Elder A****, a Knight Templar, being present, boldly asserted "that if he should see any man writing Masonry, he should consider it his duty to take measures to stop him; that as cities and churches had their laws, with a right to inflict their penalties, so Masons had their laws, with the right to inflict the penalties to them; and that the *lodge* was the place to try a Mason—that if Morgan had been writing Masonry, and his throat was cut from ear to ear, his tongue torn out by the roots, and his body buried beneath the rough sands of the sea, at low watermark, where the tide ebbs and flows twice in twenty-four hours, he could not complain in not having justice done him!" Amen, Amen, Amen, was the audible response around the room.

Various kinds of advice literature proliferated in the nineteenth century. Sex manuals were still in the future, but the age already had its various Dr. Spocks. (Selection from Mrs. L. G. Abell, *Woman in Her Various Relations*, 1851.)

MANAGEMENT OF CHILDREN

It is always well to adapt punishment to the nature of the offense, if possible. For instance, if a child insists upon climbing on a table, it will cure him entirely to set him out on the table in the middle of the room, and spread the leaves, as it will be impossible for him to get down. His situation in no time will become so very irksome, that he will have no desire to repeat the offense.

If he betrays selfishness at table, let him be served last for this reason. If he hurt anyone with a whip or plaything, it must be taken from him entirely for a season; and so on, in all the little and frequent *faults*.

Watching opportunities to curb the first determined risings of willful rebellion is an important consideration. With most children there is an era, and this often happens when the child is about emerging from babyhood, in which a struggle is made for the mastery, and the question has to be promptly decided, who is to *rule*—the child or the parent? Vigorous measures will be necessary at this juncture, and punishment, decisive and repeated, until submission on the part of the child is complete, will only answer the end desired. But one struggle will not suffice, without care, to insure obedience afterward.

Speaking of their faults has a disheartening effect, and has an unhappy influence on the feelings. Reproving a child severely in company, or holding any of its habits up to ridicule, is not well, and will tend to discourage and depress the mind.

Mere accidents should be overlooked, with a caution or warning, and the parent should discriminate between a fault and an inadvertence.

Lying and disobedience are serious faults, that may never be passed over; but the disposition and moral sense will be injured if the small offenses are treated with the same severity.

Never keep a child in suspense, and say, "I will think of it," unless you intend to grant the request, for when the expectation has been thus raised, it is harder to bear *denial*.

Great patience is necessary in all our intercourse with children. From some hidden cause, irritability and fretfulness must often be borne with, after all that we can do for their comfort. Unmoved serenity is all-important in such cases, as it can never be overcome by opposition or impatience, for it is often the result of some bodily infirmity.

Selfishness is a sin of early growth. We see it in the smallest child that stands upon its feet. He claims his own chair, his own wagon, his own toys, his own mother, if his rights are in any way invaded; and it grows with the growth, and strengthens with the strength. It is only to be overcome by an unceasing watchfulness to improve all opportunities to call out the tender feelings of kindness which all children occasionally display. It cannot be destroyed by authority, nor uprooted by commands; but can be regulated and subdued, in a measure, by calling into exercise the better feelings.

Affection should be cultivated. Parents are apt to be satisfied with the love they feel for the child, without thinking it necessary to call the same reciprocating emotion from them. The foundation of *family affection* is laid during the first ten years of childhood, and should be cherished as a plant of most tender growth. I have seen it wither and droop, for the want of care and nurture, till it became a blight upon all enjoyment, and a sting to every pleasure.

A tyrannical, and domineering, and revengeful spirit should be early crushed, or it will become a source of intolerable evil. The gentleness of Christ, the tenderness and compassion He felt, and exhibited, and taught, will touch the hearts of children, and produce the strongest impressions on their minds. It should be the maxim at all times, "Do unto others as you would have them do to you." *What can we do for children without the Bible?*

Benevolence should be taught and inculcated early. If the seed is not sown, there will be no harvest. It may be made a source of pleasure to a child to relieve the wants of the destitute. Send a child with some comfort to a poor neighbor, or a sick friend; it will bring a two-fold blessing. Accustom them to lay up their money to give to some poor object of pity, or to send Bibles to the heathen. They must be encouraged to give something that would cost them some sacrifice.

As you value a child's happiness and well-being in this life, preserve it from all unnecessary fears. Never startle them with sudden noise, or strange appearances, or ghost stories. They will do them injury that will continue for years. One alarming tale of murder, robbery, sudden death, mad dogs, etc., will leave an impression lasting as the life. We must not only do what we can to secure from alarming impressions, but cultivate resolution and fortitude to meet pain, sickness, danger, and sorrow, and to be useful in the various engagements of life. When our children are sick, while we do our utmost to relieve, to solace, and comfort them, we should mingle resolution with our tenderness, and, if necessary, combine discipline with the kindest attentions.

A sense of importance is imbibed by children, unless there is care and pains taken to learn them "to take the lowest place," and to yield in all things to superiors. We naturally incline to consider the child's comfort and happiness so *important* that we are apt to forget that the child is receiving the same impression, and will never lose the feeling that his own wants are *pre-eminent,* unless we sacrifice a little of our own feelings of tenderness to establish a better feeling in them than supreme and entire *selfishness.*

Too many playthings have a bad effect. The child who may be allowed a few simple things, and taught to use them in various ways, leaving room for the mind to act, will find more real pleasure than that afforded by the most costly toy. Disgust and dissatisfaction with every thing is often produced by too great an effort to please a child.

The sooner a child can be taught to help himself, and to help others in any little way, the better. Such exercise strengthens the faculties both of body and of mind, and will be the beginning of a habit.

"I can't" is often used as an excuse for indolence or disobedience, and should rarely be admitted, as upon resolute exertion depends success. The child can be taught to put up his own playthings, to dress himself in part, to pick up things for any one, and to wait on those who are busy, to some trifle. It will amuse and please a child more than much done merely to amuse and pacify him. It has an influence on the affections, and learns a child to help as well as to be helped, and makes him happy in pleasing others.

Teasing children has a very bad influence on their tempers and feelings. Catching them up from their play, interrupting them in their harmless and innocent pursuits and amusements, annoys and vexes them, and should never be practiced. The lives of some children are embittered, and the sunshine of their glad existence clouded, by a continuation of such unkind and injudicious treatment by mothers, or older members of a family. I have seen those that seemed to take great pleasure in this kind of amusement, but it partakes of a nature that finds its pleasure in giving pain, and is in any one a fearful trait of character.

Delicacy is a plant of choicest value, though of tenderest growth. Correct moral tastes and feelings are the greatest safeguards to all character, and nothing on this point can be correct that is not delicate. Even little children will indulge, in a small measure, in conversation bordering on indelicacy, to amuse each other and excite a laugh; but the least tendency to such a practice should be carefully watched and corrected, and, if persisted in, should be treated with severity.

An improper trick, even in infancy, should be frowned upon, and a look of serious reproof will manifest a disapprobation that will be remembered. It is only by strict and nice attention to little things that modest and refined habits are ever formed. Tell a child that God destroyed the inhabitants of Sodom for such bad behavior, and it will save them from all impure thoughts and conduct when old enough to understand.

Manners are next to religion and virtue, and should be constantly watched over, as one of the essentials in any character. Teach a child to "honor all men," to oblige, to be kind, to be respectful, and he will be pleasing of course. But allow him to follow an opposite behavior, to talk while others are conversing, to be noisy and rude, disobliging, and disobedient, and he will, of course, become an object of *disgust*. Loud talking and laughing, violent exclamations, as terrible! awful! dreadful! etc., induce a roughness of manner, as well as coarseness of mind, and will lead to vulgar habits and demeanor.

Mimicry is amusing, but will lead to an improper turn of mind, and ridicule should never be allowed.

It is essential to good breeding that children be taught by "line upon line" to express themselves well, and to speak clear, distinctly, and grammatically.

Children should be taught to sit down and rise up from the table at the same time, to wait while others are served, to be quiet, and to see delicacies without asking for them, and only to speak when they need something or are spoken to, as forwardness in talking makes children bold and unpleasing.

European travellers like Captain Marryat were usually impressed by American women and horrified by American children. (From Frederick Marryat, *A Diary in America*, 1840.)

AMERICAN BRATS

Education

. . . What is education? I consider that education commences before a child can walk: the first principle of education, the most important, and without which all subsequent are but as leather and prunella, is the lesson of *obedience*—of submitting to parental control—"*Honour thy father and thy mother!*"

Now, anyone who has been in the United States must have perceived that there is little or no parental control. This has been remarked by most of the writers who have visited the country; indeed, to an Englishman it is a most remarkable feature. How is it possible for a child to be brought up in the way that it should go, when he is not obedient to the will of his parents? I have often fallen into a melancholy sort of musing after witnessing such remarkable specimens of uncontrolled will in children; and as the father and mother both smiled at it, I have thought that they little knew what sorrow and vexation were probably in store for them, in consequence of their own injudicious treatment of their offspring. Imagine a child of three years old in England behaving thus:

"Johnny, my dear, come here," says his mama.

"I won't," cries Johnny.

"You must, my love, you are all wet, and you'll catch cold."

"I won't," replies Johnny.

"Come, my sweet, and I've something for you."

"I won't."

"Oh, Mr. ——, do, pray make Johnny come in."

"Come in, Johnny," says the father.

"I won't."

"I tell you, come in directly, sir—do you hear?"

"I won't," replies the urchin taking to his heels.

"A sturdy republican, sir," says his father to me, smiling at the boy's resolute disobedience.

Be it recollected that I give this as one instance of a thousand which I witnessed during my sojourn in the country.

It may be inquired how is it that such is the case at present, when the obedience to parents was so rigorously inculcated by the puritan fathers that, by the blue laws, the punishment of disobedience was *death?* Captain Hall ascribed it to the democracy and the rights of equality therein acknowledged; but I think, allowing the spirit of their institutions to have some effect in producing this evil, that the principal cause of it is the total neglect of the children by the father, and his absence in his professional pursuits, and the natural weakness of most mothers when their children are left altogether to their care and guidance.

Mr. Sanderson, in his *Sketches of Paris*, observes—"The motherly virtues of our women, so eulogized by foreigners, is not entitled to unqualified praise. There is no country in which maternal care is so assiduous; but also there is none in which examples of injudicious tenderness are so frequent." This I believe to be true; not that the American women are really more injudicious than those of England, but because they are not supported as they should be by the authority of the father, of whom the child should always entertain a certain portion of fear mixed with affection, to counterbalance the indulgence accorded by natural yearnings of a mother's heart.

The self-will arising from this fundamental error manifests itself throughout the whole career of the American's existence, and, consequently, it is a self-willed nation *par excellence.*

At the age of six or seven you will hear both boys and girls contradicting their fathers and mothers, and advancing their own opinions with a firmness which is very striking.

At fourteen or fifteen the boys will seldom remain longer at school. At college, it is the same thing; and they learn precisely what they please and no more. Corporal punishment is not permitted; indeed, if we are to judge from an extract I took from an American paper, the case is reversed.

The following "Rules" are posted up in a New Jersey school-house:

"No kissing girls in school-time; no *licking* the *master* during holy-days."

At fifteen or sixteen, if not at college, the boy assumes the man; he enters into business, as a clerk to some merchant, or in some store. His father's home is abandoned, except when it may suit his convenience, his salary being sufficient for most of his wants. He frequents the bar, calls for gin cocktails, chews tobacco, and talks politics. His theoretical education, whether he has profited much by it or not, is now superseded by a more practical one, in which he obtains a most rapid proficiency. I have no hestitation in asserting that there is more practical knowledge among the Americans than among any other people under the sun.

It is singular that in America, everything, whether it be of good or evil, appears to assist the country in *going ahead.* This very want of parental control, however it may affect the morals of the community, is certainly advantageous to America as far as her rapid advancement is concerned. Boys are working like men for years before they would be in England; time is money, and they assist to bring in the harvest.

But does this independence on the part of the youth of America end here? On the contrary, what at first was *independence* assumes next the form of *opposition,* and eventually that of *control.*

The young men, before they are qualified by age to claim their rights as citizens, have their societies, their book-clubs, their political meetings, their resolutions, all of which are promulgated in the newspapers; and very often the young men's societies are called upon by the newspapers to come forward with their opinions. Here is *opposition. . . .*

But what is more remarkable is the fact that society has been usurped by the young people, and the married and old people have been, to a certain degree, excluded from it. A young lady will give a ball and ask none but young men and young women of her acquaintance; not a *chaperon* is permitted to enter, and her father and mother are requested to stay upstairs, that they may not interfere with the amusement. This is constantly the case in Philadelphia and Baltimore, and I have heard bitter complaints made by the married people concerning it. Here is *control.* . . .

However, retribution follows: in their turn they marry and are ejected; they have children and are disobeyed. The pangs which they have occasioned to their own parents are now suffered by them in return, through the conduct of their own children; and thus it goes on, and will go on, until the system is changed.

Let us examine the manner in which a child is taught. Democracy, equality, the vastness of his own country, the glorious independence, the superiority of the Americans in all conflicts by sea or land, are impressed upon his mind before he can well read. All their elementary books contain garbled and false accounts of naval and land engagements, in which every credit is given to the Americans and equal vituperation and disgrace thrown upon their opponents. Monarchy is derided, the equal rights of man declared—all is invective, uncharitableness, and falsehood. . . .

And so it is; and as if this scholastic drilling were not sufficient, every year brings round the 4th of July, on which is read in every portion of the states the act of independence, in itself sufficiently vituperative, but invariably followed up by one speech (if not more) from some great personage of the village, hamlet, town, or city, as it may be, in which the more violent he is against monarchy and the English, and the more he flatters his own countrymen, the more is his speech applauded.

Every year is this drilled into the ears of American boy, until he leaves school, when he takes a political part himself, connecting himself with young men's society, where he spouts about tyrants, crowned heads, shades of his forefathers, blood flowing like water, independence, and glory. . . .

I think, after what I have brought forward, the reader will agree with me that the education of the youth in the United States is immoral.

Women

The women of America are unquestionably, physically, as far as beauty is concerned, and morally, of a higher standard than the men; nevertheless they have not that influence which they ought to possess. In my former remarks upon the women of America I have said that they are the prettiest in the world, and I have put the word *prettiest* in italics, as I considered it a term peculiarly appropriate to the American women. In many points the Americans have, to a certain degree, arrived at that equality which they profess to covet, and in no one, perhaps, more than in the fair distribution of good looks among the women. This is easily accounted for: there is not to be found, on the one hand, that squalid wretchedness, that half-starved growing up, that disease and misery, nor on the other, that hereditary refinement, that inoculation of the beautiful, from the constant association with the fine arts, that careful nurture, and constant attention to health and exercise, which exist in the dense population of the cities of the Old World and occasion those variations from extreme plainness to the perfection of beauty which are to be seen, particularly in the metropolis of England. In the United States, where neither the excess of misery nor of luxury and refinement are known, you have, therefore, a more equal distribution of good looks, and, although you often meet with beautiful women, it is but rarely that you find one that may be termed ill-favoured. The *coup-d'oeil* is, therefore, more pleasing in America—enter society and turn your eyes in any direction, you will everywhere find cause for pleasure, although seldom any of annoyance. The climate is not, however, favourable to beauty, which, compared to the English, is very transitory, especially in the eastern states; and when a female arrives at the age of thirty, its reign is, generally speaking, over.

The climate of the western states appears, however, more favourable to it, and I think I saw more handsome women at Cincinnati than in any other city of the Union; their figures were more perfect, and they were finer grown, not receiving the sudden checks to which the eastern women are exposed.

Generally speaking, but a small interval elapses between the period of American girls leaving school and their entering upon their duties as wives; but during that period, whatever it may be, they are allowed more liberty than the young people in our country, walking out without *chaperons* and visiting their friends as they please. There is a reason for this: the matrons are compelled, from the insufficiency of their domestics, to attend personally to all the various duties of housekeeping; their fathers and brothers are all employed in their respective money-making transactions, and a servant cannot be spared from American establishments; if, therefore, they are to walk out and take exercise, it must be alone, and this can be done in the United States with more security than elsewhere, from the circumstance of everybody being actively employed, and there being no people at leisure who are strolling or idling about. I think that the portion of time which elapses between the period of a young girl leaving school and being married is the happiest of her existence. I have already remarked upon the attention and gallantry shown by the Americans to the women, especially to the unmarried. This is carried to an extent which, in England, would be considered by our young women as no compliment; to a certain degree it pervades every class, and even the sable damsels have no reason to complain of not being treated with the excess of politeness; but in my opinion (and I believe the majority of the American women will admit the correctness of it) they do not consider themselves flattered by a species of homage which is paying no compliment to their good sense, and after which the usual attentions of an Englishman to the sex are by some considered as amounting to hauteur and neglect.

Be it as it may, the American women are not spoiled by this universal adulation which they receive previous to their marriage. It is not that one is selected for her wealth or extreme beauty to the exception of all others; in such a case it might prove dangerous; but it is a flattery paid to the whole sex, given to all, and received as a matter of course by all, and therefore it does no mischief. It does, however, prove what I have said at the commencement of this chapter, which is, that the women have not that influence which they are entitled to, and which, for the sake of morality, it is to be lamented that they have not; when men *respect* women they do not attempt to make fools of them, but treat them as rational and immortal beings, and this general adulation is cheating them with the shadow, while they withhold from them the substance.

I have said that the period between her emancipation from school and her marriage is the happiest portion of an American woman's existence; indeed, it has reminded me of the fêtes and amusements given in a Catholic country to a young girl previous to her taking the veil and being immured from the world; for the duties of a wife in America are from circumstances very onerous, and I consider her existence after that period as but one of negative enjoyment. And yet she appears anxious to abridge even this small portion of freedom and happiness, for marriage is considered almost as a business or, I should say, a duty, an idea probably handed down by the first settlers, to whom an increase of population was of such vital importance. . . .

Let us enter into an examination of the married life in the United States.

All the men in America are busy; their whole time is engrossed by their accumulation of money; they breakfast early and repair to their stores or counting-houses; the majority of them do not go home to dinner, but eat at the nearest tavern or oyster-cellar, for they generally live at a considerable distance from the business part of the town, and time is too precious to be thrown away. It would be supposed that they would be home to an early tea; many are, but the majority are not. After fagging, they require recreation, and the recreations of most Americans are politics and news, besides the chance of doing a little more business, all of which, with drink, are to be obtained at the bars of the principal commercial hotels in the city. The consequence is that the major portion of them come home late, tired and go to bed; early the next morning they are off to their business again. Here it is evident that the women do not have much of their husband's society; nor do I consider this arising from any want of inclination on the part of the husbands as there is an absolute necessity that they should work as hard as others if they wish to do well, and what one does, the other must do. Even frequenting the bar is almost a necessity, for it is there that they obtain all the information of the day. But the result is that the married women are left alone; their husbands are not their companions, and if they could be, still the majority of the husbands would not be suitable companions for the following reasons. An American starts into life at so early an age that what he has gained at school, with the exception of that portion brought into use from his business, is lost. He has no time for reading, except the newspaper; he becomes perfect in that, acquires a great deal of practical knowledge useful for making money, but for little else. This he must do if he would succeed, and the major portion confine themselves to such knowledge alone. But with the women it is different; their education is much more extended than that of the men, because they are more docile and easier to control in their youth; and when they are married, although their duties are much more onerous than with us, still, during the long days and evenings, during which they wait for the return of their husbands, they have time to finish, I may say, their own educations and improve their minds by reading. The consequence of this, with other adjuncts, is that their minds become, and really are, much more cultivated and refined than those of their husbands; and when the universal practice of using tobacco and drinking among the latter is borne in mind, it will be readily admitted that they are also much more refined in their persons.

These are the causes why the American women are so universally admired by the English and other nations, while they do not consider the men as equal to them either in manners or personal appearance. Let it be borne in mind that I am now speaking of the majority, and that the exceptions are very numerous; for instance, you may except one whole profession, that of the lawyers, among whom you will find no want of gentlemen or men or highly cultivated minds; indeed, the same may be said with respect to most of the liberal professions, but only so because their profession allows that time for improving themselves which the American in general, in his struggle on the race for wealth, cannot afford to spare.

The most popular dictionary published in America, *Webster's*, was originally compiled by a New Englander who passionately loved language as well as the United States. Noah Webster's nationalism extended even to proposed spelling reforms. (From Noah Webster, *Dissertations on the English Language*, 1789.)

A REFORMED MODE OF SPELLING

It has been observed by all writers on the English language, that the orthography or spelling of words is very irregular; the same letters often representing different sounds, and the same sounds often expressed by different letters. For this irregularity, two principal causes may be assigned:

1. The changes to which the pronunciation of a language is liable, from the progress of science and civilization.
2. The mixture of different languages, occasioned by revolutions in England, or by a predilection of the learned, for words of foreign growth and ancient origin.

To the first cause may be ascribed the difference between the spelling and pronunciation of Saxon words. The northern nations of Europe originally spoke much in gutturals. This is evident from the number of aspirates and guttural letters, which still remain in the orthography of words derived from those nations; and from the modern pronunciation of the collateral branches of the Teutonic, the Dutch, Scotch and German. Thus *k* before *n* was once pronounced; as in *knave, know;* the *gh* in *might, though, daughter,* and other similar words; the *g* in *reign, feign,* &c.

But as savages proceed in forming languages, they lose the guttural sounds, in some measure, and adopt the use of labials, and the more open vowels. The ease of speaking facilitates this progress, and the pronunciation of words is softened, in proportion to a national refinement of manners. This will account for the difference between the ancient and modern languages of France, Spain and Italy; and for the difference between the soft pronunciation of the present languages of those countries and the more harsh and guttural pronunciation of the northern inhabitants of Europe.

In this progress, the English have lost the sounds of most of the guttural letters. The *k* before *n* in *know,* the *g* in *reign,* and in many other words, are become mute in practice; and the *gh* is softened into the sound of *f,* as in *laugh,* or is silent, as in *brought.*

To this practice of softening the sounds of letters, or wholly suppressing those which are harsh and disagreeable, may be added a popular tendency to abbreviate words of common use. Thus *Southwark,* by a habit of quick pronunciation, is become *Suthark; Worcester* and *Leicester* are become *Wooster* and *Lester; business, bizness; colonel, curnel; cannot, will not, cant, wont.* In this manner the final *e* is not heard in many modern words, in which it formerly made a syllable. The words *clothes, cares,* and most others of the same kind, were formerly pronounced in two syllables.

Of the other cause of irregularity in the spelling of our language, I have treated sufficiently in the first Dissertation. It is here necessary only to remark, that when words have been introduced from a foreign language into the English, they have generally retained the orthography of the original, however ill adapted to express the English pronunciation. Thus *fatigue, marine, chaise,* retain their French dress, while, to represent the true pronunciation in English, they should be spelt *fateeg, mareen, shaze.* Thus thro an ambition to exhibit the etymology of words, the English, in *Philip, physic, character, chorus,* and other Greek derivatives, preserve the representatives of the original ϕ and χ; yet these words are pronounced, and ought ever to have been spelt, *Fillip, fyzzic* or *fizzic, karacter, korus.*

But such is the state of our language. The pronunciation of the words which are strictly *English,* has been gradually changing for ages, and since the revival of science in Europe, the language has received a vast accession of words from other languages, many of which retain an orthography very ill suited to exhibit the true pronunciation.

The question now occurs: ought the Americans to retain these faults which produce innumerable inconveniences in the acquisition and use of the language, or ought they at once to reform these abuses, and introduce order and regularity into the orthography of the AMERICAN TONGUE?

Let us consider this subject with some attention.

Several attempts were formerly made in England to rectify the orthography of the language. But I apprehend their schemes failed of success, rather on account of their intrinsic difficulties than on account of any necessary impracticability of a reform. It was proposed, in most of these schemes, not merely to throw out superfluous and silent letters, but to introduce a number of new characters. Any attempt on such a plan must undoubtedly prove unsuccessful. It is not to be expected that an orthography, perfectly regular and simple, such as would be formed by a "Synod of Grammarians on principles of science," will ever be substituted for that confused mode of spelling which is now established. But it is apprehended that great improvements may be made, and an orthography almost regular, or such as shall obviate most of the present difficulties which occur in learning our language, may be introduced and established with little trouble and opposition.

The principal alterations necessary to render our orthography sufficiently regular and easy, are these:

1. The omission of all superfluous or silent letters; as *a* in *bread*. Thus *bread, head, give, breast, built, meant, realm, friend*, would be spelt *bred, hed, giv, brest, bilt, ment, relm, frend*. Would this alteration produce any inconvenience any embarrassment or expense? By no means. On the other hand, it would lessen the trouble of writing, and much more, of learning the language; it would reduce the true pronunciation to a certainty; and while it would assist foreigners and our own children in acquiring the language, it would render the pronunciation uniform, in different parts of the country, and almost prevent the possibility of changes.

2. A substitution of a character that has a certain definite sound for one that is more vague and indeterminate. Thus by putting *ee* instead of *ea* or *ie*, the words *mean, near, speak, grieve, zeal*, would become *meen, neer, speek, greev, zeel*. This alteration would not occasion a moment's trouble; at the same time it would prevent a doubt respecting the pronunciation; whereas the *ea* and *ie* having different sounds, may give a learner much difficulty. Thus *greef* should be substituted for *grief; kee* for *key; beleev* for *believe; laf* for *laugh; dawter* for *daughter; plow* for *plough; tuf* for *tough; proov* for *prove; blud* for *blood;* and *draft* for *draught*. In this manner *ch* in Greek derivatives should be changed into *k;* for the English *ch* has a soft sound, as in *cherish;* but *k* always a hard sound. Therefore *character, chorus, cholic, architecture,* should be written *karacter, korus, kolic, arkitecture;* and were they thus written, no person could mistake their true pronunciation.

   Thus *ch* in French derivatives should be changed into *sh; machine, chaise, chevalier,* should be written *masheen, chaze, shevaleer;* and *pique, tour, oblique,* should be written *peek, toor, obleek*.

3. A trifling alteration in a character or the addition of a point would distinguish different sounds, without the substitution of a new character. Thus a very small stroke across *th* would distinguish its two sounds. A point over a vowel, in this manner, *ȧ*, or *ȯ*, or *ī*, might answer all the purposes of different letters. And for the dipthong *ow*, let the two letters be united by a small stroke, or both engraven on the same piece of metal, with the left hand line of the *w* united to the *o*.

These, with a few other inconsiderable alterations, would answer every purpose, and render the orthography sufficiently correct and regular.

The advantages to be derived from these alterations are numerous, great and permanent.

1. The simplicity of the orthography would facilitate the learning of the language. It is now the work of years for children to learn to spell; and after all, the business is rarely accomplished. A few men, who are bred to some business that requires constant exercise in writing, finally learn to spell most words without hesitation; but most people remain, all their lives, imperfect masters of spelling, and liable to make mistakes, whenever they take up a pen to write a short note. Nay, many people, even of education and fashion, never attempt to write a letter, without frequently consulting a dictionary.

   But with the proposed orthography, a child would learn to spell, without trouble, in a very short time, and the orthography being very regular, he would ever afterwards find it difficult to make a mistake. It would, in that case, be as difficult to spell *wrong* as it is now to spell *right*.

   Besides this advantage, foreigners would be able to acquire the pronunciation of English, which is now so difficult and embarrassing that they are either wholly discouraged on the first attempt, or obliged, after many years' labor, to rest contented with an imperfect knowledge of the subject.

2. A correct orthography would render the pronunciation of the language as uniform as the spelling in books. A general uniformity thro the United States would be the event of such a reformation as I am here recommending. All persons, of every rank, would speak with some degree of precision and uniformity. Such a uniformity in these states is very desirable; it would remove prejudice, and conciliate mutual affection and respect.

3. Such a reform would diminish the number of letters about one sixteenth or eighteenth. This would save a page in eighteen; and a saving of an eighteenth in the expense of books, is an advantage that should not be overlooked.

4. But a capital advantage of this reform in these states would be, that it would make a difference between the English orthography and the American. This will startle those who have not attended to the subject; but I am confident that such an event is an object of vast political consequence.

The alteration, however small, would encourage the publication of books in our own country. It would render it, in some measure, necessary that all books should be printed in America. The English would never copy our orthography for their own use; and consequently the same impressions of books would not answer for both countries. The inhabitants of the present generation would read the English impressions; but posterity, being taught a different spelling, would prefer the American orthography.

Besides this, a *national language* is a band of *national union*. Every engine should be employed to render the people of this country *national;*

to call their attachments home to their own country; and to inspire them with the pride of national character. However they may boast of independence, and the freedom of their government, yet their *opinions* are not sufficiently independent; an astonishing respect for the arts and literature of their parent country, and a blind imitation of its manners, are still prevalent among the Americans. Thus an habitual respect for another country, deserved indeed and once laudable, turns their attention from their own interests, and prevents their respecting themselves.

College was rather a lark in the 1850s. Aside from a very few institutions, the intellectual level was not high. (Selections from Joseph Cleaver, Jr., *Diary*, 1853–1854, and Palfrey Papers, Houghton Library, Harvard University.)

COLLEGE LIFE

Joseph Cleaver, Jr. (1833–1909)

Aug 31, 1853

Entering day at Delaware College. I set my room in order a little but found I was late for an assembly.

Sept. 1

Classes in the morning after prayers and breakfast which I did not like much and after dinner I had no classes so I set to housekeeping and felt more at home with my things about me but they look strange in a new place. We are talking of buying a shelf for our books. We look a lot better than most of the rooms where the boys have just opened their portmantos on a chair or on the floor and many have no books at all.

2

One of the boys came up before study hour and is sick for home and especially because the rain keeps us all in and it is cold and damp and dark in the College. I sounded very old and wise and made light of his feeling but it did not do him any good and when he was gone I had not been done any good either.

4

Morning prayers were very dull or over my head, and too long but I was . . . I was interrupted there and I cannot remember what I was going to say.

9

I put a great deal of time on my declamation which will be my first appearance before the Athenaean Literary Society and I want it to be good. They fired a cannon of some sort in the hall tonight and it shook all the building so that it was a long time before anyone settled. The old boys say there was a lot of it last spring meant to call attention at one end of the College when hall police is not wanted at the other end. But some do it just for sport and everyone knows the five or six who are at the bottom of most of it. Apple pie. Progress in Algebra. Licorice . . . 04.

10

I declaimed at Athenaean Literary Society and did better than I feared. I am up with Cacy, Chamberlin and Clymer to debate next week the affirmative of the question of abolishing the capital punishment.

15

There was a coffin with Professor Grover [in effigy] in it at prayers this morning. He turned the table by inviting those who thought it was funny to sit up on the mourning bench and nobody did and we all felt a little sheepy.

16

A bench gave way at prayers and made a great clatter while President Graham was speaking.

19

Slept through bells, prayers, breakfast and a part of class. Turner says I shall be called up to explain why I was out all night and though I know it is in jest I keep going over with my mind what I shall say and I almost begin to doubt my own story or my power to prove it to anybody.

20

Serenading which is against the rules but good sport or was until we got ourselves showered with cold water.

21

We learned today that we were misadvised about our serenades so that we would go to the dangerous places and it is the mystery that we have not been reported to the college. We went out again tonight but with more care and better success for we were asked in to milk and cookies.

Oct. 2

I called at Mr. Curtis's house in the afternoon and though I think I took them by surprise I was made welcome and they asked me to stay to supper and I wished I might but I did not and I wondered all the way back to College why I did not.

7

Out for a walk before bed time. I fell into an open ditch which I never saw before though it was heavily grass-grown. Wet myself through and for a minute I thought I had drowned myself.

10

Ashmead takes a bath every night and the boys on the hall burned paper in the hall and cried "Fire!" when he was covered with lather and carried his clothes away so that he ran almost to the front door that way and met Professor Boswell.

21

Set out my boots for cleaning last night and I have back a pair that are not mine and I do not think that any boy in the College ever wore them.

22

I was called in Society to substitute in debate affirmative on the question "Would it be advantagious for a young man to acquire a classical education if he did not intend to pursue a profession?" My side always loses.

Nov. 5

I am with Cacy to debate the affirmative of "It is probable that the Federal Union will dissolve in 2000 years." It seemed a good question when we wrote it down but it seems silly now when I think of debating it.

10

I was unprepared in Mathematics and tried to pretend. He [the professor] let me hang myself and then laughed with the rest at my embarrassment.

15

We almost froze at the telescope where some of us had outs [permissions] until very late. I saw no more with the telescope than without it.

16

Butternutting.

19

Too many butternuts. I was elected Treasurer of the Athenaean Literary Society.

23

They say Thatcher has been excused prayers and that has started a lot of speculation on ways to be excused.

25

I gave a little girl a kiss who was crying in the street but she cried louder and put her arms around my neck and I had a chore drying her tears and finding her way home. Now I am the butt of a lot of wit bearing on young ladies.

26

I still hear about kissing strange ladies on the street.

29

I saw my little girl of the tearful kiss and waved to her and she waved to me.

Dec. 1

There was a Nigger boy at the College this morning making his way to Wilmington and the North and asking for shelter until night but Rev. Graham would not let him stay and said the college must not break the law even when the law seems wrong and after he had said that to the boys he went away and did not ask what was done with him. So we put him in the second floor lumber room until night and when he got cold Savin took him in and the boys in his room gave him a coat and went out collecting. I gave the boots that came to me for mine and Turner calls me "Nigger lover" but would have given too I think if he had had anything to give. He left during study hour. There is a strange suppressed excitement and it is a kind of sober quiet too.

3

I was called to debate the justice of taking America from the Indians but the Nigger boy has upset my thoughts about justice.

5

DuHamel heard in Wilmington of a nigger boy being taken which sounds like our boy but not certain and did not dare ask details. Most of our boys are very sorry to hear of it and we hoped it is not the boy we helped which seems to me not to be the matter but that a black boy had been taken back from freedom to live all his life a slave. I am uncertain what I shall compose for Society. I may write about a black boy.

13

Roe walks in his sleep and he fell down the upper stairs. We were talking of the future and how God might have created a kind of man whose memory would work to the future and the past be un-knowable.

15

Playing pitch in the hall. We were reprimanded for the noise and explained that we did it to keep warm which I think did not convince him.

19

The hall is full of potato smoke which I left roasting and forgot.

21

The whole college has been in a whirl. A few have gone [home for vacation] and others are ready and waiting. I have been so anxious to go but I am a little surprised now not to be more excited than the others.

Feb. 1 [1854]

Roe went to sleep at study last night and overset his lamp which exploded and set him afire but Emanuel put it out with a blanket. Turner says Roe is the sort of a boy who would get drowned in a clearing up shower.

3

I lost this book yesterday which Biddle has just returned to me. I do not know whether I am more glad to have it again or more sorry to have it seen and recognized. Resolved to set down in future only those thoughts which do credit to someone and not idle gossip.

6

Today they got outs and put a bucket over the door and warned everybody on the hall. Roe was studying with Emanuel and needed a pencil pointed and went for his pocket knife and forgot the trap and was drowned. There was so much confusion and laughter that H. P. came up and we expected Katie [a local term denoting formal punishment] but he laughed too and sent Roe for a mop and gave him time to change his clothes.

10

We bought a lock for our coal box and put it on and when T. went out to it after supper he could not open it and we had to break it open. Lock . . . 70.

14

We made a Valentine for Ashmead as if it was from a young lady and he blushed and stammered and opened himself to a great deal of wit.

17

We have borrowed coal and when we broke open the lid this morning we found it all gone. There is much stealing on the second floor and some people who have lost nothing are suspected.

20

I traded my pocket compas for a blue leather writing case.

21

I bought ink and saw at Mr. Bunker's a gold pen with well attached.

24

Spring weather—it is very hard to stay in and study. I did not.

26

Reed showed me his likeness taken at the new shop and I mean to have one.

27

My cold is very bad. Some of the boys have been suspecting Cathcart of the stealing without any direct cause but last night his coat was taken and now he is going without one. Vindication may not be worth so much. But he has more friends than he had two days ago.

March 3

I have lost a day and I cannot remember anything about it. I am not even sure which day it was.

I have worked on my composition but I did not write what is on my mind and I cannot write what is not.

17

The men came to-day to mend the plaster in 20 but it all fell so the boys moved out and Bushnell came to sleep with us.

Turner says he understands the plaster trouble in 20 and that if Bushnell sleeps with us long we will need a new ceiling too.

18

Carlile and Row had a fire in their room this morning from starting their stove with fluid.

20

My mind must have been wandering. It wanders when I read and then I discover that I have only been reading words and have not understood it and when I read it over I do not remember even the words.

April 28

I dreamed my Mother came down a steep hill to me and had in a bucket two silver spoons and potato skins.

May 1

There were little children selling May-day baskets at the stile for a penny. I bought one for Miss M. but I did not have the courage to drop it in the daylight and now it has withered.

6

I slept badly and was waked by the night train up, wailing in the distance, and before I could go back to sleep by an even worse bawling of the down train.

8

At three hour after supper Baird who has been cultivating Church-man's friendship took him to see the creek road and when they were far out met a gang of unrecognized ruffians who admired C's clothes so much that they took them off one by one and when they had them all got him to say he was cold and built a fire for him and burned his clothes. Then they lost interest and wandered off with Baird whom they said they hated to leave alone in the woods with a wild man and he dared not follow naked but came into hall near morning by a low win-dow which was left open red with mosquito bites and scratches, white with rage and blue with cold.

13

There has been a lot of stealing of door handles in our hall and when I went to bed I found a cold nest of them at my feet.

15

There has been much knotting of bed clothes in our hall.

17

There was a Gypsy in town telling fortunes who cursed me be-cause I would not be told but told others so much that was true that if she had not cursed me I would have asked her who stole from our box.

21

Our Gypsy is back in town for stealing. The skeptical are asking why she did not foresee the result of her theft.

27

I am set to debate the affirmative of "Which affords the greater pleasure sight or hearing?" Even if it were not a silly and futile subject for discussion there is still a question as to which is the affirmative aspect.

June 3

The debate was as I expected and we lost.

14

I am pleased with a musical box that I saw at Mr. Evan's store but I have not money enough to buy it or anybody to give it to.

30

Mr. Hossinger's white bull is at the top of the college stairs and will not go down. Mr. Hossinger says whoever borrowed his bull must return him in as good condition as he took him and he will not come for him so the door has been locked and all passage is by the lower door.

July 1

The bull (and they say Mr. Hossinger) very troublesome in the night; he was still on those stairs this morning where they fed and watered him. He was taken away during Prayers so we did not see him go.

Sept. 4

Harlan reported a bee-tree south of town which we plan to raid on Saturday night.

10

There was a great ringing of the bell in the night but for no cause that we can learn unless it was that I. H. wagered G. B. P. yesterday that he could get into the belfry. He is wearing P.'s watch chain prominently today.

15

At night we went out but did not find the tree and I do not think anybody was sorry.

Nov. 20

Someone cut the bell rope during the night so everything went at odds until noon. The rope has turned up in everybody's room and is going to be found in the wrong one.

Higher Eduction

"I had the curiosity to visit Columbia College at N.Y. and a sorry place it is too. I could think of nothing but Charlestown State Prison. There is a great resemblance between them. . . ."—Jared Sparks to John G. Palfrey, May 18, 1812.

life in america

Rebecca Latimer Felton recalls her childhood on an ante-bellum Georgia plantation. Her picture of life in this part of the South is an engaging view of everyday living among more prosperous southerners. (Selection from Rebecca Felton,
Country Life in Georgia in the Days of My Youth, 1919.)

COUNTRY LIFE IN GEORGIA

It was my Georgia grandmother, Mrs. Lucy Talbot Swift, around
whom my early recollections cluster. I was often at her home and I
was a close observer of her housekeeping methods and of her abounding hospitality. The mother of eleven children, all reaching maturity
except two that lived to eleven and twelve years, her industry, her
management, and her executive ability in caring for and carrying on her
household affairs are still wonderful memories, and have continually
lingered with me as examples in the progress of my own extended life.
It was a fine specimen of a Southern planter's family and home in ante-
bellum times. Grandfather had a plantation, a grain mill and sawmill,
which kept him busy with his own duties as a provider, but it was
grandmother's skill as a homemaker, with an eye single to her domestic
duties and diligent attention to home economies, that impressed me
most in that early time of my life when I trotted around after her as she
went from the dwelling to the garden and to the milk dairy, to the
poultry house, to the loom house, to the big meat house, where rations
were issued once a day, and to the flour and meal house where there
was always a superabundance of supplies for white and colored.

She had fowls of all domestic kinds to look after, and there were
fattening pigs in the pen also. She had geese to raise feathers for the
family beds, because there were no mattresses in that early time. When
one of the children married there was a substantial outfit prepared to
set them up for limited housekeeping. There were no such things as
"comforts" eighty years ago, but quilt making was never interrupted,
winter or summer, and in early Georgia homes woolen "coverlids" woven
at home, and quilts innumerable made by hand, were the bedcoverings
in all such well-to-do Georgia homes. I distinctly remember that my
own mother made and quilted with her own nimble fingers fifty good,
serviceable, and good-looking quilts in the first ten years of her married
life.

In that early time, before there was a railroad in Georgia, our own home became a regular stopping place for travelers, and there was urgent need for beds that could meet the demand when people traveled from Savannah and regions lower down south even to Nashville, Tennessee, going north, and after stagecoaches were set going the coach expense was so great, at ten cents a mile, that the bulk of the travel was still made in carriages, carts, gigs, and on horseback. In event of stormy weather these travelers were often detained at our house. Sometimes floods in rivers and washed-out roads intercepted travel. All mules and horses and hogs brought into the state were driven from Kentucky and Tennessee, as there was no railroad in Georgia to furnish markets in southeastern Georgia.

When my grandmother, Lucy Swift, began housekeeping, wool and flax were the dependence of housekeepers for clothing their families. Silk culture was exploited in General Oglethorpe's time, but the use of cotton was handicapped. Before there were any cotton gins the cotton lint was picked from the seed by human fingers. The lint was then carded by hand, spun on homemade wheels, then reeled into what were called "hanks" by use of homemade reels; then the warp was prepared for the homemade loom by a variety of processes, all tedious and slow, and all the work done by the housemother and her helpers. In this way all the wearing apparel of the masses was constructed. Well-to-do men generally contrived to get a broadcloth coat, maybe once in a lifetime. The rest had coats of plain jeans. Silk dresses were scarce and with scanty lengths and they were only worn occasionally, at weddings or brilliant occasions. A leghorn bonnet would last a woman a lifetime, and kid slippers were the fashionable and expensive footwear of the belles of the period.

The shoe problem was an immense proposition, and the hides were generally tanned in dug-out troughs, stretched out, dressed, and dried at home. The traveling shoemaker made periodic visits, and one pair of shoes per annum was considered a liberal provision for grown-ups. Suffice to say the children as a rule all went barefooted summer and winter, and how remarkable they were for good health and lusty frame, and their longevity was astonishing. And this perplexing shoemaking problem lasted a long time. I recall with vivid memory the first time the family shoemaker measured my feet for a pair of shoes. He brought along a piece of white pine board, and I stood flat-footed on the board, while he marked a line in front of my toes with his big coarse horn-handled knife. Then he marked another line behind my heel and cautioned me that I must not draw my toes together or try to crumple up the bottom of my foot. I felt quite a somebody when the new shoes came home and I had liberty to lay aside the red-morocco baby shoes to which I had been accustomed. Stumped toes in summer and cracked heels in the winter were always in evidence with pupils during my school days, when the country child had a log cabin for a schoolroom and puncheon benches for seats, and the farmer boys and girls of the rural neighborhood wore coarse home-fashioned clothes spun and woven in looms at home. Towels, tablecloths, and shirts were made in the same slow way, and even the best-fixed families were glad to use "thrums" for towels and soft soap in a gourd to wash hands, and the family had a shelf for the washbasin outside for young and old.

A pretty white complexion was the call of that period. The young women were emphatic on this line. They were constantly busy, often with clothmaking work, but they were scrupulous in care of the skin. They wore gloves for washing dishes or when washing clothes. Tomboy girls were sometimes encountered, but the belles of Georgia enjoyed beautiful complexions. They also laced very tight, and it was fashionable to faint on occasions. Weddings were sumptuous affairs. When my mother married there was a crowded wedding at night and three more days of festivities, with a different dress for each day. "Infares" were popular, where the wedding spreads were transferred to the groom's home. Everything good to eat was bountifully furnished, meats in abundance, all sorts of home collections and concoctions topped off with pound cake and sillabub. There was always a sideboard where gin, rum, and peach brandy held distinction. Loaf sugar brought from Charleston and Augusta by wagons was uniformly present. I can remember with accurate recollection those beautiful snowy cones of white sugar encased in thick bluish-green papers, that were always in request when company came, and the sideboard drinks were set forth in generous array. "Peach and honey" was in reach of everybody that prided in their home. Those primitive farmers had abounding peach orchards, and beehives were generally in evidence more or less on Georgia farms. Everything to eat and to wear that could be grown at home was diligently cultivated, and the early fortunes of Georgians were promoted by such thrift, economy, and conservation of resources. In the summer time the drying of fruit was diligently pursued, and it was a poor and thriftless domicile which failed to supply itself with dried peaches, apples, cherries, pears, etc. My careful grandmother put up bushels of dried white English peaches, of which she often made family preserves for home consumption in the scarcer springtime.

My grandmother made all the starch she used, sometimes from whole wheat, oftener from wheat bran. Her seven girls, big and little, delighted in dainty white muslin frocks, and laundry work for thirteen in family was always going on, and insistent in that large household. She was a rare soapmaker, and every pound was prepared at home with diligent care. The meat scraps and bones were utilized and cooked with lye, drained in ash hoppers. It made perfect soap for domestic uses. Hard soap was prepared for the big house in various ways, tempered with age, and used by young and old alike. For wounds and baby usage there could be bought Castile soap, but the soaps of the multitudes were prepared at home. Except salt, iron, sugar, and coffee, everything was raised by those early Georgia planters necessary for human comfort and sustenance.

Many travelled south to observe slavery and not all were displeased with what they saw. Joseph Holt Ingraham, who wrote approvingly, was the author of dozens of popular romances. On the other hand, the slave trade was abhorred even by most southerners. (Selections from Joseph Holt Ingraham, *The South-West by a Yankee*, 1835, and Reverend R. Walsh, *Notices of Brazil*, 1831.)

THE SOUTH-WEST BY A YANKEE

Planters, particularly native planters, have a kind of affection for their Negroes, incredible to those who have not observed its effects. If rebellious they punish them—if well behaved, they not infrequently reward them. In health they treat them with uniform kindness, in sickness with attention and sympathy. I once called on a native planter— a young bachelor, like many of his class, who had graduated at Cambridge and traveled in Europe—yet Northern education and foreign habits did not destroy the Mississippian. I found him by the bedside of a dying slave, nursing him with a kindness of voice and manner, and displaying a manly sympathy with his sufferings, honorable to himself and to humanity. On large plantations hospitals are erected for the reception of the sick, and the best medical attendance is provided for them. The physicians of Natchez derive a large proportion of their incomes from attending plantations. On some estates a physician permanently resides, whose time may be supposed sufficiently taken up in attending to the health of from one to two hundred persons. Often several plantations, if the force on each is small, unite and employ one physician for the whole. Every plantation is supplied with suitable medicines, and generally to such an extent that some room or part of a room in the planter's house is converted into a small apothecary's shop. These, in the absence of the physician in any sudden emergency, are administered by the planter. Hence, the health of the slaves, so far as medical skill is concerned, is well provided for. They are well fed and warmly clothed in the winter, in warm jackets and trousers, and blanket coats enveloping the whole person, with hats or woolen caps and brogans. In summer they have clothing suitable to the season, and a ragged Negro is less frequently to be met with than in Northern cities.

No scene can be livelier or more interesting to a Northerner than that which the Negro quarters of a well-regulated plantation present on a Sabbath morning just before church hour. In every cabin the men are shaving and dressing—the women, arrayed in their gay muslins, are arranging their frizzly hair, in which they take no little pride, or investigating the condition of their children's heads—the old people, neatly clothed, are quietly conversing or smoking about their doors, and those of the younger portion who are not undergoing the affliction of the washtub, are enjoying themselves in the shade of the trees or around some little pond with as much zest as though slavery and freedom were synonymous terms. When all are dressed and the hour arrives for worship, they lock up their cabins, and the whole population of the little village proceeds to the chapel, where divine worship is performed, sometimes by an officiating clergyman and often by the planter himself, if a church member. The whole plantation is also frequently formed into a Sabbath class which is instructed by the planter or some member of his family, and often such is the anxiety of masters that they should perfectly understand what they are taught—a hard matter in the present state of African intellect—that no means calculated to advance their progress are left untried. I was not long since shown a manuscript catechism, drawn up with great care and judgment by a distinguished planter, on a plan admirably adapted to the comprehension of Negroes. The same gentleman, in conjunction with two or three neighboring planters, employs a Presbyterian clergyman to preach to the slaves, paying him a salary for his services. On those plantations which have no chapel and no regular worship on the Sabbath, Negroes are permitted to go to the nearest town to church, a privilege they seldom know how to appreciate, and prefer converting their liberty into an opportunity for marketing or visiting. Experience, however, has convinced planters that no indulgence to their slaves is so detrimental as this, both to the moral condition of the slave and the good order of the plantation, for there is no vice in which many of them will not become adepts, if allowed a temporary freedom from restraint one day in seven. Hence, this liberty, except in particular instances, is denied them on some estates, to which they are confined under easy discipline during the day, passing the time in strolling through the woods, sleeping, eating, and idling about the quarters. The evenings of the Sabbath are passed in little gossiping circles in some of the cabins, or beneath the shade of some tree in front of their dwellings, or at weddings. The Negroes are usually married by the planter, who reads the service from the gallery—the couple with their attendants standing upon the steps or on the green in front. These marriages, in the eye of the slave, are binding. Clergymen are sometimes invited to officiate by those planters who feel that respect for the marriage covenant which leads them to desire its strict observance where human legislation has not provided for it. On nuptial occasions the Negroes partake of fine suppers to which the ladies add many little delicacies and handsome presents of wearing apparel to the married pair. When the Negroes desire a clergyman to perform the ceremony for them, planters seldom refuse to comply with their request. . . .

THE SLAVE TRADE BY A YANKEE

On Friday, May 22, [1829] we were talking of this pirate at breakfast and the probability of meeting her in this place, when in the midst of our conversation a midshipman entered the cabin and said in a hurried manner that a sail was visible to the northwest on the larboard quarter. We immediately all rushed on deck, glasses were called for and set, and we distinctly saw a large ship of three masts, apparently crossing our course. It was the general opinion that she was either a large slaver or a pirate, or probably both, and Captain Arabin was strongly inclined to believe it was his friend the Spaniard from the coast of Africa, for whom we had been looking out.

All night we were pointing our glasses in the direction in which she lay, and caught occasional glimpses of her, and when morning dawned, we saw her like a speck on the horizon, standing due north. We followed in the same track; the breeze soon increased our way to eight knots, and we had the pleasure to find we were every moment gaining on her. We again sent a long shot after her, but she only crowded the more sail to escape.

We could now discern her whole equipment; her gun streak was distinctly seen along the water, with eight ports of a side; and it was the general opinion that she was a French pirate and slaver, notorious for her depredations. At twelve o'clock we were entirely within gunshot, and one of our long bow guns was again fired at her. It struck the water alongside, and then, for the first time, she showed a disposition to stop. While we were preparing a second she hove to, and in a short time we were alongside her, after a most interesting chase of thirty hours, during which we ran three hundred miles.

The first object that struck us was an enormous gun, turning on a swivel, on deck—the constant appendage of a pirate; and the next were large kettles for cooking, on the bows—the usual apparatus of a slaver. Our boat was now hoisted out, and I went on board with the officers. When we mounted her decks we found her full of slaves. She was called the *Veloz*, commanded by Captain José Barbosa, bound to Bahia. She was a very broad-decked ship, with a mainmast, schooner rigged, and behind her foremast was that large, formidable gun, which turned on a broad circle of iron, on deck, and which enabled her to act as a pirate if her slaving speculation failed. She had taken in, on the coast of Africa, 336 males and 226 females, making in all 562, and had been out seventeen days, during which she had thrown overboard 55. The slaves were all inclosed under grated hatchways between decks. The space was so low that they sat between each other's legs and [were] stowed so close together that there was no possibility of their lying down or at all changing their position by night or day. As they belonged to and were shipped on account of different individuals, they were all branded like sheep with the owner's marks of different forms. These were impressed under their breasts or on their arms, and, as the mate informed me with perfect indifference "burnt with the red-hot iron." Over the hatchway stood a ferocious-looking fellow with a scourge of many twisted thongs in his hand, who was the slave driver of the ship, and whenever he heard the slightest noise below, he shook it over them and seemed eager to exercise it. I was quite pleased to take this hateful badge out of his hand, and I have kept it ever since as a horrid memorial of reality, should I ever be disposed to forget the scene I witnessed.

As soon as the poor creatures saw us looking down at them, their dark and melancholy visages brightened up. They perceived something of sympathy and kindness in our looks which they had not been accustomed to, and, feeling instinctively that we were friends, they immediately began to shout and clap their hands. One or two had picked up a few Portuguese words, and cried out, "*Viva! Viva!*" The women were particularly excited. They all held up their arms, and when we bent down and shook hands with them, they could not contain their delight; they endeavored to scramble up on their knees, stretching up to kiss our hands, and we understood that they knew we were come to liberate them. Some, however, hung down their heads in apparently hopeless dejection; some were greatly emaciated, and some, particularly children, seemed dying.

But the circumstance which struck us most forcibly was how it was possible for such a number of human beings to exist, packed up and wedged together as tight as they could cram, in low cells three feet high, the greater part of which, except that immediately under the grated hatchways, was shut out from light or air, and this when the thermometer, exposed to the open sky, was standing in the shade, on our deck, at 89°. The space between decks was divided into two compartments 3 feet 3 inches high; the size of one was 16 feet by 18 and of the other 40 by 21; into the first were crammed the women and girls, into the second the men and boys: 226 fellow creatures were thus thrust into one space 288 feet square and 336 into another space 800 feet square, giving to the whole an average of 23 inches and to each of the women not more than 13 inches. We also found manacles and fetters of different kinds, but it appears that they had all been taken off before we boarded.

The heat of these horrid places was so great and the odor so offensive that it was quite impossible to enter them, even had there been room. They were measured as above when the slaves had left them. The officers insisted that the poor suffering creatures should be admitted on deck to get air and water. This was opposed by the mate of the slaver, who, from a feeling that they deserved it, declared they would murder them all. The officers, however, persisted, and the poor beings were all turned up together. It is impossible to conceive the effect of this eruption—517 fellow creatures of all ages and sexes, some children, some adults, some old men and women, all in a state of total nudity, scrambling out together to taste the luxury of a little fresh air and water. They came swarming up like bees from the aperture of a hive till the whole deck was crowded to suffocation from stem to stern, so that it was impossible to imagine where they could all have come from or how they could have been stowed away. On looking into the places where they had been crammed, there were found some children next the sides of the ship, in the places most remote from light and air; they were lying nearly in a torpid state after the rest had turned out. The little creatures seemed indifferent as to life or death, and when they were carried on deck, many of them could not stand.

After enjoying for a short time the unusual luxury of air, some water was brought; it was then that the extent of their sufferings was exposed in a fearful manner. They all rushed like maniacs towards it. No entreaties or threats or blows could restrain them; they shrieked and struggled and fought with one another for a drop of this precious liquid, as if they grew rabid at the sight of it.

It was not surprising that they should have endured much sickness and loss of life in their short passage. They had sailed from the coast of Africa on the 7th of May and had been out but seventeen days, and they had thrown overboard no less than fifty-five, who had died of dysentery and other complaints in that space of time, though they had left the coast in good health. Indeed, many of the survivors were seen lying about the decks in the last stage of emaciation and in a state of filth and misery not to be looked at. Even-handed justice had visited the effects of this unholy traffic on the crew who were engaged in it.

Eight or nine had died, and at that moment six were in hammocks on board, in different stages of fever. This mortality did not arise from want of medicine. There was a large stock ostentatiously displayed in the cabin, with a manuscript book containing directions as to the quantities; but the only medical man on board to prescribe it was a black, who was as ignorant as his patients.

While expressing my horror at what I saw and exclaiming against the state of this vessel for conveying human beings, I was informed by my friends, who had passed so long a time on the coast of Africa and visited so many ships, that this was one of the best they had seen. The height sometimes between decks was only eighteen inches, so that the unfortunate beings could not turn round or even on their sides, the elevation being less than the breadth of their shoulders; and here they are usually chained to the decks by the neck and legs. In such a place the sense of misery and suffocation is so great that the Negroes, like the English in the Black Hole at Calcutta, are driven to a frenzy. They had on one occasion taken a slave vessel in the river Bonny; the slaves were stowed in the narrow space between decks and chained together. They heard a horrible din and tumult among them and could not imagine from what cause it proceeded. They opened the hatches and turned them up on deck. They were manacled together in twos and threes. Their horror may be well conceived when they found a number of them in different stages of suffocation; many of them were foaming at the mouth and in the last agonies—many were dead. A living man was sometimes dragged up, and his companion was a dead body; sometimes of the three attached to the same chain, one was dying and another dead. The tumult they had heard was the frenzy of those suffocating wretches in the last stage of fury and desperation, struggling to extricate themselves. When they were all dragged up, nineteen were irrecoverably dead. Many destroyed one another in the hopes of procuring room to breathe; men strangled those next them, and women drove nails into each other's brains. Many unfortunate creatures on other occasions took the first opportunity of leaping overboard and getting rid, in this way, of an intolerable life.

In the course of one lifetime, homelife early in the nineteenth century could appear hopelessly lost in the past, as these accounts, one from Georgia and one from Ohio, suggest. The William Howells who remembered Ohio was the father of the famous critic and novelist, William Dean Howells. (Selection from William Cooper Howells, *Recollections of Life in Ohio from 1813 to 1840*, 1895.)

RECOLLECTIONS OF LIFE IN OHIO

I can hardly realize how greatly things have changed since that period, and what a primitive and simple kind of life prevailed. Particularly remarkable was the general equality and the general dependence of all upon the neighborly kindness and good offices of others. Their houses and barns were built of logs, and were raised by the collection of many neighbors together on one day, whose united strength was necessary to the handling of the logs. As every man was ready with the ax and understood this work, all came together within the circle where the raising was to be done, and all worked together with about equal skill. The best axmen were given charge of the placing of the logs on the wall, and some one of experience took the general direction. The logs of the width and length of the house were usually of different lengths. Those intended for the two sides were placed in a convenient place, some distance from the foundation; those for the ends, in another place. The first two side logs were put in place at the back and front; then the end logs were notched down in their places; then two side logs would be rolled up on skids, and notched in their places. At the corners the top of the log, as soon as it was put in place, would be dressed up by the cornerman; and when the next logs were rolled up they would be notched, which notch would be turned downwards upon the saddle made to receive it, when the cornerman would saddle that log ready for the next. This kept the logs in their places like a dovetail and brought them together so as to form a closer wall. The ends of the skids would be raised on each new log as it was laid down to make a way for the next. The logs on these skids would be rolled as long as the men could handle them from the ground, but when the wall got too high, then they would use forks, made by cutting a young notched tree, with which the logs would be pushed up. By using a fork at each end of the log, it could be pushed up with ease and safety. The men understood handling timber, and accidents seldom happened, unless the logs were icy or wet or the whisky had gone round too often. I was often at these raisings, because we had raisings of the kind to do, and it was the custom always to send one from a family to help, so that you could claim like assistance in return. At the raisings I would take the position of cornerman, if the building was not too heavy, as it was a post of honor, and my head was steady when high up from the ground. In chopping on the corners we always stood up straight, and it required a good balance.

This kind of mutual help of the neighbors was extended to many kinds of work, such as rolling up the logs in a clearing, grubbing out the underbrush, splitting rails, cutting logs for a house, and the like.

When a gathering of men for such a purpose took place there was commonly some sort of mutual job laid out for women, such as quilting, sewing, or spinning up a lot of thread for some poor neighbor. This would bring together a mixed party, and it was usually arranged that after supper there should be a dance or at least plays which would occupy a good part of the night and wind up with the young fellows seeing the girls home in the short hours or, if they went home early, sitting with them by the fire in that kind of interesting chat known as sparking.

The flax crops required a good deal of handling, in weeding, pulling, and dressing, and each of these processes was made the occasion of a joint gathering of boys and girls and a good time. As I look back now upon those times, I am puzzled to think how they managed to make such small and crowded houses serve for large parties, and how they found room to dance in an apartment of perhaps eighteen feet square, in which there would be two large beds and a trundle bed, besides the furniture, which though not of great quantity, took some room. And then, if these were small houses, they often contained large families. I have often seen three or four little heads peeping out from that part of a trundle bed that was not pushed entirely under the big bed, to get their share of the fun going on among the older ones while the big beds were used to receive the hats and bonnets and perhaps a baby or two, stowed away till the mothers were ready to go home.

One of the gatherings for joint work which has totally disappeared from the agriculture of modern times, and one that was always a jolly kind of affair, was the cornhusking. It was a sort of harvest home in its department, and it was the more jolly because it was a gathering with very little respect to persons, and embraced in the invitation men and big boys, with the understanding that no one would be unwelcome. There was always a good supper served at the husking, and as certainly a good appetite to eat it with. It came at a plentiful season, when the turkeys and chickens were fat, and a fat pig was at hand, to be flanked on the table with good bread in various forms, turnips and potatoes from the autumn stores, apple and pumpkin pies, good coffee and the like. And the cooking was always well done, and all in such bountiful abundance that no one feared to eat, while many a poor fellow was certain of a square meal by being present at a husking. You were sure to see the laboring men of the vicinity out, and the wives of a goodly number of farm hands would be on hand to help in the cooking and serving at the table. The cornhusking has been discontinued because the farmers found out that it was less trouble to husk it in the field, direct from the stalk, than to gather in the husk and go over it again. But in that day they did not know that much and therefore took the original method of managing their corn crop, which was this: as soon as the grain began to harden they would cut the stalks off just above the ears and save these tops for fodder, and if they had time they stripped all the blades off the stalks below the ears, which made very nice though costly feed. Then, as barn room was not usually overplenty, they made a kind of frame of poles, as for a tent, and thatched it, sides and top, with the corn tops placed with the tassel downward, so as to shed the rain and snow. This was called the fodder house and was built in the barnyard. Inside they would store the blades in bundles, the husks, and the pumpkins that were saved for use in the winter. The fodder house was commonly made ten feet high and as long as was necessary, and it was used up through the winter by feeding the fodder to the cattle, beginning at the back, which would be temporarily closed by a few bundles of the tops. It would thus serve as a protection for what might be stored in it till all was used up. The fodder house was, of all things, a favorite place for the children to hide in and play. When the season for gathering the corn came the farmers went through the fields and pulled off the ears and husks together, throwing them upon the ground in heaps, whence they were hauled into the barnyard and there piled up in a neat pile of convenient length, according to the crop, and say four or five feet high, rising to a sharp peak from a base about six feet. Care was taken to make this pile of equal width and height from end to end, so that it would be easily and fairly divided in the middle by a rail laid upon it.

When the husking party had assembled they were all called out into line, and two fellows, mostly ambitious boys, were chosen captains. These then chose their men, each calling out one of the crowd alternately, till all were chosen. Then the heap was divided, by two judicious chaps walking solemnly along the ridge of the heap of corn, and deciding where the dividing rail was to be laid, and, as this had to be done by starlight or moonlight at best, it took considerable deliberation, as the comparative solidity of the ends of the heap and the evenness of it had to be taken into account. This done, the captains placed a good steady man at each side of the rail, who made it a point to work through and cut the heap in two as soon as possible; and then the two parties fell to husking, all standing with the heap in front of them, and throwing the husked corn on to a clear space over the heap, and the husks behind them. From the time they begin till the corn was all husked at one end, there would be steady work, each man husking all the corn he could, never stopping except to take a pull at the stone jug of inspiration that passed occasionally along the line; weak lovers of the stuff were sometimes overcome, though it was held to be a disgraceful thing to take too much. The captains would go up and down their lines and rally their men as if in a battle, and the whole was an exciting affair. As soon as one party got done, they raised a shout, and hoisting their captain on their shoulders, carried him over to the other side with general cheering. Then would come a little bantering talk and explanation why the defeated party lost, and all would turn to and husk up the remnants of the heap. All hands would then join to carry the husks into the fodder house. The shout at hoisting the captain was the signal for bringing the supper on the table, and the huskers and the supper met soon after. These gatherings often embraced forty or fifty men. If the farmhouse was small it would be crowded, and the supper would be managed by repeated sittings at the table. At a large house there was less crowding and more fun, and if, as was often the case, some occasion had been given for an assemblage of the girls of the neighborhood, and particularly if the man that played the fiddle should attend, after the older men had gone there was very apt to be a good time. There was a tradition that the boys who accidentally husked a red ear and saved it would be entitled to a kiss from somebody. But I never knew it to be necessary to produce a red ear to secure a kiss where there was a disposition to give or take one.

A portrait of woman's life on the moving—endlessly moving—frontier is Harriet Connor Brown's reminiscences about her grandmother. (From Harriet Connor Brown, *Grandmother Brown's Hundred Years,* 1929.)

GRANDMOTHER BROWN ON THE FRONTIER

After periods at the Brice House or in Logan or Somerset, we were always glad to get back to our own father's dear old home. Nowhere else did we have the same conveniences. We did most of our work there in the summer kitchen. That was where we had the big brick oven. We used to fire it twice a week and do a sight o' baking all at once. We'd make a hot fire in the oven, and then, when the bricks were thoroughly heated, we'd scrape out all the coals with a big iron scraper, dump the coals into the fireplace, and shove in the roasts and fowls, the pies and bread. At other times 'we'd use the open fireplace. It wasn't nearly so difficult to work by as people think. When we went to keeping house in 1845, Dan'l and I, he bought me a little iron stove, a new thing in those days. It was no good, and would only bake things on one side. I soon went back to cooking at an open fireplace.

You know the look of andirons, crane, spit, reflectors. Our heavy iron vessels were swung from chains. When we wanted to lift the iron lids off, we'd have to reach in with a hook and swing them off. They had a flange around the edge. Many of our dishes were baked in Dutch ovens on the hearth. We used to bake Indian pone—that is, bread made of rye and corn meal—that way. We would set it off in a corner of the hearth covered with coals and ashes, and that it would bake slowly all night long. In the morning the crust would be thick but soft—oh, *so* good.

For roasting meat we had reflectors. Some joints we roasted in our big iron kettles with a bit of water. And others we put on three-legged gridirons which could be turned. These had a little fluted place for the gravy to run down. Chickens we could split down the back and lay on the gridiron with a plate and flatirons on top to hold them down. Oh, how different, how different, is everything now, encumbered with conveniences!

The difference between those who were naturally clean and orderly and those who were not was perhaps more marked in those days than it is now. It was so easy, for instance, since we had no screens, to let the flies spoil everything. My mother just wouldn't have it so. We weren't allowed to bring apples into the house in summer, because apples attract flies. If any of us dropped a speck of butter or cream on the floor, she had to run at once for a cloth to wipe it up. Our kitchen floor was of ash, and Ma was very proud of keeping it white. In the summer kitchen the floor was of brick, and it was expected to be spotless also. At mealtime someone stood and fanned to keep the flies away while the others ate. When Sister Libbie went to housekeeping, she had little round-topped screens for every dish on her table. This was considered quite stylish. Ma used to set some tall thing in the centre of her table, spread a cloth over it, and slip food under until we were ready to sit down. As soon as the meal was finished, all curtains had to be pulled down and the flies driven from the darkened room.

Our dishes for common use were white with blue edges. The finer ones were a figured blue. I remember, also, a large blue soup tureen with a cover and a blue, long-handled ladle, all very handsome.

Our forks were two-tined. They weren't much good for holding some things. But if we used our knives for conveying food to our mouths it had to be done with the back of the knife towards the face. We had no napkins. We used our handkerchiefs. Tablecloths were made of cotton diaper especially woven for the purpose. The first white bed-spread I ever had was made of two widths of that same cotton whitened on the grass.

In warm weather we washed outdoors under the quince bushes. We used our well water. It was so soft, it was just beautiful. We'd draw a barrel of water, put one shovel of ashes into it, and it would just suds up like soft water, so white and clean. We used soft soap, of course. Our starch was of two kinds—either made from a dough of flour worked round and round until it was smooth and fine or made from grated potato cooked to the right consistency.

Ma put us girls to work early. It was taken as a matter of course that we should learn all kinds of housework. I know that before I was seven years old I used to wash the dishes. But our mother had village girls to help her also. I remember one Ann Fierce who was with us for years, but it seems to me that Sister Libbie and I usually did the washing. There was need of many hands to get all the work done. It required more knowledge to do the things for everyday living than is the case nowadays. If one wants light now, all one has to do is pull a string or push a button. Then, we had to pick up a coal with tongs, hold it against a candle, and blow. And one had to make the candles, perhaps.

I remember the first matches that I ever saw. Someone handed me a little bunch of them, fastened together at the bottom in a solid block of wood about a half inch square. "Lucifer matches" they called them. I tore one off and set the whole thing afire.

Some people had tinder boxes. Some kept a kind of punk which would give off a spark when struck with steel or knife. Generally speaking, people kept the fire on their hearthstones going year in and year out.

We did not make our candles at home, but got them usually from Uncle Dean, who made candles for the town. I used to love to watch him and Aunt Maria at work dipping candles—she with the hot tallow in a big kettle on the hearth, he with stillyards beside him, weighing carefully. Occasionally we had some sperm candles made of fine whale tallow. Besides candles, people sometimes burned sperm or whale oil in little lamps that looked like square-topped candlesticks. In the square top was a place for a bowl that would hold perhaps a half pint of oil.

Even without candle making, there was certainly a plenty to do to keep life going in those days. Baking, washing, ironing, sewing, kept us busy. Not to mention the spinning and weaving that had to be done before cloth was available for the seamstress.

My mother used to spin. She made beautiful fine thread. She taught Sister Libbie how to spin, but decided, before my turn came, that spinning was doomed to become a lost art, and that I might be better employed in some other way. I used to love to watch her at the spinning wheel. She had two wheels, lovely big ones. She used a wheel boy to turn her wheel. I can just close my eyes and see Ma standing over there spinning a thread as far as from here to the bed—say, twelve feet long.

My mother and her sister had some beautiful woolen cloth of their own spinning and weaving. Part of the thread was made with the open, part with the crossed, band. They colored it with butternut bark, but the two kinds would never color alike, so that part of it was a light and part a dark brown. They wove it into a plaid and had it pressed, and then they made fine dresses out of it to wear to church. I remember, too, that my mother raised flax, spun it into linen, wove it into cloth,—colored blue in the yarn,—made it up into a dress for me which she embroidered in white above the hem. I wish I had kept that dress to show my children the beautiful work of their grandmother.

Ma used to use Aunt Betsy's loom sometimes. When I was eight years old, she wove me a plaid dress of which I was very proud. I remember the pattern: eight threads of brown, then one of red, one of blue, one of red, then brown again, both in the warp and in the woof. It made the prettiest flannel, and that dress lasted me for years.

Women made their own designs for cloth as well as for dresses in those days. If a woman had taste, she had a chance to show it in her weaving. But, oh, it was hard work. You never saw warping bars, did you? Clumsy things, long as a bed. On them work was prepared for the loom. You had to draw each thread through a reed. I used to love to watch my mother weaving, her shuttle holding the spool with yarn shooting through the warp, then back the other way. When she had woven as far as she could reach, she would bend below the loom and wind the woven cloth into a roll beneath. Blankets made at home used to last a long, long time. Homespun things were good.

We had all the things that were really necessary for our comfort in those days, and we had quite as much leisure as people have now. Always, too, we had time to attend church and Sunday school.

Lester Frank Ward, later one of the pioneer figures of American sociology, had more important things on his mind than sociology when he kept this diary—in French—when he was 19 years old and in love. It is rare to find such intimate portraits of mid-nineteenth century life. (Selection from Lester Frank Ward, *Diary*, 1860–1862.)

LESTER FRANK WARD (1841-1913), *Diary*

July 9 [1860]

I cultivated the corn this morning for the first time this year. I was a little annoyed with the horse's not keeping to the row. In the afternoon I gathered and bound the sheaves.

When the night came I had a fine time playing on the violin while Baxter played the tambourine. My heart was very light regarding the girl whom I loved, and whom I no longer esteem.

July 11

I went to the Post Office to look for the promised letter from the girl, but did not find it, so I came to the conclusion that I never wished to see her again. My heart is light. I was almost sick cutting the corn all this morning.

My girl, I am going to abandon you eternally, you whom I have loved so deeply! It will kill me, but let me perish.

August 19, Sunday morning

Hearing mention of an Episcopal meeting at six o'clock in the evening I decided to attend it. After having finished a letter I went to Sunday School and finally to the girl's, taking her a music book. I talked with her for an hour or two and she entertained me wonderfully —when I returned and got something to eat, I went to church.

Mr. Douglas, the minister, after having gone through all the ceremonies which belong to this church (which were, incidentally, very interesting to me) preached a very practical and profound sermon. The girl was there, and as I passed the stairs which lead to the gallery I saw her standing on the steps. It was a very awkward maneuver to approach her and ask for her company to another service.

But I accomplished it casually, and she could not refuse. We went at once to another church, chatting and enjoying ourselves marvelously. She fascinated me. I remembered my previous love. What a charming girl. If I could once more press my lips on hers and draw from them my soul's satisfaction!

We returned in the evening talking all the time but more gravely than before. We arrived at the door, I entered with her, she lit a lamp and we sat down together talking, but I could not keep myself from feasting my eyes ardently and with intensity on the object of beauty and attraction at my side.

Girl, I thought, if you were true to me, what a happy man I should be! I took the hand which I loved, and looked at it. We spoke little more from that moment, while I looked steadily at her face and was conquered.

I could no longer keep my place. Leaning forward I received her sweet and tender form in my arms and in an instant her face was covered with kisses. What a sublime scene! Who could have words to express my emotions?

And there we bathed ourselves in the passion of love until the crowing of cocks announced that it was day.

September 22

I could not sing long with her without feeling my trapped heart dart forth and come to rest in her loving breast. At half past three I parted from her amid thousands of kisses. I have forgotten to remark that I collected forty sets of hubs on Monday for myself. Tuesday and Wednesday I worked on the fallow land, and Wednesday evening went to a meeting of the choir in town.

I escorted the girl to her home which I did not leave until three. We had considerable difficulty with the lamp, which finally went out at the critical moment when it started to rain so that I could not go home.

Taking her by the hand, I attempted to find the door but in the shadows we stumbled over a shoemaker's bench, and embracing her I sat down with her on the bench, where we remained about an hour, embracing, caressing, hugging and kissing. O bliss! O love! O passion pure, sweet and profound! What more do I want than you?

Tuesday I finished 45 sets of hubs of which twenty are reserved for me. Wednesday and Saturday I worked on the fallow land, which we have finished.

(Evening)

It was with great difficulty that I finally succeeded in obtaining a team-license to go and sell my hubs. I am going to leave tomorrow afternoon. My route will be down the river to Standing Stone &c and I am determined not to sell a single hub without getting something useful to me now.

Friday evening [February 15, 1861]

The girl and I had a very sweet time. I kissed her on her soft breasts, and took too many liberties with her sweet person, and we are going to stop. It is a very fascinating practice and fills us with very sweet, tender and familiar sentiments, and consequently makes us happy. But the difficulty is that we might become so addicted in that direction that we might go too deep and possibly confound ourselves by the standards of virtue.

July 16

I have just finished a day's work and am going up on the mountain. Yesterday afternoon I worked on the mountain cutting hay. Sunday evening before I went to sleep I was summoned to watch beside the corpse of Madame Partner. I found my darling there. We had a good time watching until broad daylight.

I accompanied the girl home, and she insisted on my staying there and getting a little sleep, but she came into my room to give me my socks and to kiss me a little, and her mother found her there and she said several things concerning us which made me angry and I got up and soon left the house. I shall never spend another night there.

August 4 [1862]

I shall resume with the narration of the events of this week. Sunday, being here, I was happy with my girl. We walked to May's and had a good time. On the way back we went to church to hear an Episcopal discourse by Mr. Brush. Not very good.

Monday morning I went to Towanda to buy some kerosene oil and do several other errands. I had been convinced by something I had read in the *Tribune* that I was exempt from military service, but I found that the *Tribune* was mistaken.

Immediately my intention was changed, and again I resolved to go to war. On my return I found Ed Owen who had already enrolled, and as I came here with him in his carriage, I found occasion to write my name among the brave men of Pennsylvania. I brought all my things from John's here this morning.

That same evening I joined the company, and Tuesday we all went to Towanda to elect officers. Every man who can is going to war, and everything is very exciting. But one more event is needed to crown the catalogue, and yesterday was the day.

Wednesday, August 13

I had to register my marriage! What? I, married? True enough.

My heart's darling whom I have loved so long, so constantly, so franti-
cally, is mine! We are keeping it a secret, but it has been guessed, but
not yet discovered. How sweet it is to sleep with her!

This song of the gold rushers of 1849 became the state song of Washington later
in the nineteenth century. Its hero abandons the pursuit of gold for more solid
riches in the Northwest.

CALIFORNIA—"ACRES OF CLAMS"

1 I've wandered all over this country
   Prospecting and digging for gold;
   I've tunneled, hydraulicked, and cradled,
   And I have been frequently sold.

   Chorus
   And I have been frequently sold,
   And I have been frequently sold—
   I've tunneled, hydraulicked, and cradled,
   And I have been frequently sold!

2 For one who got rich by mining
   I saw there were hundreds grew poor;
   I made up my mind to try farming,
   The only pursuit that is sure.

   Chorus
   The only pursuit that is sure,
   The only pursuit that is sure—
   I made up my mind to try farming,
   The only pursuit that is sure!

3 I rolled up my grub in my blanket,
   I left all my tools on the ground,
   I started one morning to shank it
   For the country they call Puget Sound.

   Chorus
   For the country they call Puget Sound,

For the country they call Puget Sound—
I started one morning to shank it
For the country they call Puget Sound!

4 No longer the slave of ambition,
I laugh at the world and its shams,
And think of my happy condition
Surrounded by acres of clams.

Chorus
Surrounded by acres of clams,
Surrounded by acres of clams—
And think of my happy condition
Surrounded by acres of clams!

Richard Henry Dana, a Harvard boy who dropped out of school and went to sea, presented a startling realistic picture of the life of common seamen. (Selection from Richard Henry Dana, *Two Years Before the Mast*, 1840.)

AT SEA

For several days the captain seemed very much out of humor. Nothing went right, or fast enough for him. He quarreled with the cook, and threatened to flog him for throwing wood on deck; and had a dispute with the mate about reeving a Spanish burton; the mate saying that he was right, and had been taught how to do it by a man *who was a sailor!* This, the captain took in dudgeon and they were at sword's points at once.

But his displeasure was chiefly turned against a large heavy-molded fellow from the middle States who was called Sam. This man hesitated in his speech, and was rather slow in his motions, but was a pretty good sailor, and always seemed to do his best; but the captain took a dislike to him, thought he was surly and lazy; and "if you once give a dog a bad name"—as the sailor phrase is—"he may as well jump overboard." The captain found fault with everything this man did, and hazed him for dropping a marline-spike from the main yard, where he was at work. This, of course, was an accident, but it was set down against him.

The captain was on board all day Friday, and everything went on hard and disagreeably. "The more you drive a man the less he will do" was as true with us as with any other people. We worked late Friday night and were turned to early Saturday morning. About ten o'clock the captain ordered our new officer, Russell, who by this time had become thoroughly disliked by all the crew, to get the gig ready to take him ashore.

John, the Swede, was sitting in the boat alongside, and Russell and myself were standing by the main hatchway, waiting for the captain, who was down in the hold, where the crew were at work, when we heard his voice raised in violent dispute with somebody, whether it was with the same mate or one of the crew I could not tell; and then came blows and scuffling. I ran to the side and beckoned to John, who came up, and we leaned down the hatchway; and though we could see no one, yet we knew that the captain had the advantage, for his voice was loud and clear.

"You see your condition! You see your condition! Will you ever give me any more of your *jaw*?" No answer, and then came wrestling and heaving, as though the man was trying to turn him.

"You may as well keep still, for I have got you," said the captain. Then came the question, "Will you ever give me any more of your jaw?"

"I never gave you any, sir," said Sam; for it was his voice that we heard, though low and half choked.

"That's not what I ask you. Will you ever be impudent to me again?"

"I never have been," said Sam.

"Answer my question, or I'll make a spread eagle of you! I'll flog you, by G–d."

"I'm no Negro slave," said Sam.

"Then I'll make you one," said the captain; and he came to the hatchway, and sprang on deck, threw off his coat, and rolling up his sleeves, called out to the mate: "Seize that man up, Mr. A⎯⎯! Seize him up! Make a spread eagle of him! I'll teach you all who is master aboard!"

The crew and officers followed the captain up the hatchway, and after repeated orders the mate laid hold of Sam, who made no resistance, and carried him to the gangway.

"What are you going to flog that man for, sir?" said John, the Swede, to the captain.

Upon hearing this, the captain turned upon him, but knowing him to be quick and resolute, he ordered the steward to bring the irons, and calling upon Russell to help him, went up to John.

"Let me alone," said John. "I'm willing to be put in irons. You need not use any force"; and putting out his hands, the captain slipped the irons on, and sent him aft to the quarter-deck. Sam by this time was *seized up*, as it is called, that is, placed against the shrouds, with his wrists made fast to the shrouds, his jacket off, and his back exposed. The captain stood on the break of the deck, a few feet from him, and a little raised, so as to have a good swing at him, and held in his hand the bight of a thick, strong rope. The officers stood round, and the crew grouped together in the waist.

All these preparations made me feel sick and almost faint, angry and excited as I was. A man—a human being, made in God's likeness—fastened up and flogged like a beast! A man, too, whom I had lived with and eaten with for months, and knew almost as well as a brother.

The first and almost uncontrollable impulse was resistance. But what was to be done? The time for it had gone by. The two best men were fast, and there were only two besides myself, and a small boy of ten or twelve years of age. And then there were (besides the captain) three officers, steward, agent, and clerk. But besides the numbers, what is there for sailors to do? If they resist, it is mutiny; and if they succeed and take the vessel, it is piracy. If they ever yield again, their punishment must come; and if they do not yield, they are pirates for life. If a sailor resist his commander, he resists the law, and piracy or submission are his only alternatives. Bad as it was, it must be borne. It is what a sailor ships for.

Swinging the rope over his head, and bending his body so as to give it full force, the captain brought it down upon the poor fellow's back. Once, twice—six times. "Will you ever give me any more of your jaw?" The man writhed with pain, but said not a word. Three times more. This was too much, and he muttered something which I could not hear; this brought as many more as the man could stand; when the captain ordered him to be cut down, and go forward.

"Now for you," said the captain, making up to John and taking his irons off. As soon as he was loose, he ran forward to the forecastle. "Bring that man aft," shouted the captain. The second mate, who had been a shipmate of John's stood still in the waist, and the mate walked slowly forward; but our third officer, anxious to show his zeal, sprang forward over the windlass, and laid hold of John; but he soon threw him from him.

At this moment I would have given worlds for the power to help the poor fellow, but it was all in vain. The captain stood on the quarter-deck, bare-headed, his eyes flashing with rage, and his face as red as blood, swinging the rope, and calling out to his officers, "Drag him aft!—Lay hold of him! I'll *sweeten* him!" etc., etc.

The mate now went forward and told John quietly to go aft, and he, seeing resistance in vain, threw the blackguard third mate from him; said he would go aft of himself, that they should not drag him; and went up to the gangway and held out his hands; but as soon as the captain began to make him fast, the indignity was too much, and he began to resist; but the mate and Russell holding him, he was soon seized up.

When he was made fast, he turned to the captain, who stood turning up his sleeves and getting ready for the blow, and asked him what he was to be flogged for. "Have I ever refused my duty, sir? Have you ever known me to hang back, or to be insolent, or not to know my work?"

"No," said the captain, "it is not that I flog you for; I flog you for your interference—for asking questions."

"Can't a man ask a question here without being flogged?"

"No," shouted the captain; "nobody shall open his mouth aboard this vessel, but myself"; and began laying the blows upon his back, swinging half round before each blow, to give it full effect. As he went on his passion increased and he danced about the deck calling out as he swung the rope: "If you want to know what I flog you for, I'll tell you. It's because I like to do it!—because I like to do it! It suits me! That's what I do it for!"

The man writhed under the pain, until he could endure it no longer, when he called out, with an exclamation more common among foreigners than with us—"Oh, Jesus Christ, oh, Jesus Christ!"

"Don't call on Jesus Christ," shouted the captain. *"He can't help you. Call on Captain T*____. He's the man! He can help you! Jesus Christ can't help you now!"

At these words, which I never shall forget, my blood ran cold. I could look on no longer. Disgusted, sick, and horror-struck, I turned away and leaned over the rail, and looked down into the water. A few rapid thoughts of my own situation, and of the prospect of future revenge, crossed my mind; but the falling of the blows and the cries of the man called me back at once.

At length they ceased, and turning round, I found that the mate, at a signal from the captain, had cut him down. Almost doubled up with pain, the man walked forward and went down into the forecastle. Every one else stood still at his post, while the captain, swelling with rage and with the importance of his achievement, walked the quarter-deck, and at each turn, as he came forward, calling out to us:

"You see your condition! You see where I've got you all, and you know what to expect! You've been mistaken in me—you didn't know what I was! Now you know what I am!"—"I'll make you toe the mark, every soul of you, or I'll flog you all, fore and aft, from the boy up!"—

"You've got a driver over you! Yes, a *slave driver, a Negro driver!* I'll see who'll tell me he isn't a Negro slave!"

With this and the like matter, equally calculated to quiet us and to allay any apprehension of future trouble, he entertained us for about ten minutes, when he went below. Soon after, John came aft, with his bare back covered with stripes and wales in every direction, and dreadfully swollen, and asked the steward to ask the captain to let him have some salve or balsam to put upon it.

"No," said the captain, who heard him from below; "tell him to put his shirt on, that's the best thing for him, and pull me ashore in the boat. Nobody is going to lay up on board this vessel."

He then called to Mr. Russell to take those two men and two others in the boat and pull him ashore. I went for one. The two men could hardly bend their backs, and the captain called to them to "give way," "give way!" but finding they did their best, he let them alone. The agent was in the stern sheet, but during the whole pull—a league or more—not a word was spoken.

We landed; the captain, agent, and officer went up to the house, and left us with the boat. I, and the man with me, stayed near the boat, while John and Sam walked slowly away, and sat down on the rocks. They talked some time together, but at length separated, each sitting alone.

I had some fears of John. He was a foreigner, and violently tempered, and under suffering; and he had his knife with him, and the captain was to come down alone to the boat. The captain was probably armed, and if either of them had lifted a hand against him, they would have had nothing before them but flight, and starvation in the woods of California, or capture by the soldiers and Indian bloodhounds whom the offer of twenty dollars would have set upon them.

After the day's work was done, we went down into the forecastle and ate our plain supper; but not a word was spoken. It was Saturday night; but there was no song—no "sweethearts and wives." A gloom was over everything.

The two men lay in their berths, groaning with pain, and we all turned in, but, for myself, not to sleep. A sound coming now and then from the berths of the two men showed that they were awake, as awake they must have been, for they could hardly lie in one posture a moment; the dim, swinging lamp of the forecastle shed its light over the dark hole in which we lived; and many and various reflections and purposes coursed through my mind.

I thought of our situation, living under a tyranny; of the character of the country we were in; of the length of the voyage, and of the uncertainty attending our return to America; and then if we should return, of the prospect of obtaining justice and satisfaction for these poor men; and vowed that if God should ever give me the means, I would do something to redress the grievances and relieve the sufferings of that poor class of beings, of whom I then was one.

manners

In the 1820s more and more urban families were growing prosperous enough to have servants. But economic opportunity tended to draw them into more remunerative activities quickly. Therefore guides to handling servants and managing households proliferated, some aimed at the mistresses of houses and others at the maids. (Selections from Robert Roberts, *The House Servants' Directory*, 1828.)

HOUSE SERVANTS' DIRECTORY

Behaviour of Servants at Their Meals

Now, my friends, having had the pleasure and gratification of bringing ye in perfect order to wait on your superiors, I will therefore give you some advice and observations on behaviour and propriety at your own meals. In all families there is or should be a proper time for the meals in the kitchen, so as not to interfere with the parlour hours, as the servants are generally busy at that time. All the help should be ready, if possible, to sit down together at their meals, unless they are hindered by their employers; therefore you should strive to regulate your work, so as to be ready to sit down together, and not be loitering round as some do, which often is the cause of sad contention and confusion; for where one comes now and another at another time, it interferes with the cook's business, and hinders her from getting her work done in proper season.

Therefore, you should all sit down together thankfully; not to quarrel and dispute with each other, as very often is the case in families, and murmuring that the provisions are not good enough; this I have often seen myself to be the case, with those that had scarcely ever seen or known the comfort of eating a good meal, before they entered a gentleman's service. How wicked must be such conduct towards God, who has made their cups to run over with good things; and how ungrateful must it be to their employers, who provide bountifully to make them comfortable.

In the next place you should always be careful of every thing belonging to your employers, and never make waste of any thing you possibly can avoid. Whenever you draw beer, cider, or the like for dinner, never draw more than you think is wanted; for it is better to go twice than to make waste, and the old saying is a true one, "that a wilful waste often makes a woful want;" this I have often seen fulfilled, in those that have been extravagant and wasteful of the provisions under their charge.

My young friends, supposing you were in your employer's situation, and servants under your command, and your property in their charge, should you not think them very wicked and dishonest, when wasting your property and provisions? only put this to your own feelings, and it will give you full insight how you should act towards your employers; and how you should manage the property that is put under your trust.

Now, my friends, I shall trespass no longer by these remarks, but give you some few observations how you should conduct yourself at table, when at meals. Make it your study always to be clean at meal times; never talk much while eating; be polite and help all round before yourself. Never begin any vulgar conversation at such or any time. I have known some servants that were so rude, and void of all discretion, as to use the most vulgar conversation during meal times, which was a disgrace to any being, and ought not to be suffered in a gentleman's family. Always behave respectfully, and never stand up before the others are done, unless your business calls you. When done dinner, put by your chair; never leave your things about for others to wait on you, for in this station every one should attend to their own business. When done, you should always offer up a blessing for the good you have received; for we are ordered by the Lord to receive every thing with thanksgiving and prayer; therefore my friends, I sincerely hope that these examples will become beneficial to all who may study them. I shall now conclude these remarks and instructions, and give some hints to servants in general on their dress.

Hints to House Servants on Their Dress

Now, David, in the first place I shall address myself particularly to you, and give you a few hasty remarks on the propriety of servants in dressing, &c. There is no class of people that should dress more neat and clean than a house servant, because he is generally exposed to the eyes of the public; but his dress, though neat and tidy, should not be foppish or extravagant. A man that lives in a family should have two or three changes of light clothes for the summer, that he may always appear neat and clean. You should likewise have a good suit of clothes on purpose to wear while waiting on dinner, as there is nothing that looks more creditable than to see a servant well dressed at dinner. It is a credit to himself and the family whom he has the honour to serve. Make it a rule always to brush your dinner suit, when your morning's work is done, and every thing put in order, that you may have them ready when you want to dress for dinner.

You should never wear thick shoes or boots in the parlour, or waiting on dinner. You should have a pair of light pumps, on purpose for dinner, and a pair of slippers is the best thing you can wear in the morning, as they are easy to your feet while running about and doing your morning's work; likewise you are free from making a noise to disturb the family before they are up. You must always be very clean in your person, and wash your face and comb your hair, &c.

In the next place wash your feet at least three times per week, as in summer time your feet generally perspire; a little weak vinegar and water, or a little rum is very good for this use, as it is a stimulant, and there is no danger of taking cold after washing in either. Servants being generally on the foot throughout the day, it must cause perspiration, which makes a bad smell, which would be a very disagreeable thing to yourself and the company on whom you wait.

Now, David, there is one thing more that I must caution you against, that is, running in debt for fine clothes, &c. There are many servants that practise this to their utter ruin, all through pride and vanity, striving even to outvie their master. This is a very unbecoming thing in a servant, and no one would do so but an ignorant person and one that does not know his place: because, in the first place, his circumstances do not allow it. I never find fault with a servant to dress well, and always to be clean and tidy, but he should not be extravagant, or go above his ability. I have known several servants who dressed so foppish that it looked quite ridiculous, and myself have seen those very same servants afterwards in a perfect state of poverty, and without a dollar to help themselves. Consider, my young friend, that when sickness comes on, and no friends or relations to look to you, and no money laid up to support you, then what good does all your fine clothes? does not your pride then make you repent of your folly, and wish that you had been more careful of your money; instead of spending it to support your ignorant pride and folly? It absolutely makes me think of the fable of the frog and the ox; where the poor conceited frog puffed himself up, thinking to be as large as the ox, but at length he burst. This was all through pride and folly; and this I compare to a servant that strives to be in fashion, and spend all his money; then sickness comes on, and he sinks in poverty and death, and is no more thought of than the poor frog. But, my young friend, I sincerely hope that this never may be the case with you, nor any other that has to earn a living in this capacity; for the holy scripture says, that "the servant must not be above his master!" therefore I hope you will follow those examples.

There once was a right way to do everything, even being socially graceful about the loss of a limb. Guides to correct etiquette attained vast popularity from the age of Jackson through the century. (Selection from Clifton Furness, ed., *The Genteel Female*, 1931.)

LETTER WRITING AND ETIQUETTE—A SAMPLING

Letter Congratulating a Friend upon Finding a Lost Child

MY DEAR MRS. WILTON:

Mr. Baird has just come in with the good news that you have found darling Essie, poor little frightened child! I *must* send a word or two to say how glad I was that your agony of fright and suspense has ended so happily. Nothing but illness could have kept me from you at such a crucial time, and I have suffered most cruelly with anxiety and inability to go to you. But thanks to an over-ruling Providence, your little darling is once more safe in your arms. God bless Essie!

Most sincerely do I congratulate you.

Affectionately,
ELLEN BAIRD.

Answer to a Letter of Condolence on the Loss of a Limb

MY DEAR MRS. STACEY:

My right arm being still spared me, I can write you myself in answer to your loving letter of sympathy. I am not very graceful just now in my movements, and feel decidedly, lop-sided, but dear Mother and Marion will scarcely let me miss my deleted arm and hand, they are so quick to guess my wants, so constant in their care of me.

When I think of the "might have been," and recall the scenes of horror in which so many of my fellow-travellers lost their lives, I am most deeply grateful that my own loss was so comparatively slight.

I am learning to make one limb do the work of two, and my general health is quite restored, so you see I am not so very much to be pitied, though it is very sweet to me to know my friends are so sorry for me.

Hoping to see you soon, maimed as I am,

Ever yours affectionately,
MARY JANE LEVY.

A Letter From An Abandoned Female: To Mrs. M. Wharton

Tuesday

My Honored and Dear Mamma,

In what words, in what language shall I address you? Repentance comes too late, when it cannot prevent the evil lamented. For your kindness, your more than maternal affection toward me, from my infancy to the present moment, a long life of filial duty and unswerving rectitude could hardly compensate. Your kind endeavors to promote my happiness have been repaid by the inexcusable folly of sacrificing it. The various emotions of shame, and remorse, penitence and regret, which torture and distract my guilty breast, exceed description. Yes, madam, your Eliza has fallen, fallen, indeed! She has become the victim of her own indiscretion, and of the intrigue and artifice of a designing libertine, who is the husband of another. She is polluted, and no more worthy of her parentage. At present, I cannot see you. The effect of my crime is too obvious to be longer concealed, to elude the invidious eye of curiosity. This night, therefore, I leave your hospitable mansion. Oh, that the grave were this night to be my lodging! Then I should lie down and be at rest.

Farewell, my dear mamma! pity and pray for your ruined child; and be assured, that affection and gratitude will be the last sentiments, which expire in the breast of your repenting daughter,

ELIZA WHARTON.

Love at First Sight

DEAR MISS HAWLEY:

You will, I trust, forgive this abrupt and plainly spoken letter. Although I have been in your company but once, I cannot forbear writing to you in defiance of all rules of etiquette. Affection is sometimes of slow growth, but sometimes it springs up in a moment. I left you last night with my heart no longer my own. I cannot, of course, hope that I have created any interest in you, but will you do me the great favor to allow me to cultivate your acquaintance? Hoping that you may regard me favorably, I shall await with much anxiety your reply. I remain

Yours Devotedly,

BENSON GOODRICH.

Unfavorable Reply

MR. GOODRICH.

Sir: Your note was a surprise to me, considering that we had never met until last evening, and that then our conversation had been only on commonplace subjects. Your conduct is indeed quite strange. You will please be so kind as to oblige me by not repeating the request, allowing this note to close our correspondence.

MARION HAWLEY.

Favorable Reply

MR. GOODRICH.

Dear Sir: Undoubtedly I ought to call you severely to account for your declaration of love at first sight, but I really cannot find it in my heart to do so, as I must confess that, after our brief interview last evening, I have thought much more of you that I should have been willing to have acknowledged had you not come to the confession first. Seriously speaking, we know but very little of each other yet, and we must be very careful not to exchange our hearts in the dark. I shall be happy to receive you here, as a friend, with a view to our further acquaintance. I remain, dear sir,

MARION HAWLEY.

Lady's Refusal to a Young Man Addicted to Intemperance

MR. SPELLMAN.

Dear Sir:

You kind invitation to accompany you to the opera, to-morrow evening, is received. Under ordinary circumstances, I would be delighted to go with you, believing you at heart to be really a most excellent gentleman. I regret to add, however, that I have undoubted evidence of the fact that you are becoming addicted to the use of the wine-cup. I regard it entirely unsafe for any young lady to continue an intimacy with a young man upon whom is growing the habit of intemperance. With an earnest prayer for your reformation, ere it be too late, I beg you to consider our intimacy at an end.

Respectfully,

HELEN SANFORD.

Behaviour at Concerts and Operas

As soon as you are seated, lay aside wraps, get your opera-glass in readiness, and compose yourself for the evening. The true lover of music does not turn around with every movement in the audience, nor laugh and talk during the performance of any of the numbers. Those who have no music in their souls, but who go to the opera to see the styles and be seen themselves, should remember that etiquette demands of them an entire submission to the rules of time and place. They must listen to the strains that delight other ears in decorous silence . . . and suppress all criticisms until they are beyond the reach of censure from those who are appreciative listeners. Nothing is more ill-bred than the whisperings and tittering of those who are unable to discern the difference between Meyerbeer and Handel. The intensity of feeling displayed by musical people towards those who rudely shatter the silver sphere of sound is appreciated only by the music lover. In an exaltation of sentiment that lifts the spirit almost out of the body, the ear attuned to the lingering melody hears some commonplace voice remark, "We had puddin' for dinner yesterday." Mrs. Stowe relates that she once attended a concert where, just as the music had sunk to a calm of sweetest melody, she heard a female voice say, "I always cook mine in vinegar!"

Piano-Playing

Amateur performers upon the piano should thoroughly commit to memory a few pieces to play independently of notes, as to take sheet-music to a party is a hint that they expect to be invited to play. If possible, have the voice in good condition also, so as not to be obliged to complain of a cold. To eat a small amount of horse-radish just previous to reading, singing or speaking, will quite effectually remove hoarseness.

Any lady-guest being invited to play the piano, it is courtesy for the gentleman nearest her to offer his arm and escort her to the instrument. While she is playing he will hold her bouquet, fan and gloves, and should also turn the leaves if he can readily read music, but he should not attempt it otherwise.

Habits and Manners which Indicate Gentility when Eating

The dinner-hour will completely test the refinement, the culture and good breeding which the lady may possess.

Sit upright, neither too close nor too far away from the table.

Open and spread upon your lap or breast a napkin, if one is provided—otherwise a handkerchief.

Do not be in haste; compose yourself; put your mind into a pleasant condition, and resolve to eat slowly.

Keep the hands from the table until your time comes to be served It is rude to take knife and fork in hand and commence drumming on the table while you are waiting.

Grace will be said by someone present, and the most respectful attention and quietude should be observed until the exercise is passed.

By interchange of thought, much valuable information may be acquired at the table. With social chit-chat and eating, the meal-time should always be prolonged from thirty minutes to an hour.

If soup comes first, and you do not desire it, you will simply say, "No, I thank you," but make no comment; or you may take it and eat as little as you choose. The other course will be along soon.

The soup should be eaten with a medium-sized spoon, so slowly and carefully that you will drop none upon your person or the table-cloth. Making an effort to get the last drop, and all unusual noise when eating, should be avoided.

If furnished with potatoes in small dishes, you will put the skins back into the dish again. Where there are side-dishes all refuse should be placed in them—otherwise potato-skins will be placed upon the table-cloth. If possible, avoid depositing waste matter upon the cloth.

The knife, which is now only used for cutting meat, mashing potatoes, and for a few other purposes at the table, is no longer placed to the mouth by those who give attention to the etiquette of the table; the advantage being that there is less danger to the mouth from using the fork.

What Should Be Avoided When Calling

Do not stare around the room.
Do not take a dog or small child. . . .
Do not lay aside the bonnet. . . .
Do not make a call of ceremony on a wet day. . . .
Do not touch the piano, unless invited to do so.
Do not handle ornaments. . . .
Do not remove the gloves. . . .
Do not, if a lady call upon a gentleman . . . unless he may be a confirmed invalid.

How-to-do-it books have a long history.

Homely Recipes for Genteel Housewives

To kill worms in children: Take sage, boil it with milk to a good tea, turn it to whey with alum or vinegar, and give the whey to the child, if the worms are not knotted in the stomach, and it will be a sure cure. If the worms are knotted in the stomach, it will kill the child.

Cure for puking up food: Take an old pipe, and powder the same—take from half to a teaspoonful on an empty stomach in the morning.

For female weakness or weaknesses: Take two or two and a half pails full of double tansy closely packed in a pot, put on a tin still, draw out two quarts of essence, add a quarter of spirits or less, so as to keep it, cork it up. Take a glass at a time, half an hour before eating two or three times a day, and thus continue till you take a quart or more. If you use single tansy you must use twice the quantity above mentioned.

Lydia Sigourney was the most popular woman poet of her age—one rich in popular women poets. She mined a rich vein of romantic sentiment. These outpourings of sentimental verse are dreadful to modern tastes, but contemporaries bought them and apparently read them. (From Lydia Sigourney, *The Token*, 1834.)

A SENTIMENTAL POEM

The Orphans

'Sister, when I go to rest,
The last image in my breast
Is of a hand that gently spread
The covering o'er my cradle bed;
And of a bosom soft and kind,
On which my infant head reclined.
And ever, when I wake, my theme,
As of some dear and blissful dream,
Is of a tone prolong'd and clear,
Sweet and birdlike to my ear,
Of a fond kiss,—it was not thine—
And murmur of the Name divine—
Sister, you remember well—
Tell me of our parents, tell.'

'Alas, of him, our early guide,
Few tints hath memory's scroll supplied.
A tender smile, a glance, whose pain

Could well my wayward moods restrain.
Fair gifts that still unsullied shine,
In childhood's books some pencill'd line,
And then a burst of bitter woe—
Knell, coffin, and procession slow—
And this is all of him who sleeps
Where yonder drooping willow weeps.
But of that blessed one who gave
Our father to the lowly grave,
So strong with every thought is wove
The tireless teachings of her love,
With every fibre of the mind,
So close her sigh, her prayer entwined,
That my whole being's secret store
Seems by her pencil written o'er:—
And if, within my heart there springs
Some chasten'd love of holy things,
She sow'd the seed, with mild control,
That patient florist of the soul.
    'Sweetest, let me dry thy tear,
Thou art like that mother dear,
And I fain would be thee,
What that mother was to me.'

entertainment

Domesticity became a virtual ideology for women: manners, home, and children would define their lives. Yet the revolt against domesticity begins in this generation as well, as both the women's rights movement and songs like "Life is a Toil" illustrate. (Selections from National Magazine, *Heart Songs*, 1909.)

DOMESTICITY

Be Kind to the Loved Ones at Home

1   Be kind to thy father, for when thou wert young,
Who lov'd thee so fondly as he?
He caught the first accents that fell from thy tongue,
And joined in thy innocent glee.
Be kind to thy father, for now he is old,
His locks intermingled with gray;
His footsteps are feeble, once fearless and bold,
Thy father is passing away.

2   Be kind to thy mother, for lo! on her brow
May traces of sorrow be seen;
Oh, well may'st thou cherish and comfort her now,
For loving and kind hath she been.
Remember thy mother, for thee will she pray,
As long as God giveth her breath;
With accents of kindness then cheer her lone way,
E'en to the dark valley of death.

3   Be kind to thy brother, his heart will have dearth,
If the smile of thy joy be withdrawn;
The flowers of feeling will fade at their birth,
If the dew of affection be gone.
Be kind to thy brother, wherever you are,
The love of a brother shall be
An ornament purer and richer by far
Than pearls from the depth of the sea.

4   Be kind to thy sister, not many may know
    The depth of true sisterly love;
    The wealth of the ocean lies fathoms below
    The surface that sparkles above.
    Be kind to thy father, once fearless and bold,
    Be kind to thy mother so near;
    Be kind to thy brother, nor show thy heart cold,
    Be kind to thy sister so dear.

Life Is A Toil

1   One day as I wandered, I heard a complaining,
    and saw an old woman, the picture of gloom.
    She gazed at the mud on her doorstep (t'was raining)
    and this was her song as she wielded her broom:

Chorus
"Oh, life is a toil and love is a trouble,
And beauty will fade and riches will flee.
Oh, pleasures they dwindle and prices they double,
And nothing is as I could wish it to be.

2   "It's sweeping at six and it's dusting at seven;
    It's victuals at eight and it's dishes at nine.
    It's potting and panning from ten to eleven;
    We scarce break our fast till we plan how to dine.

3   "There's too much of worriment goes in a bonnet;
    There's too much of ironing goes in a shirt.
    There's nothing that pays for the time you waste on it;
    There's nothing that lasts us but trouble and dirt.

4   "In March it is mud, it is snow in December;
    The mid-summer breezes are loaded with dust.
    In fall the leaves litter; in rainy September
    The wallpaper rots and the candlesticks rust.

5   "Last night in my dreams I was stationed forever
    On a far litle isle in the midst of the sea.
    My one chance for life was a ceaseless endeavor
    To sweep off the waves ere they swept over me.

6   "Alas, 'twas no dream, for ahead I behold it;
     I know I am helpless my fate to avert."
     She put down her broom and her apron she folded,
     Then lay down and died, and was buried in dirt.

Some things never seem to change. . . . (From *National Intelligencer*, Washington, D.C., November 20, 1805.)

HAIR AGAIN

Before a general court martial, of which lieut. col. Freeman was president, held at New Orleans on the 1st, and continued to the 10th of July, 1805, col. Thomas Butler, of the 2d Regiment of Infantry, was tried on the following charges, viz.

Charge 1st—Wilful, obstinate and continued disobedience of the general order of the 30th of April, 1801, for regulating the cut of the hair, and also disobedience to the order of 1st Feb. 1804.

Specification—By refusing to conform the cut of his hair, to the general order of the 30th April, 1801, as directed in the order of the 1st Feb. 1804, contumaciously resisting the authority of these orders, after he had been tried by a general court martial, found guilty of disobedience of the general order of the 30th April, 1801, and sentenced to be reprimanded in general orders.

Charge 2d—Mutinous conduct.

Specification—By appearing publicly in command of the troops, in the city of New Orleans, with his hair cued in direct and open violation of the general order of the 30th of April, 1801, and of the 1st Feb. 1804 —thereby giving an example of disrespect and contempt to the orders and authority of the commanding general, tending to dissever the bands of military subordination, to impair the forces of those obligations by which military men are bound to obedience, and to excite a spirit of sedition and mutiny in the army of the United States.

The prisoner pleaded not guilty, and the court passed the following sentence, viz.

The court having maturely weighed and considered what hath appeared before them in evidence, during the course of the prosecution, as well as what the prisoner, Col. Thomas Butler, hath urged in his defence are of opinion that he is guilty of wilful, obstinate and continued disobedience to the general order of the 30th of April, 1801, for regulating the cut of the hair, and also of disobedience to the general order of the 1st Feb. 1804, as set forth in the first charge and specification, whereon he has been arraigned; the court also finds him guilty of mutinous conduct, in appearing publicly in command of the troops at the city of New Orleans, with his hair cued, in direct and open violation of the general order of the 30th of April, 1801, and 1st Feb. 1804, as stated in the 2d charge and part of the 2d specification; and thereupon they do in consequence adjudge and sentence him to be suspended from all command, pay and emoluments for the space of twelve calendar months, to commence from and immediately after the promulgation of this sentence. The General confirms the sentence of the general court martial, and the court is dissolved.

(signed) Jas. Wilkinson

Phineas T. Barnum, the legendary American showman, was a master at generating publicity and at conning the semi-literate public of his day. His saying that "There's a sucker born every minute" has inspired generations of Americans. (Selection from P. T. Barnum, *Struggles and Triumphs*, 1884.)

PHINEAS T. BARNUM

I thoroughly understood the art of advertising, not merely by means of printer's ink, which I have always used freely, and to which I confess myself so much indebted for my success, but by turning every possible circumstance to my account. It was my monomania to make the Museum the town wonder and town talk. I often seized upon an opportunity by instinct, even before I had a very definite conception as to how it should be used, and it seemed, somehow, to mature itself and serve my purpose. As an illustration, one morning a stout, hearty-looking man came into my ticket-office and begged some money. I asked him why he did not work and earn his living? He replied that he could get nothing to do, and that he would be glad of any job at a dollar a day. I handed him a quarter of a dollar, told him to go and get his breakfast and return, and I would employ him, at light labor, at a dollar and a half a day. When he returned I gave him five common bricks.

"Now," said I, "go and lay a brick on the sidewalk, at the corner of Broadway and Ann street; another close by the Museum; a third diagonally across the way, at the corner of Broadway and Vesey street, by the Astor House; put down the fourth on the sidewalk, in front of St. Paul's Church, opposite; then, with the fifth brick in hand, take up a rapid march from one point to the other, making the circuit, exchanging your brick at every point, and say nothing to any one.

"What is the object of this?" inquired the man.

"No matter," I replied; "all you need to know is that it brings you fifteen cents wages per hour. It is a bit of my fun, and to assist me properly you must seem to be as deaf as a post; wear a serious countenance; answer no questions; pay no attention to any one; but attend faithfully to the work, and at the end of every hour, by St. Paul's clock, show this ticket at the Museum door; enter, walking solemnly through every hall in the building; pass out, and resume your work."

With the remark that it was "all one to him, so long as he could earn his living," the man placed his bricks, and began his round. Half an hour afterwards, at least five hundred people were watching his mysterious movements. He had assumed a military step and bearing, and, looking as sober as a judge, he made no response whatever to the constant inquiries as to the object of his singular conduct. At the end of the first hour, the sidewalks in the vicinity were packed with people, all anxious to solve the mystery. The man, as directed, then went into the Museum, devoting fifteen minutes to a solemn survey of the halls, and afterwards returning to his round. This was repeated every hour till sundown, and whenever the man went into the Museum a dozen or more persons would buy tickets and follow him, hoping to gratify their curiosity in regard to the purpose of his movements. This was continued for several days—the curious people who followed the man into the Museum considerably more than paying his wages—till finally the policeman, to whom I had imparted my object, complained that the obstruction of the sidewalk by crowds, had become so serious that I must call in my "brick man." This trivial incident excited considerable talk and amusement; it advertised me; and it materially advanced my purpose of making a lively corner near the Museum.

The stories illustrating merely my introduction of novelties would more than fill this book, but I must make room for a few of them.

An actor, named La Rue, presented himself as an imitator of celebrated histrionic personages, including Macready, Forrest, Kemble, the elder Booth, Kean, Hamblin and others. Taking him into the green-room for a private rehearsal, and finding his imitations excellent, I engaged him. For three nights he gave great satisfaction, but early in the fourth evening he staggered into the Museum so drunk that he could hardly stand, and in half an hour he must be on the stage! Calling an assistant, we took La Rue between us, and marched him up Broadway as far as Chambers street, and back to the lower end of the Park, hoping to sober him. At this point we put his head under a pump, and gave him a good ducking, with visible beneficial effect—then a walk around the Park, and another ducking,—when he assured me that he should be able to give his imitations "to a charm."

"You drunken brute," said I, "if you fail, and disappoint my audience, I will throw you out of the window."

He declared that he was "all right," and I led him behind the scenes, where I waited with considerable trepidation to watch his movements on the stage. He began by saying:

"Ladies and gentlemen: I will now give you an imitation of Mr. Booth, the eminent tragedian."

His tongue was thick, his language somewhat incoherent, and I had great misgivings as he proceeded; but as no token of disapprobation came from the audience, I began to hope he would go through with his parts without exciting suspicion of his condition. But before he had half finished his presentation of Booth, in the soliloquy in the opening act of Richard III, the house discovered that he was very drunk, and began to hiss. This only seemed to stimulate him to make an effort to appear sober, which, as is usual in such cases, only made matters worse, and the hissing increased. I lost all patience, and going on the stage and taking the drunken fellow by the collar, I apologized to the audience, assuring them that he should not appear before them again. I was about to march him off, when he stepped to the front, and said:

"Ladies and gentlemen: Mr. Booth often appeared on the stage in a state of inebriety, and I was simply giving you a truthful representation of him on such occasions. I beg to be permitted to proceed with my imitations."

The audience at once supposed it was all right, and cried out, "go on, go on": which he did, and at every imitation of Booth, whether as Richard, Shylock, or Sir Giles Overreach, he received a hearty round of applause. I was quite delighted with his success; but when he came to imitate Forrest and Hamblin, necessarily representing them as drunk also, the audience could be no longer deluded; the hissing was almost deafening, and I was forced to lead the actor off. It was his last appearance on my stage.

I determined to make people talk about my Museum; to exclaim over its wonders; to have men and women all over the country say: "There is not another place in the United States where so much can be seen for twenty-five cents as in Barnum's American Museum." It was the best advertisement I could possibly have, and one for which I could afford to pay. I knew, too, that it was an honorable advertisement, because it was as deserved as it was spontaneous. And so, in addition to the permanent collection and the ordinary attractions of the stage, I labored to keep the Museum well supplied with transient novelties; I exhibited such living curiosities as a rhinoceros, giraffes, grizzly bears, ourangoutangs, great serpents and whatever else of the kind money would buy or enterprise secure.

It was the world's way then, as it is now, to excite the community with flaming posters, promising almost everything for next to nothing. I confess that I took no pains to set my enterprising fellow-citizens a better example. I fell in with the world's way; and if my "puffing" was more persistent, my advertising more audacious, my posters more glaring, my pictures more exaggerated, my flags more patriotic and my transparencies more brilliant than they would have been under the management of my neighbors, it was not because I had less scruple than they, but more energy, far more ingenuity, and a better foundation for such promises. In all this, if I cannot be justified, I at least find palliation in the fact that I presented a wilderness of wonderful, instructive and amusing realities of such evident and marked merit that I have yet to learn of a single instance where a visitor went away from the Museum complaining that he had been defrauded of his money. Surely this is an offset to any eccentricities to which I may have resorted to make my establishment widely known.

Very soon after introducing my extra exhibitions, I purchased for $200, a curiosity which had much merit and some absurdity. It was a model of Niagara Falls, in which the merit was that the proportions of the great cataract, the trees, rocks, and buildings in the vicinity were mathematically given, while the absurdity was in introducing "real water" to represent the falls. Yet the model served a purpose in making "a good line in the bill"—an end in view which was never neglected—and it helped to give the Museum notoriety. One day I was summoned to appear before the Board of Croton Water Commissioners, and was informed that as I paid only $25 per annum for water at the Museum, I must pay a large extra compensation for the supply for my Niagara Falls. I begged the board not to believe all that appeared in the papers, nor to interpret my showbills too literally, and assured them that a single barrel of water, if my pump was in good order, would furnish my falls for a month.

It was even so, for the water flowed into a reservoir behind the scenes, and was forced back with a pump over the falls. On one occasion, Mr. Louis Gaylord Clark, the editor of the *Knickerbocker,* came to view my Museum, and introduced himself to me. As I was quite anxious that my establishment should receive a first-rate notice at his hands, I took pains to show him everything of interest, except the Niagara Falls, which I feared would prejudice him against my entire show. But as we passed the room, the pump was at work, warning me that the great cataract was in full operation, and Clark, to my dismay, insisted upon seeing it.

"Well, Barnum, I declare, this is quite a new idea; I never saw the like before."

"No?" I faintly inquired, with something like reviving hope.

"No," said Clark, "and I hope, with all my heart, I never shall again."

But the *Knickerbocker* spoke kindly of me, and refrained from all allusions to "the Cataract of Niagara, with real water." Some months after, Clark came in breathless one day, and asked me if I had the club with which Captain Cook was killed? As I had a lot of Indian war clubs in the collection of aboriginal curiosities, and owing Clark something on the old Niagara Falls account, I told him I had the veritable club, with documents which placed its identity beyond question, and I showed him the warlike weapon.

"Poor Cook! Poor Cook!" said Clark, musingly. "Well, Mr. Barnum," he continued, with great gravity, at the same time extending his hand and giving mine a hearty shake, "I am really very much obliged to you for your kindness. I had an irrepressible desire to see the club that killed Captain Cook, and I felt quite confident you could accommodate me. I have been in half a dozen smaller museums, and as they all had it, I was sure such a large establishment like yours would not be without it."

A few weeks afterwards, I wrote to Clark that if he would come to my office I was anxious to consult him on a matter of great importance. He came, and I said:

"Now, I don't want any of your nonsense, but I want your sober advice."

He assured me that he would serve me in any way in his power, and I proceeded to tell him about a wonderful fish from the Nile, offered to me for exhibition at $100 a week, the owner of which was willing to forfeit $5,000, if, within six weeks, this fish did not pass through a transformation in which the tail would disappear and the fish would then have legs.

"Is it possible!" asked the astonished Clark.

I assured him that there was no doubt of it.

Thereupon he advised me to engage the wonder at any price; that it would startle the naturalists, wake up the whole scientific world, draw in the masses, and make $20,000 for the Museum. I told him I thought well of the speculation, only I did not like the name of the fish.

"That makes no difference whatever," said Clark; "what is the name of the fish?"

"Tadpole," I replied, with becoming gravity, "but it is vulgarly called 'pollywog.'"

"Sold, by thunder!" exclaimed Clark, and he left.

A curiosity, which in an extraordinary degree served my ever-present object of extending the notoriety of the Museum, was the so-called "Feejee Mermaid." It has been supposed that this mermaid was manufactured by my order, but such is not the fact. I was known as a successful showman, and strange things of every sort were brought to me from all quarters, for sale or exhibition. In the summer of 1842, Mr. Moses Kimball, of the Boston Museum, came to New York and showed me what purported to be a mermaid. He had bought it from a sailor, whose father, a sea captain, had purchased it in Calcutta, in 1822, from some Japanese sailors. I may mention here that this identical preserved specimen was exhibited in London in 1822, as I fully verified in my visit to that city in 1858, for I found an advertisement of it in an old file of the London *Times,* and a friend gave me a copy of the *Mirror,* published by J. Limbird, 335 Strand, November 9, 1822, containing a cut of this same creature and two pages of letterpress describing it, together with an account of other mermaids said to have been captured in different parts of the world. The *Mirror* stated that this specimen was "the great source of attraction in the British metropolis, and three to four hundred people every day paid their shilling to see it."

This was the curiosity which had fallen into Mr. Kimball's hands. I requested my naturalist's opinion of the genuineness of the animal, and he said he could not conceive how it could have been manufactured, for he never saw a monkey with such peculiar teeth, arms, hands, etc., and he never saw a fish with such peculiar fins; but he did not believe in mermaids. Nevertheless, I concluded to hire this curiosity and to modify the general incredulity as to the possibility of the existence of mermaids, and to awaken curiosity to see and examine the specimen, I invoked the potent power of printer's ink.

Since Japan has been opened to the outer world, it has been discovered that certain "artists" in that country manufacture a great variety of fabulous animals, with an ingenuity and mechanical perfection well calculated to deceive. No doubt my mermaid was a specimen of this curious manufacture. I used it mainly to advertise the regular business of the Museum, and this effective indirect advertising is the only feature I can commend, in a special show of which, I confess, I am not proud. Newspapers throughout the country copied the mermaid notices, for they were novel and caught the attention of readers. Thus was the fame of the Museum, as well as the mermaid, wafted from one end of the land to the other. I was careful to keep up the excitement, for I knew that every dollar sown in advertising would return in tens, and perhaps hundreds, in a future harvest, and after obtaining all the notoriety possible by advertising and by exhibiting the mermaid at the Museum, I sent the curiosity throughout the country, directing my agent to everywhere advertise it as "From Barnum's Great American Museum, New York." The effect was immediately felt; money flowed in rapidly, and was readily expended in more advertising.

When I became proprietor of the establishment, there were only the words: "American Museum," to indicate the character of the concern; there was no bustle or activity about the place; no posters to announce what was to be seen;— the whole exterior was as dead as the skeletons and stuffed skins within. My experiences had taught me the advantages of advertising. I printed whole columns in the papers, setting forth the wonders of my establishment. Old "fogies" opened their eyes in amazement at a man who could expend hundreds of dollars in announcing a show of "stuffed monkey skins"; but these same old fogies paid their quarters, nevertheless, and when they saw the curiosities and novelties in the Museum halls, they, like all other visitors, were astonished as well as pleased, and went home and told their friends and neighbors, and thus assisted in advertising my business.

Other and not less effective advertising,—flags and banners,—began to adorn the exterior of the building. I kept a band of music on the front balcony and announced "Free Music for the Million." People said, "Well, that Barnum is a liberal fellow to give us music for nothing," and they flocked down to hear my outdoor free concerts. But I took pains to select and maintain the poorest band I could find—one whose discordant notes would drive the crowd into the Museum, out of earshot of my outside orchestra. Of course, the music was poor. When people expect to get "something for nothing" they are sure to be cheated. Powerful Drummond lights were placed at the top of the Museum, which, in the darkest night, threw a flood of light up and down Broadway, from the Battery to Niblo's, that would enable one to read a newspaper in the street. These were the first Drummond lights ever seen in New York, and they made people talk, and so advertised my Museum.

The Road to Riches

The American Museum was the ladder by which I rose to fortune. Whenever I cross Broadway at the head of Vesey street, and see the *Herald* building and that gorgeous pile, the Park Bank, my mind's eye recalls that less solid, more showy edifice which once occupied the site, and was covered with pictures of all manner of beasts, birds and creeping things, and in which were treasures that brought treasures and notoriety and pleasant hours to me. The Jenny Lind enterprise was more audacious, more immediately remunerative, and I remember it with a pride which I do not attempt to conceal; but instinctively I often go back and live over again the old days of my struggles and triumphs in the American Museum.

The Museum was always open at sunrise, and this was so well known throughout the country that strangers coming to the city would often take a tour through my halls before going to breakfast or to their hotels. I do not believe there was ever a more truly popular place of amusement. I frequently compared the annual number of visitors with the number officially reported as visiting (free of charge) the British Museum in London, and my list was invariably the larger. Nor do I believe that any man or manager ever labored more industriously to please his patrons. I furnished the most attractive exhibitions which money could procure; I abolished all vulgarity and profanity from the stage, and I prided myself upon the fact, that parents and children could attend the dramatic performances in the so-called Lecture Room, and not be shocked or offended by anything they might see or hear; I introduced the "Moral Drama," producing such plays as "The Drunkard," "Uncle Tom's Cabin," "Moses in Egypt," "Joseph and his Brethren," and occasional spectacular melodramas produced with great care at considerable outlay.

Mr. Sothern, who has since attained such wide-spread celebrity at home and abroad as a character actor, was a member of my dramatic company for one or two seasons. Mr. Barney Williams began his theatrical career at the Museum, occupying, at first, quite a subordinate position, at a salary of ten dollars a week. During the past twelve or fifteen years, I presume his weekly receipts, when he has acted, have been nearly $3,000. The late Miss Mary Gannon also commenced at the Museum, and many more actors and actresses of celebrity have been, from time to time, engaged there. What was once the small Lecture Room was converted into a spacious and beautiful theater, extending over the lots adjoining the Museum, and capable of holding about three thousand persons. The saloons were greatly multiplied and enlarged, and the "egress" having been made to work to perfection, on holidays I advertised Lecture Room performances every hour through the afternoon and evening, and consequently the actors and actresses were dressed for the stage as early as eleven o'clock in the morning, and did not resume their ordinary clothes till ten o'clock at night. In these busy days the meals for the company were brought in and served in the dressing-rooms and green-rooms, and the company always received extra pay.

I confess that I liked the Museum mainly for the opportunities it afforded for rapidly making money. Before I bought it, I weighed the matter well in my mind, and was convinced that I could present to the

American public such a variety, quantity and quality of amusement, blended with instruction, "all for twenty-five cents, children half price," that my attractions would be irresistible, and my fortune certain. I myself relished a higher grade of amusement, and I was a frequent attendant at the opera, first-class concerts, lectures, and the like; but I worked for the million, and I knew the only way to make a million from my patrons was to give them abundant and wholesome attractions for a small sum of money.

About the first of July, 1842, I began to make arrangements for extra novelties, additional performances, a large amount of extra advertising, and an out-door display for the "Glorious Fourth." Large parti-colored bills were ordered, transparencies were prepared, the free band of music was augmented by a trumpeter, and columns of advertisements, headed with large capitals, were written and put on file.

I wanted to run out a string of American flags across the street on that day, for I knew there would be thousands of people passing the Museum with leisure and pocket-money, and I felt confident that an unusual display of national flags would arrest their patriotic attention, and bring many of them within my walls. Unfortunately for my purpose, St. Paul's Church stood directly opposite, and there was nothing to which I could attach my flag-rope, unless it might be one of the trees in the church-yard. I went to the vestrymen for permission to so attach my flag-rope on the Fourth of July, and they were indignant at what they called my "insulting proposition"; such a concession would be "sacrilege." I plied them with arguments, and appealed to their patriotism, but in vain.

Returning to the Museum, I gave orders to have the string of flags made ready, with directions at daylight on the Fourth of July to attach one end of the rope to one of the third-story windows of the Museum, and the other end to a tree in St. Paul's churchyard. The great day arrived, and my orders were strictly followed. The flags attracted great attention. By half-past nine Broadway was thronged, and about that time two gentlemen, in a high state of excitement, rushed into my office, announcing themselves as injured and insulted vestrymen of St. Paul's Church.

"Keep cool, gentlemen," said I; "I guess it is all right."

"Right!" indignantly exclaimed one of them, "do you think it is right to attach your Museum to our Church! We will show you what is 'right' and what is law, if we live till to-morrow; those flags must come down instantly."

"Thank you," I said, "but let us not be in a hurry. I will go out with you and look at them, and I guess we can make it all right."

Going into the street, I remarked: "Really, gentlemen, these flags look very beautiful; they do not injure your tree; I always stop my balcony music for your accommodation whenever you hold week-day services, and it is but fair that you should return the favor."

"We could indict your 'music,' as you call it, as a nuisance, if we chose," answered one vestryman, "and now I tell you that if these flags are not taken down in ten minutes, I will cut them down."

His indignation was at boiling point. The crowd in the street was dense, and the angry gesticulation of the vestryman attracted their attention. I saw there was no use in trying to parley with him or coax him, and so, assuming an angry air, I rolled up my sleeves and exclaimed, in a loud tone,

"Well, Mister, I should just like to see you dare to cut down the American flag on the Fourth of July; you must be a 'Britisher' to make such a threat as that; but I'll show you a thousand pairs of Yankee hands in two minutes, if you dare to attempt to take down the stars and stripes on this great birth-day of American freedom!"

"What's that John Bull a-saying?" asked a brawny fellow, placing himself in front of the irate vestryman. "Look here, old fellow," he continued, "if you want to save a whole bone in your body, you had better slope, and never dare to talk again about hauling down the American flag in the city of New York."

Throngs of excited, exasperated men crowded around, and the vestryman, seeing the effect of my ruse, smiled faintly and said, "Oh, of course it is all right," and he and his companion quietly edged out of the crowd.

On that Fourth of July, at one o'clock P.M., my Museum was so densely crowded that we could admit no more visitors, and we were compelled to stop the sale of tickets. Looking down into the street it was a sad sight to see the thousands of people who stood ready with their money to enter the Museum, but who were actually turned away. It was exceedingly harrowing to my feelings. Rushing down stairs, I told my carpenter and his assistants to cut through the partition and floor in the rear and to put in a temporary flight of stairs so as to let out people by that egress into Ann street. By three o'clock the egress was opened, and a few people were passed down the new stairs, while a corresponding number came in at the front. But I lost a large amount of money that day by not having sufficiently estimated the value of my own advertising, and consequently not having provided for the thousands who had read my announcements and seen my outside show, and had taken the first leisure day to visit the Museum. I had learned one lesson, however, and that was to have the egress ready on future holidays.

Early in the following March I received notice from some of the Irish population that they meant to visit me in great numbers on "St. Patrick's day in the morning." "All right," said I to my carpenter, "get your egress ready for March 17"; and I added, to my assistant manager: "If there is much of a crowd, don't let a single person pass out at the front, even if it were St. Patrick himself; put every man out through the egress in the rear." The day came, and before noon we were caught in the same dilemma as we were on the Fourth of July; the Museum was jammed, and the sale of tickets was stopped. I went to the egress and asked the sentinel how many hundreds had passed out?

"Hundreds," he replied, "why only three persons have gone out by this way and they came back, saying that it was a mistake and begging to be let in again."

"What does this mean?" I inquired; "surely thousands of people have been all over the Museum since they came in."

"Certainly," was the reply, "but after they have gone from one saloon to another, and have been on every floor, even to the roof, they come down and travel the same route over again."

At this time I espied a tall Irish woman with two good-sized children whom I had happened to notice when they came early in the morning."

"Step this way, madam," said I, politely, "you will never be able to get into the street by the front door without crushing these dear children. We have opened a large egress here, and you can pass by these rear stairs into Ann street and thus avoid all danger."

"Sure," replied the woman, indignantly, "an' I'm not going out at all, at all, nor the children aither, for we've brought our dinners and we are going to stay all day."

Further investigation showed that pretty much all of my visitors had brought their dinners with the evident intention of literally "making a day of it." No one expected to go home till night; the building was overcrowded, and meanwhile hundreds were waiting at the front entrance to get in when they could. In despair I sauntered upon the stage behind the scenes, biting my lips with vexation, when I happened to see the scene-painter at work and a happy thought struck me: "Here," I exclaimed, "take a piece of canvas four feet square, and paint on it, as soon as you can, in large letters,

To the Egress

Seizing his brush, he finished the sign in fifteen minutes, and I directed the carpenter to nail it over the door leading to the back stairs. He did so, and as the crowd, after making the entire tour of the establishment, came pouring down the main stairs from the third story, they stopped and looked at the new sign, while some of them read audibly: "To the Aigress."

"The Aigress," said others, "sure that's an animal we haven't seen," and the throng began to pour down the back stairs only to find that the "Aigress" was the elephant, and that the elephant was all out o'doors, or so much of it as began with Ann street. Meanwhile, I began to accommodate those who had long been waiting with their money at the Broadway entrance.

Money poured in upon me so rapidly that I was sometimes actually embarrassed to devise means to carry out my original plan for laying out the entire profits of the first year in advertising. I meant to sow first and reap afterwards. I finally hit upon a plan which cost a large sum, and that was to prepare large oval oil paintings to be placed between the windows of the entire building, representing nearly every important animal known in zoology. These paintings were put on the building in a single night, and so complete a transformation in the appearance of an edifice is seldom witnessed. When the living stream rolled down Broadway the next morning and reached the Astor House corner, opposite the Museum, it seemed to meet with a sudden check. I never before saw so many open mouths and astonished eyes. Some people were puzzled to know what it all meant; some looked as if they thought it was an enchanted palace that had suddenly sprung up; others exclaimed, "Well, the animals all seem to have 'broken out' last night," and hundreds came in to see how the establishment survived the sudden eruption.

From that morning the Museum receipts took a jump forward of nearly a hundred dollars a day, and they never fell back again.

Stephen Collins Foster is one of the few nineteenth-century songwriters whose works are still played. Many of his songs were written for minstrel shows, the most popular form of midcentury entertainment, and contain the kind of good-natured patronizing of blacks that is no longer tolerable. His love songs were written, essentially, for amateurs to sing at home—unlike so much of the popular music of the twentieth century. (Selections from National Magazine, *Heart Songs*, 1909.)

STEPHEN FOSTER SONGS

Massa's in de Cold Ground

1   Round de meadows am a-ringing
    De darkey's mournful song,
    While de mockingbird am singing,
    Happy as de day am long.

Where de ivy am a-creeping
O'er de grassy mound,
Dare old massa am a-sleeping,
Sleeping in de cold, cold ground.

Chorus

Down in de cornfield
Hear dat mournful sound;
All de darkeys am a-weeping,
Massa's in de cold, cold ground.

2 When de autumn leaves were falling,
When de days were cold,
'Twas hard to hear old massa calling,
Cayse he was so weak and old.
Now de orange trees am blooming,
On de sandy shore,
Now de summer days am coming,
Massa neber calls no more.

3 Massa make de darkeys love him,
Cayse he was so kind;
Now, dey sadly weep above him,
Mourning cayse he leave dem behind.
I cannot work before tomorrow,
Cayse de teardrop flow;
I try to drive away my sorrow,
Pickin' on de old banjo.

The Old Folks at Home

1 Way down upon the Swanee ribber,
Far, far away,
Dere's wha my heart is turning ebber,
Dere's wha de old folks stay;
All up and down de whole creation,
Sadly I roam,
Still longing for de old plantation,
And for de old folks at home.

Chorus

All de world am sad and weary,

Eb'rywhere I roam,
Oh! darkies, how my heart grows weary,
Far from the old folks at home.

2   All round the little farm I wander'd,
When I was young,
Den many happy days I squander'd,
Many de songs I sung;
When I was playing wid my brudder,
Happy was I.
Oh! take me to my kind old mudder,
Dere let me live and die.

3   One little hut among de bushes,
One dat I love,
Still sadly to my mem'ry rushes,
No matter where I rove;
When will I see de bees a humming,
All round de comb!
When will I hear de banjo tumming
Down in my good old home.

Beautiful Dreamer

1   Beautiful dreamer, wake unto me,
Starlight and dewdrops are waiting for thee;
Sounds of the rude world heard in the day,
Lull'd by the moonlight, have all pass'd away!
Beautiful dreamer, queen of my song,
List while I woo thee with soft melody;
Gone are the cares of life's busy throng,
Beautiful dreamer, awake unto me!
Beautiful dreamer, awake unto me.

2   Beautiful dreamer, out of the sea
Mermaids are chanting the wide lorelie;
Over the streamlet vapors are borne,
Waiting to fade at the bright coming morn.
Beautiful dreamer, beam on my heart,
E'en as the morn on the streamlet and sea;
Then will all clouds of sorrow depart,
Beautiful dreamer, awake unto me!
Beautiful dreamer, awake unto me.

Jeanie with the Light Brown Hair

1 I dream of Jeanie with the light brown hair,
Borne, like a vapor, on the summer air;
I see her tripping where the bright streams play,
Happy as the daisies that dance on her way.
Many were the wild notes her merry voice would pour,
Many were the blithe birds that warbled them o'er:
Oh! I dream of Jeanie with the light brown hair,
Floating, like a vapor, on the soft summer air.

2 I long for Jeanie with the daydawn smile,
Radiant in gladness, warm with winning guile;
I hear her melodies, like joys gone by,
Sighing 'round my heart o'er the fond hopes that die;
Sighing like the night wind and sobbing like the rain,
Wailing for the lost one that comes not again:
Oh! I long for Jeanie and my heart bows low,
Nevermore to find her where the bright waters flow.

3 I sigh for Jeanie, but her light form strayed
Far from the fond hearts 'round her native glade;
Her smiles have vanished and her sweet songs flown,
Flitting like the dreams that have cheered us and gone.
Now the nodding wild flow'rs may wither on the shore
While her gentle fingers will cull them no more:
Oh! I sigh for Jeanie with the light brown hair,
Floating, like a vapor, on the soft summer air.

Old Black Joe

1 Gone are the days when my heart was young and gay,
Gone are my friends from the cotton fields away,
Gone from the earth to a better land I know,
I hear their gentle voices calling "Old Black Joe."

Chorus

I'm coming, I'm coming, for my head is bending low:
I hear those gentle voices calling "Old Black Joe."

2 Why do I weep when my heart should feel no pain,
Why do I sigh that my friends come not again,
Grieving for forms now departed long ago?
I hear their gentle voices calling "Old Black Joe."

3   Where are the hearts once so happy and so free,
The children so dear that I held upon my knee?
Gone to the shore where my soul has longed to go.
I hear their gentle voices calling "Old Black Joe."

The logic of the minstrel shows is simplicity itself: people could make clowns of themselves in blackface in a way that they could not without. These shows were among the most popular entertainments from the 1830s to well after the Civil War. They frequently parodied high culture, as in these Shakespearean takeoffs below. (Selections from Charles Haywood, ed., *Negro Minstrelsy and Shakespearean Burlesque*, 1966.)

BLACK MINSTRELSY

Hamlet: Air—"Jim Crow"

Oh! 'tis consummation
   Devoutly to be wished
To end your heart-ache by a sleep,
   When likely to be dish'd.
Shuffle off your mortal coil,
   Do just so,
Wheel about, and turn about,
   And jump Jim Crow.

Oh! I've seen the guilty creatures
   A sitting at the play,
That struck so to the soul, they did
   Their malefactions say.
Shuffle off your mortal coil,
   And just so,
Show 'em that the play's the thing,
   And jump Jim Crow.

'Tilda Horn

Now I go about, down in the mouth, and stockings down at heel;
Like Massa Shakespeare's Hamlet, too, I'm
   touch'd up here I feel.
His uncle gave him good advice—mine took
   my clothes in pawn;

And all to raise the cash to dress—deceitful
'Tilda Horn.
Oh! this wool I could pull, this poor heart is
so full.

Chorus
But fretting won't do for a darkie of this
figure—
Time enough for that when he gets a little
bigger;
Dancing with the yellow girls and shucking
out the corn,
Will make him forget 'Tilda Horn.

Since the Shakespeare's coming in my head,
I'm like Othello, too,
The victim of my jealous fears, I don't know
what to do;
Desdemona lost his handkerchief—that wasn't
much to lose;
But 'Tilda took my 'bacca-box, my shirts and
Sunday shoes.
Now I stray all the day, from the gay far away.

Chorus.—But fretting won't do, &c.

This dialect humor is a little hard to read, although nowhere near so difficult as the dialect humor about Irishmen, Germans, and blacks that was also popular in mid-nineteenth century. Perhaps slightly educated readers derived satisfaction from being able to detect spelling errors. Besides, much genuine humor got written in this peculiar form which had become a literary convention. (Selections from Charles F. Browne, ed., *Selected Works of Artemus Ward*, 1924.)

DIALECT HUMOR

One of Mr. Ward's Business Letters

To the Editor of the———

Sir—I'm movin along—slowly along—down tords your place. I want you should rite me a letter, sayin how is the show bizniss in your

place. My show at present consists of three moral Bares, a Kangaroo
(a amoozin little Raskal—t'would make you larf yerself to deth to see
the little cuss jump up and squeal) wax figgers of G. Washington Gen.
Taylor John Bunyan Capt. Kidd and Dr. Webster in the act of killin
Dr. Parkman, besides several miscellanyus moral wax statoots of celebrated piruts & murderers, &c., ekalled by few & exceld by none. Now
Mr. Editor, scratch orf a few lines sayin how is the show bizniss down
to your place. I shall hav my hanbills dun at your offiss. Depend upon
it. I want you should git my hanbills up in flamin stile. Also git up a
tremenjus excitemunt in yr. paper 'bowt my onparaleld Show. We must
fetch the public sumhow. We must wurk on their feelins. Cum the moral
on 'em strong. If it's a temprance community tell 'em I sined the pledge
fifteen minits arter Ise born, but on the contery ef your people take their
tods, say Mister Ward is as Jenial a feller as we ever met, full of con-
wiviality, & the life an sole of the Soshul Bored. Take, don't you? If
you say anythin abowt my show say my snaiks is as harmliss as the new
born Babe. What a interestin study it is to see a zewological animil like
a snaik under perfeck subjecshun! My kangaroo is the most larfable little
cuss I ever saw. All for 15 cents. I am anxyus to skewer your inflooounce.
I repeet in regard to them hanbills that I shall git 'em struck orf up to
your printin office. My perliteral sentiments agree with yourn exackly.
I know thay do, becawz I never saw a man whoos didn't.

Respectively yures, A. Ward

P.S.—You scratch my back & Ile scratch your back.

Interview with President Lincoln

I hav no politics. Nary a one. I'm not in the bisiness. If I was
I spose I should holler versiffrusly in the streets at nite and go home
to Betsy Jane smellen of coal ile and gin, in the mornin. I should go to
the Poles arly. I should stay there all day. I should see to it that my
nabers was thar. I should git carriges to take the kripples, the infirm
and the indignant thar. I should be on guard agin frauds and sich. I
should be on the look out for the infamus lise of the enemy, got up
just be4 elecshun for perlitical effeck. When all was over and my can-
dydate was elected, I should move heving & arth—so to speak—until I
got orfice, which if I didn't git a orfice I should turn round and abooze
the Administration with all my mite and maine. But I'm not in the bisniss. I'm in a far more respecful bisniss nor what pollertics is. I wouldn't
giv two cents to be a Congresser. The wuss insult I ever received was
when sertin citizens of Baldinsville axed me to run fur the Legislater.
Sez I, "My frends, dostest think I'd stoop to that there?" They turned as
white as a sheet. I spoke in my most orfullest tones, & they knowd I

wasn't to be trifled with. They slunked out of site to onct.

There4, havin no politics, I made bold to visit Old Abe at his humstid in Springfield. I found the old feller in his parler, surrounded by a perfeck swarm of orfice seekers. Knowin he had been capting of a flat boat on the roarin Mississippy I thought I'd address him in sailor lingo, so sez I "Old Abe, ahoy! Let out yer main-suls, reef hum the forecastle & throw yer jib-poop overboard! Shiver my timbers, my harty!" (N.B. This is ginuine mariner langwidge. I know, becawz I've seen sailor plays acted out by them New York theater fellers.) Old Abe lookt up quite cross & sez, "Send in yer petition by & by. I can't possibly look at it now. Indeed, I can't. It's onpossible sir!"

"Mr. Linkin, who do you spect I air?" sed I.

"A orfice-seeker, to be sure?" sed he.

"Wall, sir," sed I, "you s never more mistaken in your life. You hain't gut a orfis I'd take under no circumstances. I'm A Ward. Wax figgers is my perfeshun. I'm the father of Twins, and they look like me—*both of them.* I cum to pay a frendly visit to the President eleck of the United States. If so be you wants to see me say so—if not, say so, & I'm orf like a jug handle."

"Mr. Ward, sit down. I am glad to see you, Sir."

"Repose in Abraham's Buzzum!" sed one of the orfice seekers, his idee bein to git orf a goak at my expense.

"Wall," sez I, "ef all you fellers repose in that there Buzzum thare'll be mity poor nussin for sum of you!" whereupon Old Abe buttoned his weskit clear up and blusht like a maidin of sweet 16. Jest at this pint of the conversation another swarm of orfice-seekers arrove & cum pilin into the parler. Sum wanted post orfices, sum wanted collectorships, sum wantid furrin missions, and all wanted sumthin. I thought Old Abe would go crazy. He hadn't more than had time to shake hands with 'em, before another tremenjis crowd cum porein onto his premises. His house and dooryard was now perfeckly overflowed with orfice seekers, all clameruss for a immejit interview with Old Abe. One man from Ohio, who had about seven inches of corn whisky into him, mistook me for Old Abe and addrest me as "The Pra-hayrie Flower of the West!" Thinks I *you* want a offiss putty bad. Another man with a gold heded cane and a red nose told Old Abe he was "a seckind Washington & the Pride of the Boundliss West."

Sez I, "Squire, you wouldn't take a small post-offis if you could git it, would you?"

Sez he, "a patrit is abuv them things, sir!"

"There's a putty big crop of patrits this season, aint there Squire?" sez I, when *another* crowd of offiss seekers pored in. The house, dooryard, barn & woodshed was now all full, and when *another* crowd cum

I told 'em not to go away for want of room as the hog-pen was still empty. One patrit from a small town in Michygan went up on top of the house, got into the chimney and slid down into the parler where Old Abe was endeverin to keep the hungry pack of orfice-seekers from chawin him up alive without benefit of clergy. The minit he reached the fire-place he jumpt up, brusht the soot out of his eyes, and yelled: "Don't make eny pintment at the Spunkville postoffiss till you've read my papers. All the respectful men in our town is signers to that there dockyment!"

"Good God!" cride Old Abe, "the cum upon me from the skize—down the chimneys, and from the bowels of the yearth!" He hadn't more'n got them words out of his delikit mouth before two fat offiss-seekers from Wisconsin, in endeverin to crawl atween his legs for the purpuss of applyin for the tollgateship at Milwawky, upsot the President eleck & he would hev gone sprawlin into the fire-place if I hadn't caught him in these arms. But I hadn't morn'n stood him up strate before another man cum crashin down the chimney, his head strikin me vilently agin the inards and prostratin my voluptoous form onto the floor. "Mr. Linkin," shoutid the infatooated being, "my papers is signed by every clergyman in our town, and likewise the skoolmaster!"

Sez I, "you egrejis ass," gittin up & brushin the dust from my eyes, "I'll sign your papers with this bunch of bones, if you don't be a little more keerful how you make my bread basket a depot in the futer. How do you like that air perfumery?" sez I, shuving my fist under his nose. "Them's the kind of papers I'll giv you! Them's the paper's *you* want!"

"But I workt hard for the ticket; I toiled night and day! The patrit should be rewarded!"

"Virtoo," sed I, holdin' the infatooated man by the coat-collar, "virtoo, sir, is its own reward. Look at me!" He did look at me, and qualed be4 my gase. "The fact is," I continued, lookin' round on the hungry crowd, "there is scarcely a offiss for every ile lamp carrid round durin' this campane. I wish thare was. I wish thare was furrin missions to be filled on varis lonely Islands where eppydemics rage incessantly, and if I was in Old Abe's place I'd send every mother's son of you to them. What air you here for?" I continnered, warmin up considerable, "can't you giv Abe a minit's peace? Don't you see he's worrid most to death? Go home, you miserable men, go home & till the sile! Go to peddlin tin-ware—go to choppin wood—go to bilin' sope—stuff sassengers—black boots—git a clerkship on sum respectable manure cart —go round as original Swiss Bell Ringers—becum 'origenal and only' Campbell Minstrels—go to lecturin at 50 dollars a nite—imbark in the peanut bizniss—*write for the Ledger*—saw off your legs and go round givin concerts, with techin appeals to a charitable public, printed on your handbills—anything for a honest living, but don't come round here drivin Old Abe crazy by your outrajis cuttings up! Go home. Stand not upon the order of your goin', but go to onct! If in five minits from this time," sez I pullin' out my new sixteen dollar huntin cased watch, and brandishin' it before their eyes, "Ef in five minits from this time a single sole of you remains on these here premises, I'll go out to my cage near by, and let my Boy Constructor loose! & ef he gits amung you, you'll think old Solferino has cum again and no mistake!" You ought to hev seen them scamper, Mr. Fair. They run orf as tho Satun his self was arter them with a red hot ten pronged pitchfork. In five minits the premises was clear.

"How kin I ever repay you, Mr. Ward, for your kindness?" sed Old Abe, advancin and shakin me warmly by the hand. "How kin I ever repay you, sir?"

"By givin the whole country a good, sound administration. By poerin' ile upon the troubled waturs, North and South. By pursooin' a patriotic, firm, and just course, and then if any State wants to secede, let 'em Sesesh!"

"How 'bout my Cabinit, Mister Ward?" sed Abe.

"Fill it up with Showmen sir! Showmen is devoid of politics. They hain't got any principles! They know how to cater for the public. They know what the public wants, North & South. Showmen, sir, is honest men. Ef you doubt their literary ability, look at their posters, and see small bills! Ef you want a Cabinit as is a Cabinit fill it up with showmen, but don't call on me. The moral wax figger perfeshun musn't be permitted to go down while there's a drop of blood in these vains! A. Linkin, I wish you well! Ef Powers or Walcutt wus to pick out a model for a beautiful man, I scarcely think they'd sculp you; but ef you do the fair thing by your country you'll make as putty a angel as any of us! A. Linkin, use the talents which Nature has put into you judishusly and firmly, and all will be well! A. Linkin, adoo!"

He shook me cordyully by the hand—we exchanged picters, so we could gaze upon each others' liniments when far away from one another—he at the hellum of the ship of State, and I at the hellum of the show bizniss—admittance only 15 cents.

reform

A little theatricality never hurt a reform movement, as Henry Ward Beecher, one of the most theatrical of ministers, demonstrated in Brooklyn in 1847.

BEECHER'S SLAVE AUCTION

Slavery since the early days of New York was the source of frequent discussions. Slave markets had been established and abolished, and pulpit and press had never ceased to discuss the all-important subject. When in 1847 Mr. [Henry Ward] Beecher became the pastor of Plymouth Church, Brooklyn, he frankly stated that he intended to oppose slavery. The majority of the church members agreed with him, but the majority of the people of New York and Brooklyn sympathized with the Southerners, regarding slavery as a patriarchal institution that gave the people of the South leisure to develop into charming ladies and eloquent politicians. Mr. Beecher encountered bitter opposition, and was abused as a Negro worshiper. He was threatened with personal violence, and a mob was formed in New York to tear down his church. Amid these excitements he conceived the idea of giving to the people who came to hear him preach an object lesson in Southern slavery. His idea was that he would sell a slave in Plymouth Church, so that everybody could see what slave dealing really meant, and might be stirred to help to pay for the liberation of some victims of the system.

The first slave auction in Plymouth Church was held on June 1, 1856. Mr. Beecher's intention had become known, and although the service did not begin until after ten o'clock, people had gathered by hundreds two hours before, until the streets on both sides of the church were literally jammed and carriages had to stop a block distant. Thousands had to turn away without gaining admission. When Mr. Beecher appeared on the platform a deathlike stillness fell upon the great audience, and after a short Scriptural introduction Mr. Beecher informed the congregation that a young woman had been sold by her own father, to be sent South.

"She was bought by a slave trader for twelve hundred dollars, and he has offered to give you the opportunity of purchasing her freedom. She has given her word of honor to return to Richmond if the money be not raised, and, slave though she be called, she is a woman who will keep her word.—Now, Sarah, come up here, so that all may see you."

When the young woman ascended to the pulpit and sank into a chair by Mr. Beecher's side, he assumed the look and manner of a slave auctioneer calling for bids.

"Look," he exclaimed, "at this marketable commodity—human flesh and blood like yourselves! You see the white blood of her father in her regular features and high, thoughtful brow. Who bids? You will have to pay extra for that white blood, because it is supposed to give intelligence. Stand up, Sarah! Now look at her trim figure and her wavy hair! How much do you bid for them. She is sound of wind and limb— I'll warrant her! Who bids? Her feet and hands—hold them out, Sarah —are small and finely formed. What do you bid for her? She is a Christian woman—I mean a praying nigger—and that makes her more valuable, because it insures her docility and obedience to your wishes. 'Servants, obey your masters,' you know. Well, she believes in that doctrine. How much for her?—Will you allow this praying woman to be sent back to Richmond to meet the fate for which her father sold her? If not, who bids?"

The impression produced by these words is indescribable. Mr. Beecher once told Mr. Robert Bonner that he could have been an actor, and his acting as auctioneer was perfect. People held their breath as he proceeded:

"Come now! We are selling this woman, you know, and a fine specimen, too. Look at her; see for yourselves. Don't you want her? Now, then, pass the baskets and let us see."

The congregation was wrought up to the highest pitch. Women became hysterical; men were almost beside themselves. For a half-hour money was heaped into the contribution boxes; women took off their jewelry and rings, bracelets and brooches were piled one upon the other. Men unfastened their watches, and some threw coin and bank notes upon the pulpit; and above all the confusion Mr. Beecher's powerful voice rang out:

"In the name of Christ, men and women, how much do you bid?"

At this point a gentleman arose and shouted that several members would make up the deficiency whatever it might be. The wildest demonstrations of enthusiasm followed. The collection was found to be more than sufficient to purchase the freedom of Sarah, who was established in a little home of her own at Peekskill, New York. This slave auction was the most remarkable of the many that later took place in Plymouth Church, and undoubtedly was a very effective means of opening the eyes of the people to the horrors of slavery.

The underground railroad was far more mythical than most Americans think, since runaway slaves never had much organized assistance and did most of what they did on their own. But a few people, largely Quakers, did help many slaves to freedom and they became part of an enduring legend. (From *The Reminiscences of Levi Coffin,* 1876.)

AN UNDERGROUND RAILROAD

In the winter of 1826–27 fugitives began to come to our house, and as it became more widely known on different routes that the slaves fleeing from bondage would find a welcome and shelter at our house and be forwarded safely on their journey, the number increased. Friends in the neighborhood who had formerly stood aloof from the work, fearful of the penalty of the law, were encouraged to engage in it when they saw the fearless manner in which I acted and the success that attended my efforts. They would contribute to clothe the fugitives and would aid in forwarding them on their way but were timid about sheltering them under their roof; so that part of the work devolved on us. . . .

I soon became extensively known to the friends of the slaves, at different points on the Ohio River where fugitives generally crossed, and to those northward of us on the various routes leading to Canada. Depots were established on the different lines of the underground railroad, south and north of Newport, and a perfect understanding was maintained between those who kept them. Three principal lines from the South converged at my house, one from Cincinnati, one from Madison, and one from Jeffersonville, Indiana. The roads were always in running order, and the connections were good, the conductors active and zealous, and there was no lack of passengers. Seldom a week passed without our receiving passengers by this mysterious road. We found it necessary to be always prepared to receive such company and properly care for them. We knew not what night or what hour of the night we would be roused from slumber by a gentle rap at the door. Outside in the cold or rain there would be a two-horse wagon loaded with fugitives, perhaps the greater part of them women and children. I would invite them in a low tone to come in, and they would follow me into the darkened house without a word, for we knew not who might be watching and listening. When they were all safely inside and the door fastened, I would cover the windows, strike a light, and build a good fire. By this time my wife would be up and preparing victuals for them, and in a short time the cold and hungry fugitives would be made comfortable. I would accompany the conductor of the train to the stable and care for the horses that had, perhaps, been driven twenty-five or thirty miles that night through the cold and rain. The fugitives would rest on pallets before the fire the rest of the night. Frequently wagonloads of passengers from the different lines have met at our house, having no previous knowledge of each other. The companies varied in number, from two or three fugitives to seventeen.

The pursuit was often very close, and we had to resort to various stratagems in order to elude the pursuers. Sometimes a company of fugitives were scattered and secreted in the neighborhood until the hunters had given up the chase. At other times their route was changed and they were hurried forward with all speed. It was a continual excitement and anxiety to us, but the work was its own reward.

As I have said before, when we knew of no pursuit and the fugitives need to rest or to be clothed or were sick from exposure and fatigue, we have kept them with us for weeks or months. A case of this kind was that of two young men who were brought to our house during a severe cold spell in the early part of winter. They had been out in the snow and ice, and their feet were so badly frozen that their boots had to be cut off, and they were compelled to lie by for three months, being unable to travel. Doctor Henry H. Way, who was always ready to minister to the fugitives, attended them, and by his skillful treatment their feet were saved, though for some time it was thought that a surgical operation would have to be performed. The two men left us in the spring and went on to Canada. They seemed loath to part from us and 'manifested much gratitude for our kindness and care. The next autumn one of them returned to our house, saying that he felt so much indebted to us that he had come back to work for us to try to repay us, in some measure, for what we had done for him. I told him that we had no charge against him and could not receive anything for our attention to him while he was sick and helpless, but if he thought he would be safe, I would hire him during the winter at good wages. He accepted this offer and proved to be a faithful servant. He attended night school and made some progress in learning. He returned to Canada in the spring.

Many of the fugitives came long distances, from Alabama, Mississippi, Louisiana, in fact from all part of the South. Sometimes the poor hunted creatures had been out so long, living in woods and thickets, that they were almost wild when they came in and so fearful of being betrayed that it was some time before their confidence could be gained and the true state of their case learned. Although the number of fugitives that I aided on their way was so large, not one, so far as I ever knew, was captured and taken back to slavery. Providence seemed to favor our efforts for the poor slaves and to crown them with success.

At another time when I was in the city accompanied by my wife and daughter, Hiram S. Gillmore, a noted abolitionist and one of my particular friends, asked me if I knew of any person in from the country with a wagon who would take a fugitive slave girl out to a place of safety. He then gave me the outlines of her story. She had come from Boone County, Kentucky, having run away because she learned that she was to be sold to the far South. Knowing that she would be pursued and probably retaken if she started northward immediately, she conceived a plan like that adopted by Cassie and Emmeline when they ran away from Legree in *Uncle Tom's Cabin.* She hid herself in the interior of a large straw pile near her master's barn, having previously arranged apertures for air and a winding passage with concealed entrance by which her fellow servants who brought her food could enter. Here she remained six weeks, while her master with a posse of men scoured the country in search for her. Like Cassie who looked from her hiding place in the garret and heard the discomfited Legree swearing at his ill luck as he returned from the unsuccessful pursuit, this young woman could hear in her hiding place in the straw pile the noise of horses' feet and the sound of talking as her master and his men returned from their fruitless search for her. When the hunt was over, she stole out and made her way safely to the Ohio River, crossed in a skiff, and reached the house of a family of abolitionists in Cincinnati, where she was kindly received and furnished with comfortable clothing.

In answer to the inquiry of Hiram S. Gillmore I replied that I was there in a carriage and would take her out if she would be ready when I called for her at nine o'clock next morning. At the appointed time we started. The young slave woman was nearly white, was well dressed, and presented quite a ladylike appearance.

At the end of the first day's travel we stopped about four miles above Hamilton, at a private house, the residence of one of my friends —a Democrat, by the way—who had often invited me to call at his house with my wife and pay his family a visit. The gentleman's daughter ran out to meet us and I said to her: "Well, Ellen, I have brought my wife with me this time; now guess which of these ladies she is."

She looked from one to the other, hardly able to decide; but finally, judging perhaps from the Quaker bonnet my wife wore, decided on the right one. The gentleman and his wife now came out to meet us, and when I introduced the young lady with us as a fugitive slave, they were full of surprise and curiosity, having never seen a fugitive slave before.

I told them her story and then said to my friend:

"Will she be safe here tonight, Thomas?"

"I reckon so," was the reply.

"I don't want any *reckon* about it," I rejoined; "I shall put her in thy care, and I don't want thee to let anybody capture her." She was kindly treated.

Next morning—it being the Sabbath day—we went on about eight miles to West Elkton, a Friends' settlement, to attend meeting and spend the day. Meeting had just commenced when we arrived. My wife took the fugitive into meeting with her and seated her by her side. This was the first time the girl had ever attended a Quaker meeting. At its close I introduced her to a number of our friends as a runaway slave from Kentucky. She was the first that had been seen at that place, and a mysterious influence seemed to invest her at once. Men lowered their voices as if in awe when they inquired about her, and some of them seemed alarmed, as if there was danger in the very air that a fugitive slave breathed. I spoke in a loud, cheerful tone and asked: "Why do you lower your voices? Are you afraid of anything? Have you blood-hounds among you? If so, you ought to drive them out of your village."

This public exposition of a fugitive slave at Friends' meeting and in the village seemed to have a good effect in the place, for West Elkton afterward became one of our best underground railroad depots and the timid man first alluded to became one of the most zealous workers on the road.

The women's rights movement, when it organized in 1848, at a convention in Seneca Falls, New York, adopted what was by this time a folk theme—an updating of the Declaration of Independence. The noble words of Jefferson had passed into the common culture. (From Elizabeth Cady Stanton, *Seneca Falls Declaration of Sentiments*, July 19, 1848.)

A WOMAN'S DECLARATION OF INDEPENDENCE

When, in the course of human events, it becomes necessary for one portion of the family of man to assume among the people of the earth a position different from that which they have hitherto occupied, but one to which the laws of nature and of nature's God entitle them, a decent respect to the opinions of mankind requires that they should declare the causes that impel them to such a course.

We hold these truths to be self-evident: that all men and women are created equal; that they are endowed by their Creator with certain inalienable rights; that among these are life, liberty, and the pursuit of happiness; that to secure these rights governments are instituted, deriving their just powers from the consent of the governed. Whenever any form of government becomes destructive of these ends, it is the right of those who suffer from it to refuse allegiance to it, and to insist upon the institution of a new government, laying its foundation on such principles, and organizing its powers in such form, as to them shall seem most likely to effect their safety and happiness. Prudence, indeed, will dictate that governments long established should not be changed for light and transient causes; and accordingly all experience hath shown that mankind are more disposed to suffer while evils are sufferable, than to right themselves by abolishing the forms to which they are accustomed. But when a long train of abuses and usurpations, pursuing invariably the same object, evinces a design to reduce them under absolute despotism, it is their duty to throw off such government, and to provide new guards for their future security. Such has been the patient sufferance of the women under this government, and such is now the necessity which constrains them to demand the equal station to which they are entitled.

The history of mankind is a history of repeated injuries and usurpations on the part of man toward woman, having in direct object the establishment of an absolute tyranny over her. To prove this, let facts be submitted to a candid world. . . .

Now, in view of this entire disfranchisement of one-half the people of this country, their social and religious degradation—in view of the unjust laws above mentioned, and because women do feel themselves aggrieved, oppressed, and fraudulently deprived of their most sacred rights, we insist that they have immediate admission to all the rights and privileges which belong to them as citizens of the United States.

In entering upon the great work before us, we anticipate no small amount of misconception, misrepresentation, and ridicule; but we shall use every instrumentality within our power to effect our object. We shall employ agents, circulate tracts, petition the state and national legislatures, and endeavor to enlist the pulpit and the press in our behalf. We hope this convention will be followed by a series of conventions embracing every part of the country.

Resolutions

Resolved, That all laws which prevent woman from occupying such a station in society as her conscience shall dictate, or which place her in a position inferior to that of man, are contrary to the great precept of nature, and therefore of no force or authority.

Resolved, That woman is man's equal—was intended to be so by the Creator, and the highest good of the race demands that she should be recognized as such. . . .

Resolved, That it is the duty of the women of this country to secure to themselves their sacred right to the elective franchise. . . .

Resolved, That the speedy success of our cause depends upon the zealous and untiring efforts of both men and women for the overthrow of the monopoly of the pulpit and for the securing to women an equal participation with men in the various trades, professions, and commerce.

Resolved, therefore, That, being invested by the Creator with the same capabilities and the same consciousness of responsibility for their exercise, it is demonstrably the right and duty of woman, equally with man, to promote every righteous cause by every righteous means; and especially in regard to the great subjects of morals and religion, it is self-evidently her right to participate with her brother in teaching them, both in private and in public, by writing and by speaking, by any instrumentalities proper to be used, and in any assemblies proper to be held; and this being a self-evident truth growing out of the divinely implanted principles of human nature, any custom or authority adverse to it, whether modern or wearing the hoary sanction of antiquity, is to be regarded as a self-evident falsehood, and at war with mankind.

The typical reformer of the pre-Civil War period attempted to convert his listeners by pure argument—moral suasion. If people changed their beliefs, it was hoped, they would change their actions as well; they would stop whatever sin they were committing. In the temperance crusade, this happened quite often: emotional appeals persuaded tens of thousands to stop drinking. Modern techniques to deal with alcoholism are not that different from what we find almost a century and a half ago. (Selection from *A Second Declaration of Independence,* 1841.)

TEMPERANCE: PRO

When from the depths of human misery, it becomes possible for a portion of the infatuated victims of appetite to arise, and dissolve the vicious and habitual bonds which have connected them with *inebriety* and degradation, and to assume among the temperate and industrious of the community, the useful, respectable and appropriate stations, to which the laws of Nature, and of Nature's God entitle them, an anxious regard for the safety of their former companions; and the welfare of society requires, that they should declare the causes that impel them to such a *Reformation!*

We hold these truths to be self-evident; that all men are created *temperate;* that they are endowed by their Creator with certain natural and innocent desires; that among these are the appetite for COLD WATER and the pursuit of happiness! that to secure the gratification of these propensities fountains and streams are gushing and meandering from the hills and vales, benignly and abundantly abroad among men, deriving their just powers from their beneficial adaptation to the natures of all the varieties of animal organization, that whenever any form of substituted artificial beverage becomes destructive of these natures, it is the right of the recipients to proscribe—to alter, or to abolish it and to return to the use of that crystal element, which alone of all that has come to us from Eden, still retains all its primitive purity and sweetness, demonstrating its benefits on such principles, and testing its powers in such quantities, and under such circumstances, as to them shall seem most likely to effect their safety and happiness.

Habit indeed will dictate, that indulgences long established cannot be forborne, or changed for slight and transient causes; and accordingly all experience hath shown, that "inebriates" are more disposed to suffer the evils of intoxicating drinks, while the temptations of intoxicating drinks are around them and sufferable, than to right themselves, by abandoning the *Dram Shops,* to which they are accustomed. But when a long train of abuses, and gradually excessive and habitual potations of these destructive stimulants, prompting invariably still greater and greater indulgences, evinces a tendency to reduce them under absolute despotism, despondency, and death, it is their right— it is their duty—and as they now by blessed experience know, it is their power, to throw off such habits, and to provide new guards for their future security in *total abstinence* and *pure water.* Such has been the cruel sufferance of these Inebriates; and such is now the necessity which constrains them to alter their former habits of using intoxicating drinks—to reform—and to refrain from the use of them all, henceforth and forever, *entirely.* The history of the *Reign of Alcohol* is a history of repeated injuries—brutalities—vices—diseases—and enormities, all having in direct object the absolute ruin, both temporal and eternal, of all his votaries! To prove this, let facts be submitted to a candid world. . . .

We, therefore, the Reformed Inebriates of the United States of America, for the celebration of the 4th of July, 1841, throughout the Union assembled, appealing to the Supreme Judge of the world for support in the maintenance of our pledges, do, in the name, and by the authority of all the *Washington Total Abstinence Societies* of these States, solemnly publish and declare, that the members of these blessed and blessing Washingtonian Fraternities, are, and of right ought to be, temperate, free and independent citizens; that they are absolved from all allegiance to the ALCOHOLIC CROWN, and that all social intercourse, or connection, or fellowship, between them and any and all of the numerous branches of the *Alcoholic Family,* is, and ought to be totally dissolved; and that as free, temperate, reformed, and independent citizens, they have full power to levy war against all the Alcoholic Legions—conclude peace when the same are vanquished and exterminated—contract alliances for the accomplishment of their objects—establish commerce in the deeds of benevolence and charity, and to do all other acts and things which reformed, temperate, free, and independent citizens may of right do.

And for the support of this Declaration, with a firm reliance on the protection of Divine Providence, we mutually pledge to each other our adhesion to PURE WATER, TOTAL ABSTINENCE, and the CAUSE OF HUMANITY.

Come Home, Father

1 Father, dear father, come home with me now!
The clock in the steeple strikes one;
You said you were coming right home from the shop,
As soon as your day's work was done.
Our fire has gone out—our house is all dark—
And mother's been watching since tea,
With poor brother Benny so sick in her arms,
And no one to help her but me . . .
Come home! come home! come home!
Please, father, dear father, come home.

Chorus

Hear the sweet voice of the child,

Which the nightwinds repeat as they roam!
Oh, who could resist this most pleading of prayers?
"Please, father, dear father, come home!"

2 Father, dear father come home with me now!
The clock in the steeple strikes two;
The night has grown colder, and Benny is worse,
But he has been calling for you.
Indeed he is worse—Ma says he will die,
Perhaps before morning shall dawn;
And this is the message she sent me to bring—
"Come quickly, or he will be gone."
Come home! come home! come home!
Please, father, dear father, come home.

3 Father, dear father, come home with me now!
The clock in the steeple strikes three;
The house is so lonely—the hours are so long
For poor weeping mother and me.
Yes, we are alone—poor Benny is dead,
And gone with the angels of light;
And these were the very last words that he said—
"I want to kiss Papa goodnight."
Come home! come home! come home!
Please, father, dear father, come home.

Even temperance produced its backlash. Historical accounts generally dwell far more on reformers than on antireformers like Tom Flynn. (Selection from *Reminiscences of the Old Fire Laddies*, 1885.)

TEMPERANCE: CON

Tom Flynn's Temperance Lecture

. . . When the old Chatham Theater [just above Roosevelt Street] was in the height of its popularity, Tom Flynn and Charley Thorn were its owners. Flynn was one of the best of the old-school actors, and the most successful Irish comedian that ever stepped upon a stage. He was a heavy drinker, though he managed always to promptly attend to business and play his parts without a blemish. It was along in the early Forties that a crusade against rum was organized in this city, and the movement was known as the "Washingtonian Battery against Rum." Though organized and for a time confined entirely to doing good in this city, the work gradually spread itself throughout the whole country, and no temperance movement ever before or since met with such enthusiastic success. Entire engine companies in this city were known to sign the pledge in a body, and beautiful silk banners were presented to each company when they joined the crusade. . . . It was during the excitement consequent upon these meetings that it was suggested that the old Chatham be secured for revival meetings.

"I have been seriously thinking over this tippling business," said Flynn to the committee who waited upon him, "and I cannot fail noticing the great good which this temperance revival is causing among thousands in this city. Its good effects have reached even so rum-soaked a sinner as myself, and I am desirous of doing something for the cause. You can not only have the theater on certain occasions for meetings, but I will address the first gathering that is called together there under the auspices of the Washingtonians."

When the announcement was made public that Tom Flynn was to address a temperance meeting, it created the greatest surprise and wide-spread comment. The day, or rather afternoon, finally arrived when the great actor was to renounce rum and tell his audience the reason why. The theater was packed from pit to dome, the very aisles being jammed almost to suffocation with solid humanity. The stage was set with a scene from *The Drunkard's Home,* and near the footlights was placed a table, upon which rested a half-filled glass pitcher and a tumbler. At the appointed hour Flynn, wreathed in his most genial smile, came upon the stage, and the thunder of applause which greeted him never awakened such echoes before in the old theater. Filling his glass from the pitcher, Flynn drank the contents in one draught, and then proceeded with his lecture. He was a brilliant and voluble talker, and his fund of anecdotes never seemed to be exhausted. The pathos and eloquence with which he pictured step by step the drunkard's path down the abyss of moral ruin, I will never forget; neither will I forget the laughter I enjoyed while listening to his side-splitting anecdotes. Such an audience was never seen. One moment the sobs of men and women were distinctly audible throughout the whole building while Flynn drew one of his inimitable pictures of the curse of rum. At the next moment everybody was holding his or her sides in a strong effort to save themselves from bursting with laughter. Flynn finally reached the peroration of his lecture, and a finer burst of eloquence I never listened to. The audience was fairly worked to the highest pitch of seemingly religious enthusiasm, and the lecturer continued for two hours to talk uninterruptedly. At the end of that time, he was seen to totter at the close of one of his sentences and then fall fainting upon the stage. Such excitement was never manifested in a public gathering before or since; and while some attendants carried Flynn around to the old New England Hotel, the audience dispersed to their homes, loud in their praises of the reformed actor. Some of the temperance people, however, managed to get upon the stage, and in nosing about discovered that the pitcher which was supposed to contain water actually contained gin—old swan gin, which was Tom's favorite beverage; and putting two and two together, they concluded that Flynn had been drawing inspiration for his lecture from the camp of the enemy, and that his exhaustion and final collapse were not due so much from the mental strain of the lecture as from the seductive and exhausting contents of the pitcher. The story soon got out, and though it caused many to laugh, it made Flynn very unpopular with some at the time. The object of the joke was to prevent the temperance people from again asking for the use of the theater, and they never did.

The communitarian movements of the antebellum period experimented with new sexual relations as well as new economic ones. Robert Dale Owen glimpsed the emerging concern for reducing the size of families that urbanization and industrialization typically produce. (Selection from Robert Dale Owen, *Moral Physiology*, 1831.)

THE COMMUNITARIAN MOVEMENT

Among the various instincts which contribute to man's preservation and well-being, the instinct of reproduction holds a distinguished rank. It peoples the earth; it perpetuates the species. Controlled by reason and chastened by good feeling, it gives to social intercourse much of its charm and zest. Directed by selfishness or governed by force, it is prolific of misery and degradation. . . .

Like other instincts, it may assume a selfish, mercenary or brutal character. But, in itself, it appears to me the most social and least selfish of all our instincts. It fits us to give, even while receiving, pleasure; and, among cultivated beings, the former power is ever more highly valued than the latter. Not one of our instincts affords larger

scope for the exercise of disinterestedness, and the best moral sentiments of our race. . . .

It is a serious question—and surely an exceedingly proper and
important one—whether man can obtain, and whether he is benefited
by obtaining control over this instinct. IS IT DESIRABLE, THAT IT SHOULD
NEVER BE GRATIFIED WITHOUT AN INCREASE TO POPULATION? OR, IS IT
DESIRABLE, THAT, IN GRATIFYING IT, MAN SHALL BE ABLE TO SAY WHETHER
OFFSPRING SHALL BE THE RESULT OR NOT? . . .

The population question has of late years occupied much attention,
especially in Great Britain. It was first prominently brought forward
and discussed, in 1798, by Malthus, an English clergyman. . . .

He asserts, that in most countries population at this moment
presses against the means of subsistence; and that, in all countries, it
has a tendency so to do. He recommends, as a preventive of the growing evil, celibacy till a late age, say thirty years; and he asserts, that unless
this "moral restraint" is exerted, vice, poverty, and misery, will and
must remain as checks to population. . . .

The most enlightened observers of mankind are agreed that nothing contributes so positively and immediately to demoralize a nation,
as when its youth refrain, until a late period, from forming disinterested
connections with those of the other sex. The frightful increase of prostitutes, the destruction of health, the rapid spread of intemperance, the
ruin of moral feelings, are, to the mass, the *certain* consequences. Individuals there are who escape the contagion; individuals whose better
feelings revolt, under *any* temptation, from the mercenary embrace, or
the Circean cup of intoxication; but these are exceptions only. The mass
will have their pleasures: the pleasures of intellectual intercourse, of
unbought affection, and of good taste and good feeling, if they can;
but if they cannot, then such pleasures (alas! that language should be
perverted to entitle them to the name!) as the sacrifice of money and
the ruin of body and mind can purchase.

But this is not all. Not only is Malthus' proposition fraught with
immorality, in that it discountenances to a late age those disinterested
sexual connections which can alone save youth from vice; but it is *im-
practicable*. Men and women will scarcely pause to calculate the
chances they have of affording support to the children ere they become
parents: how, then, should they stop to calculate the chances of the
world's being overpeopled? Mr. Malthus may say what he pleases, they
never will make any such calculation; and it is folly to expect they
should.

Let us observe, then: *unless some more ascetic and more practicable species of "moral restraint" be introduced,* vice and misery will

ultimately become the inevitable lot of man. He can no more escape them, than he can the light of the sun, or the stroke of death. . . .

What would be the probable effect, in social life, if mankind obtained and exercised a control over the instinct of reproduction?

My settled conviction is—and I am prepared to defend it—that the effect would be salutary, moral, civilizing; that it would prevent many crimes, and more unhappiness; that it would lessen intemperance and profligacy; that it would polish the manners and improve the moral feelings; that it would relieve the burden of the poor, and the cares of the rich; that it would most essentially benefit the rising generation, by enabling parents generally more carefully to educate, and more comfortably to provide for, their offspring. . . .

Is it not notorious, that the families of the married often increase beyond what a regard for the young beings coming into the world, or the happiness of those who give them birth, would dictate? In how many instances does the hard-working father, and more especially the mother of a poor family, remain slaves throughout their lives, tugging at the oar of incessant labour, toiling to live, and living only to die; when, if their offspring had been limited to two or three only, they might have enjoyed comfort and comparative affluence! How often is the health of the mother—giving birth, every year, perchance, to an infant—happy, if it be not twins!—and compelled to toil on, even at those times when nature imperiously calls for some relief from daily drudgery—how often is the mother's comfort, health, nay, her life, thus sacrificed! Or when care and toil have weighed down the spirit, and at last broken the health of the father, how often is the widow left, unable with the most virtuous intentions to save her fatherless offspring from becoming degraded objects of charity, or profligate votaries of vice! . . .

. . . is it not most plainly, clearly, incontrovertibly *desirable,* that parents *should have the power* to limit their offspring, whether they choose to exercise it or not? Who *can* lose by their having this power? and how many *may* gain—may gain competency for themselves, and the opportunity carefully to educate and provide for their children? . . .

If the moral feelings were carefully cultivated—if we were taught to consult, in everything, rather the welfare of those we love than our own, how strongly would these arguments be felt! No man ought even to desire that a woman should become the mother of his children, unless it was her express wish, and unless he knew it to be for her welfare, that she should. Her feelings, her interests, should be for him in this matter *an imperative law.* She it is who bears the burden, and therefore with her also should the decision rest. Surely it may well be a question whether it be desirable, or whether any man ought to ask, that the whole life of an intellectual, cultivated woman, should be spent in bearing a family of twelve or fifteen children—to the ruin, perhaps, of her constitution, if not to the overstocking of the world. No man ought to require or expect it. . . .

Thus, inasmuch as the scruple of incurring heavy responsibilities deters from forming moral connections, and encourages intemperance and prostitution, the knowledge which enables man to limit his offspring would, in the present state of things, save much unhappiness and prevent many crimes. Young persons sincerely attached to each other, and who might wish to marry, would marry early; merely resolving not to become parents until prudence permitted it. The young man, instead of solitary toil or vulgar dissipation, would enjoy the society and the assistance of her he has chosen as his companion; and the best years of life, whose pleasures never return, would not be squandered in riot, or lost through mortification. . . .

But there are other cases, it will be said, where the knowledge of such a check would be mischievous. If young women, it will be argued, were absolved from the fear of consequences, they would rarely preserve their chastity. Unlegalized connections would be common and seldom detected. Seduction would be facilitated. . . .

That chastity which is worth preserving is not the chastity that owes its birth to fear and ignorance. If to enlighten a woman regarding a simple physiological fact will make her a prostitute, she must be especially predisposed to profligacy. But it is a libel on the sex. Few, indeed, there are, who would continue so miserable and degrading a calling, could they escape from it. For one prostitute that is made by inclination, ten are made by necessity. Reform the laws—equalize the comforts of society, and you need withhold no knowledge from wives and daughters. It is want, not knowledge, that leads to prostitution. . . .

I know that parents often think it right and proper to withhold from their children—especially from their daughters—facts the most influential on their future lives, and the knowledge of which is essential to every man and woman's well-being. Such a course has ever appeared to me ill-judged and productive of very injurious effects. A girl is surely no whit better for believing, until her marriage night, that children are found among the cabbage-leaves in the garden. . . .

Among the modes of preventing conception which may have prevailed in various countries, that which has been adopted, and is now practised by the cultivated classes on the continent of Europe, by the French, the Italians, and, I believe, by the Germans and Spaniards, consists of complete withdrawal, on the part of the man, immediately previous to emission. *This is, in all cases, effectual.* It may be objected, that the practice requires a mental effort and a partial sacrifice. I reply, that, in France, where men consider this (as it ought ever to be considered, when the interests of the other sex require it,) a *point of honour,* all young men learn to make the necessary effort; and custom renders it easy, and a matter of course. As for the sacrifice, shall a trifling, . . . diminution of physical enjoyment be suffered to outweigh the most important considerations connected with the permanent welfare of those who are the nearest and dearest to us? Shall it be suffered to outweigh a regard for the comfort, the well-being—in some cases, the *life* of those whom we profess to love?—The most selfish will hesitate deliberately to reply in the affirmative to such questions as these. . . .

The most practical of philosophers, Franklin, interprets chastity to mean, *the regulated and strictly temperate satisfaction, without injury to others, of those desires which are natural to all healthy adult beings. . . .*

The promotion of such chastity is the chief object of the present work. It is all-important for the welfare of our race, that the reproductive instinct should never be selfishly indulged; never gratified at the expense of the well-being of our companions. A man who, in this matter, will not consult, with scrupulous deference, the slightest wishes of the other sex; a man who will ever put his desires in competition with theirs, and who will prize more highly the pleasure he receives than that he may be capable of bestowing—such a man appears to me, in the essentials of character, a brute. . . .

Human beings of whatever sex or class! examine dispassionately and narrowly the influence which the control here recommended will produce throughout society. Reflect whether it will not lighten the burdens of one sex, while it affords scope for the exercise of the best feelings of the other. Consider whether its tendency be not benignant and elevating; conducive to the exercise of practical virtue, and to the permanent welfare of the human.

country and city

Americans conceded the primacy of agriculture even when they moved to cities or created an economy in which the farmer profited less and less from his labors. But in the early nineteenth century there was still some reality to the agrarian ideal that Americans held into the twentieth century, long after it had ceased to describe very much about American life. (Selection from Jesse Buel, *The Farmer's Companion*, 1840.)

THE IMPORTANCE OF AGRICULTURE

There is no business of life which so highly conduces to the prosperity of a nation, and to the happiness of its entire population, as that of cultivating the soil. Agriculture may be regarded, says the great Sully, as the breasts from which the state derives support and nourishment. Agriculture is truly our nursing mother, which gives food, and growth, and wealth, and moral health and character to our country. It may be considered the great wheel which moves all the machinery of society; and that whatever gives to this a new impulse communicates a corresponding impetus to the thousand minor wheels of interest which it propels and regulates. While the other classes of the community are directly dependent upon agriculture for a regular and sufficient supply of the means of subsistence, the agriculturist is able to supply all the absolute wants of life from his own labors, though he derives most of his pleasures and profits from an interchange of the products of labor with the other classes of society. Agriculture is called the parent of arts, not only because it was the first art practiced by man, but because the other arts are its legitimate offspring and cannot continue long to exist without it. It is the great business of civilized life, and gives employment to a vast majority of almost every people.

The substantial prosperity of a country is always in the ratio of its agricultural industry and wealth. Commerce and manufactures may give temporary consequence to a state, but these are always a precarious dependence. They are effeminating and corrupting; and, unless backed by a prosperous agricultural population, they engender the elements of speedy decay and ruin. . . .

Great Britain has now become ascendant in commerce and manufactures, yet her greatness in these sources of power and opulence is primarily and principally owing to the excellent condition of her agriculture; without which she would not be able to sustain her manufacturers or her commerce, in their present flourishing state, or long retain her immense foreign possessions, or anything like her present population. . . .

A *country* can only continue long prosperous and be truly independent when it is sustained by agricultural intelligence, agricultural industry, and agricultural wealth. Though its commerce may be swept from the ocean—and its manufactures perish—yet, if its soil is tilled, and well tilled, by an independent yeomanry, it can still be made to yield all the absolute necessaries of life; it can sustain its population and its independence; and when its misfortunes abate, it can, like the trunkless roots of a recently cut down tree, firmly braced in, and deriving nourishment from the soil, send forth a new trunk, new branches, new foliage, and new fruits; it can rear again the edifice of its manufacturer, and spread again the sails of its commerce.

But agriculture is beneficial to a state in proportion as its labors are encouraged, enlightened, and honored—for in that proportion does it add to national and individual wealth and happiness.

Agriculture feeds all. Were agriculture to be neglected, population would diminish, because the necessaries of life would be wanting. Did it not supply more than is necessary for its own wants, not only would every other art be at a stand, but every science and every kind of mental improvement would be neglected. Manufactures and commerce originally owed their existence to agriculture. Agriculture furnishes, in a great measure, raw materials and subsistence for the one and commodities for barter and exchange for the other. In proportion as these raw materials and commodities are multiplied, by the intelligence and industry of the farmer and the consequent improvement of the soil, in the same proportion are manufactures and commerce benefited—not only in being furnished with more abundant supplies, but in the increased demand for their fabrics and merchandise. The more agriculture produces, the more she sells—the more she buys; and the business and comfort of society are mainly influenced and controlled by the result of her labor.

Agriculture, directly or indirectly, pays the burdens of our taxes and our tolls, which support the government, and sustain our internal improvements; and the more abundant her means, the greater will be her contributions. The farmer who manages his business ignorantly and slothfully, and who produces from it only just enough for the subsistence of his family, pays no tolls on the transit of his produce and but a small tax upon the nominal value of his lands. Instruct his mind and awaken him to industry, by the hope of distinction and reward, so that he triples the products of his labor, the value of his lands is increased in a corresponding ratio, his comforts are multiplied, his mind disenthralled, and two thirds of his products go to augment the business and tolls of our canals and roads. If such a change in the situation of one farm would add one hundred dollars to the wealth and one dollar to the tolls of the state, what an astonishing aggregate would be produced, both in capital and in revenue, by a similar improvement upon 250,000 farms, the assumed number in the State of New York. The capital would be augmented 25 millions, and the revenue two hundred and fifty thousand dollars per annum.

Agriculture is the principal source of our wealth. It furnishes more productive labor, the legitimate source of wealth, than all the other employments in society combined. The more it is enlightened by science, the more abundant will be its products; the more elevated its character, the stronger the incitements to pursue it. Whatever, therefore, tends to enlighten the agriculturist tends to increase the wealth of the state and the means for the successful prosecution of the other arts and the sciences, now indispensable to their profitable management.

Agriculturists are the guardians of our freedom. They are the fountains of political power. If the fountains become impure, the stream will be defiled. If the agriculturist is slothful, and ignorant, and poor, he will be spiritless and servile. If he is enlightened, industrious, and in prosperous circumstances, he will be independent in mind, jealous of his rights, and watchful for the public good. His welfare is identified with the welfare of the state. He is virtually fixed to the soil; and has, therefore, a paramount interest, as well as a giant power, to defend it from the encroachment of foreign or domestic foes. If his country suffers, he must suffer; if she prospers, he too may expect to prosper. Hence, whatever tends to improve the intellectual condition of the farmer, and to elevate him above venal temptation, essentially contributes to the good order of society at large and to the perpetuity of our country's freedom.

Agriculture is the parent of physical and moral health to the state, it is the salt which preserves from moral corruption. Not only are her labors useful in administering to our wants, and in dispensing the blessing of abundance to others, but she is constantly exercising a salutary influence upon the moral and physical health of the state and in perpetuating the republican habits and good order of society. While rural labor is the great source of physical health and constitutional vigor to our population, it interposes the most formidable barrier to the demoralizing influence of luxury and vice. We seldom hear of civil commotions, of crimes, or of hereditary disease, among those who are steadily engaged in the business of agriculture. Men who are satisfied with the abundant and certain resources of their own labor, and their own farms, are not willing to jeopard these enjoyments by promoting popular tumult, or tolerating crime. The more we promote the interest of the agriculturist, by developing the powers of his mind, and elevating his moral views, the more we shall promote the virtue and happiness of society.

The facts which are here submitted must afford ample proof that agriculture is all-important to us as a nation; and that our prosperity in manufactures, in commerce, and in the other pursuits of life, will depend, in a great measure, upon the returns which the soil makes to agricultural labor. It therefore becomes the interest of every class to cherish, to encourage, to enlighten, to honor, and to reward those who engage in agricultural pursuits. Our independence was won by our yeomanry, and it can only be preserved by them.

The early factories appeared to most observers, such as the Englishwoman Harriet Martineau, unalloyed blessings. The negative image of the "dark, satanic Mills" came later. (Selection from Harriet Martineau, *Society in America*, 1837.)

FACTORY LIFE: A FOREIGNER'S VIEW

I visited [1834] the corporate factory establishment at Waltham, within a few miles of Boston. The Waltham Mills were at work before those of Lowell were set up. The establishment is for the spinning and weaving of cotton alone, and the construction of the requisite machinery. Five hundred persons were employed at the time of my visit. The girls earn two, and sometimes three, dollars a week, besides their board. The little children earn one dollar a week. Most of the girls live in the houses provided by the corporation, which accommodate from six to eight each. When sisters come to the mill, it is a common practice for them to bring their mother to keep house for them and some of their companions, in a dwelling built by their own earnings. In this case, they save enough out of their board to clothe themselves, and have their two or three dollars a week to spare. Some have thus cleared off mortgages from their fathers' farms; others have educated the hope of the family at college; and many are rapidly accumulating an independence. I saw a whole street of houses built with the earnings of the girls, some with piazzas and green Venetian blinds, and all neat and sufficiently spacious.

The factory people built the church, which stands conspicuous on the green in the midst of the place. The minister's salary (eight hundred dollars last year) is raised by a tax on the pews. The corporation gave them a building for a lyceum, which they have furnished with a good library, and where they have lectures every winter—the best that money can procure. The girls have, in many instances, private libraries of some merit and value.

The managers of the various factory establishments keep the wages as nearly equal as possible, and then let the girls freely shift about from one to another. When a girl comes to the overseer to inform him of her intention of working at the mill, he welcomes her, and asks how long she means to stay. It may be six months, or a year, or five years, or for life. She declares what she considers herself fit for and sets to work accordingly. If she finds that she cannot work so as to keep up with the companion appointed to her, or to please her employer or herself, she comes to the overseer, and volunteers to pick cotton, or sweep the rooms, or undertake some other service that she can perform.

The people work about seventy hours per week on the average. The time of work varies with the length of the days, the wages continuing the same. All look like well-dressed young ladies. The health is good, or rather (as this is too much to be said about health anywhere in the United States) it is no worse than it is elsewhere.

These facts speak for themselves. There is no need to enlarge on the pleasure of an acquaintance with the operative classes of the United States.

The shoemaking at Lynn is carried on almost entirely in private dwellings, from the circumstance that the people who do it are almost all farmers or fishermen likewise. A stranger who has not been enlightened upon the ways of the place would be astonished at the number of small square erections, like miniature schoolhouses, standing each as an appendage to a dwelling house. These are the shoeshops, where the father of the family and his boys work, while the women within are employed in binding and trimming. Thirty or more of these shoeshops may be counted in a walk of half a mile. When a Lynn shoe manufacturer receives an order, he issues the tidings. The leather is cut out by men on his premises; and then the work is given to those who apply for it—if possible, in small quantities, for the sake of dispatch. The shoes are brought home on Friday night, packed off on Saturday, and in a fortnight or three weeks are on the feet of dwellers in all parts of the Union. The whole family works upon shoes during the winter, and in the summer the father and sons turn out into the fields or go fishing. I know of an instance where a little boy and girl maintained the whole family, while the earnings of the rest went to build a house. I saw very few shabby houses. Quakers are numerous in Lynn. The place is unboundedly prosperous, through the temperance and industry of the people. The deposits in the Lynn Savings Bank in 1834 were about thirty-four thousand dollars, the population of the town being then four thousand. Since that time, both the population and the prosperity have much increased. It must be remembered too that the mechanics of America have more uses for their money than are open to the operatives of England. They build houses, buy land, and educate their sons and daughters.

It is probably true that the pleasures and pains of life are pretty equally distributed among its various vocations and positions, but it is difficult to keep clear of the impression which outward circumstances occasion, that some are eminently desirable. The mechanics of these Northern States appear to me the most favored class I have ever known. In England, I believe the highest order of mechanics to be, as a class, the wisest and best men of the community. They have the fewest base and narrow interests; they are brought into sufficient contact with the realities of existence without being hardened by excess of toil and care; and the knowledge they have the opportunity of gaining is of the best kind for the health of the mind. To them, if to any, we may look for public and private virtue. The mechanics of America have nearly all the same advantages, and some others. They have better means of living; their labors are perhaps more honored; and they are republicans, enjoying the powers and prospects of perfectly equal citizenship. The only respect in which their condition falls below that of English artisans of the highest order is that the knowledge which they have commonly the means of obtaining is not the equal value. The facilities are great; schools, lyceums, libraries, are open to them; but the instruction imparted there is not so good as they deserve. Whenever they have this, it will be difficult to imagine a mode of life more favorable to virtue and happiness than theirs.

There seems to be no doubt among those who know both England and America that the mechanics of the New World work harder than those of the Old. They have much to do besides their daily handicraft business. They are up and at work early about this, and when it is done, they read till late, or attend lectures, or perhaps have their houses to build or repair, or other care to take of their property. They live in a state and period of society where every man is answerable for his own fortunes and where there is therefore stimulus to the exercise of every power.

What a state of society it is when a dozen artisans of one town—Salem—are seen rearing each a comfortable one-story (or, as the Americans would say, two-story) house, in the place with which they have grown up! when a man who began with laying bricks criticizes, and sometimes corrects, his lawyer's composition; when a poor errand boy becomes the proprietor of a flourishing store before he is thirty; pays off the capital advanced by his friends at the rate of two thousand dollars per month, and bids fair to be one of the more substantial citizens of the place! Such are the outward fortunes of the mechanics of America.

There must have been a time when Americans were serious about stamping out prostitution and gambling in their cities, as shown in descriptions of these riots and investigations.

NIGHT LIFE

Portland Whorehouse Riot

(1825)

We are again called upon to record the proceedings of a disgraceful riot, making the third which has occurred in this town, in the space of little more than a year, and the last of a more atrocious and aggravated character than either of the former, inasmuch as deadly weapons were used and life taken. If these affairs are suffered to go on at this rate, Portland will soon receive and *deserve* the name of mob-town. It is high time something effectual was done to put a stop to occurrences of this kind. If we have laws sufficient to preserve order in the community, let them be enforced; if we have not, let application be made to the Legislature for the enactment of laws of a more severe and efficacious nature. We have generally been in the habit of considering the standard of public morals in this town as high and tense as in any of our seaport towns, and are at a loss to account for the repetition of scenes which indicate a want of moral energy in the community, and which are universally condemned, though not prevented. . . . *Every* good citizen should make it his business, and be willing to raise his voice and his hand against these enormous outrages upon the peace and security of society. It is said most of the offenders in this last riot were foreigners, principally Irishmen. Be it so, it does not remove the stain from the reputation of the town; public peace has been outraged, no matter by whom . . .

These outrageous riots and highhanded breaches of the peace have grown out of a well-meant, but ill advised step of some individuals about a year ago to do what they no doubt thought a good deed. There was . . . a nest of little, mean, filthy boxes, of that description commonly called houses of ill-fame, tenanted by the most loathsome and vicious of the human species, and made a common resort for drunken sailors and the lowest off-scouring of society. These buildings in the heart of the town were an *eye-sore* to the neighborhood, and even the owners of some of the buildings wished them torn away. . . . Instead of taking the proper steps of the law to abate these nuisances, a company of laboring people, truckmen, boys &c. understanding the feelings of the owners and the wishes of the neighbors, assembled in the evening, turned out the tenants and tore the buildings to the ground, while some hundreds of citizens stood looking on and sanctioning the whole proceeding by their presence and their silence. The operators in this transaction becoming a little warm and excited, grew over zealous in the good work and repaired to other parts of the town and demolished other buildings of a like character. The affair passed off and but little was said or done about it. But the example was left to work its effect upon the minds of lower classes of people, the idle, the mischievous, and the vicious, and having learnt their lesson they began last spring to put it in practice. It was a kind of sport that had peculiar attractions for idle roaring boys and raw Irishmen; and the watchword being past, a throng assembled one night and tore several more houses of ill-fame, *all for public good*, mind ye; till coming to a long 2 story house in Crabtree's wharf, which contained several families, and which proved so firmly built that they were unable to pull it down, and in their zeal for serving the public they set it on fire, and the whole town was alarmed in the dead of night by the ringing of bells and the cry of fire. It was now thought to be rather a serious matter and the feelings of the citizens were very much excited. The selectmen called a town meeting, and a committee was appointed to investigate the subject and to commence legal prosecutions. Accordingly several were arrested, examined, and bound over for trial. One black man, not being able to procure bonds, was committed to jail for a few months until the Common Pleas was in session. All of them were finally discharged without any penalty, and it was thought, the law had shown its *teeth* at the rioters, they would be deterred from a repetion of their offenses.

But time has proved the opinion fallacious. . . . On Saturday night last, the *reformers* attacked a two story house on Fore Street occupied by a colored barber by the name of Gray. Gray had been convicted at the Common Pleas Court of keeping a house of ill-fame, and had appealed to the Supreme Court which is now in session, and in which he has also been convicted the present week. But the mob chose to render more speedy justice than the laws would do and accordingly on Saturday night they threw a few rocks into Gray's house, broke the windows, &c., but either from the want of sufficient forces or from meeting more resistance than they expected, they desisted till Monday evening, when they renewed their attack with increased force. In the meantime Gray had armed himself with guns and other weapons. He and his family, with some others remained in the house. In the course of the assault, the mob fired guns into the house, and guns were fired from the house upon the mob. Which fired first we are not informed. One man in the street, an Englishman by the name of Joseph Fuller, was killed almost instantly and six or eight others were wounded, some severely. After this the crowd soon dispersed. We examined the house on Tuesday morning, and found the windows mostly stove in, rocks scattered about the floors and lead shot in the plastering opposite the windows.—From Portland (Maine) *Eastern Argus,* November 11, 1825.

Pay As You Enter

Proceeding from the subterranean apartments below to view the rooms in the upper stories, a class of tenant house occupants was stumbled upon, for the amelioration of whose condition the [legislative] Committee, [appointed to examine into the construction of tenement houses] hardly deemed themselves commissioned. The staid chairman was quietly taking the lead, not venturing hardly to ask a question without a prefatory apology, when, passing into a room on the fourth floor, he was proceeding to open the bedroom door.

"No, sir, don't you do it," uttered a big, coarse woman; "I don't care who you are—no one opens that door unless he pays first!"

The chairman did not open the door, but while he looked amazed, together with the other rural members of the Committee, the dozen female occupants of the room set up a general laugh, the import of which was unmistakable. The chairman beat a hasty retreat, followed by two other members of the committee and Mr. Downing.—From Mobile *Commercial Register,* July 10, 1835.

Vicksburg Gamblers (1835)

For years past, professional gamblers, destitute of all sense of moral obligations . . . have made Vicksburg their place of rendezvous—and, in the very bosom of our society, boldly plotted their vile and lawless machinations. . . .

Our streets everywhere resounded with the echoes of their drunken and obscene mirth, and no citizen was secure from their villainy. Frequently in armed bodies, they have disturbed the good order of public assemblages, insulted our citizens, and defied our civil authorities. Thus had they continued to grow bolder in their wickedness, and more formidable in their numbers, until Saturday, the fourth of July, instant, when our citizens had assembled together with a corps of Vicksburg volunteers, at the barbecue to celebrate the day by the usual festivities. After dinner, and during the delivery of the toasts, one of the officers attempted to enforce order and silence at the table, when one of these gamblers, whose name is Cakler, who had impudently thrust himself into the company, insulted the officer, and struck one of the citizens. Indignation immediately rose high, and it was only by the interference of the commandant that he was saved from instantaneous punishment. He was, however, permitted to retire, and the company dispersed.

The military corps proceeded to the public square of the city, and information was received that Cakler was coming up armed, and resolved to kill one of the volunteers who had been most active in expelling him from the table. Knowing his desperate character—two of the corps instantly stepped forward and arrested him. A loaded pistol, a large knife and a dagger were found on his person, all of which he had procured since he had separated from the company. To liberate him would have been to devote several of the most respectable members of the company to his vengeance, and to proceed against him at law would have been mere mockery, inasmuch, as not having had the opportunity of consummating his design, no adequate punishment could have been inflicted on him. Consequently it was determined to take him into the woods and *Lynch* him—which is a mode of punishment provided for such as become obnoxious in a manner which the law cannot reach. He was immediately carried out under a guard, attended by a crowd of respectable citizens—tied to a tree, punished with stripes—tarred and feathered; and ordered to leave the city in forty-eight hours.—From *Frank Leslie's Illustrated Newspaper*, Vol. I (March 29, 1856), No. 16, p. 246.

Every age cherishes its "low life," clucks over it, excoriates it, does everything but put an end to it or ignore it. As in so much of American history, the choicest lowlife was in New York. The area here described later produced that monarch among gangsters of the 1920s, Al Capone. (From C. C. Foster, *New York by Gas-Light*, 1850.)

NEW YORK BY GAS-LIGHT

Thomas Carlyle, the great Scotchman, looked up to the starry midnight and exclaimed with a groan, " 'Tis a sad sight!" What would have been his exclamation had he stood, reader, where you and I now stand—in the very center of the "Five Points,"—knowing the moral geography of the place,—and with that same midnight streaming its glories down upon his head! *This* is, indeed, a sad, an awful sight—a sight to make the blood slowly congeal and the heart to grow fearful and cease its beatings. Here, whence these streets diverge in dark and endless paths, whose steps take hold on hell—here is the very type and physical semblance, in fact, of hell itself. Moralists no longer entertain a doubt that the monster vice of humanity is licentiousness—the vice teeming with destruction and annihilation to the race itself—pervading all classes,—inextinguishable either by repressive laws or by considerations of personal safety. . . .

So, then, we are standing at midnight in the center of the Five Points. Over our heads is a large gas-lamp, which throws a strong light for some distance around, over the scene where once complete darkness furnished almost absolute security and escape to the pursued thief and felon, familiar with every step and knowing the exits and entrances to every house. In those days an officer, even with the best intentions, was often baffled at the very moment when he thought he had his victim most secure. Some unexpected cellar-door, or some silent-sliding panel, would suddenly receive the fugitive and thwart the keenest pursuit. Now, however, the large lamp is kept constantly lighted, and a policeman stands ever sentinel to see that it is not extinguished. The existence of this single lamp has greatly improved the character of the whole location and increased the safety of going through the Points at night. Those, however, whose purposes are honest, had better walk a mile round the spot, on their way home, than cross through.

Opposite the lamp, eastwardly, is the "Old Brewery"—a building so often described that it has become as familiar as the Points themselves—in print. We will not, therefore, attempt another description of that which has already been so well depicted. The building was originally, previous to the city being built up so far, used as a brewery. But when the population increased and buildings, streets and squares grew up and spread out all around it, the owner—shrewd man, and very respectable church deacon—found that he might make a much larger income from his brewery than by retaining it for the manufacture of malt liquor. It was accordingly floored and partitioned off into small apartments, and rented to persons of disreputable character and vile habits, who had found their inevitable way gradually from the "Golden Gate of Hell," through all the intermediate haunts of prostitution and drunkenness, down to this hell-like den—little less dark, gloomy and terrible than the grave itself, to which it is the prelude. Every room in every story has its separate family or occupant, renting by the week or month and paying in advance. In this one room, the cooking, eating and sleeping of the whole family, and their visitors, are performed. Yes—*and their visitors:* for it is no unusual thing for a mother and her two or three daughters—all of course prostitutes—to receive their "men" at the same time and in the same room—passing in and out and going through all the transaction of their hellish intercourse, with a sang froid at which devils would stand aghast and struck with horror.

All the houses in this vicinity, and for some considerable distance round—yes, every one—are of the same character, and are filled in precisely the same manner. The lower stories are usually occupied as drinking and dancing rooms: and here, soon as evening sets in, the inmates of the house, dressed in most shocking immodesty, gather. The bar sends forth its poisonous steam—the door is flung wide open, if the weather will permit it; and the women, bare-headed, bare-armed and bare-bosomed, stand in the doorway or on the side-walk, inviting passers-by, indiscriminately, to enter, or exchanging oaths and obscenity with the inmates of the next house, similarly employed. The walkers in these haunts are mostly sailors, negroes and the worst of loafers and vagabonds, who are enticed and perhaps even dragged in by the painted Jezebels, made to "treat," and then invited to the dance—every room being provided with its fiddler, ready to tune up his villainous squeaking for sixpence a piece and a treat at the end of the figure. The liquor is of course of the most abominable description, poison and fire; and by the time the first dance is concluded, the visitor feels his blood on fire —all his brutal appetites are aroused, and he is ready for any thing. The first object is to produce stupefying intoxication. More drinking is proposed—then more dancing—then drink, and so on, until the poor victim loses what little human sense and precaution he is endowed withal, and hurries his partner off in a paroxysm of drunken lust. Of course if he has any money or valuables on his person he is completely robbed. If his clothes are decent they are stripped off him and a pair of tattered trowsers put on, when he is kicked into the street by a back door, and found by the policemen just in time for the loafer's reveillé at the Tombs, at day-light. Sometimes the victim is not quite so drunk as is supposed, and doesn't submit quietly to the touching operation. Another glass—or if he refuses, a good "punch" on the head—settles the question for him, with speediest logic, and the problem is solved at once.

In the cellars of these houses are the "oyster saloons,"etc., etc. for the accommodation of thieves, burglars, low gamblers and vagabonds in general, who haunt these quarters, and whose "pals" are up-stairs carrying on the game of prostitution. They are usually kept open nearly all night, because the population forming the principal class of their customers burrow in their secret holes and dens all day, and only venture out at night. Indeed, this is mostly true of all the inhabitants in this region. They are the obscene night-birds who flit and howl and hoot by night, and whose crimes and abominations make them shun the light of day—nor merely because they fear detection, but because day is hateful to them. Dropping in from their expeditions of the night—some from picking pockets at the theaters, some from general prowling after what they can pick up about town, and others from more important and regularly-ordered expeditions of robbery or burglary or arson,—they recognize each other with a sullen nod or gather in noisy riot, as the humor takes them. If a stranger enter, they immediately reconnoiter, and if they conclude that he is worth picking, they immediately commence their game. The most usual one is to get up a pretended dispute and call upon the stranger to decide. Often card-tricks or thimbles are introduced, and the conspirators bet carelessly and largely against each other—pulling out and showing pocket-books well crammed with counterfeit or worthless bills. If the stranger is not fully aware of the character of those among whom he has fallen, he is a "goner." If none of the ordinary tricks will answer, as a last resource they get up a sham row and fight, in the course of which general scramble the pigeon is pretty sure of being plucked to the last feather, and most likely left bleeding and senseless in the street.

Leading off easterly from the big gas-lamp we have mentioned, is a little three-cornered piece of ground about the size of a village potato-patch, enclosed in whitewashed palings, containing half-a-dozen stunted trees. This is the "Regent's Park" of that neighborhood, and the walk by which it is surrounded is continually crowded in pleasant evenings by couples chaffering and carrying on their infamous bargains —reminding one of the reverse of rural life with all its innocent blandishments and moonlight love-walks beneath the whispering trees. Indeed throughout the entire realm of metropolitan degradation one is incessantly struck with the ghastly resemblances to the forms of virtue and purity, everywhere starting out before him. There is no virtue nor innocence of a beauteous life which is not reflected in the dark sea of licentiousness and dissipation—though in an inverted position, like the images of green shores and pleasant trees in the turbid waters of the wild-rolling river.

A few steps from the Points is a little alley terminating in a blind court or *cul-de-sac*, into which is constantly pouring a stream of mephitic air which never finds an outlet nor an escape, save into the lungs of those who inhale it. This alley is called "Cow Bay," and is chiefly celebrated in profane history as being the battle-field of the negroes and police. Of course the negroes form a large and rather controlling portion of the population of the Points, as they bear brutalization better than the whites, (probably from having been so long used to it!) and retain more consistency and force of character, amid all their filth and degradation. They manage, many of them, to become house-keepers and landlords, and in one way and another scrape together a good deal of money. They associate upon at least equal terms with the men and women of the parish, and many of them are regarded as desirable companions and lovers by the "girls." They most of them have either white wives or white mistresses, and sometimes both; and their influence in the community is commanding. But they are savage, sullen, reckless dogs, and are continually promoting some "muss" or other, which not unfrequently leads to absolute riot. Two memorable occasions, at least, have recently occured in which "Cow Bay" was rendered classic ground by the set fights which took place within its purlieus between the police and the fighting-men among the Ethiopian tribes. Both commenced at dusk and lasted for over an hour,—giving occasion for the display of individual prowess and feats of arms before which the Chronicles of the veracious Froissart sink into insignificance. But as we do not aspire to the historian's bays, we must leave the details to the imagination of our readers, in the good old-fashioned way of those who attempt a description to which their powers are unequal. It is related, however, that the police were for a long time unable to make headway against the furious onslaught of the blacks, who received the official clubs so liberally rattled about their heads, without flinching, and returned the charge with stones and brickbats, so gallantly that several of the protectors of the city had already knocked under, and the whole body began actually to give way—when the renowned Captain Smith bethought him that Cuffee's tender point was not the head, but the SHIN. Passing the word in a whisper to his men to strike low, he himself aimed a settler at the understandings of a gigantic negro who led the assualt upon his wing, and brought him instantly, with a terrific yell of agony, to the ground. A shout of triumph, and a simultaneous movement of the police, as if they were mowing, soon decided the contest, and covered the shores and gutters of "Cow Bay" with the sprawling forms of the tender-shinned Africans. Once afterward the very same thing happened, with precisely similar results: and since, the woolly-heads are kept in tolerable subjection. If they ever become troublesome let but a policeman grasp his club tightly and take aim at the shins, and the ground is cleared in a twinkling.

Another peculiar and description-worth feature of the Five Points are the "fences," or shops for the reception and purchase of stolen goods. These shops are of course kept entirely by Jews, and are situated in a row, in Orange street, near the Points. One who has never seen the squalid undercrust of a fine city would be at a loss to derive any adequate idea, even from the most graphic description, of the sort of building in which the great business of living and trafficking *can* be carried on. If the reader is a farmer, however, we shall succeed tolerably well in conveying some notion of what we mean. Let him imagine forty or fifty cow-sheds got together in line, furnished with dismal-looking little windows, half broken in and patched up with old newspapers— let him imagine half a hundred of these establishments, we say, standing in a row, with a dark paved street and an uneven narrow brick sidewalk in front, and he will not be far behind the reality of the place where we now stand.

These beggarly little shanties all have pretensions to being considered shops, and in each the front window is heaped up with an indiscriminate indescribableness of wares. Here is a drugstore, with a big bottle of scarlet water in the window, throwing a lurid glare out into the dark. The next is a clothing-store, another hardware, another gentlemen's furnishing, &c., &c. They are all, however, devoted to the one branch of trade, in all its varieties—the purchase of stolen goods. Whatever may be the sign in the window, the thief who has grabbed a watch, prigged a handkerchief or robbed a store, brings his booty confidently in and receives his money for it. Perhaps not at a very high figure—but then, you know, "de peoplesh ish very poor in dis neighborhood, and we can't kif much—and besides we don't really want 'em at all." The felon, of course, anxious to have them off his hands, sells them at any price. Whatever may be the article purchased, the first care is naturally to destroy its identity, rub out its ear-marks, and thus prepare it against being claimed by the owner and the purchase of stolen goods fastened upon the "fence." If it is a coat or garment of any kind, the seams are carefully ripped open, the facings, linings, &c., &c. changed, and the whole hastily stitched together again and disposed to the best advantage on the shelves or in the window. If the article purchased is jewelry, it is immediately melted, and converted into bullion,—the precious stones, if there be any, carefully put aside. The most troublesome and dangerous articles are watches—and these the "fence" generally hesitates to have anything to do with, recommending his customer to the pawn-broker, who usually is not much less a rascal than himself. From particular customers, however, whose delicate organizations and long experience render them peculiarly successful in the watch business, the "fence" is willing to receive these dainty wares—although at a terrible sacrifice, and even then never keeping them on hand longer than is necessary to get safely to the pawn-broker's.

In the rear of each of these squalid shops is a wretched apartment or two, combining the various uses of sleeping, eating, cooking and living, with the other performances necessary for carrying on the operations of the front shop. They are generally densely inhabited— the descendants of Israel being as celebrated for fecundity as cats or

Irish women. And here it is proper to state one of the most remarkable facts we have encountered in the course of our metropolitan investigations. However low the grade or wretched the habitation—and the latter are generally filthy to abomination—of the Jew, the race always retains the peculiar physical conformation constituting that peculiar style of beauty for which his tribe has been celebrated from remotest antiquity. The roundness and suppleness of limb, the elasticity of flesh, the glittering eye-sparkle—are as inevitable in Jew or Jewess, in whatever rank of existence, as the hook of the nose which betrays the Israelite as the human kite, formed to be feared, hated and despised, yet to prey upon mankind.

We could not expect to convey any tolerable idea of the Five Points were we to omit all attempt at describing one of their most remarkable and characteristic features—the great wholesale and retail establishment of Mr. Crown, situated on the corner opposite "Cow Bay." A visit of exploration through this place we regard as one of our most noteworthy experiences in life. The building itself is low and mean in appearance, although covering a good deal of ground. It contains three low stories—the upper one being devoted to the same species of life and traffic as all the other houses in the neighborhood. It is with the two lower stories, however, that we have at present to do—these being occupied as the store. The entrance is on both streets; and, although entirely unobstructed by any thing but the posts that sustain the walls above, it is not without difficulty that we effect an entrance, through the baskets, barrels, boxes, Irishwomen and sluttish house-keepers, white, black, yellow and brown, thickly crowding the walk, up to the very threshold—as if the store were too full of its commodities and customers, and some of them had tumbled and rolled out-doors. On either hand piles of cabbages, potatoes, squashes, egg-plants, tomatoes, turnips, eggs, dried apples, chestnuts and beans rise like miniature mountains round you. At the left hand as you enter is a row of little boxes containing anthracite and charcoal, nails, plug-tobacco, &c. &c. which are dealt out in any quantity, from a bushel or a dollar to a cent's-worth. On a shelf near by is a pile of fire-wood, seven sticks for sixpence, or a cent apiece, and kindling-wood three sticks for two cents. Along the walls are ranged upright casks containing lamp-oil, molasses, rum, whisky, brandy, and all sorts of cordials, (carefully manufactured in the back room, where a kettle and furnace, with all the necessary instruments of spiritual devilment are provided for the purpose.) The cross-beams that support the ceiling are thickly hung with hams, tongues, sausages, strings of onions, and other light and airy articles, and at every step you tumble over a butter-firkin or a meal-bin. Across one end of the room runs a "long, low, black" counter, armed at either end with bottles of poisoned fire-water, doled out at three cents a glass to the loafers and bloated women who frequent the place—while the shelves behind are filled with an uncatalogueable jumble of candles, all-spice, crackers, sugar and tea, pickles, ginger, mustard, and other kitchen necessaries. In the opposite corner is a shorter counter filled with three-cent pies, mince, apple, pumpkin and custard—all kept smoking hot—where you can get a cup of coffee with plenty of milk and sugar, for the same price, and buy a hat-full of "Americans with Spanish wrappers" for a penny.

Groping our way through the back room, where the furnace and other machineries are kept—and which may be appropriately termed the laboratory of the concern—we mount a short ladder, and squeeze our way amid piles of drying tobacco, cigar-boxes, tubs, buckets, bales and bundles, of all imaginable shapes and uses, into a little room, similarly filled, but in a corner of which room has been dug for a single cot, upon which lie a heap of rags that evidently have never been washed nor disturbed since they were first slept under, save by the nightly crawlings in and out of the clerk of the premises, and the other inhabitants. Here too is a diminutive iron safe, containing the archives and valuables of the establishment—perhaps silver spoons, rings, watches, and other similar properties—who knows?

One thing is at least certain—the proprietor of this store has amassed a large fortune in a few years, by the immense per centage of profit realized on his minute sales. His customers, living literally from hand to mouth, buy the food they eat and even the fire and whisky that warms them, not only from day to day, but literally from hour to hour. Of many commodities a large proportion sticks to the measure, and on others the profit is incredible—often reaching as high as five or six hundred per cent. No credit—not for a moment—is given to any one, and everything is bought for cash and at the cheapest rates and commonest places.

Well—it is nearly dawn, and we might still prolong our stay upon the Points, there being no lack of subjects well worth our investigation and study. But this is enough for once. To-morrow night—should the fancy take us, for we bind ourselves to nothing—we will return and look in at some of the regular dance-houses and public places in this neighborhood—especially the well known "Dickens' Place," kept by Pete Williams, which, like other more aristocratic establishments, was shut up during the summer, "on account of the cholera." Before we leave this dreadful place—at once the nucleus and consummation of prostitution—we will state a fact or two and make a few reflections bearing generally on the subject. The great source whence the ranks of prostitution are replenished is young women from the country, who, seduced and in the way of becoming mothers, fly from home to escape infamy, and rush to the city with anguish and desperation in their hearts. Either murdering their infants as soon as born, or abandoning them upon a doorstep, they are thenceforth ready for any course of crime that will procure them a living,—or, if they still have struggling scruples, necessity soon overcomes them. As an instance of this we were recently informed of a case where thirteen unmarried mothers came from Canada to New-York a few weeks before their confinement, and were all sent to the Asylum. Of these thirteen poor, deserted, heart-broken creatures, eleven are now inhabitants of the Five Points or the immediate neighborhood. How has society punished the respectable seducers and destroyers of these women?

Another fact is that those who once enter into this diabolical traffic are seldom saved. The poison is active as lightning, and produces a kind of moral insanity, during which the victim is pleased with ruin and rejects the hand outstretched to save her. We have avoided no pains nor labor in our researches on this subject, and we wish all virtuous and benevolent men and women to mark well our words:— After a woman once enters a house of prostitution and leads the life of all who dwell there, *it is too late*. The woman is transformed to a devil and there is no hope for her. There may be, and doubtless are, exceptions to this rule, but we are convinced they must be rare. When a woman has once nerved herself to make the fatal plunge, a change comes over her whole character; and sustained by outraged love transmuted to hate, by miscalculating yet indomitable pride, by revenge, and by a reckless abandonment to the unnatural stimulus and excitement of her new profession, her fate is fixed. Take heed, then, philanthropists, and fathers and mothers, and husbands, whose wives and daughters have drank deeply of that damning draught of ambition for dress and display, that makes so many prostitutes! Expend all your watchfulness and tenderness and care upon your charges *before* they fall. Lay open to them with a bold and faithful hand the horrors of the career which lies before them, unless they learn to unlearn vanity and to learn content. For one whose hair is gray, and whose heart has often and often bled for grief at sight of so many beautiful creatures wrecked and cast away forever, in the wild pursuit after admiration, tells you that vanity and a love for social distinction are the rocks upon which these noble vessels, freighted with the wealth of immortal souls, have foundered. Strive, oh young woman! whose heart pants with envy at the gay equipages and fine dresses of the more fortunate or more guilty sisters who glitter by you—strive to win to your bosom the sweet and gentle goddess Content. So shall memory and hope embalm your life and time shall crown you alone with blessings.

Underworld slang is a frequent forerunner of common expressions and remains perennially fascinating to respectable citizens. (Selection from *Gangster Slang of the 1850's,* 1928.)

UNDERWORLD SLANG

The following slang terms are from *"Vocabulum, or, The Rogue's Lexicon,"* by George W. Matsell, Special Justice and Chief of the New York Police. It was first published in 1859 by George W. Matsell & Company, proprietors of the *National Police Gazette.* It is interesting to note that of the words and phrases which are still in use, the meaning of many has entirely changed. Others, however, retain their ancient meanings, and have been appropriated by the modern wise-cracker:

Ace of Spades. A widow.
Active citizen. A louse.
Addle-cove. A foolish man.
Alamort. Confounded; struck dumb; unable to say or do anything.
Ankle. The mother of a child born out of wedlock.
Anointed. Flogged.
Autum. A church.
Autum bawler. A parson.

Baby paps. Caps.
Ballum-rancum. A ball where all the dancers are thieves and prostitutes.
Balsam. Money.
Bandog. A civil officer.
Baptized. Liquor that has been watered.
Barking irons. Pistols.
Barrel fever. Delirium tremens.
Bat. A prostitute who walks the street only at night.
Beak. A magistrate; a judge.
Beans. Five dollar gold pieces.
Ben. A vest.
Benjamin. A coat.
Bens. Fools.
Billy Noodle. A soft fellow who believes all the girls are in love with him.
Bingo. Liquor.
Bingo-boy. A drunken man.

Bingo-mort. A drunken woman.
Black-box. A lawyer.
Black ointment. Raw meat.
Bleak. Handsome. "The moll is bleak"; the girl is handsome.
Bleak mort. A pretty girl.
Bloke. A man.
Blowen. The mistress of a thief.
Bludget. A female thief.
Blue ruin. Bad gin.
Blunt. Money.
Boke. The nose.
Boodle. A quantity of bad money.
Booly dog. A policeman.
Bouncer. A fellow who robs while bargaining with the storekeeper.
Brads. Money.
Brass. Money
Broads. Cards.
Broken leg. A woman who has a child out of marriage.
Bucks-face. A cuckold.
Bull. A locomotive.
Bully. A lump of lead tied in the corner of a kerchief.
Buzz. To search for and steal.

Cab moll. A woman who keeps a bad house.
Cad. A baggage smasher; a railroad conductor.
Cain and Abel. A table.
Can. A dollar.
Canary bird. A convict.
Captain Heeman. A blustering fellow.
Captain Toper. A smart highwayman.
Caravan. Plenty of money.
Casa. A house.
Case. A dollar.
Castor. A hat.
Cat. A prostitute; a cross old woman.
Century. One hundred dollars.
Charley. A gold watch.
Charley Prescot. A vest.
Chink. Money.
Chips. Money.
Church. A place where the markings on stolen jewelry are changed.
City College. The Tombs.
Clout. A handkerchief.
Conk. The nose.
Cove or covey. A man.
Cow. A dilapidated prostitute.
Cows and kisses. The ladies.
Crib. A house.
Crokus. A doctor.
Crusher. A policeman.
Cull. A man; sometimes a partner.
Cymbal. A watch.

The large influx of Irish immigrants in the 1840s and 1850s produced an outpouring of prejudice such as this song describes.

No Irish Need Apply

1   I'm a decent boy just landed from the town of Ballyfad;
I want a situation and I want it very bad.
I have seen employment advertised, "It's just the thing," says I,
But the dirty spalpeen ended with "No Irish need apply."
"Whoo," says I, "that is an insult, but to get the place I'll try."
So I went to see the blackguard with his "No Irish need apply."
Some do think it a misfortune to be christened Pat or Dan,
But to me it is an honor to be born an Irishman.

2   I started out to find the house; I got there mighty soon.
I found the old chap seated; he was reading the Tribune.
I told him what I came for, when he in a rage did fly.
"No!" he says, "You are a Paddy, and no Irish need apply."
Then I gets my dander rising, and I'd like to black his eye
For to tell an Irish gentleman "No Irish Need Apply."

3   I couldn't stand it longer so a-hold of him I took,
And I gave him such a beating as he'd get at Donnybrook,
He hollered "Milia Murther," and to get away did try,
And swore he'd never write again "No Irish Need Apply."
Well, he made a big apology; I told him then goodbye,
Saying, "When next you want a beating, write 'No Irish Need
    Apply.'"

the civil war and after

Like flowers sprouting from a gravesite, the terrible Civil War bred marvelous music that Americans sang for generations. "Dixie" below is not strictly speaking a Civil War song, since it had been around a long time by then, but it became the unofficial rebel anthem. (From National Magazine, *Heart Songs*, 1909.)

PATRIOTIC SONGS

Dixie

1   I wish I was in de land ob cotton,
Old times dar am not forgotten,
Look away! Look away! Look away! Dixie Land.
In Dixie Land whar I was born in,
Early on one frosty mornin',
Look away! Look away! Look away! Dixie Land.

Chorus
Den I wish I was in Dixie, Hooray! Hooray!
In Dixie Land I'll take my stand,
To lib and die in Dixie, Away, Away,
Away down south in Dixie, Away, Away,
Away down south in Dixie.

2   Old Missus marry "Will de Weaber,"
Willium was a gay deceaber;
Look away! Look away! Look away! Dixie Land.
But when he put his arm around 'er,
He smiles as fierce as a fortypounder,
Look away! Look away! Look away! Dixie Land.

3   His face was sharp as a butcher's cleaber,
But dat did not seem to greab'er;
Look away! Look away! Look away! Dixie Land.
Old Missus acted de foolish part,
And died for a man dat broke her heart,
Look away! Look away! Look away! Dixie Land.

4   Now here's a health to the next old Missus,
An all de gals dat want to kiss us;
    Look away! etc.
But if you want to drive 'way sorrow,
Come and hear dis song to-morrow,
    Look away! etc.

5   Dar's buckwheat cakes an' Ingun' batter,
Makes you fat or a little fatter;
    Look away! etc.
Den hoe it down an scratch your grabble,
To Dixie's land I'm bound to trabble,
    Look away! etc.

The Bonnie Blue Flag

1   We are a band of brothers, and native to the soil,
Fighting for the property we gain'd by honest toil;
And when our rights were threaten'd the cry rose near and far,
Hurrah for the Bonnie Blue Flag, that bears a Single Star.

Chorus
Hurrah! Hurrah! for Southern Rights, Hurrah!
Hurrah! for the Bonnie Blue Flag, that bears a single Star.

2   As long as the old Union was faithful to her trust,
Like friends and like brothers, kind were we and just;
But now, when Northern treachery attempts our rights to mar,
We hoist on high the Bonnie Blue Flag, that bears a Single Star.

3   First, gallant South Carolina nobly made the stand;
Then came Alabama, who took her by the hand;
Next, quickly Mississippi, Georgia and Florida,
All rais'd on high the Bonnie Blue Flag that bears a Single Star.

4   Ye men of valor, gather round the Banner of the Right,
Texas and fair Louisiana join us in the fight;
Davis, our loved President, and Stephens, statesman rare,
Now rally round the Bonnie Blue Flag that bears a Single Star.

5   And here's to brave Virginia! the Old Dominion State
With the young Confederacy at length has linked her fate;
Impell'd by her example, now other states prepare
To hoist on high the Bonnie Blue Flag that bears a Single Star.

6   Then here's to our Confederacy, strong we are and brave,
    Like patriots of old, we'll fight our heritage to save;
    And rather than submit to shame, to die we would prefer,
    So cheer for the Bonnie Blue Flag that bears a Single Star.

7   Then cheer, boys, cheer, raise the joyous shout,
    For Arkansas and North Carolina now have both gone out;
    And let another rousing cheer for Tennessee be given—
    The Single Star of the Bonnie Blue Flag has grown to be Eleven.

Chorus for 7
Hurrah! Hurrah! for Southern Rights, Hurrah!
Hurrah! for the Bonnie Blue Flag has gain'd th' Eleventh Star.

Battle Hymn of the Republic

1   Mine eyes have seen the glory of the coming of the Lord;
    He is tramping out the vintage where the grapes of wrath
      are stored;
    He hath loosed the fateful lightning of his terrible quick sword:
    His truth is marching on.

Chorus
Glory, glory, hallelujah!
Glory, glory, hallelujah!
Glory, glory, hallelujah!
His truth is marching on.

2   I have seen him in the watchfires of a hundred circling camps;
    They have builded Him an altar in the evening dews and damps;
    I have read his righteous sentence by the dim and flaring lamps:
    His day is marching on.

3   I have read a fiery gospel, writ in burnished rows of steel,
    "As ye deal with my contemners, so with you my grace shall deal;
    Let the Hero, born of woman, crush the serpent with his heel,
    Since God is marching on.

4   He has sounded forth the trumpet that shall never call retreat;
    He is sifting out the hearts of men before his judgment seat;
    O, be swift, my soul, to answer Him! be jubilant, my feet:
    Our God is marching on.

5   In the beauty of the lilies Christ was born across the sea,
With a glory in His bosom that transfigures you and me;
As He died to make men holy, let us die to make men free,
While God is marching on.

John Brown's Body

1   John Brown's body lies a-mould'ring in the grave,
John Brown's body lies a-mould'ring in the grave,
John Brown's body lies a-mould'ring in the grave,
His soul is marching on!
  Glory, glory, hallelujah!
  Glory, glory, hallelujah!
  Glory, glory, hallelujah!
  His soul is marching on!

2   The stars of heaven are looking kindly down,
  On the grave of old John Brown! Cho.—Glory, etc.

3   He's gone to be a soldier in the army of the Lord!
  His soul is marching on. Cho.—Glory, etc.

4   John Brown's knapsack is strapped upon his back!
  His soul is marching on. Cho.—Glory, etc.

John Brown's Body (Another Version)

1   Old John Brown lies a-mouldering in the grave,
Old John Brown lies slumbering in his grave—
But John Brown's soul is marching with the brave,
His soul is marching on.
  Glory, glory, hallelujah!
  Glory, glory, hallelujah!
  Glory, glory, hallelujah!
  His soul is marching on!

2   He has gone to be a soldier in the army of the Lord,
He is sworn as a private in the ranks of the Lord—
He shall stand at Armageddon with his brave old sword,
When Heaven is marching on.
  Glory, glory, hallelujah, etc.
  For Heaven is marching on.

3   He shall file in front where the lines of battle form—
He shall face to front when the squares of battle form—
Time with the column, and charge with the storm,
Where men are marching on,
   Glory, glory, hallelujah, etc.
   True men are marching on.

4   Ah, foul tyrants! do ye hear him where he comes?
Ah, black traitors! do ye know him as he comes?
In thunder of the cannon and roll of the drums,
As we go marching on.
   Glory, glory, hallelujah, etc.
   We all go marching on.

5   Men may die, and moulder in the dust—
Men may die, and arise again from dust,
Shoulder to shoulder, in the ranks of the Just,
When Heaven is marching on.
   Glory, glory, hallelujah, etc.
   The Lord is marching on.—H. H. Brownell

The Battle Cry of Freedom

1   Yes, we'll rally around the flag, boys, we'll rally once again,
Shouting the battle cry of Freedom,
We will rally from the hillside, we'll gather from the plain,
Shouting the battle cry of Freedom.

Chorus
The Union forever, Hurrah boys, Hurrah!
Down with the traitor, Up with the star;
While we rally around the flags boys, rally once again,
Shouting the battle cry of Freedom.

2   We are springing to the call of our brothers gone before,
Shouting the battle cry of Freedom,
And we'll fill the vacant ranks with a million freemen more,
Shouting the battle cry of Freedom.

3   We will welcome to our numbers the loyal true and brave,
Shouting the battle cry of Freedom,
And altho' they may be poor, not a man shall be a slave,
Shouting the battle cry of Freedom.

4   So we're springing to the call from the East and from the West,
Shouting the battle cry of Freedom,
And we'll hurl the rebel crew from the land we love the best,
Shouting the battle cry of Freedom.

The war also produced its share of popular literature. They expressed the emotions of men and women in the crisis. (Selections from Francis Brown, *Bugle Echoes*, 1868; and Frank Moore, *Anecdotes, Poetry and Incidents of the War,* 1866.)

SOME CIVIL WAR POEMS

Enlisted To-day

I KNOW the sun shines, and the lilacs are blowing,
    And summer sends kisses by beautiful May;
Oh! to see all the treasures the spring is bestowing,
    And think—my boy Willie enlisted to-day.

It seems but a day since at twilight, low humming,
    I rocked him to sleep with his cheek upon mine,
While Robby, the four-year-old, watched for the
            coming
Of father, adown the street's indistinct line.

It is many a year since my Harry departed,
        To come back no more in the twilight or dawn;
And Robby grew weary of watching, and started
        Alone on the journey his father had gone.

It is many a year—and this afternoon, sitting
        At Robby's old window, I heard the band play,
And suddenly ceased dreaming over my knitting,
        To recollect Willie is twenty to-day.

And that, standing beside him this soft May-day morning,
        The sun making gold of his wreathed cigar smoke,
I saw in his sweet eyes and lips a faint warning,
        And choked down the tears when he eagerly spoke:

"Dear mother, you know how these Northmen are crowing,
    They would trample the rights of the South in the dust;
The boys are all fire; and they wish I were going—"
    He stopped, but his eyes said, "Oh, say if I must!"

I smiled on the boy, though my heart it seemed breaking,
    My eyes filled with tears, so I turned them away,
And answered him, "Willie, 'tis well you are waking—
    Go, act as your father would bid you, to-day!"

I sit in the window, and see the flags flying,
    And drearily list to the roll of the drum,
And smother the pain in my heart that is lying,
    And bid all the fears in my bosom be dumb.

I shall sit in the window when summer is lying
    Out over the fields, and the honey-bee's hum
Lulls the rose at the porch from her tremulous sighing,
    And watch for the face of my darling to come.

And if he should fall—his young life he has given
    For freedom's sweet sake; and for me, I will pray
Once more with my Harry and Robby in heaven
    To meet the dear boy that enlisted to-day.—*Anonymous.*

Three Hundred Thousand More

[In answer to President Lincoln's call, issued July 2, 1862, for 300,000 additional men, to serve three years]

We are coming, Father Abraham, three hundred thousand more,
From Mississippi's winding stream and from New England's shore;
We leave our ploughs and workshops, our wives and children dear,
With hearts too full for utterance, with but a silent tear;
We dare not look behind us, but steadfastly before:
We are coming, Father Abraham, three hundred thousand more!

If you look across the hill-tops that meet the northern sky,
Long moving lines of rising dust your vision may descry;
And now the wind, an instant, tears the cloudy veil aside,
And floats aloft our spangled flag in glory and in pride,
And bayonets in the sunlight gleam, and bands brave music pour:
We are coming, Father Abraham, three hundred thousand more!

If you look all up our valleys where the growing harvests shine,
You may see our sturdy farmer boys fast forming into line;
And children from their mother's knees are pulling at the weeds,
And learning how to reap and sow against their country's needs;
And a farewell group stands weeping at every cottage door:
We are coming, Father Abraham, three hundred thousand more!

You have called us, and we're coming, by Richmond's bloody tide
To lay us down, for Freedom's sake, our brothers' bones beside,
Or from foul treason's savage grasp to wrench the murderous blade,
And in the face of foreign foes its fragments to parade.
Six hundred thousand loyal men and true have gone before:
We are coming, Father Abraham, three hundred thousand more!

—Anonymous.

Paddy on Sambo as a Soldier

BY PRIVATE MILES O'REILLY
AIR: *"The Low-Backed Car."*

Some tell us 'tis a burning shame
To make the naygurs fight,
An' that the thrade of bein' kilt
Belongs but to the white;
But as for me, upon my sowl!
So liberal are we here,
I'll let Sambo be murdered in place of myself
On every day in the year!
    On every day in the year, boys,
    And every hour in the day,
    The right to be kilt I'll divide wid him,
    An' divil a word I'll say.

In battle's wild commotion
I shouldn't at all object
If Sambo's body should stop a ball
That was comin' for me direct;
And the prod of a Southern bagnet,
So liberal are we here,
I'll resign, and let Sambo take it,
On every day in the year!
    On every day in the year, boys,

And wid none of your nasty pride,
All my right in a Southern bagnet prod
Wid Sambo I'll divide.

The men who object to Sambo
Should take his place and fight;
And it's better to have a naygur's hue
Than a liver that's wake an' white.
Though Sambo's black as the ace of spades,
His finger a thrigger can pull,
And his eye runs straight on the barrel-sights
From under his thatch of wool!
　　So hear me all, boys, darlings,—
　　Don't think I'm tippin' you chaff,—
　　The right to be kilt I'll divide wid him,
　　And give him the largest half!

The Southern Cross

BY ST. GEORGE TUCKER

O, say, can you see, through the gloom and the storm,
More bright for the darkness, that pure constellation?
Like the symbol of love and redemption its form,
As it points to the haven of hope for the nation.
How radiant each star! as they beacon afar.
Giving promise of peace, or assurance in war;
'Tis the Cross of the South, which shall ever remain
To light us to Freedom and Glory again.

How peaceful and blest was America's soil,
Till betrayed by the guile of the Puritan demon,
Which lurks under Virtue, and springs from its coil,
To fasten its fangs in the life-blood of freemen!
Then loudly appeal to each heart that can feel,
And crush the foul viper 'neath Liberty's heel;
And the Cross of the South shall forever remain
To light us to Freedom and Glory again.

'Tis the emblem of peace, 'tis the day-star of hope,
Like the sacred Labarum, which guided the Roman:
From the shores of the Gulf to the Delaware's slope,
'Tis the trust of the free, and the terror of foemen.

Fling its folds to the air, while we boldly declare
The rights we demand, or the deeds that we dare;
And the Cross of the South shall forever remain
To light us to Freedom and Glory again.

But, if peace should be hopeless, and justice denied,
And war's bloody vulture should flap his black pinions,
Then gladly to arms! while we hurl, in our pride,
Defiance to tyrants, and death to their minions,
With our front to the field, swearing never to yield,
Or return like the Spartan in death on our shield;
And the Cross of the South shall triumphantly wave
As the flag of the free, or the pall of the brave.

The Civil War was a great thing for newspapermen. Their audience was riveted on the progress of the war to the virtual exclusion of all else and they had remarkable freedom to dig for information and present what they found. William Tecumseh Sherman, one of the great northern generals, in this letter of February 18, 1863, to his brother United States Senator John Sherman, laments the military difficulties this could at times cause. The conflict between the press and the constituted authorities is nothing new. (From Rachel Thorndike Sherman, ed., *The Sherman Letters*, 1894.)

THE GENERAL AND THE NEWSPAPERS

My Dear Brother:

We have reproached the South for arbitrary conduct in coercing their people; at last we find we must imitate their example. We have denounced their tyranny in filling their armies with conscripts, and now we must follow her example. We have denounced their tyranny in suppressing freedom of speech and the press, and here, too, in time, we must follow their example. The longer it is deferred the worse it becomes. Who gave notice of McDowell's movement on Manassas and enabled Johnston so to reinforce Beauregard that our army was defeated? The press. Who gave notice of the movement on Vicksburg? The press. Who has prevented all secret combinations and movements against our enemy? The press. . . .

In the South this powerful machine was at once scotched and used by the Rebel government, but in the North was allowed to go free.

What are the results? After arousing the passions of the people till the two great sections hate each other with a hate hardly paralleled in history, it now begins to stir up sedition at home, and even to encourage mutiny in our armies. What has paralyzed the Army of the Potomac? Mutual jealousies kept alive by the press. What has enabled the enemy to combine so as to hold Tennessee after we have twice crossed it with victorious armies? What defeats and will continue to defeat our best plans here and elsewhere? The press.

I cannot pick up a paper but tells of our situation here, in the mud, sickness, and digging a canal in which we have little faith. But our officers attempt secretly to cut two other channels, one into Yazoo by an old pass and one through Lake Providence into Tensas, Black, Red, etc., whereby we could turn not only Vicksburg, Port Hudson, but also Grand (Gulf), Natchez, Ellis Cliff, Fort Adams, and all the strategic points on the main river; and the busy agents of the press follow up and proclaim to the world the whole thing, and instead of surprising our enemy we find him felling trees and blocking passages that would without this have been in our possession, and all the real effects of surprise are lost. I say with the press unfettered as now we are defeated to the end of time. 'Tis folly to say the people must have news.

Every soldier can and does write to his family and friends, and all have ample opportunities for so doing; and this pretext forms no good reason why agents of the press should reveal prematurely all our plans and designs. We cannot prevent it. Clerks of steamboats, correspondents in disguise or openly, attend each army and detachment, and presto! appear in Memphis and St. Louis minute accounts of our plans and designs. These reach Vicksburg by telegraph from Hernando and Holly Springs before we know of it. The only two really successful military strokes out here have succeeded because of the absence of newspapers, or by throwing them off the trail. Halleck had to make a simulated attack on Columbus to prevent the press giving notice of his intended move against Forts Henry and Donelson. We succeeded in reaching the Post of Arkansas before the correspondents could reach the papers.

General Sherman's remark that "War is Hell" has remained one kind of last word on the subject. Certainly Sherman's credentials for making the statement are unimpeachable. His burning of Atlanta and his march through Georgia to the sea established in every mind the meaning of modern war. In the excerpts below, Sherman refuses a plea to spare Atlanta, and a Southern lady remembers the results of his subsequent march of destruction. (From the *Memoirs of General William T. Sherman, II,* 1887; and Eliza F. Andrews, *The War-Time Journal of a Georgia Girl,* 1908.)

ATLANTA, GEORGIA, SENTENCED TO DESTRUCTION

Gentlemen: I have your letter of the 11th, in the nature of a petition to revoke my orders removing all the inhabitants from Atlanta. I have read it carefully, and give full credit to your statements of the distress that will be occasioned, and yet shall not revoke my orders, because they were not designed to meet the humanities of the case, but to prepare for the future struggles in which millions of good people outside of Atlanta have a deep interest.

We must have peace, not only at Atlanta, but in all America. To secure this, we must stop the war that now desolates our once happy and favored country. To stop war, we must defeat the rebel armies which are arrayed against the laws and Constitution that all must respect and obey. To defeat those armies, we must prepare the way to reach them in their recesses, provided with the arms and instruments which enable us to accomplish our purpose.

Now, I know the vindictive nature of our enemy, that we may have many years of military operations from this quarter; and, therefore, deem it wise and prudent to prepare in time. The use of Atlanta for warlike purposes is inconsistent with its character as a home for families. There will be no manufactures, commerce, or agriculture here for the maintenance of families, and sooner or later want will compel the inhabitants to go. Why not go now, when all the arrangements are completed for the transfer, instead of waiting till the plunging shot of contending armies will renew the scenes of the past month? Of course, I do not apprehend any such thing at this moment, but you do not suppose this army will be here until the war is over. I cannot discuss this subject with you fairly, because I cannot impart to you what we propose to do, but I assert that our military plans make it necessary for the inhabitants to go away, and I can only renew my offer of services to make their exodus in any direction as easy and comfortable as possible.

You cannot qualify war in harsher terms than I will. War is cruelty, and you cannot refine it; and those who brought war into our country deserve all the curses and maledictions a people can pour out. I know I had no hand in making this war, and I know I will make more sacrifices today than any of you to secure peace. But you cannot have peace and a division of our country. If the United States submits to a division now, it will not stop, but will go on until we reap the fate of Mexico, which is eternal war.

The United States does and must assert its authority, wherever it once had power; for, if it relaxes one bit to pressure, it is gone, and I believe that such is the national feeling. This feeling assumes various shapes, but always comes back to that of Union. Once admit the Union, once more acknowledge the authority of the national Government, and, instead of devoting your houses and streets and roads to the dread uses of war, I and this army become at once your protectors and supporters, shielding you from danger, let it come from what quarter it may. I know that a few individuals cannot resist a torrent of error and passion, such as swept the South into rebellion, but you can point out, so that we may know those who desire a government, and those who insist on war and its desolation.

You might as well appeal against the thunderstorm as against these terrible hardships of war. They are inevitable, and the only way the people of Atlanta can hope once more to live in peace and quiet at home, is to stop the war, which can only be done by admitting that it began in error and is perpetuated in pride.

We don't want your Negroes, or your horses, or your houses, or your lands, or anything you have, but we do want and will have a just obedience to the laws of the United States. That we will have, and, if it involves the destruction of your improvements, we cannot help it.

You have heretofore read public sentiment in your newspapers, that live by falsehood and excitement; and the quicker you seek for truth in other quarters, the better. I repeat then that, by the original compact of government, the United States had certain rights in Georgia, which have never been relinquished and never will be; that the South began war by seizing forts, arsenals, mints, custom-houses, etc., etc., long before Mr. Lincoln was installed, and before the South had one jot or tittle of provocation.

I myself have seen in Missouri, Kentucky, Tennessee, and Mississippi, hundreds of thousands of women and children fleeing from your armies and desperadoes, hungry and with bleeding feet. In Memphis, Vicksburg, and Mississippi, we fed thousands upon thousands of the families of rebel soldiers left on our hands, and whom we could not see starve.

Now that war comes home to you, you feel very different. You deprecate its horrors, but did not feel them when you sent carloads of soldiers and ammunition, and molded shells and shot, to carry war into Kentucky and Tennessee, to desolate the homes of hundreds and thousands of good people who only asked to live in peace at their old homes, and under the government of their inheritance.

But these comparisons are idle. I want peace, and believe it can only be reached through union and war, and I will ever conduct war with a view to perfect and early success.

But, my dear sirs, when peace does come, you may call on me for anything. Then will I share with you the last cracker, and watch with you to shield your homes and families against danger from every quarter.

Now you must go, and take with you the old and feeble, feed and nurse them, and build for them, in more quiet places, proper habitations to shield them against the weather until the mad passions of men cool down, and allow the Union and peace once more to settle over your old homes at Atlanta. Yours in haste,

W. T. Sherman, Major-General commanding

THE "BURNT COUNTRY"

December 24, 1864.—About three miles from Sparta [Georgia] we struck the "Burnt Country," as it is well named by the natives, and then I could better understand the wrath and desperation of these poor people. I almost felt as if I should like to hang a Yankee myself. There was hardly a fence left standing all the way from Sparta to Gordon. The fields were trampled down and the road was lined with carcasses of horses, hogs, and cattle that the invaders, unable either to consume or to carry away with them, had wantonly shot down, to starve out the people and prevent them from making their crops. The stench in some places was unbearable; every few hundred yards we had to hold our noses or stop them with the cologne Mrs. Elzey had given us, and it proved a great boon.

The dwellings that were standing all showed signs of pillage, and on every plantation we saw the charred remains of the gin-house and packing-screw, while here and there lone chimney-stacks, "Sherman's sentinels," told of homes laid in ashes. The infamous wretches! I couldn't wonder now that these poor people should want to put a rope round the neck of every red-handed "devil of them" they could lay their hands on.

Hay ricks and fodder stacks were demolished, corn-cribs were empty, and every bale of cotton that could be found was burnt by the savages. I saw no grain of any sort, except little patches they had spilled when feeding their horses and which there was not even a chicken left in the country to eat. A bag of oats might have lain anywhere along the road without danger from the beasts of the fields, though I cannot say it would have been safe from the assaults of hungry man.

Crowds of [Confederate] soldiers were tramping over the road in both directions; it was like traveling through the streets of a populous town all day. They were mostly on foot, and I saw numbers seated on the roadside greedily eating raw turnips, meat skins, parched corn—anything they could find, even picking up the loose grains that Sherman's horses had left. I felt tempted to stop and empty the contents of our provision baskets into their laps, but the dreadful accounts that were given of the state of the country before us made prudence get the better of our generosity.

Before crossing the Oconee [River] at Milledgeville we ascended an immense hill, from which there was a fine view of the town, with Governor Brown's fortifications in the foreground and the river rolling at our feet. The Yankees had burnt the bridge; so we had to cross on a ferry. There was a long train of vehicles ahead of us, and it was nearly an hour before our turn came; so we had ample time to look about us. On our left was a field where thirty thousand Yankees had camped hardly three weeks before. It was strewn with the debris they had left behind, and the poor people of the neighborhood were wandering over it, seeking anything they could find to eat, even picking up grains of corn that were scattered around where the Yankees had fed their horses. We were told that a great many valuables were found there at first, plunder that the invaders had left behind, but the place had been picked over so often by this time that little now remained except tufts of loose cotton, piles of half-rotted grain, and the carcasses of slaughtered animals, which raised a horrible stench. Some men were plowing in one part of the field, making ready for next year's crop.

Walt Whitman in his Civil War writings did essentially what nearly everyone in the nation was trying to do: to find some way to cope with the brutal facts of a war between brothers. Whitman's particular courage was to confront the suffering of the war directly and struggle to personal terms with it. (From *Specimen Days*, 1882–83.)

AFTER THE BATTLES: THE NORTH

Wartime Letters

December 23 to 31, 1862.—The results of the late battle are exhibited everywhere about here in thousands of cases, (hundreds die every day,) in the camp, brigade, and division hospitals. These are merely tents, and sometimes very poor ones, the wounded lying on the ground, lucky if their blankets are spread on layers of pine or hemlock twigs, or small leaves. No cots; seldom even a mattress. It is pretty cold. The ground is frozen hard, and there is occasional snow. I go around from one case to another. I do not see that I do much good to these wounded and dying; but I cannot leave them. Once in a while some youngster holds on to me convulsively, and I do what I can for him; at any rate, stop with him and sit near him for hours, if he wishes it.

Besides the hospitals, I also go occasionally on long tours through the camps, talking with the men, &c. Sometimes at night among the groups around the fires, in their shebang enclosures of bushes. These are curious shows, full of characters and groups. I soon get acquainted anywhere in camp, with officers or men, and am always well used. Sometimes I go down on picket with the regiments I know best. As to rations, the army here at present seems to be tolerably well supplied, and the men have enough, such as it is, mainly salt pork and hard tack. Most of the regiments lodge in the flimsy little shelter-tents. A few have built themselves huts of logs and mud, with fire-places.

January, '63.—Left camp at Falmouth, with some wounded, a few days since, and came here by Aquia creek railroad, and so on government steamer up the Potomac. Many wounded were with us on the cars and boat. The cars were just common platform ones. The railroad journey of ten or twelve miles was made mostly before sunrise. The soldiers guarding the road came out from their tents or shebangs of bushes with rumpled hair and half-awake look. Those on duty were walking their posts, some on banks over us, others down far below the level of the track. I saw large cavalry camps off the road. At Aquia creek landing were numbers of wounded going north. While I waited some three hours, I went around among them. Several wanted word sent home to parents, brothers, wives, &c., which I did for them, (by mail the next day from Washington.) On the boat I had my hands full. One poor fellow died going up.

I am now remaining in and around Washington, daily visiting the hospitals. Am much in Patent-office, Eighth street, H street, Armory-square, and others. Am now able to do a little good, having money, (as almoner of others home,) and getting experience. To-day, Sunday afternoon and till nine in the evening, visited Campbell hospital; attended specially to one case in ward I, very sick with pleurisy and typhoid fever, young man, farmer's son, D. F. Russell, company E, 60th New York, downhearted and feeble; a long time before he would take any interest; wrote a letter home to his mother, in Malone, Franklin county, N. Y., at his request; gave him some fruit and one or two other gifts;

envelop'd and directed his letter, &c. Then went thoroughly through ward 6, observ'd every case in the ward, without, I think, missing one; gave perhaps from twenty to thirty persons, each one some little gift, such as oranges, apples, sweet crackers, figs, &c.

Thursday, Jan. 21.—Devoted the main part of the day to Armory-square hospital; went pretty thoroughly through wards F, G, H, and I; some fifty cases in each ward. In ward F supplied the men throughout with writing paper and stamp'd envelope each; distributed in small portions, to proper subjects, a large jar of first-rate preserv'd berries, which had been donated to me by a lady—her own cooking. Found several cases I thought good subjects for small sums of money, which I furnish'd. (The wounded men often come up broke, and it helps their spirits to have even the small sum I give them.) My paper and envelopes all gone, but distributed a good lot of amusing reading matter; also, as I thought judicious, tobacco, oranges, apples, &c. Interesting cases in ward I; Charles Miller, bed 19, company D, 53d Pennsylvania, is only sixteen years of age, very bright, courageous boy, left leg amputated below the knee; next bed to him, another young lad very sick; gave each appropriate gifts. In the bed above, also, amputation of the left leg; gave him a little jar of raspberries; bed 1, this ward, gave a small sum; also to a soldier on crutches, sitting on his bed near. . . . (I am more and more surprised at the very great proportion of youngsters from fifteen to twenty-one in the army. I afterwards found a still greater proportion among the southerners.)

Evening, same day, went to see D. F. R., before alluded to; found him remarkably changed for the better; up and dress'd—quite a triumph; he afterwards got well, and went back to his regiment. Distributed in the wards a quantity of note-paper, and forty or fifty stamp'd envelopes, of which I had recruited my stock, and the men were much in need. . . .

Letter Writing.—When eligible, I encourage the men to write, and myself, when called upon, write all sorts of letters for them, (including love letters, very tender ones.) Almost as I reel off these memoranda, I write for a new patient to his wife. M. de F., of the 17th Connecticut, company H, has just come up (February 17th) from Windmill point, and is received in ward H, Armory-square. He is an intelligent looking man, has a foreign accent, black-eyed and hair'd, a Hebraic appearance. Wants a telegraphic message sent to his wife, New Canaan, Conn. I agree to send the message—but to make things sure I also sit down and write the wife a letter, and despatch it to the postoffice immediately, as he fears she will come on, and he does not wish her to, as he will surely get well.

Saturday, January 30th.—Afternoon, visited Campbell hospital. Scene of cleaning up the ward, and giving the men all clean clothes— through the ward (6) the patients dressing or being dress'd—the naked upper half of the bodies—the good-humor and fun—the shirts, drawers, sheets of beds, &c., and the general fixing up for Sunday. Gave J. L. 50 cents.

Wednesday, February 4th.—Visited Armory-square hospital, went pretty thoroughly through wards E and D. Supplied paper and en- velopes to all who wish'd—as usual, found plenty of men who needed those articles. Wrote letters. Saw and talk'd with two or three members of the Brooklyn 14th regt. A poor fellow in ward D, with a fearful wound in a fearful condition, was having some loose splinters of bone taken from the neighborhood of the wound. The operation was long, and one of great pain—yet, after it was well commenced, the soldier bore it in silence. He sat up propp'd—was much wasted—had lain a long time quiet in one position (not for days only but weeks,) a blood- less, brown-skinn'd face, with eyes full of determination—belong'd to a New York regiment. There was an unusual cluster of surgeons, medical cadets, nurses, &c., around his bed—I thought the whole thing was done with tenderness, and done well. In one case, the wife sat by the side of her husband, his sickness typhoid fever, pretty bad. In another, by the side of her son, a mother—she told me she had seven children, and this was the youngest. (A fine, kind, healthy, gentle mother, good-looking, not very old, with a cap on her head, and dress'd like home—what a charm it gave to the whole ward.) I liked the woman nurse in ward E—I noticed how she sat a long time by a poor fellow who just had, that morning, in addition to his other sickness, bad hemorrhage—she gently assisted him, reliev'd him of the blood, holding a cloth to his mouth, as he coughed it up—he was so weak he could only just turn his head over on the pillow.

One young New York man, with a bright, handsome face, had been lying several months from a most disagreeable wound, receiv'd at Bull Run. A bullet had shot him right through the bladder, hitting him front, low in the belly, and coming out back. He had suffer'd much —the water came out of the wound, by slow but steady quantities, for many weeks—so that he lay almost constantly in a sort of puddle—and there were other disagreeable circumstances. He was of good heart, however. At present comparatively comfortable, had a bad throat, was delighted with a stick of horehound candy I gave him, with one or two other trifles.

February 23.—I must not let the great hospital at the Patent-office pass away without some mention. A few weeks ago the vast area of the second story of that noblest of Washington buildings was crowded close with rows of sick, badly wounded and dying soldiers. They were placed in three very large apartments. I went there many times. It was a strange, solemn, and, with all its features of suffering and death, a sort of fascinating sight. I go sometimes at night to soothe and relieve particular cases. Two of the immense apartments are fill'd with high and ponderous glass cases, crowded with models in minature of every kind of utensil, machine or invention, it ever enter'd into the mind of man to conceive; and with curiosities and foreign presents. Between these cases are lateral openings, perhaps eight feet wide and quite deep, and in these were placed the sick, besides a great long double row of them up and down through the middle of the hall. Many of them were very bad cases, wounds and amputations. Then there was a gallery running above the hall in which there were beds also. It was, indeed, a curious scene, especially at night when lit up. The glass cases, the beds, the forms lying there, the gallery above, and the marble pavement under foot—the suffering, and the fortitude to bear it in various degrees—occasionally, from some, the groan that could not be repress'd—sometimes a poor fellow dying, with emaciated face and glassy eye, the nurse by his side, the doctor also there, but no friend, no relative—such were the sights but lately in the Patent-office. . . .

Let me specialize a visit I made to the collection of barrack-like one-story edifices, Campbell hospital, out on the flats, at the end of the then horse railway route, on Seventh street. There is a long building appropriated to each ward. Let us go into ward 6. It contains to-day, I should judge, eighty or a hundred patients, half sick, half wounded. The edifice is nothing but boards, well whitewash'd inside, and the usual slender-framed iron bedsteads, narrow and plain. You walk down the central passage, with a row on either side, their feet towards you, and their heads to the wall. There are fires in large stoves, and the prevailing white of the walls is reliev'd by some ornaments, stars, circles, &c., made of evergreens. The view of the whole edifice and occupants can be taken at once, for there is no partition. You may hear groans or other sounds of unendurable suffering from two or three of the cots, but in the main there is quiet—almost a painful absence of demonstration; but the pallid face, the dull'd eye, and the moisture on the lip, are demonstration enough. Most of these sick or hurt are evidently young fellows from the country, farmers' sons, and such like. Look at the fine large frames, the bright and broad countenances, and the many yet lingering proofs of strong constitution and physique. Look at the patient and mute manner of our American wounded as they lie in such a sad collection; representatives from all New England, and from New York, and New Jersey, and Pennsylvania—indeed from all the States and all the cities—largely from the west. Most of them are entirely without friends or acquaintances here—no familiar face, and hardly a word of judicious sympathy or cheer, through their sometimes long and tedious sickness, or the pangs of aggravated wounds. . . .

May, '63.—As I write this, the wounded have begun to arrive from Hooker's command from bloody Chancellorsville. I was down among the first arrivals. The men in charge told me the bad cases were yet to come. If that is so I pity them, for these are bad enough. You ought to see the scene of the wounded arriving at the landing here at the foot of Sixth street, at night. Two boat loads came about half-past seven last night. A little after eight it rain'd a long and violent shower. The pale, help-less soldiers had been debark'd, and lay around on the wharf and neighborhood anywhere. The rain was, probably, grateful to them; at any rate they were exposed to it. The few torches light up the spectacle. All around—on the wharf, on the ground, out on side places—the men are lying on blankets, old quilts, &c., with bloody rags bound round heads, arms, and legs. The attendants are few, and at night few out-siders also—only a few hardwork'd transportation men and drivers. (The wounded are getting to be common, and people grow callous.) The men, whatever their condition, lie there, and patiently wait till their turn comes to be taken up. Near by, the ambulances are now arriving in clusters, and one after another is call'd to back up and take its load. Extreme cases are sent off on stretchers. The men generally make little or no ado, whatever their sufferings. A few groans that cannot be suppress'd, and occasionally a scream of pain as they lift a man into the ambulance. To-day, as I write, hundreds more are ex-pected, and to-morrow and the next day more and so on for many days. Quite often they arrive at the rate of 1000 a day.

May 12.—There was part of the late battle at Chancellorsville, (second Fredericksburg,) a little over a week ago, Saturday night and Sunday, under Gen. Joe Hooker, I would like to give just a glimpse of —(a moment's look in a terrible storm at sea—of which a few suggestions are enough, and full details impossible.) The fighting had been very hot during the day, and after an intermission the latter part, was resumed at night, and kept up with furious energy till 3 o'clock in the morning. That afternoon (Saturday) an attack sudden and strong by Stonewall Jackson had gain'd a great advantage to the southern army, and broken our lines, entering us like a wedge, and leaving things in that position at dark. But Hooker at 11 at night made a desperate push, drove the secesh forces back, restored his original lines, and resumed his plans. This night scrimmage was very exciting, and afforded countless strange and fearful pictures. The fighting had been general both at Chancellorsville and northeast of Fredericksburg. (We hear of some poor fighting, episodes, skedaddling on our part. I think not of it. I think of the fierce bravery, the general rule.) One corps, the 6th, Sedgewick's, fights four dashing and bloody battles in thirty-six hours, retreating in great jeopardy, losing largely but maintaining itself, fighting with the sternest desperation under all circumstances, getting over the Rappahannock only by the skin of its teeth, yet getting over. It lost many, many brave men, yet it took vengeance, ample vengeance.

But it was the tug of Saturday evening, and through the night and Sunday morning, I wanted to make a special note of. It was largely in the woods, and quite a general engagement. The night was very pleasant, at times the moon shining out full and clear, all Nature so calm in itself, the early summer grass so rich, and foliage of the trees —yet there the battle raging, and many good fellows lying helpless, with new accessions to them, and every minute amid the rattle of muskets and crash of cannon, (for there was an artillery contest too,) the red life-blood oozing out from heads or trunks or limbs upon that green and dew-cool grass. Patches of the woods take fire, and several of the wounded, unable to move, are consumed—quite large spaces are swept over, burning the dead also—some of the men have their hair and beards singed—some, burns on their faces and hands—others holes burnt in their clothing. The flashes of fire from the cannon, the quick flaring flames and smoke, and the immense roar—the musketry so general, the light nearly bright enough for each side to see the other—the crashing, tramping of men—the yelling—close quarters—we hear the secesh yells—our men cheer loudly back, especially if Hooker is in sight —hand to hand conflicts, each side stands up to it, brave, determin'd as demons, they often charge upon us—a thousand deeds are done worth to write newer greater poems on—and still the woods on fire—still many are not only scorch'd—too many, unable to move, are burn'd to death.

Then the camps of the wounded—O heavens, what scene is this? —is this indeed *humanity*—these butchers' shambles? There are several of them. There they lie, in the largest, in an open space in the woods, from 200 to 300 poor fellows—the groans and screams—the odor of blood, mixed with the fresh scent of the night, the grass, the trees—that

slaughter-house! O well is it their mothers, their sisters cannot see them
—cannot conceive, and never conceiv'd, these things. One man is shot
by a shell, both in the arm and leg—both are amputed—there lie the
rejected members. Some have their legs blown off—some bullets through
the breast—some indescribably horrid wounds in the face or head, all
mutilated, sickening, torn, gouged out—some in the abdomen—some
mere boys—many rebels, badly hurt—they take their regular turns with
the rest, just the same as any—the surgeons use them just the same.
Such is the camp of the wounded—such a fragment, a reflection afar off
of the bloody scene—while over all the clear, large moon comes out
at times softly, quietly shining. Amid the woods, that scene of flitting
souls—amid the crack and crash and yelling sounds—the impalpable
perfume of the woods—and yet the pungent, stifling smoke—the radiance
of the moon, looking from heaven at intervals so placid—the sky so
heavenly—the clear-obscure up there, those buoyant upper oceans—a few
large placid stars beyond, coming silently and languidly out, and then
disappearing—the melancholy, draperied night above, around. And there,
upon the roads, the fields, and in those woods, that contest, never one
more desperate in any age or land—both parties now in force—masses
—no fancy battle, no semi-play, but fierce and savage demons fighting
there—courage and scorn of death the rule, exceptions almost none.

What history, I say, can ever give—for who can know—the mad,
determin'd tussle of the armies, in all their separate large and little
squads—as this—each steep'd from crown to toe in desperate, mortal
purports? Who know the conflict, hand-to-hand—the many conflicts
in the dark, those shadowy-tangled, flashing-moonbeam'd woods—the
writhing groups and squads—the cries, the din, the cracking guns and
pistols—the distant cannon—the cheers and calls and threats and awful
music of the oaths—the indescribable mix—the officers' orders, persuasions, encouragements—the devils fully rous'd in human hearts—the
strong shout, *Charge, men, charge*—the flash of the naked sword, and
rolling flame and smoke? And still the broken, clear and clouded
heaven—and still again the moonlight pouring silvery soft its radiant
patches over all. Who paint the scene, the sudden partial panic of the
afternoon, at dusk? Who paint the irrepressible advance of the second
division of the Third corps, under Hooker himself, suddenly order'd up
—those rapid-filing phantoms through the woods? Who show what moves
there in the shadows, fluid and firm—to save, (and it did save,) the
army's name, perhaps the nation? as there the veterans hold the field.
(Brave Berry falls not yet—but death has mark'd him—soon he falls.)

Of scenes like these, I say, who writes—whoe'er can write the story? Of
many a score—aye, thousands, north and south, of unwrit heroes, un-

known heroisms, incredible, impromptu first-class desperations—who tells? No history ever—no poem sings, no music sounds, those bravest men of all—those deeds. No formal general's report, nor book in the library, nor column in the paper, embalms the bravest, north or south, east or west. Unnamed, unknown, remain, and still remain, the bravest soldiers. Our manliest—our boys—our hardy darlings; no picture gives them. Likely, the typic one of them (standing, no doubt, for hundreds, thousands,) crawls aside to some bush-clump, or ferny tuft, on receiving his death-shot—there sheltering a little while, soaking roots, grass and soil, with red blood—the battle advances, retreats, flits from the scene, sweeps by—and there, haply with pain and suffering (yet less, far less, than is supposed,) the last lethargy winds like a serpent round him—the eyes glaze in death—none recks—perhaps the burial-squads, in truce, a week afterwards, search not the secluded spot—and there, at last, the Bravest Soldier crumbles in mother earth, unburied and unknown. . . .

Multiply the above by scores, aye hundreds—verify it in all the forms that different circumstances, individuals, places, could afford—light it with every lurid passion, the wolf's, the lion's lapping thirst for blood—the passionate, boiling volcanoes of human revenge for comrades, brothers slain—with the light of burning farms, and heaps of smutting, smouldering black embers—and in the human heart everywhere black, worse embers—and you have an inkling of this war.

The South, as C. Vann Woodward the distinguished Southern historian has observed, is the only part of the United States that knows what it is to experience defeat. Mark Twain had long ago observed that Southerners dated experience from the Confederacy much as other people used "B.C." and "A.D." And the legend lives on: here are two responses to the night they drove old Dixie down. (Selections from Arthur C. Inman, ed., *Soldier of the South, General Pickett's War Letters to His Wife,* 1928; Mrs. S. A. B. Putnam, *Richmond During the War,* 1867.)

AFTER THE BATTLES: THE SOUTH

General George Pickett reflects on imminent surrender in a letter to his wife:

I would have your life, my darling, all sunshine, all brightness. I would have no sorrow, no pain, no fear come to you but all

To be as cloudless, save with rare and roseate shadows
As I would thy fate.

And yet the very thoughts of me that come to you must bring all that I would spare you.

Tomorrow may see our flag furled, forever.

Jackerie, our faithful old mail carrier, sobs behind me as I write. He bears tonight this—his last—message from me to you. He is commissioned with three orders, which I know you will obey as fearlessly as the bravest of your brother soldiers. Keep up a stout heart. Believe that I shall come back to you. Know that God reigns. After tonight, you will be my whole command—staff, field officers, men—all.

Lee's surrender is imminent. It is finished. Through the suggestion of their commanding officers as many of the men as desire are permitted to cut through and join Johnston's army. The cloud of despair settled over all on the 3rd, when the tidings came to us of the evacuation of Richmond and its partial loss by fire. The homes and families of many of my men were there, and all knew too well that with the fall of our capital, the last hope of success was over. And yet, my beloved, these men as resolutely obeyed the orders of their commanding officers as if we had just captured and burned the Federal capitol.

The horrors of the march from Five Forks to Amelia Court House, and thence to Sailor's Creek, beggar all description. For forty-eight hours the man or officer who had a handful of parched corn in his pocket was most fortunate. We reached Sailor's Creek on the morning of the 6th—weary, starving, despairing.

Sheridan was in our front, delaying us with his cavalry, according to his custom, until the infantry should come up. Mahone was on our right; Ewell on our left. Mahone was ordered to move on, and we were ordered to stand still. The movement of Mahone left a gap which increased as he went on. Huger's battalion of artillery, in attempting to cross the gap, was being swept away, when I pushed on with two of my brigades across Sailor's Creek.

We formed line of battle across an open field, holding it against repeated charges of Sheridan's dismounted cavalry. At about 3 o'clock, the infantry which Sheridan had been looking for came up, completely hemming us in. Anderson ordered me to draw off my brigades to the rear and to cut our way out in any possible manner that we could. Wise's brigade was deployed in the rear to assist us but was charged upon on all sides by the enemy, and, though fighting manfully to the last, was forced to yield. Two of my brigadiers, Corse and Hunton, were taken prisoners. The other two barely escaped, and my life, by some miracle, was spared. And by another miracle, greater still, I escaped capture.

A squadron of the enemy's cavalry was riding down upon us, two of my staff and myself, when a small squad of my men recognized me and, risking their own lives, rallied to our assistance and suddenly delivered a last volley into the faces of the pursuing horsemen, checking them for a moment. But in that one moment we, by the speed of our horses, made our escape. Ah, my darling, the sacrifice of that little band of men was like unto that which was made at Calvary.

It is finished! Ah, my beloved division! Thousands of them have gone to their eternal home, having given up their lives for the cause they knew to be just. The others, alas, heartbroken, crushed in spirit, are left to mourn its loss. Well, it is practically all over now. We have poured out our blood, and suffered untold hardships and privations, all in vain. And now, well—I must not forget, either, that God reigns.

Richmond Receives the News

The morning of the 2d of April, 1865, dawned brightly over the capital of the Southern Confederacy. A soft haze rested over the city, but above that, the sun shone with the warm pleasant radiance of early spring. The sky was cloudless. No sound disturbed the stillness of the Sabbath morn, save the subdued murmur of the river, and the cheerful music of the church bells. The long familiar tumult of war broke not upon the sacred calmness of the day. Around the War Department, and the Post Office, news gatherers were assembled for the latest tidings, but nothing was bruited that deterred the masses from seeking their accustomed places in the temples of the living God. At St. Paul's church the usual congregation was in attendance. President Davis occupied his pew.

It was again the regular monthly return for the celebration of the sacrament of the Lord's Supper. The services were progressing as usual, no agitation nor disturbance withdrew the thoughts from holy contemplation, when a messenger was observed to make his way up the aisle, and to place in the hands of the President a sealed package. Mr. Davis arose, and was noticed to walk rather unsteadily out of the church. An uneasy whisper ran through the congregation, and intuitively they seemed possessed of the dreadful secret of the sealed dispatch—the unhappy condition of General Lee's army and the necessity for evacuating Richmond. The dispatch stated that this was inevitable unless his lines could be reformed before eight o'clock that evening.

The direful tidings spread with the swiftness of electricity. From lip to lip, from men, women, children and servants, the news was bandied, but many received it at first, as only a "Sunday sensation rumor."

Friend looked into the face of friend to meet only an expression of incredulity; but later in the day, as the truth, stark and appalling, con-
fronted us, the answering look was that of stony, calm despair. Late in
the afternoon the signs of evacuation became obvious to even the most
incredulous. Wagons were driven furiously through the streets, to the
different departments, where they received as freight, the archives of the
government, and carried them to the Danville Depot, to be there con-
veyed away by railroad.

Thousands of the citizens determined to evacuate the city with the
government. Vehicles commanded any price in any currency possessed
by the individuals desiring to escape from the doomed capital. The streets
were filled with excited crowds hurrying to the different avenues for
transportation, intermingled with porters carrying huge loads, and wagons
piled up with incongruous heaps of baggage, of all sorts and descriptions.
The banks were all open, and depositors were busily and anxiously collecting their specie deposits, and directors were as busily engaged in
getting off their bullion. Millions of dollars of paper money, both State
and Confederate, were carried to the Capitol Square and buried.

Night came on, but with no sleep for human eyes in Richmond.
Confusion worse confounded reigned, and grim terror spread in wild
contagion. The City Council met, and ordered the destruction of all
spirituous liquors, fearing lest, in the excitement, there would be temptation to drink, and thus render our situation still more terrible. In the
gutters ran a stream of whiskey, and its fumes filled and impregnated
the air. After night-fall Richmond was ruled by the mob. In the principal
business section of the city they surged in one black mass from store to
store, breaking them open, robbing them, and in some instances (it is
said) applying the torch to them.

In the alarm and terror, the guards of the State Penitentiary fled
from their posts, and numbers of the lawless and desperate villains in-
carcerated there, for crimes of every grade and hue, after setting fire to
the workshops, made good the opportunity for escape, and donning garments stolen wherever they could get them, in exchange for their prison
livery, roamed over the city like fierce, ferocious beasts. No human
tongue, no pen, however gifted, can give an adequate description of
the events of that awful night.

While these fearful scenes were being enacted on the streets, in-
doors there was scarcely less excitment and confusion. Into every house
terror penetrated. Ladies were busily engaged in collecting and secreting
all the valuables possessed by them, together with cherished correspondence, yet they found time and presence of mind to prepare a few comforts for friends forced to depart with the army or the government. Few
tears were shed; there was no time for weakness or sentiment. The grief

was too deep, the agony too terrible to find vent through the ordinary channels of distress. Fathers, husbands, brothers and friends clasped their loved ones to their bosoms in convulsive and agonized embraces, and bade an adieu, oh, how heart-rending! perhaps, thought many of them, forever.

At midnight the train on the Danville Railroad bore off the officers of the Government, and at the same hour many persons made their escape on the canal packets, and fled in the direction of Lynchburg.

But a still more terrible element was destined to appear and add to the horrors of the scene. From some authority—it seems uncertain what—an order had been issued to fire the four principal tobacco warehouses. They were so situated as to jeopardize the entire commercial portion of Richmond. At a late hour of the night, Mayor Mayo had dispatched, by a committee of citizens, a remonstrance against this reckless military order. But in the mad excitement of the moment the protest was unheeded. The torch was applied, and the helpless citizens were left to witness the destruction of their property. The rams in the James River were blown up. The "Richmond," the "Virginia" No. 2 and the "Beaufort" were all scattered in fiery fragments to the four winds of heaven. The noise of these explosions, which occurred as the first grey streaks of dawn broke over Richmond, was like that of a hundred cannon at one time. The very foundations of the city were shaken; windows were shattered more than two miles from where these gun-boats were exploded, and the frightened inhabitants imagined that the place was being furiously bombarded. The "Patrick Henry," a receiving ship, was scuttled, and all the shipping at the wharves was fired except the flag-of-truce steamer "Allison."

As the sun rose on Richmond, such a spectacle was presented as can never be forgotten by those who witnessed it. To speed destruction, some malicious and foolish individuals had cut the hose in the city. The fire was progressing with fearful rapidity. The roaring, the hissing, and the crackling of the flames were heard above the shouting and confusion of the immense crowd of plunderers who were moving amid the dense smoke like demons, pushing, rioting and swaying with their burdens to make a passage to the open air. From the lower portion of the city, near the river, dense black clouds of smoke arose as a pall of crape to hide the ravages of the devouring flames, which lifted their red tongues and leaped from building to building as if possessed of demoniac instinct, and intent upon wholesale destruction. All the railroad bridges, and Mayo's Bridge, that crossed the James River and connected with Manchester, on the opposite side, were in flames.

The most remarkable scenes, however, were said to have occurred at the commissary depot. Hundreds of Government wagons were loaded with bacon, flour and whiskey, and driven off in hot haste to join the retreating army. In a dense throng around the depot stood hundreds of men, women and children, black and white, provided with anything in which they could carry away provisions, awaiting the opening of the doors to rush in and help themselves. A cascade of whiskey streamed from the windows. About sunrise the doors were thrown open to the populace, and with a rush that seemed almost sufficient to bear off the building itself, they soon sweep away all that remained of the Confederate commissariat of Richmond.

By this time the flames had been applied to or had reached the arsenal, in which several hundred car loads of loaded shell were left. At every moment the most terrific explosions were sending forth their awful reverberations, and gave us the idea of a general bombardment. All the horrors of the final conflagration, when the earth shall be wrapped in flames and melt with fervent heat, were, it seemed to us, prefigured in our capital.

At an early hour in the morning, the Mayor of the city, to whom it had been resigned by the military commander, proceeded to the lines of the enemy and surrendered it to General Godfrey Weitzel, who had been left by General Ord, when he withdrew one-half of his division to the lines investing Petersburg, to receive the surrender of Richmond.

As early as eight o'clock in the morning, while the mob held possession of Main Street, and were busily helping themselves to the contents of the dry goods stores and other shops in that portion of the city, and while a few of our cavalry were still to be seen here and there in the upper portions, a cry was raised: "The Yankees!" The Yankees are coming!" Major A. H. Stevens, of the Fourth Massachusetts Cavalry, and Major E. E. Graves, of his staff, with forty cavalry, rode steadily into the city, proceeded directly to the Capital, and planted once more the "Stars and Stripes"—the ensign of our subjugation—on that ancient edifice. As its folds were given to the breeze, while still we heard the roaring, hissing, crackling flames, the explosions of the shells and the shouting of the multitude, the strains of an old, familiar tune floated upon the air—a tune that, in days gone by, was wont to awaken a thrill of patriotism. But now only the most bitter and crushing recollections awoke within us, as upon our quickened hearing fell the strains of "The Star Spangled Banner." For us it was a requiem for buried hopes.

As the day advanced, Weitzel's troops poured through the city. Long lines of negro cavalry swept by the Exchange Hotel, brandishing their swords and uttering savage cheers, replied to by the shouts of those of their own color, who were trudging along under loads of plunder, laughing and exulting over the prizes they had secured from the wreck of the stores, rather than rejoicing at the more precious prize of freedom which had been won for them. On passed the colored troops, singing, "John Brown's body is mouldering in the grave," etc.

By one o'clock in the day, the confusion reached its height. As soon as the Federal troops reached the city they were set to work by the officers to arrest the progress of the fire. By this time a wind had risen from the south, and seemed likely to carry the surging flames all over the northwestern portion of the city. The most strenuous efforts were made to prevent this, and the grateful thanks of the people of Richmond are due to General Weitzel and other officers for their energetic measures to save the city from entire destruction.

The Capitol Square now presented a novel appearance. On the south, east, and west of its lower half, it was bounded by burning buildings. The flames bursting from the windows, and rising from the roofs, were proclaiming in one wild roar their work of destruction. Myriads of sparks, borne upward up by the current of hot air, were brightening and breaking in the dense smoke above. On the sward of the Square, fresh with the emerald green of early spring, thousands of wretched creatures, who had been driven from their dwellings by the devouring flames, were congregated. Fathers and mothers, and weeping, frightened children sought this open space for a breath of fresh air. But here, even, it was almost as hot as a furnace. Intermingled with these miserable beings were the Federal troops in their garish uniform, representing almost every nation on the continent of Europe, and thousands of the *Corps d'Afrique*. All along on the north side of the Square were tethered the horses of the Federal cavalry, while, dotted about, were seen the white tents of the sutlers, in which there were temptingly displayed canned fruits and meats, crackers, cheese, etc.

The roaring, crackling and hissing of the flames, the bursting of shells at the Confederate Arsenal, the sounds of instruments of martial music, the neighing of the horses, the shoutings of the multitude, in which could be distinctly distinguished the coarse, wild voices of the negroes, gave an idea of all the horrors of Pandemonium. Above all this scene of terror, hung a black shroud of smoke through which the sun shone with a lurid angry glare like an immense ball of blood that emitted sullen rays of light, as if loth to shine over a scene so appalling.

Remembering the unhappy fate of the citizens of Columbia and other cities of the South, and momentarily expecting pillage, and other evils incidental to the sacking of a city, great numbers of ladies sought the proper miiltary authorities and were furnished with safeguards for the protection of themselves and their homes. These were willingly and generously furnished, and no scene of violence is remembered to have been committed by the troops which occupied Richmond.

Throughout the entire day, those who had enriched themselves by plundering the stores were busy in conveying off their goods. Laughing and jesting negroes tugged along with every conceivable description of merchandise, and many an astute shopkeeper from questionable quarters of Richmond thus added greatly to his former stock.

The sun had set upon this terrible day before the awful reverberations of exploding shells at the arsenal ceased to be heard over Richmond. The evening came on. A deathlike quiet pervaded the late heaving and tumultuous city, broken only by the murmuring waters of the river. Night drew her sable mantle over the mutilated remains of our beautiful capital, and we locked, and bolted, and barred our doors; but sleep had fled our eyelids. All night long we kept a fearful vigil, and listened with beating heart and quickened ears for the faintest sound that might indicate the development of other and more terrible phases of horror. But from all these we were mercifully and providentially spared. . . .

Comic creations like Artemus Ward, Major Jack Downing, and the peculiarly named Petroleum V. Nasby were popular during the Civil War era and provided an effective avenue for political commentary and satire. They offered freedom for an observer to say things that he might not have been willing to utter in a more straightforward manner. (From Petroleum V. Nasby [David Locke], "Swingin Round the Cirkle," 1867.)

RECONSTRUCTION: A COMIC'S VIEW

The Reconstructed meet to Congratulate the Country upon the Result of the Memphis Outbreak.—The Reverend discourses upon the Nigger, and runs against a Snag.

CONFEDRIT × ROADS
(which is in the Stait uv Kentucky),
May 12, 1866.

The news from Memphis filled the soles uv the Dimocrisy uv Kentucky with undilooted joy. There, at last, the Ethiopian wuz taught that to him, at least, the spellin book is a seeled volume, and that the gospel is not for him, save ez he gits it filtered through a sound, constooshnel, Dimekratic preacher. We met at the Corners last nite to jollify over the brave acts uv our Memphis frends, and I wuz the speeker. I addressed them on the subjick uv the nigger,—his wants, needs, and capacities,—a subjick, permit me to state, I flatter myself I understand.

Probably no man in the Yoonited States hez given the nigger more study, or devoted more time to a pashent investigashen uv this species uv the brute creashen, than the undersigned. I have contemplated him sittin and standin, sleepin and wakin, at labor and in idleness,—in every shape, in fact, ceptin ez a free man, wich situashen is too disgustin for a proud Caucashen to contemplate him; and when he ariz before my mind's eye in that shape, I alluz shuddrin away.

I hed proceeded in my discourse with a flowin sale. It's easy demonstratin anythin yoor awjence wants to beleeve, and wich their interest lies in. For instants, I hev notist wicked men, who wuz somewhat wedded to sin, genrally lean toward Universalism; men heavily developed in the back uv the neck are easily convinst uv the grand trooths uv free love; and them ez is too fond uv makin money to rest on the seventh day, hev serious doubts ez to whether the observance uv the Sabbath is bindin onto em. I, not likin to work at all, am a firm beleever in slavery, and wood be firmer ef I cood get start enuff to own a nigger.

I hed gone on and proved concloosively, from a comparison uv the fizzikle structer uv the Afrikin and the Caucashen, that the nigger wuz a beast, and not a human bein; and that, consekently, we hed a perfeck rite to catch him, and tame him, and yoose him ez we do other wild animals. Finishin this hed uv my discourse, I glode easily into a history uv the flood; explained how Noer got tite and cust Ham, condemnin him and his posterity to serve his brethren forever, wich I insisted give us an indubitable warranty deed to all uv em for all time

I warmed up on this elokently. "Behold, my brethren, the beginnin uv Dimocrasy," I sed. "Fust, the wine (which wuz the antetype of our whisky) wuz the beginnin. Wine (or whisky) wuz necessary to the foundation uv the party, and it wuz forthcomin. But the thing was not complete. It did its work on Noer, but yet there wuz a achin void. There was no *Nigger* in the world, and without nigger there could be no Dimocracy. Ham, my friends, wuz born a brother uv Japhet, and wuz like unto him, and, uv course, could not be a slave. Whisky wuz the instrument to bring him down; and it fetched him. Ham looked upon his father, and was cust; and the void wuz filled. THERE WUZ NIGGER AND WHISKY, and upon them the foundashuns uv the party wuz laid, broad and deep. Methinks, my brethren, when Ham went out from the presence uv his father, black in the face ez the ace uv spades (ef I may be allowed to yoose the expression), bowing his back to the burdens Shem and Japhet piled onto him with alacrity, that Democracy, then in the womb uv the future, kicked lively, and clapped its hands. There wuz a nigger to enslave, and whisky to bring men down to the pint uv enslavin him. There wuz whisky to make men incapable uv labor; whisky to accompany horse racin, and poker playin, and sich rational amoosements, and a nigger cust especially that he mite sweat to furnish the means. Observe the fitniss uv things. Bless the Lord, my brethren, for whisky and the nigger; for, without em, there could be no Dimocrisy, and yoor beloved speaker mite hev owned a farm in Noo Jersey, and bin a votin the whig ticket to-day."

At this pint, a venerable old freedman, who wuz a sittin quietly in the meetin, ariz, and asked ef he mite ask a question. Thinkin what a splendid opportoonity there wood be uv demonstratin the sooperiority uv the Caucashen over the Afrikin race, I answered "Yes," gladly.

"Well, Mas'r," sed the old imbecile, "is I a beest?"

"My venerable friend, there aint nary doubt uv it."

"Is my old woman a old beastesses, too?"

"Indubitably," replied I.

"And my children—is they little beasts and beastesses?"

"Onquestionably."

"Den a yaller feller ain't but a half a beast, is he?"

"My friend," sed I, "that question is———"

"Hold on," sed he; "wat I wanted to git at is dis: dere's a heap uv yaller fellers in dis section, whose fadders must hev bin white men; and, ez der mudders wuz all beastesses, I want to know whedder dar ain't no law in Kentucky agin———"

"Put him out!" "Kill the black wretch!" shouted a majority uv them who hed bin the heaviest slave owners under the good old patriarkle system, and they went for the old reprobate. At this pint, a officer uv the Freedmen's Bureau, who we hedn't observed, riz, and, bustin with laughter, remarked that his venerable friend shood have a chance to be heerd. We respeck that Burow, partikelerly ez the officers generally hev a hundred or two bayonets within reech, and, chokin our wrath, permitted ourselves to be further insulted by the cussed nigger, who, grinnin from ear to ear, riz and perceeded.

"My white friends," sed he, "dar pears to be an objection to my reference to de subjeck uv dis mixin with beasts, so I won't press de matter. But I ask yoo, did Noer hev three sons?"

"He did," sed I.

"Berry good. Wuz dey all brudders?"

"Uv course."

"Ham come from the same fadder and mudder as the odder two?"

"C-e-r-t-i-n-l-y."

"Well, den, it seems to me—not fully understandin the skripters—dat if we is beasts and beastesses, dat you is beasts and beastesses also, and dat, after all, we is brudders." And the disgustin old wretch threw his arms around my neck, and kissed me, callin me his "long lost brudder."

The officer uv the Freedmen's Bureau laft vosiferously, and so did a dozen or two soljers in the crowd likewise; and the awjence slunk out without adjournin the meetin, one uv em remarkin, audibly, that he had notised one thing, that Dimocrisy wuz extremely weak whenever it undertook to defend itself with fax or revelashun. For his part, he'd done with argyment. He wanted niggers, because he cood wallop em, and make em do his work without payin em, wich he coodent do with white men.

I left the meetin house convinst that the South, who worked the niggers, leavin us Northern Dimokrats to defend the system, hed the best end uv the bargain.

Petroleum V. Nasby,
Lait Paster uv the Church of the Noo Dispensashun.

This humorous portrayal of the Indian wars of the 1870s was no joke: it expresses what most Americans seemed to have thought of Indians. (From *Bill Nye's History of the United States*, 1894.)

THE INDIAN WARS: A COMIC VIEW

In 1876 the peaceful Sioux took an outing, having refused to go to their reservation in accordance with the treaty made with the Great Father at Washington, D. C., and regular troops were sent against them.

General Custer, with the 7th Regiment, led the advance, and General Terry aimed for the rear of the children of the forest up the Big Horn. Here, on the 25th of June, without assistance, and with characteristic courage, General Custer attacked the enemy, sending Colonel Reno to fall on the rear of the village.

Scarcely enough of Custer's own command with him at the time lived long enough to tell the story of the battle. General Custer, his two brothers, and his nephew were among the dead. Reno held his ground until reinforced, but Custer's troops were exterminated.

It is said that the Sioux rose from the ground like bunch-grass and swarmed up the little hill like a pest of grasshoppers, mowing down the soldiers with the very newest and best weapons of warfare, and leaving nothing at last but the robbed and mutilated bodies lying naked in the desolate land of the Dakotah.

The Fenimore Cooper Indian is no doubt a brave and highly intellectual person, educated abroad, refined and cultivated by foreign travel, graceful in the grub dance or scalp walk-around, yet tender-hearted as a girl, walking by night fifty-seven miles in a single evening

to warn his white friends of danger. The Indian introduced into literature was a bronze Apollo who bathed almost constantly and only killed
white people who were unpleasant and coarse. He dressed in new and
fresh buckskins, with trimming of same, and his sable hair hung glossy
and beautiful down the coppery-billows of muscles on his back.

The real Indian has the dead and unkempt hair of a busted buggy-
cushion filled with hen feathers. He lies, he steals, he assassinates, he
mutilates, he tortures. He needs Persian powder long before he needs
the theology which abler men cannot agree upon. We can, in fact, only
retain him as we do the buffalo, so long as he complies with the statutes.
But the red brother is on his way to join the cave-bear, the three-toed
horse, and the ichthyosaurus in the great fossil realm of the historic
past. Move on, maroon brother, move on!

Every age, someone once said, gets the heroes it deserves. With some sanitizing,
Commodore Vanderbilt became a representative of the Captains of Industry
that the age learned to admire and that provided images of success for young
men. (Selection from William A. Croffut, *The Vanderbilts and the Story of Their
Fortune*, 1886.)

A CAPTAIN OF INDUSTRY

This is a history of the Vanderbilt family, with a record of their
vicissitudes, and a chronicle of the method by which their wealth has
been acquired. It is confidently put forth as a work which should fall
into the hands of boys and young men—of all who aspire to become
Captains of Industry or leaders of their fellows in the sharp and wholesome competitions of life.

In preparing these pages, the author has had an ambition, not
merely to give a biographical picture of sire, son, and grandsons and
descendants, but to consider their relation to society, to measure the
significance and the influence of their fortune, to ascertain where their
money came from, to inquire whether others are poorer because they
are rich, whether they are hindering or promoting civilization, whether
they and such as they are impediments to the welfare of the human
race. A correct answer to these questions will solve half of the problems
which most eagerly beset this generation.

This story is an analogue of the story of all American successes.
When Commodore Vanderbilt visited Europe in 1853 at the head of his

family, he seemed to defy classification. He was apparently neither lord nor commoner. He was too democratic for a grandee; too self-poised for a plebeian. He was untitled, but his yacht surpassed in size and splendor the ocean vehicles of monarchs. No expense was too great to be indulged, no luxury too choice to be provided, but he moved modestly and without ostentation, with the serene composure of a prince among his equals. There were wealthy English citizens who could have afforded a similar outlay, but they would have been sneered at and charged with pretentiousness and vanity, with aping customs rightly monopolized by the nobility. They would have been rated as snobs, cads, upstarts, and would have been twitted with their humble origin, as if an improvement of one's condition were a reproach instead of an honor.

But the cruising Commodore came from a land where prevalent conditions and not antecedents are considered; where a coat-of-arms is properly regarded as a foolish affectation; where a family's "descent" is of no importance, and its ascent of all importance; where the wheel of fortune runs rapidly around and every man is not only permitted but required to stand for what he is. . . .

America is the land of the self-made man—the empire of the parvenu. Here it is felt that the accident of birth is of trifling consequence; here there is no "blood" that is to be coveted save the red blood which every masterful man distills in his own arteries: and here the name of parvenu is the only and all-sufficient title of nobility. So here, if nowhere else in the world, should such a dominant man without hesitation or apology assume the place to which he is entitled, in commerce or the industrial arts, in professional life or society. . . .

[Cornelius Vanderbilt] dressed no better than his clerk, and ate less than his coachman. He drank chiefly milk. He could sleep in only one room, like others. He had little taste for books, and not time enough to read the newspapers. Envy and ignorance had raised up an army of enemies about him. The public press stormed at him like a harridan and covered the dead walls with infamous caricatures, representing him as a vampire, a dragon, a Gorgon, a Silenus, a Moloch, a malevolent Hurlothrumbo. He was a victim of insomnia and indigestion. The jockey, Anxiety, rode him with whip and spur. He was in constant peril of apoplexy. He could not take needful exercise by walking in the Park for fear of being accosted by tramps or insulted by socialistic philosophers. Every week his life was threatened by anonymous letters. He kept a magnificent servants' boarding-house on Fifth Avenue, where he made his home, and superbly equipped a stable, whose advantages inured chiefly to the benefit of his employés. He organized the finest picture-gallery in America for the enjoyment of lovers of art, but was compelled to limit his hospitality by the fact that some of the guests rifled the conservatory of its choicest flowers, scratched the Meissoniers with the ends of their parasols, invaded the private apartments of the mansion, and carried away portable things as souvenirs of the visit. An enormous fortune is a heavy burden to bear. To be very rich invites attacks, cares, responsibilities, intrusions and annoyances for which there is no adequate offset.

A man like Commodore Vanderbilt, indeed, has the large satisfaction of feeling that he has given the human race a magnificent endowment in adding to the wealth of the world. He was not a juggler, who managed by a cunning trick to transfer to himself the wealth of others; he created property that did not before have an existence. When he stepped from the deck upon land, the best railroads in the United States had been paralyzed and driven to bankruptcy by blunderers and plunderers. They were largely in the hands of men who cared nothing for them except as they could be made serviceable in the reckless games of Wall Street. Whether they could meet the demands of traffic was regarded by these desperate gamblers as of no consequence. Thieves had pillaged the Erie road till its stock was sold for three cents on a dollar. Michigan Southern was at 5, and Erie at 6.

The Commodore introduced a new policy. Instead of taking money out of the roads, he put millions into them. Instead of breaking them down he built them up. Instead of robbing them, he renovated them and raised them from the grave. He equipped them anew, trusting that the public would respond and give him his money back. He dragged together worthless fragments and made them one; he consolidated parallel roads that were apart and belonged together; he cut down every possible expense, and subjected them to the economic supervision of one despotic will. He fearlessly staked all upon the venture, and upon the belief that the war for the Union would end in the defeat of Secession.

In both he was right. The South was beaten. The public responded. The stock mounted to par and beyond. His roads had all they could do, and he made millions a year from the investment of his marvelous brain. And he made these millions as legitimately as an artisan fashions a hat from wool, or a chair from wood. He received better pay than the artisan, not only because he risked his money where the mechanic risks nothing, but because he invested his consummate brain.

One of the commonest and most pernicious errors is the assumption that the human hand is the chief factor in the creation of wealth, and from this error springs much of the noisy remonstrance of our time. It is not the hand, but the brain, that is the real creator. It was Michael Angelo that built St. Peter's, not the forgotten workmen who, executing the will of the great master, borne to them through a dozen skilled architects and master-artisans, hewed the stone to lines that had been accurately drawn for them. The unit of service underlying all is the faithful workman; but a brigade of workmen cannot do as much effective good as is done by one strong and intelligent capitalist, whose money employs and whose sagacity directs and renders fruitful the sterile hand. The chief productiveness of the world is due mainly to the skill that plans, the audacity that risks, and the prescience that sees through the heart of the future. So to those captains of industry who succeed in their financial ventures should go that premium called profit which society offers to superior foresight.

It used to be thought by all that as wealth accumulated men decayed; that the love of money was the root of all evil; that avarice was a vice; that the world would be better off if the division of property could be more nearly equal; that great riches were a curse to society; that the millionaire capitalist was a sort of bandit-king who plundered the people by methods which were sometimes legal but always highly immoral, and under whose tyrannical exactions industry was paralyzed and laboring men were impoverished.

But it is now known that the desire to own property is the chief difference between the savage and the enlightened man; that aggregations of money in the hands of individuals are an inestimable blessing to Society, for without them there could be no public improvements or private enterprises, no railroads or steamships, or telegraphs; no cities, no leisure class, no schools, colleges, literature, art—in short no civilization. The one man to whom the community owes most is the capitalist, not the man who gives, but the man who saves and invests, so that his property reproduces and multiplies itself instead of being consumed.

It is now known that civilization is the result of labor put in motion by wealth; that wealth springs from self-denial; that self-denial springs from avarice; and that avarice is the child of an aspiring discontent.

It used to be thought that consolidation was a menace to the people, and that great "Monopolies," as they were called, ought to be forbidden by law. It is now known that such consolidation is a public benefit; that the man who owns a thousand houses rents them cheaper than he who owns but one or two; that the greatest oil company in the world furnishes oil cheaper than it was ever furnished before, or could be by any other means of distribution; that the Western Union Telegraph Company sends dispatches far cheaper than they were sent by any of the score of companies from which it sprung, and cheaper than they are sent by any of the telegraphs in the world which are owned and operated by governments; that A. T. Stewart greatly reduced the profits and losses of merchandising and the cost of goods to the consumer, and that, therefore, while he crushed out small dealers, his career was a tremendous public benefit; that the New York Central Railroad, the net result of the combination of many roads, carries passengers at lower fares than any other road in the world—lower even than is required by law—and transports freight so cheaply that it has driven from successful competition a canal that was built by the State and is free to all! The government has reduced the price of postage only one-half in a quarter of a century, and delivers letters at a loss of millions of dollars a year; but freight from Chicago to New York costs less than a quarter what it did then, and desperate competition keeps the rate at the lowest possible point.

It is to the obvious advantage of society that reproductive wealth shall be concentrated in few hands; for the larger its aggregations the smaller the toll which it will exact from society, for the privilege of its use. And before Socialists can rationally demand an abolition of the competitive system and a reconstruction of the industrial methods of society, they must exhibit one railroad somewhere in the world which is owned by a state and managed as wisely and thriftily as are the roads which are allied to the name of Vanderbilt.